MW01098195

A PEOPLE'S CONSTITUTION

HISTORIES OF ECONOMIC LIFE

Jeremy Adelman, Sunil Amrith,
and Emma Rothschild, Series Editors

A People's Constitution

THE EVERYDAY LIFE OF LAW IN THE INDIAN REPUBLIC

ROHIT DE

PRINCETON UNIVERSITY PRESS

PRINCETON & OXFORD

Published by Princeton University Press
41 William Street, Princeton, New Jersey 08540
6 Oxford Street, Woodstock, Oxfordshire OX20 1TR

press.princeton.edu

Library of Congress Control Number: 2018948540
ISBN 978-0-691-17443-3

British Library Cataloging-in-Publication Data is available

Editorial: Amanda Peery
Production Editorial: Kathleen Cioffi
Jacket Design: Layla MacRory
Jacket illustrations by author
Production: Erin Suydam
Publicity: Jodi Price
Copyeditor: Judith Antonelli

This book has been composed in Arno

Printed on acid-free paper. ∞

Printed in the United States of America

10 9 8 7 6 5 4 3 2 1

CONTENTS

ABBREVIATIONS

AIR *All India Reporter*

ASMH Association for Social and Moral Hygiene

BPA Bombay Prohibition Act, 1949

CrLJ *Criminal Law Journal*

CSSAAME *Comparative Studies of South Asia, Africa, and the Middle East*

CWMG *Collected Works of Mahatma Gandhi*

ESA Essential Supplies Act, 1946

ILR *India Law Reports*

IOR India Office Records

NAI National Archives of India

NMML Nehru Memorial Museum and Library

MSA Maharashtra State Archives

SC Supreme Court of India

SCR *Supreme Court Reports*

SCRR Supreme Court Record Room

SITA Suppression of Immoral Traffic in Women and Girls Act, 1956

A PEOPLE'S CONSTITUTION

Introduction

IN DECEMBER 1950 Mohammed Yasin, a young Muslim vegetable vendor in the small town of Jalalabad in north India, was in distress. He had received notification that the town government was implementing a new set of bylaws licensing the sale of various commodities and was providing only one license for the sale of vegetables in the town area. This license had been issued to a Hindu merchant, granting him a virtual monopoly over the vegetable trade in Jalalabad, which forced Yasin and other vegetable vendors to sell their goods after paying the license holder a certain fee. Yasin petitioned the Supreme Court to issue a writ of mandamus directing the town committee not to prohibit the petitioner from carrying on his trade. A writ of mandamus is an order issued by a superior court to compel a lower authority or government officer to perform mandatory or administrative duties correctly. Yasin's lawyer argued that not only was the new regulation ultra vires (i.e., beyond the powers of the municipality), it also violated Yasin's rights to a trade and an occupation, conferred by the Constitution of India.

As a vegetable vendor from a minor town, Yasin appears to be a nondescript bystander as the grand narratives of Indian history—independence, partition, elections, the integration of princely states—play out around him. Why should he be interesting to us today? Yasin is one of the first Indians to present himself before the new Indian Supreme Court as a rights-bearing citizen. His problem and its solution both emerge from India's new constitutional republican order and represent a phenomenon that is the subject of this book.[1]

Yasin's constitutional adventure highlights three features, this book argues, that form the basis for Indian constitutionalism. First, the Constitution mattered as a limit to or a structure for daily living. Second, this constitutional engagement included large numbers of ordinary Indians, often from minorities or subaltern groups. Third, a significant number of these constitutional encounters were produced through the new Indian state's attempt to regulate market relations.

India became independent at the stroke of midnight on August 15, 1947. Three years later the Constituent Assembly, whose members were nominated by elected provincial legislatures, promulgated a new constitution declaring the state to be a "sovereign democratic republic." This was a remarkable achievement for that time.[2] The Indian Constitution was written over a period of four years by the Constituent Assembly. Dominated by the Congress Party, India's leading nationalist political organization, the assembly sought to include a wide range of political opinions and represented diversity by sex, religion, caste, and tribe. This achievement is striking compared to other states that were decolonized. Indians wrote the Indian Constitution, unlike the people of most former British colonies, like Kenya, Malaysia, Ghana, and Sri Lanka, whose constitutions were written by British officials at Whitehall. Indian leaders were also able to agree upon a constitution, unlike Israeli and Pakistani leaders, both of whom elected constituent assemblies at a similar time but were unable to reach agreement on a document.

The Indian Constitution is the longest surviving constitution in the postcolonial world, and it continues to dominate public life in India. Despite this, its endurance has received little attention from scholars.[3] Although there are a handful of accounts of constitution making and constitutional design, the processes through which a society comes to adopt a constitution still remain underexplored.[4] Constitutions mark transformations of polity and codify moments of revolutionary change. Yet we have little idea of how Indians understood and experienced the new order marked by a constitution.

This is despite the fact that constitutional debates had dominated newspaper headlines in all major Indian languages since the 1920s. The process of drafting in 1946 evoked a great deal of interest across the country, and the Constituent Assembly was flooded with telegrams, postcards, and petitions from schoolboys to housewives to postmasters, staking claims, making demands, and offering suggestions for the constitutional draft.[5] Thousands of Indians followed Mohammed Yasin in invoking the Constitution in the courts. These cases included situations of dire necessity (e.g., a Muslim man who, on being informed of his imminent deportation to Pakistan, smashed his tumbler and injured his face and hands to give his lawyer time to file a writ petition while he was receiving medical treatment);[6] situations of mundane everyday life (e.g., an irate Bengali college professor who protested the rise in Calcutta tram fares by challenging the legality of the notification);[7] and leaps of imagination (e.g., a petitioner who demanded that the country switch to matrilineal succession and that all state documents require the name of the mother rather than the father.[8] As we shall see, the Constitution did not descend upon the people; it was produced and reproduced in everyday encounters. From the earliest days of India's independence, citizens' political action influenced the court and reveals a long history of public-interest litigation driven by litigants rather than judges.

Despite the centrality of the Constitution to public and private lives in South Asia, it remains "ill served by historical imagination" and its history understudied.[9] It is partly because Indian constitutionalism defies easy explanations. Constitutionalism is based on the desirability of the rule of law rather than the arbitrary rule of men, but both seem to exist simultaneously in India. On the one hand, India has a visibly vibrant constitutional culture. The Indian Supreme Court has been frequently described as the most powerful constitutional court in the world, exercising wide powers of judicial review.[10] A constitutional court is the final authority on interpreting the Constitution and is tasked with ensuring that its limits are not transgressed. Aided by a robust bar, supported by the state, and enjoying tremendous public support, the courts have come to play an all-pervasive role in public life, so much so that scholars argue that "there is not a single important issue of political life in India that has not, by accident or design, been profoundly shaped by the Supreme Court's interventions."[11] The state is frequently taken to task, and governmental decisions that violate the constitutional limits are challenged and overturned. More significantly, self-imaginings, interests, identities, rights, and injuries of citizens have become saturated with the constitutional language, and even radical social and political movements are constrained to engage with law and constitutional structures. Marginalized groups, including Dalits and tribals, have transformed the constitution into a public resource through the construction of monumental public statuary commemorating the constitutional promise of equality or through installing stone slabs in villages outlining the constitutional safeguards to tribal areas.[12] Class struggles increasingly morph into class-action cases.[13]

On the other hand, the preponderance of constitutional language and rhetoric stands in sharp contrast to the systemic failure of both the government and the citizens to follow the law. Since the eighteenth century, corruption, expense, and chronic delays have been endemic to the legal system, much of which functions in a language incomprehensible to a majority of Indians.[14]

Levels of civil litigation have fallen since independence, indicating that people avoid the courts when resolving private disputes.[15]

This visible dialectic of "law and disorder" is similar to processes that have been observed in other states since the 1990s. Jean and John Comaroff argue that the law is increasingly ascribed with having a life force of its own, and the people's faith in it is sustained because "the promulgation of a New Legal Order . . . signals a break with the past, with its embarrassments, nightmares, torments, and traumas."[16] Courts emerged as powerful juristocracies across the world.[17] This growing faith in constitutionalism is attributed not merely to regime change but also to neoliberalism and the growth of transnational and human rights networks in the 1990s.[18] Both neoliberalism and globalization lead to a greater dispersal of governance and the fragmentation of state authority, granting law a greater communicative force.[19]

The imbrications of the Constitution in daily life and the judicialization of politics have a considerably longer history in India that predates not just newly democratic Africa and Eastern Europe but also older democracies like Canada and New Zealand. Within days of the adoption of the new Constitution, thousands of citizens began invoking the Constitution when challenging state action. This book recovers a new genealogy of conditions in which citizen action drove politics into the courts. Conflicts with the state that had been negotiated through a variety of channels in colonial India, from street politics to backroom negotiations, began to migrate to the courts. Whereas the global judicialization of the 1990s emerged during the withdrawal of state authority, these legal and constitutional channels for conflict emerged at a moment of state expansion and of consolidation.

This book explores how the Indian Constitution, a document with alien antecedents that was a product of elite consensus, became part of the experience of ordinary Indians in the first decade of independence. It traces the process through which the Constitution emerged as the dominant field for politics. It recognizes that constitutions exist in a normative universe, a "world of right and wrong, of lawful and unlawful, of valid and void," in the words of Robert Cover. This normative universe is constructed by the force of "interpretive commitments—some small and private, others immense and public."[20] This book breaks new methodological ground by studying the Constitution through the daily interpretive acts of ordinary people as well as judges and state officials. Using previously unexplored archives at the Supreme Court, this book charts how the Constitution came to dominate, structure, frame, and constrain everyday life in India.

The Constitution as Triumph

What changed when the Constituent Assembly enacted the Constitution that declared India to be a sovereign democratic republic? Depending on whom you ask, you get two broadly different stories.

The first story is the triumphant institutional one, cherished by lawyers and politicians alike, that is perhaps best described by the Indian Supreme Court: "at one stroke territorial allegiances were wiped out and the past obliterated, . . . at one moment in time the new order was born with its new allegiances, springing from the same source all grounded on the same basis, the sovereign will of the peoples of India with no class, no caste, no race, no creed, no distinction, no reservation."[21] Constitutional theorists have attributed the success of the Constitution to its moment of founding, the installation of a popular nationalist movement that was led by farsighted leaders committed to the rule of law.[22]

In the last decade, intellectual historians and political theorists have made an effort to come to the rescue of the Indian Constitution and rehabilitate it as "a moral document embodying an ethical vision."[23] They have engaged with the Constitution's text and debates in the Constituent Assembly as sites for the enactment of basic oppositions in political theory: the tension between constitutionalism and popular democracy, between individual and group rights, or between religious freedom and secularism. This small but significant body of work has opened up the Indian Constitution both to scholars who are seeking the core values that undergird the Indian polity and to those seeking an archive of political theory from the Global South.[24]

The institution of adult suffrage and the institutionalization of the social revolution are the markers of radical change in the Indian Constitution. The institutionalization of universal franchise was a revolutionary act in a deeply hierarchical society—especially when franchise had only recently been extended to women, people of color, and working-class men in various "mature" Western democracies.[25] Franchise without restrictions was a sharp break from the very limited franchise linked to communal identities and property qualifications that had been provided through various colonial reforms.[26] As Sunil Khilnani evocatively describes it, the imaginative potency of democracy lies "in its promise to bring the alien and powerful machine like that of the state under the control of human will, and to enable a community of political equals before constitutional law to make their own history."[27]

More remarkably, the question of economic and social deprivation was made central to the Indian Constitution. The preamble to the Constitution guaranteed social, economic, and, finally, political justice to all citizens. The Constitution itself laid the ground for land reform by limiting the right to property, provided for constitutionally permitted affirmative action, abolished untouchability and human trafficking, allowed for special provisions to be made for women and children, and gave rights to religious and linguistic minority groups. Under the Directive Principles of State Policy, the Constitution laid out what it called the fundamental principles of governance: the equitable distribution of resources, a free and compulsory education for children, equal wages for men and women, fair work conditions and a living wage, the prohibition of alcohol, the abolition of child labor, and the improvement of nutrition and public health.[28] Despite the implicit hierarchy in the implementation of fundamental rights and of the Directive Principles of State Policy, Indian jurist Bhimrao Ramji (B. R.) Ambedkar reassured the Constituent Assembly that "the intention of the Assembly is that in future both [the] legislature and the executive should not merely pay lip-service to these principles enacted in this part but that they should be made the basis of all executive and legislative action that may be taken thereafter in the matter of governance of the country."[29]

The Directive Principles of State Policy incorporated a wide range of constitutional aspirations, from economic questions to moral precepts.[30] It also linked freedom to the removal of social and economic inequality.[31] Promising social and economic change through a liberal constitution was a unique experiment in India; it challenged liberal theorists' formulation that every attempt to resolve social questions of inequality and material destitution by political means would lead to terror and absolutism.[32]

Despite their celebration of the radical departures of the constitutional text, intellectual historians remain cautious about the impact of the Constitution. They have reiterated that the Constitution was an elite project. In their narrative, the institution of democracy through the Constitution did not emerge from popular pressure, nor was it wrested from a state; Indian democracy, in their view, was a gift to the people of India by their political elite. Sunil Khilnani cautions us that the powerful ideas of democracy and equality persuaded few outside "intellectual and English-speaking circles" and did not have the backing of any particular powerful group.[33]

In the celebratory story of the Indian Constitution, the main heroes are its charismatic and dedicated founding fathers who enshrined the principles of the nationalist movement into the constitutional document and largely abided by it.[34] As the sheen wore off the next generation of politicians, scholars focused on the Supreme Court as the site for strengthening constitutional values and cheered the activism of Indian judges.[35]

The Constitution as Illusion

Unlike the official narrative of the Indian Constitution, many have seen the document as a mirage and its promise as illusory. The excitement and despair produced by the Constitution is perhaps best described by Sadaat Hasan Mano, one of the finest writers in Urdu in the twentieth century, in his short story "Naya Kanoon" (The New Constitution).[36] The protagonist of the story, Ustaad Mangu, is a *tanga* (horse-drawn cart) driver in Lahore, a classic subaltern figure who is aware and excited about the buzz on the street about the passage of the Government of India Act of 1935, which promised to bring greater self-government to Indians. Throughout the story Mangu is elated at the passing of the new act, and he imagines that it will send the Englishmen "scurrying back into their holes." On the day the act is promulgated, Mangu is assaulted by an English customer for daring to ask for a high fare. Mangu retaliates by landing blows upon the surprised Englishman and shouting, "Well, sonny boy, it is our Raj now. . . . Those days are gone, friends, when they ruled the roost. There is a new constitution now, fellows, a new constitution." Mangu is surprised to find himself seized by two policemen, who drag him away to the police station. The story closes with the following lines: "All along the way, and even inside the station, he kept screaming, 'New constitution, new constitution!' but nobody paid any attention to him. 'New constitution, new constitution! What rubbish are you talking? It's the same old constitution.' And he was locked up."

Why is this short story about the Government of India Act relevant to a discussion on India's postcolonial Constitution? In recent years, historians and constitutional scholars have turned to Mangu's story as a metaphor for independence and the Constitution as a "spectacle of emancipation, i.e., the gap between the vision of emancipation that the law promises and the reality of violence that the law performs."[37] Aamir Mufti describes it as a "lesson in the discrepancy between subaltern struggles and bourgeois aspirations," in which the subaltern, blinded by the bourgeois project of reform, tries to claim his new rights and is quickly repressed.[38] The comparison is particularly tempting because the Constitution of India in 1950 almost identically reproduced two-thirds of the text of the Government of India Act of 1935, the "new constitu-tion" in Manto's story.

A skepticism of transformative constitutional change was expressed repeat-edly, beginning with the members of the Constituent Assembly. They pointed to the absence of a popularly elected assembly and the limits of its representation. The people had little input on the largely oligarchic process of constitution making.[39]

Despite the incorporation of universal adult suffrage and a bill of rights, the legal framework of the Indian republic remained rooted in colonial laws and institutions that were designed for centralized control.[40] The text that the new Constitution reproduced verbatim from the colonial Government of India Act included its controversial emergency power that allowed the central govern-ment to proclaim a situation of emergency and suspend fundamental rights, restrict access to courts, extend the life of parliament, and dissolve elected state assemblies.[41] Contrary to constitutional traditions that sought to protect in-dividuals from the state, the Indian Constitution empowered the state to trans-form society and the economy.

Thus the new fundamental rights could be constitutionally circumscribed on the grounds of maintaining the sovereignty and integrity of India, the security of the state, good foreign relations, public order, public health, and decency and morality, among others.[42] Somnath Lahiri, the sole Communist Party member in the Constituent Assembly, remarked that "many of these fundamental rights have been framed from the point of view of a police con-stable."[43] The institutions of colonial government—the police, the army, the judiciary, and the district administration—continued largely unchanged.

Critics pointed out that the easy procedures for amending the Constitution made it an extremely malleable document. A simple two-thirds majority of parliament was all that was required to amend the Constitution, a task made easier by the dominance of a single party until the 1980s.[44] How could the con-stitutional text restrain the state's actions, if it could be altered to suit the state's purposes? The Indian Constitution has been amended ninety-seven times to date. It was amended seventeen times in its first fourteen years, the period this book examines. At least half of these amendments curtailed judicial review or amended fundamental rights in order to reverse the impact of a Supreme Court judgment.[45]

Another illusory claim is that the Constitution was not authentically Indian or organic to India and thus remained outside the sphere of the people.[46] This echoes critiques by several members of the Constituent Assembly who had argued that the Constitution was an alien document that would fail to work because it was made in "slavish imitation" of Western constitutions.[47] A disappointed member regretfully said, "We wanted the music of the veena or the sitar, but we have the music of an English band."[48] Even the authors of the Constitution remained painfully aware that its founding notions were not available as actual experiences to the majority of its citizens. In his closing speech to the Constituent Assembly, Ambedkar observed that with the commencement of the Constitution, India entered a life of contradictions, recognizing equality in political life but denying, by reason of social and economic structures, equality in other spheres.[49] There seems to be an uneasy consensus that the Constitution reflects a gap between the elites comfortable with Weberian rationality and the people whose everyday discourse was not structured through formal rationality at all.[50]

The Republic of Writs

Rather than promoting either the celebratory or tragic stories of constitutional change, this book presents a contrary argument: the Indian Constitution profoundly transformed everyday life in the Indian republic. Moreover, this process was led by some of India's most marginal citizens rather than by elite politicians and judges. It shows that the Constitution, a document in English that was a product of elite consensus, came so alive in the popular imagination that ordinary people attributed meaning to its existence, took recourse through it, and argued with it.

In 1951, the year after the Constitution had come into force, the chief minister of the state of Hyderabad agitatedly wrote the following to the government in Delhi:

> An extraordinary tendency has been noticed recently for all sorts of people to take cases up to the High Court citing provisions in the constitution relating to what are termed fundamental rights; a Pakistani woman has asked for a stay of an order erred on her by police asking her to leave the state for non-possession of a valid permit, . . . while two displaced teachers who were asked to pass a test of a regional language have prayed for the issue of a writ of mandamus questioning the validity of an order.[51]

The situation in Hyderabad was not unique. Much to the surprise of politicians and bureaucrats across the country, Indians from all walks of life began flooding the courts and the public sphere with claims based on the Constitution.

The situation in Hyderabad was remarkable because that state had been integrated into the Indian state only recently and was, in effect, still under military rule.

Despite the apprehensions about it, the Indian Constitution quickly came to dominate public life in India. The objective of this book is to study "constitutional consciousness" as it exists in people's minds. The book charts the dialectic between the Indian Constitution as "politics of state desire" and the Constitution as "articulating insurgent orders of expectations from the state."[52] The former describes how the founders of the Constitution and succeeding governments imagined the Constitution would operate. The latter is generated by people who have their own expectations and make their own demands of the Constitution.

In service to this project of dialectical mapping, this book turns to a set of provisions in the Constitution that have largely been ignored, despite marking a clear break from the colonial past, in addition to the radical provisions of equality discussed above. These are the provisions that provide the right to constitutional remedies, which allowed any citizen of India to petition the Supreme Court for the enforcement of fundamental rights granted in the Constitution.[53] The powers granted to the state and provincial high courts (i.e., the appellate courts) were even wider: they were empowered to issue remedies in forms of writs against the state for the violation of fundamental rights, legal rights, and "any other matter."[54] Although political scientists and historians have discussed the substance of the fundamental-rights provisions, they have largely ignored the section of remedies as mere procedure. However, with just one stroke these supposedly procedural provisions of the Constitution empowered citizens to challenge laws and administrative action before the courts and greatly enhanced the powers of judicial review.

The introduction of these new remedies occurred just as the state was beginning to expand and intervene in everyday lives in an effort to achieve social and economic transformation. This led to a massive explosion of litigation before the Indian courts, which both the state and the judiciary were unprepared for. Almost all litigation in colonial India was civil litigation, often property disputes, between two or more private parties. Civil litigation rates actually declined after independence, whereas litigation against the state increased exponentially.[55] The inclusion of constitutional remedies in the form of a wide writ jurisdiction of the courts in newly independent India radically transformed the practices of governance in ways the Constitution drafters did not expect. As the new state consciously sought to mold the behavior of its citizens,

many of them found their livelihoods and ways of life challenged. The postcolonial state drew its legitimacy from its democratic mandate and development
agenda, making it particularly hard for electoral minorities to challenge its
agenda publicly. A range of individuals disaffected with the policies of the new
state, ranging from municipal sweepers to maharajahs, resorted to the courts
through writ jurisdiction.

The popularity of the courts arose not only from the nature of the remedies
available but also from the speedier hearing accorded to writ petitions in a
system rife with endemic delays.[56] Valued at a flat fee, the writ petition was
also a much cheaper remedy than most forms of civil litigation. In 1950 the Supreme Court heard more than 600 writ petitions. Its immediate predecessor,
the Federal Court, had heard 169 cases in eleven years. By 1962 the Supreme
Court had heard 3,833 such cases.[57] In contrast, over the same twelve-year
period the US Supreme Court (with more than a century of history and influence) heard only 960 such cases. In the first fifty years of American independence, the US Supreme Court had heard about 40 cases, not even 1 a year. The
dockets at the Indian Supreme Court, which were more accessible, grew even
more exponentially. The wide original and appellate jurisdiction of the high
courts, along with the comparatively simple procedural requirements for filing
petitions, brought a greater diversity of disputes before the Indian courts than
were brought before Western constitutional courts.

The writ petition therefore reveals the extent to which the state could penetrate everyday life as well as the point at which this interference would compel
a citizen to petition the court. The adversarial nature of the litigation system
forced each side to put forth its claims explicitly, making visible the emerging
conceptual vocabulary of democracy. The constitutional court becomes the
perfect lens to see top-down and bottom-up conceptualizations of constitutional
law in interaction.[58] The constitutional courtroom thus becomes an archive of
citizenship, a space in which the individual and the state can converse with each
other.[59]

The new Supreme Court's office was inside the houses of parliament, in the
chamber formerly used by Indian princes for their meetings (fig. 0.1). The court
was one of three chambers (the others being the House of the People and the
Council of States). Chief Justice Harilal Kania and the majority of his brother
judges had served on the Federal Court of India, which had been set up in 1937.
Although the Federal Court was the first court to exercise appellate jurisdiction throughout India, for the majority of its existence it had only three judges
and its jurisdiction was heavily circumscribed.[60] The coat of arms of the various

FIG. 0.1. Inaugural Sitting of Judges of the Supreme Court of India in the former Chamber of Princes, 1950. Ministry of Information and Broadcasting Photo Division.

princely states looked down upon the original eight judges as they deliberated their cases. In 1956, emphasizing their growing disagreement with the legislature, the now eleven judges moved to their own seventeen-acre complex a mile away.

The location of the Supreme Court in Delhi was a controversial decision. Despite being declared the capital of British India in 1911, the city remained a sleepy government town. There was no vibrant local bar, and the city lacked legal autonomy, coming under the jurisdiction of the Lahore High Court until 1947 and under the Punjab High Court until 1966. Metropolitan lawyers from Bombay, Allahabad, and Calcutta, though sneering at the Delhi bar, began to set up second establishments in Delhi because of the growing number of appeals. The early Supreme Court bar was small, populated largely by refugee lawyers from West Pakistan. The new judges had served a decade or longer on the provincial high courts and on the Federal Court, to which they had been appointed by the colonial government.

The Indian court system consisted of three levels (fig. 0.2). Just below the Supreme Court were the high courts, many of them established since the eighteenth century and housed within neo-Gothic structures at the center of major cities. However, the new Constitution greatly widened their jurisdictions and powers over the provinces. Half a dozen new high courts were established within the former princely states. The new Supreme Court and the newly empowered high courts sat at the apex of a judicial system whose lower ranks continued to be staffed by executive magistrates.

Below the high courts was the district judiciary, the first point of contact in the legal system for most citizens. It comprised bureaucrats who performed executive functions such as revenue collection and maintenance of law and order and who dispensed justice. As the administration grew more complex, the state established specialized

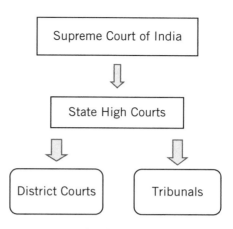

FIG. 0.2. Hierarchy of courts in India after 1950.

tribunals with judges and experts to look into areas like income tax. Only the high courts and Supreme Court exercised constitutional jurisdiction; the district courts were the site where the conflicts originated or where cases generated by the new constitutional interpretations of the appellate (high) courts were lodged.

The Constitution laid down the separation of the judiciary from the executive as a goal, but its achievement was a slow process, finally accomplished in the early 1970s.[61] Therefore, the courts exercising constitutional jurisdiction formed a clearly demarcated space that operated at a different register.

Indian litigants had attempted to approach the colonial judiciary for redress from the colonial executive. There was a brief period in the late eighteenth century when the judiciary in Calcutta and Bombay clashed repeatedly in an attempt to impose order on an unruly legal frontier.[62] However, much of this confrontation was framed in terms of a liberal imperial justice that positioned a judiciary representing the interests of the British Crown and Parliament against a corrupt and unruly East India Company governance.[63]

The narrative of judicial review in colonial India is one of constant erosion of authority over executive actions. The British Parliament curtailed the jurisdiction of the Supreme Court of Calcutta in 1781 and made the Governor's Executive Council the final body of appeal for all areas outside the city of Calcutta. These limitations were extended to Madras in 1800 and Bombay in 1823.[64] With the end of the company-state in 1857 and the enactment of the Indian High Courts Act of 1861, the powers of the high courts were pruned, and these confrontations became rarer. Chief Justice Ameer Ali of the Calcutta

High Court was driven to wryly remark that his court had all the powers of the King's Bench in England, provided that "England in India was confined to (a) Calcutta and (b) to British subjects, i.e., servants of the Crown."[65]

Before the Constitution was enacted, only the high courts of Calcutta, Bombay, and Madras had the jurisdiction to issue writs (Allahabad received its writ jurisdiction in the 1920s), and even this was available to and enforceable against only individuals and authorities within the city limits, as determined in the eighteenth century. The courts outside presidency towns (provincial capitals) had no power to issue writs. Even this limited remedy was a subject of much contestation from the executive, and the scope of writs was eroded, which led to the belief that a writ of liberty was a contradiction in a regime of conquest.[66]

Further legislation sought to render the government immune from prosecution. Various indemnity clauses made it mandatory to acquire the consent of the governor-general before the institution of proceedings against government officials, and the courts were precluded from investigating the validity of government orders.[67] All matters relating to revenue or its collection were excluded from the jurisdiction of the high courts, ensuring that the chief objective of the colonial government remained unhindered.

Indian nationalists and liberal reformers repeatedly made demands (which the colonial government consistently ignored) for greater power and autonomy to be granted to the judiciary and for the establishment of a Supreme Court with broad powers.[68] Judicial review was expressly included in the constitutional text not just to provide remedies for breach of fundamental rights but also to open the actions of the entire executive to scrutiny. The original draft of the Constitution had revoked the immunity of the government for writs only to the extent that they violated the fundamental-rights provisions. B. R. Ambedkar proposed what he described as a "small but consequential amendment"; it provided that "nothing in this clause revoking governmental immunity shall be construed as restricting the right of any person to bring action against the government of India."[69] Alladi Krishnaswami Ayyar, who served on the committee that drafted the powers of the Supreme Court, emphasized that Ambedkar's amendment clarified the right of aggrieved individuals to petition the high court for writs not just when fundamental rights were violated but also whenever the government overstepped the limits of its power in exercising its quasi-judicial authority or in implementing statutory provisions.[70] Article 225 of the Constitution expressly stated that the high courts were granted jurisdiction over questions of revenue collection, destroying one of the oldest bulwarks of executive immunity.

It is curious that the Congress Party–dominated Constituent Assembly voluntarily granted such significant powers of judicial review, for they were rightly suspicious of the judiciary and emboldened by public support. The answer lies partly in the nationalist accusation that the British were violating the rule of law in practice. A new regime would set itself apart from the colonial regime by reclaiming and instituting the rule of law. More cynical readings suggest that the judicial review was uncontroversial in the absence of a strong tradition of judicial interference with the executive.[71] A closer reading of the workings of the assembly makes it clear that several members, particularly practicing lawyers, saw it almost as a natural step.[72]

The Supreme Court of India: A Public and Secret Archive

The Supreme Court of India is located on seventeen acres in the heart of New Delhi (fig. 0.3). Built in 1958 and designed by Ganesh Bhikaji Deolalikar, the first Indian to head the Public Works Department, the white and red sandstone complex closely mimics the architectural style of the colonial public buildings in New Delhi. The complex itself is shaped to symbolize the scales of justice. A majestic red sandstone staircase directs visitors and the public gaze toward a high colonnaded gallery that wraps around the building.

Much of the public business of the court is carried out at this level. The colonnade leads to multiple wood-paneled courtrooms hung with portraits of legal luminaries. Litigants, visitors, clerks, and interns mill around the courtroom. Bored policemen desultorily pat down visitors and confiscate the occasional mobile phone. The judges, preceded by magnificently turbaned ushers in gilded uniforms, move through their own private red-carpeted corridors, where conversation is carried out in hushed tones. Stoic court officials in black jackets fill up the offices in both wings, slowly moving reams of paperwork. Cutting through all the spaces are hundreds of black-robed lawyers, arguing, gossiping, and occasionally sprinting between courtrooms with their robes billowing around them. This is the public view of the court, emphasized by the dozen odd OB vans and television crews that are almost permanently parked in the lawn across the main staircase. The Supreme Court is a designated court of record and is required to preserve its records for all eternity. Its final judgments are public and are scrutinized extensively by lawyers and reported

FIG. 0.3. The newly built Supreme Court of India, 1958. Ministry of Information and Broadcasting Photo Division.

in newspapers. A recent study showed that more articles in leading English newspapers discussed the Supreme Court than the parliament or the prime minister.[73]

However, underneath the public archive, buried in the basement, is the Supreme Court Record Room, which stores the entire proceedings of the cases: the arguments made by the lawyers, the affidavits and evidence produced before the court, transcripts of witness statements, maps of crime scenes, the occasional bloodstained physical evidence, and so on. In 2010 I became the first scholar to work with materials in this "secret" archive.

The aura of secrecy around the Supreme Court Record Room (and the record rooms of the lower courts) is partly physical, in terms of difficulty of access, and partly methodological, in terms of its value as a source. No formal procedure exists for researchers to consult Supreme Court records; access is granted at the discretion of the registrar. Furthermore, legal scholars emphasize the final reported judgment because it is the only document with future consequences and precedent value. The chief justice of India, who very generously gave me permission to consult the records and work in the court, was bemused by my goal. "The judgments are available online," he reminded me twice, emphasizing that I need not spend several months in the musky interior of the record room. Court officials, while personally welcoming me, were unsure where to place me. The usual visitors to the record room were Advocates-on-Record who wanted to consult a specific file on a case that was usually subject to a continuing litigation, and these individuals left within a few minutes after cross-checking details. In the absence of a designated space for research, it was decided that I would be allotted the workspace of whichever official was on leave that particular day. Over the course of six months, I, along with cloth bundles of files, moved through a series of offices in the court complex. This book is grounded in the exploration of this archive, both as a physical space and a discursive one.[74]

In order to understand the process of constitutional change, I sought early challenges to the new regulatory authorities and legislation that were set up as part of the state project to transform society and the economy, which emerged as critical cases. These cases became important as legal precedents and also resonated outside the legal sphere, in the form of discussions within the government or in the public sphere. Thus some, like the cow slaughter case, were repeatedly and frequently cited by early law textbooks and commentators; others, like the prostitution case, generated anxious correspondence between bureaucrats in state archives; still others, like the Prohibition case, were extensively discussed in newspapers and cartoons. The constitutional archive, while centered in the record room, is much larger than the records it contains.

Another important feature of this archive that became apparent to me was that the challenges to particular regulatory laws were dominated by individuals who belonged to the same caste or community. Since South Asian names mark both religion and caste, I first noticed this phenomenon when looking at the registers of case names, but a close examination of the case file showed that litigants almost always identified themselves by the community they belonged to. Minority communities (of caste and religion) appeared to be overrepresented in the courts, which shows that they took the state's obligations to protect them seriously. This book provides evidence that electoral minorities—that is, members of communities that were unlikely to represent themselves through electoral democracy because of class, sex, or race—were overrepresented before the courts in constitutional cases. Central to the construction of the constitutional order is a distinctive form of subalternity generated with the installation of electoral democracy through the tension between legislation and judicial review.

Although such a study cannot be exhaustive, this book attempts to capture the broadest range possible of regulatory measures and geographical distribution, ranging from Bombay to Bengal and covering large cities, small towns, and rural settings. Much of the existing scholarship on the Constitution is organized on the evolution of particular rights, largely property, free speech, and religious liberty, and is written to explain the evolution of that particular right to the present moment. This book's analytic frame is the new regulatory state that emerged in the 1950s, and it pays considerable attention to the under-explored areas of civil liberties (e.g., freedom of profession) as well as the field of administrative law. Questions over the right to property, religion, equality and free speech are also explored.[75]

Book Schema

This book seeks to demonstrate how constitutionalism became the governing frame in postcolonial India through a social history of constitutional and ad-ministrative processes. It does so through the minutiae of multiple constitu-tional encounters between citizens and the postcolonial state rather than through the construction of a teleological narrative.

The four numbered chapters are each named after a leading case that domi-nates the field. This is in tribute to both the formal discipline of common law adjudication, which is organized around legal cases, and the genre of popular legal writing. Legal thrillers like the Perry Mason novels of Earle Stanley Gardner or the courtroom dramas of John Mortimer remain popular in India. Lawyers like Khalid Latif (K. L.) Gauba and Kailas Nath Katju wrote best-selling and salacious titled narratives of famous trials.[76]

Each chapter is framed around a particular set of constitutional cases and performs three tasks. First, it uncovers the deepening reach of the Constitu-tion in everyday life. At the heart of each case is an attempt to transform the daily life of the citizen, be it through changing food practices, drinking habits, access to clothing, or sexual behavior. Through an engagement with quotidian practices, each chapter also highlights the changes or lack thereof during the transition from the colonial to the postcolonial. Second, in recognition of the plurality of citizen experiences with the Constitution, the analysis focuses on a different citizen political subject in each case. Chapters 1 and 2 deal with new spheres of regulation, prohibition, and market controls, whereas chapters 3 and 4 focus on how older regulatory debates over prostitution and beef eating became transformed in independent India. Finally, each chapter is also repre-sentative of a new form of legal strategy or technique that emerged in the period.

Chapter 1 is built on the litigation over the imposition of a draconian Pro-hibition regime on Bombay and focuses on the emerging practice of the test case. It also highlights how constitutional cases came to affect everyday legal-ity. The Prohibition laws in Bombay and other provinces, brought in to enforce

Article 47 of the Constitution, were among the earliest attempts by the post-colonial state to regulate the everyday life of its citizens. The Prohibition policy was a critical aspect of the attempt of the state to fashion a postcolonial identity for itself by freeing its citizens from what it called the foreign practice of drinking. However, it relied on the mechanisms of the colonial state for its implementation, opening up questions about state involvement in private life and the role of the police in a democracy. Given that the majority of litigants were Parsis (Indian Zoroastrians), a community with strong links to the liquor trade, this chapter explores the emerging idea of public interest and the relationship between liberty, property, and community identity. The chapter also demonstrates how even minimal legal victories were able to erode the state's confidence in its abilities.

Chapter 2 examines a series of administrative law challenges to the Essential Commodities Act. Independent India retained commodity controls that were established to meet wartime shortages but had become a permanent instrument for addressing the needs of the developmentalist state. The system of commodity controls exemplified the permit-license-quota Ra, a form of economic regulation that characterized the Nehruvian state, and sought to discipline the market economy by criminalizing economic offenses. Economic offenders, often petty traders from the Marwari community who were denied political legitimacy, sought to challenge this new criminal law through the language of constitutionalism. Complicating the view that this system of controls contributed to a culture of corruption, this chapter argues that judicial review of administrative action, the hallmark of the rule of law in a state, emerged in India from this illegality and culture of corruption.

Although the first two chapters focus on the new fields of politics (Prohibition and economic controls, respectively) that were generated by the Constitution, the subsequent two chapters focus on how the enactment of the Constitution transformed politics dating back to the nineteenth century.

Chapter 3 examines the transformation of the political agitation over cow protection by the enactment of the Constitution. Although the debate over cow protection had always been framed in terms of the religious rights of Hindus and Muslims, the Constitution met the demands for cow protection on ostensibly neutral economic grounds and laid it down in Article 48 as a directive principle of state policy. After partition and democratic elections, the new elected state governments of north India enacted strict laws prohibiting cow slaughter and criminalizing the consumption of beef. This chapter examines a writ petition brought by three thousand Muslim butchers—possibly

India's first class-action suit—that challenged these bans through a language of economic rights rather than religious freedom. It examines how religious freedom, minority rights, and political mobilization were transformed through the emergence of the Constitution as a site for politics.

Chapter 4 explores the new laws against prostitution, enacted to enforce Article 23 of the Constitution, which sought to end the trafficking of women. For nationalists and leaders of the Indian women's movement, independence meant the achievement of constitutional and legal equality and the emergence of the republican female citizen as a moral, productive member of society. However, legislators and social workers were confronted by a different conception of freedom when sex workers began to file constitutional challenges to the antitrafficking laws. They asserted their constitutional right to a trade or a profession and to freedom of movement around the country, and they challenged the procedural irregularities in the new statutes. The chapter demonstrates that despite the sex workers' minimal success in the courts, this litigation prompted mobilization and associational politics outside the court and brought rights language into the everyday life of the sex trade. This is evident from the deep anxieties this largely unsuccessful litigation created for politicians, bureaucrats, and middle-class women's activists.

The epilogue underscores the three connected themes that emerge from the cases: the process through which the Constitution emerged as an organizational assumption and a background threat for the state; the greater acceptability of procedural over substantive challenges to government action; and the origins of constitutional consciousness among certain citizens.

Demonstrating the early emergence of the constitutional field through the acts of marginal citizens, this book challenges the established narrative of the rise of judicial power in India as well as theories of juristocracy globally, which locate this shift in the 1980s and identify the main actors as judges, politicians, and international nongovernmental organizations (NGOs).

Rethinking the People's Constitution: The Constitution

The title of this book, A People's Constitution, refers to how we understand constitutions and imagine people's relationship to them. Constitutional and administrative history has long been out of fashion in India. This is in complete contrast to the United States, the other nation with a long history of constitutionalism and a powerful Supreme Court, where constitutional history threatens to crowd out other bodies of legal history. The dry and voluminous tomes that exist on the subject in India date back to the 1960s; they are consulted largely by those preparing for government service examinations or serve as treatises for practicing lawyers tracing the evolution of a doctrine.[77] Judges are central, and judgments are the final word. The historian's neglect of constitutional law arises from its identification with elite histories and linear narratives. This book makes a methodological shift by focusing on the contingency of constitutional law and the processes of mediation and translation.

The Constitution as Practice

This book argues that by asking "What did the court do?" in a certain case, we fail to consider the real contestations among judges, litigants, lawyers, and other actors in the presentation of legal claims. To understand how constitutional law works in India, then, it is necessary to understand what people (whether legal officials or ordinary citizens) believe law is and what they do with this knowledge as they make decisions in their daily lives.[78] An equally frustrating query is "Who won the case?" Although the question is tempting, it is reductive and often unhelpful in explaining people's repeated engagement with law. This book challenges the idea that constitutional interpretation is the monopoly of state elites and recognizes that that there are various ways of reading and interpreting the text.[79]

This book challenges the singular truth produced by a judgment-driven narrative by emphasizing the contingency and the contestation that make up the process of litigation. People who decided not to go to court are as important as subjects of study as people who did go to court when faced with a similar dispute. Similarly, this book pays equal attention to the losers in constitutional litigation, exploring what their vision of the correct constitutional order would have been. Legal losses are not always understood as such outside the legal arena. The book examines the afterlife of a court case, not just through its circulation as legal precedent but also through its effect on the lower courts, executive practices, and popular memory. This wider canvas shifts constitutional law away from a teleological project to an arena for struggle.[80]

The Constitution as Archive

What changed with the adoption of a written constitution? What did it mean to be a citizen of a sovereign republic? What did freedom mean to citizens of the Indian state? The answers to these questions remain surprisingly elusive.

The Indian state after independence has received little historical attention compared to both its colonial predecessor and its more recent past. Until recently,
disciplinary divisions marked the study of India before independence as the
province of historians; after independence, political scientists and anthropolo-
gists dominate.[81] Research was also stymied by poor record keeping and other
archival practices of the postcolonial states. State documents after independence, the mainstay of histories of colonial India, have rarely been transferred
to the archives.[82]

This book focuses on the two decades that have been described as the Nehruvian period, which begins with Jawaharlal Nehru's appointment as prime
minister in 1947 and ends with his death in 1964. Politically, the Congress Party,
headed by Nehru (whose leadership was virtually unchallenged after 1952),
held office continuously in the central government at Delhi and in almost all
state and local bodies. In contrast to contemporary India, which is dominated
by neoliberal economic policies and the increased visibility of a politics of identity based on caste and religion, the Nehruvian period has been defined as
dominated by a consensus on socialism, secularism, and nonalignment.[83]
Through centralized planning and modern developmental projects, the primary
aims of the state were to combat poverty and to reduce India's dependence on
Britain. Its politics were seen as modern and liberal and were dominated by
debates about class rather than identity. Its foreign policy was based on principled nonalignment between the Eastern and Western blocs during the Cold
War and an opposition to militarization.[84]

We still know very little about the Nehruvian state.[85] We know particularly
little about the role of provincial and local governments, let alone the quotidian
lives of ordinary citizens.[86] However, these constitutional cases are valuable
for the breadth of interactions between state and citizen that it makes visible.
The Supreme Court Record Room provides a new archive of postcolonial
India, and its files contain a variety of documents, including affidavits, government memoranda, newspaper reports, and printed material, that were submitted to the court for evidence. Given the spotty coverage of records in the state
archives for this period, the court's record room becomes even more valuable.[87]
These materials open up the cultural practices of the Nehruvian state, the institutionalization of law and legal discourse as the authoritative language
of the state, and the "materialization of the state in . . . signs and rituals" and in
the practical language of governance (i.e., assertion of territorial sovereignty,
development, and management of the national economy).[88]

The emerging scholarship on Nehru's India has focused on how citizens encountered the state in various places. As a result, studies on state formation in postcolonial India have focused on the centralized formation of cultural production from above, either through an analysis of debates among "powerful state actors" about state-produced documentaries, organization of parades, and new practices of town planning or by tracing the intellectual history of the new consensus on an Indian model of development that emerged among elites.[89] There is an assumption that most citizens remained outside these elite discussions altogether and were increasingly puzzled by their terms. Even though figures like Nehru were aware of the gap and constantly sought to explain the operations of the state and democratic politics to the people, they were caught within their own conceptual language and the limitations of the intelligibility of English.[90]

There is a broad consensus that in the absence of a mechanism of representation, the colonial state relied more on oppressive power and less on self-discipline. The logic of racial difference made it impossible to create a modern liberal state without superseding the conditions of colonial rule.[91] This book examines the nature of postcolonial governance: how regimes and techniques that were predicated on racial difference worked when discrimination was erased and popular representation introduced.

The ambition of the postcolonial state was to reshape both society and the economy. New instrumentalities were created to plan, review, and monitor these programs, and thousands of new laws were enacted by all levels of government. Of the 437 pieces of central-government legislation passed in a century and a half and found in a compilation of civil laws made in 1958, 140 were passed in the first decade of independence. In addition, 73 of the 191 acts involving penal sanctions belonged to the same period.[92] The majority dealt with social or economic regulation or administrative process, whereas only 28 of the approximately 400 colonial laws could be identified as such.[93] The Constitution created a powerful central government with vast revenue-raising powers and virtually blanket powers of legislation. The Planning Commission was established to create overall plans within which a "protective but realistic socialism would be created." The economy was subjected to regulatory control, perhaps more stringent than that of the agencies set up by President Franklin D. Roosevelt as part of the New Deal. A huge public sector would make the manufacture and production of goods and services so vital that they could not be left to the vagaries of private enterprise, and a new import policy would ensure a measure of austerity for the national good for the Indian middle classes.[94] The police powers of the state expanded massively at the same time that democratic processes were being implemented. Police powers are deeply rooted in the idea of public welfare, and by tracing changes in police power this book uncovers the transition from the colonial idea of the public to a postcolonial public. The familiar story of the state is of tax collectors marching into villages, social workers teaching housewives about nutritious diets, doctors vaccinating babies, and forest dwellers being displaced to make big dams. This book shows a different side of the experience, when the people not only refused to pay the tax but also started making claims against the state that used the state's own vocabulary.

The most visible practices of citizenship in Nehru's India have been those of refugees and of people displaced by partition. Research in this area has been aided by the preservation of the records of the Ministry of Refugee and Rehabilitation, unlike other ministries, as well as multiple projects to record the oral histories of partition survivors. The refugee experience offers two models of state society relations: one that recognizes the helplessness of individual citizens in the face of bureaucratic violence and decisions from above, and one that emphasizes the active agency of refugees, who used collective action to persuade lower-level officials to deviate from the letter of the law.[95] Drawing on both approaches, this book turns to the emergence of the Constitution as a field in which the state imagination and citizen agency would interact.[96]

The archive of litigation captures a broad spectrum of everyday interactions between the different levels of the state and its citizens. In 1958 the Law Commission report on the administration of justice argued that since

> the country stagnated for one hundred and fifty years of foreign rule, our legislatures are now trying to advance the nation in all directions. In their zeal to achieve quick results, they have not infrequently enacted legislation interfering with the vital and daily functions of the citizen. In order that their policies may go forward uninterrupted they have endeavored to entrench the executive and succumbed to the temptation of restricting the powers of the court.[97]

As the new state sought to implement its policies through laws and administrative action, those affected by it frequently appeared before the courts. The docket might include an association of printers challenging the state government's takeover of textbook production;[98] a schoolgirl refusing to comply with a government order forcing her to study in her mother tongue;[99] a widow protesting the requisitioning of her apartment by the rationing office;[100] a Hindu man unable to take a second wife because of marriage law reform;[101] and a Communist Party newspaper editor facing censorship by the central government.[102] It is not surprising, therefore that citizens "make of the rituals, representations, and laws imposed on them something quite different from what their originators had in mind."[103]

The Constitution as Democratic Practice

Unlike studies on how the state was produced from above, the Constitution opens up ways that the state is undone and negotiated from below. As this book demonstrates, constitutional litigation provided an option for citizens to insert themselves into an elite conversation. The writ petition and the new Constitution compelled state authorities, including high-ranking bureaucrats and ministers, to come to court to defend their policies. It also required them to respond specifically to the claims made by the litigants. The constitutional courtroom is distinctly different in form and content from the records of the executive or the legislature; here, instead of citizens encountering the state, the state suddenly encounters its citizens.

The courtroom was therefore the space of the unexpected. A study of the Supreme Court in the mid-1960s showed that two-thirds of the cases involved a level of government on one side and an individual or a private party on the other side. The government lost fully 40 percent of its cases in this category of litigation. Moreover, in 487 of these 3,272 decisions, the validity of certain legislation had been explicitly attacked by the private party in the dispute, and in 128 of these instances the legislation was held unconstitutional or otherwise invalid in its entirety (twenty-seven state laws, four laws) or in part (seventy state laws, twenty-seven central laws). The study concluded that "few, if any, other governments in the world fare as poorly in encounters with their citizens before the nation's highest judicial tribunal."[104] It is the uncertainty of the encounter in the courtroom that makes it a valuable archive, for law is the arena in which abstract new principles run up against the messiness of social change.[105]

Rethinking the People's Constitution: The People

The people who inhabit books on constitutional law are judges, lawyers, and the occasional politician. In doctrine-driven scholarship, judges emerge as the central actors, and little attention is paid to the actual litigants or to the

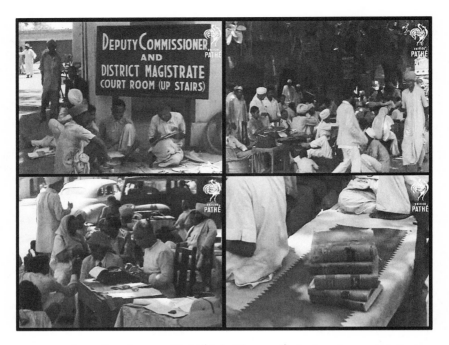

FIG. 0.4. Scenes from *Lawyers of Delhi* (Pathe Films, 1948) of refugee lawyers and clients conducting business on the streets outside the Delhi district courts.

histories of the disputes. It is not surprising, therefore, that the major debates over constitutional law in India have been framed around the question of judicial intervention or activism: What is the appropriate role for judges in a democracy?[106] This book makes a methodological shift away from the approaches distinguished above and toward a social history of constitutional law. In seeking to integrate the subjects of Indian social history (subaltern actors and everyday life) and Indian constitutional law (high politics, judges, and political theory), I draw upon the methods of constitutional ethnography to "better understand how constitutional systems operate by identifying the mechanisms through which governance is accomplished and the strategies through which governance is attempted, experienced, resisted, and revised, taken in their historical depth and cultural context (fig. 0.4)."[107]

The central actor in this book is the citizen litigant, who has received little attention as a political actor in South Asian history. Litigants, and even litigation itself as a mode of political action, have easily been labeled bourgeois in India; as such, litigation has been regarded as an activity unavailable to the majority of the population. The popular argument is that the bulk of democratic politics in the postcolonial world, particularly India, lies in the realm of political society in contrast to civil society. Whereas civil-society politics are marked by modern associations such as autonomy, deliberative decision making, and individual rights and operate through formal institutions like the courts and the media, political-society politics "make their claims on government, and in turn are governed not within the framework of stable constitutionally defined rights and law, but rather through temporary, contextual, and unstable arrangements arrived at through direct political negotiations."[108] Law is regarded with suspicion here because its application seeks to disrupt the tacit acceptance of illegalities, such as squatting or vending without a license.

This book challenges the above view as an empirical fact, showing that thousands of individuals who turned to the court were from groups that were marginalized both socially and economically in independent India. Although only a few could be considered to be absolutely poor, many participated in the informal economy or were rendered marginal because of their religion or their sex. This diverse group of litigants included prostitutes, Muslim butchers, Hindu refugees, Muslims who had been evicted from their homes, vegetable vendors, and even the occasional peasant rebel. This book does not suggest that litigation was an option available to all citizens of India but only argues that access to it was not determined solely by one's socioeconomic class.

Unlike litigation in the United States, to which it is often compared, strategic litigation in India was not driven by NGOS or public-interest law firms. For organizing legal campaigns nationally, there was no Indian equivalent to the American Civil Liberties Union in the United States or the Haldane Society of Socialist Lawyers in Britain. The lawyers who appear in this book are largely ordinary lawyers, handling a range of different matters, who were approached by their clients. However, India at the time of independence had at least 72,425 legal practitioners.[109] Although the number might seem small relative to India's population, it was the second highest in the world after the United States and was striking, compared to most newly independent states of Asia and Africa. For instance, on the eve of independence, Indonesia had only 36 native lawyers. China reported only 3,000 lawyers in 1957, despite having a comparable population to India's. The situation in the former British colonies was equally dire, with expatriate Indians making up most of the non-European legal profession in eastern and southern Africa.

By the 1940s the Indian legal profession had come to constitute a fairly well-defined professional public, with common journals, association meetings, and lobbying groups. Lawyers who represented opposite sides and the judges who heard them continued to share professional and social bonds. It is this bond that the book explores in order to contextualize legal professionals as mediators. In the decade after independence, lawyers, judges, and legal academics were consciously engaged in examining the problems of the Indian legal system. Through commission reports, journal articles, biographies, and newspaper editorials, they spoke as lawyers expressing their concerns and visions for the new legal regime.

The People as Postcolonial Citizens

How were the claims and strategies of Indians as postcolonial citizens different from their claims as colonial subjects? Rights claims and rights consciousness in India did not emerge with the enactment of the Constitution. The challenges in a search for rights consciousness arise from the fragmented nature of the public sphere in colonial India. Indians were seen to lack the Liberty Tree of British imaginings. In his history of liberal thought in India, Christopher Bayly has emphasized how everyday encounters in colonial India informed the debates among both British and Indian intellectuals over the rights of Indians. For instance, cases of lascars (Indian seamen) in Britain who were damaging ships in response to mistreatment opened up a debate over the rights of Indians and their relationship to British property.[110] Demanding access to new professions and jurisdictions across the empire, Indians formulated and laid claim to various universalist ideas of citizenship even when it was being denied to them.[111] However, these forms of rights and claim making were limited in significant ways.

First, even the most persuasive advocate of these British Indian claims had little ability to enforce them. The powers of the courts were trimmed, and the limited representative government that existed had minimal powers. Thus a majority of these claims were expressed through the petitioning of various authorities, a practice that later nationalists would pejoratively describe as mendicant liberalism. Early Indian liberals adopted a juridical model of justice, but they saw the British Crown and Parliament as their court, where they could make appeals against the despotic local colonial government.[112]

Second, in the absence of guaranteed liberties, many of these claims had to be made with great subtlety, through "parody, innuendo, and indirect criticism," and the claimants had to search for new forums in the absence of representative institutions and in view of the elusiveness of the law.[113] Finally, Bayly makes an important distinction between claims made by rights-bearing individuals (which formed the basis of Indian liberalism) and claims made by holders of "ancient customary liberties."[114]

The demand for the protection of "ancient customary liberties," made by subjects ranging from Hindu widows insisting on their inheritance rights to temple authorities resisting taxation, formed the more broad-based secondary order of rights claims in colonial India. This order drew on promises made by the colonial government, in 1772 and 1858, to apply Hindu and Muslim religious laws to matters concerning marriage and inheritance. These promises became a point of furious contestation between the state and various groups of citizens. The colonial state's interference in the private domain was resisted by many nationalists, who viewed the incipient nation as enjoying sovereignty and superiority in the inner domain of family, culture, and community while conceding the colonial state's dominance in the outer domain.[115] As recent scholarship has argued, the administration of Hindu and Muslim law did not merely resurrect scriptural authority but transformed it through liberal ideas of equality, women's rights, and difference.[116] Tanika Sarkar argues that rights were developed from messy encounters between scriptural law and the Anglo-American legal system rather than from any form of systematic political thinking.[117] Unlike the West, where group rights emerged within established civic communities, in colonial India rights were accorded to groups before the formation of a civic community, that is, the nation.[118]

The Constitution transformed both orders of rights. It brought forward a written code that explicitly granted rights to all citizens. Citizens belonging to a broad range of classes presented themselves before the state as rights-bearing individuals, in contrast to petitioners seeking to have some rights recognized or propagandists working through innuendo or shadows. The difference is not merely semantic. Rights claims in colonial India were first a question of recognition—that is, of whether the subject had a right—whereas under the new Constitution they became a question of enforcement, based on an assumption that the existence of rights was already guaranteed. A legally enforceable right is distinct from the same right framed as a moral claim or as a privilege granted by the benevolent colonial state.

Furthermore, the distinction between claims made as rights-bearing individuals and those made as holders of customary liberties became difficult to sustain after independence. The argument for noninterference with custom and tradition had been based on the fragmented authority between the alien state and its communities. However, with independence the state moved from the outer sphere to encompass all areas of life. The Constitution explicitly recognized religion and family as arenas for transformation. The right to practice and profess one's religion was limited on several grounds, including public order, morality, and health.[119]

The most drastic change from the precolonial system was the displacement of a normative inequality as the foundation for the conceptions of rights in India. Rights under the colonial government were determined by caste, class, and sex and drew on custom.[120] The Constitution, however, heralded a formal equality between all citizens and created a common source of rights for all. However, as the constitutional founders recognized, this did not herald immediate social transformation. Given the limited history of individual rights claims in colonial and precolonial India, from what source did the new postcolonial rights claims emerge?

The People, Property, and the Market

The cornerstone of the colonial legal system and classical liberal theory was the protection of individual property rights. Property law thus became the framework within which status-based community identities could be incorporated into state-recognized individual rights.[121] The language of property rights was called on even when other rights were at stake—for instance, disputes over religious ritual and authority were settled by appealing to property titles.[122] David Gilmartin and Jonathan Ocko argue that property law provided the model for the notions of rights in colonial India and linked the individual and indigenous conceptions of identity together. Thus, religious and customary privileges came to be conceptualized as forms of individual property. It was not surprising that the only right guaranteed in the colonial Government of India Act of 1935 was the right to property.[123]

However, the right to property itself became a ground for contestation in the Constituent Assembly. Several members argued in favor of weaker property rights to allow the state to bring about land reforms and redistribute property. Although the Constitution guaranteed the right to hold, acquire, and dispose of property, the right was subject to several limitations. Confronted with early court decisions striking down land reform law as violating the right to property, parliament sought to successively amend the Constitution and narrow the right. The very first amendment to the Constitution in 1951 granted the state the power to acquire property for "public purposes" or to "secure property management." Laws implementing such acquisitions were declared immune to judicial review and fundamental-rights challenges. The right to property continued to be eroded until the 42nd Amendment in 1978 deleted it entirely from the fundamental-rights section.[124]

How did a rights order that was predicated on the right to property turn into a system in which property was the least secure right? This book uncovers a process of translation in which claims to property were increasingly coded as the right to freedom of expression, privacy, or equality. This move reversed the logic of the colonial order of rights in which various claims had to be translated through the right to property.

So how did the colonial rule of property change with independence? Based on archival findings, this book argues that the market replaced property as the basis for the new rights order. This challenges the political economy narratives about the Constitution that have almost exclusively considered real property (i.e., urban and agricultural land). The market had emerged as an object of governance in colonial India in the late nineteenth century but became central to the postcolonial state's imagination as it sought to simultaneously industrialize and redistribute property. Building on Ritu Birla's work on the imbrication of culture with economy, this book shows how the new order of rights grew out of questions of consumption, production, and retail.[125]

Studies of democracy in independent India have predominantly focused on elections and representation and have given little attention to the judicial process. This book considers writ petitions against new government initiatives that sought to radically transform the state as critical events. A *critical event* is an event through which new modes of action emerge that redefine traditional categories and that can be acquired by a variety of political groups.[126] These critical events form a new genealogy of Indian constitutionalism that emerges from the everyday acts from citizens. Thus, to use the words of Hannah Arendt, this book explores the process by which the Constitution emerged as a hybrid realm where "private interests assumed public significance."[127]

1

The Case of the Constable's Nose

POLICING PROHIBITION IN BOMBAY

THE SUMMER OF 1951 was an exceptionally hot one in Bombay. On May 29, Behram Khurshed Pesikaka, a middle-age government servant, left home after dinner for a drive around south Bombay to escape the oppressive heat. As he returned to his home on Wodehouse Road at 9:30 p.m., some people "emerged from behind a stationary vehicle and suddenly stepped out on the path of his jeep."[1] Although he braked and swerved, he was unable to avoid them, and his jeep knocked down three members of a Sindhi family.[2] The two women were hit by one of the front wheels, and the man was dragged some distance by the bumper. The police constable on the scene reported that Pesikaka's breath smelled of alcohol. Pesikaka was accordingly charged under the Indian Penal Code for rash and negligent driving as well as under the newly enacted Bombay Prohibition Act (BPA), which had made the consumption of alcohol without a license an offense.

During the trial the neighborhood watchman, an independent witness, testified that Pesikaka was driving at ordinary speed and exercising adequate care. Furthermore, the medical evidence confirmed that even though Pesikaka had smelled of alcohol, his pupils reacted to light, his speech was coherent, he was well behaved, and he could walk in a straight line. The police doctor testified that Pesikaka had not been acting under the influence of alcohol. Despite the serious injuries that he had inflicted on the victims, Pesikaka was acquitted of the charges of rash and negligent driving.[3] However, the High Court decided to convict him under the BPA.[4] The court held that the gist of the offense under the BPA lay in the mere consumption of liquor without a permit. It was entirely irrelevant whether the person who consumed liquor was drunk and incapable. Once the prosecution established that liquor was consumed, the burden of proof was on the accused to show that he had not consumed liquor illegally. Pesikaka, who was sentenced to one year in Arthur Road Jail, was one of hundreds of thousands of people convicted under the BPA. By the time the Prohibition regime was liberalized in 1964, more than four hundred thousand people had been convicted under Prohibition.[5] Pesikaka's lawyers petitioned the Supreme Court of India by challenging the constitutionality of the Prohibition laws.

Prohibition laws in Bombay and in other provinces were among the earliest attempts by the postcolonial state to regulate the everyday life of its citizens. Prohibition had been written into the Constitution as a goal for the new state.[6] This policy was a critical aspect of the state's attempt to fashion a postcolonial identity for itself while relying for its implementation on mechanisms of the colonial state. Central to the issue of drinking alcohol was the question of individual freedom. Yet even though the decision to drink was an exercise of will, the act of drinking could lead to a loss of self-control. The regulation of alcohol required the restriction of its movement and the creation of locations where drinks could and could not be consumed, limiting the freedom of movement of people and property. Thus the imposition of Prohibition had to be reconciled with the new constitutional rights to property, life, and liberty.

Compared to authoritarian regimes, liberal states have a greater difficulty enacting systems to control their citizens' habits of consumption.[7] The state machinery and the mechanisms of government that had been developed in the colonial period did not have to represent the will of the subject. But these constituted the physical and ideological apparatus available to the postcolonial government, which sought to represent popular will.

The regulation of alcohol is an extremely productive example of how the major modes of governance interacted with one another. As an American study of Prohibition suggested, there are "few major problems of public administration which do not emerge in striking fashion with the governmental effort to control the consumption of alcohol."[8] The act of drinking is governed by social and moral codes, religious rituals, and individual desires that differ widely across the population. It is simultaneously managed through medicalization, criminal law, licensing and zoning regulations, taxation, and health and safety regulations.

Despite the history of alcohol regulation since the nineteenth century and a prominent campaign for Prohibition, there is very little known about the subject.[9] Most scholars have understood the history of Prohibition in India as a state or bourgeois project to transform the culture and practice of drinking in India, and they have looked to the strategies of resistance and co-optation that were adopted by the lower classes. Studies on the consumption of alcohol on the tribal population near Bombay have found that despite a short-lived temperance movement among tribal people (which sought to financially hurt moneylenders and landowners), drinking practices remained unchanged even in the face of coercive efforts by the state and co-optation by the nationalists. Social histories of Prohibition emphasize the resilience of the masses in their resistance to the bourgeois politics of Prohibition. Thus the failure of Prohibition and temperance is predicated on the gap between the masses and the state.

Pesikaka's case, and the dozens of legal challenges that preceded and followed it, demonstrate a way of citizen engagement with the state that did not turn on the notion of this gap. The Constitution, in these cases, was not an external force but a structure within which Prohibition could be resisted and negotiated. Pesikaka's case is significant for two reasons. First, it offers an extremely well-documented example of how citizens could find themselves in the grip of Prohibition laws while going about their everyday lives. Second, Pesikaka's constitutional strategy marked an important shift in how the legal system could be used to subvert the regime of Prohibition. The emergence and end of Prohibition in the 1950s was structured through these court cases and under the shadow of the Constitution. Pesikaka's case marked a turning point, when the debate about Prohibition moved from the question regulating individuals or populations to the question of regulating the state itself.

The Constitution transformed the debate over Prohibition in ways that the Constitution drafters had not anticipated. Central to the constitutionalization of the question was the reformulated idea of the public interest and its relationship to private interests. This chapter examines the history of alcohol regulation in India and seeks to locate Bombay's Prohibition policy among the larger apparatus of the postcolonial welfare state. It then moves to discuss the three distinctive forms of Prohibition litigation that emerged: the substantive constitutional challenge to the imposition of Prohibition, the procedural challenge to the implementation of Prohibition, and the impact of this self-conscious constitutional litigation on everyday criminal cases. Finally, it examines the effect of this litigation on the state's confidence in its ability to transform society through law.

Toward the Moral Nation: Prohibition
and Nationalism

The Bombay Prohibition Act, under which Pesikaka was arrested, was a strict and draconian piece of legislation enacted as part of the total Prohibition policy adopted by the Congress Party government in Bombay in 1946. The government decided to introduce total Prohibition throughout the state over four years through a gradual cut in consumption of 25 percent a year.[10] To this end, the BPA was enacted in 1949. It prohibited "the import, export, transport, manufacture, sale, purchase, possession, use, or consumption of any intoxicant, hemp, or the tapping of any toddy-producing tree, except . . . in accordance with the terms and conditions of a license, permit, pass, or authorization granted under the Act."[11] The criminalization of both the consumption and the possession of alcohol marks the BPA as a radical departure from the Prohibition regimes in the United States, Europe, and Canada, which focused on production and distribution.

Why did the BPA look so different from other contemporary experiments with Prohibition?[12] The answer lies in the fact that the production and sale of alcohol in India had become a state project in colonial India. In Bombay it had been regulated by the Bombay Abkari Act of 1878 (*Abkari* literally meant "hard water"). The Abkari Act was essentially a revenue act that sought to generate maximum revenue with minimum compensation. Motivated by a need to increase profits, the government held a monopoly over the sale of liquor and auctioned licenses for the privilege to make and sell liquor in specific areas. Successful bidders then delegated their rights to selected village-level liquor dealers who did the actual jobs of manufacture and sale. This created a class of middlemen, often outsiders to the village economy, who had the incentive to raise liquor revenues. The Parsi community, which had access to other sources of capital, came to dominate the liquor trade in province of Bombay. We will return to the effects of the involvement of the Parsis in the liquor trade later in the chapter.[13]

The Bombay Abkari Act had brought in a centralized system of distilleries and promoted new drinking practices, because village-based alcohol production provided more opportunities for revenue evasion. For instance, toddy (made from the sap of palm trees), the most popular form of liquor, was subject to prohibitive taxes because it had a short shelf life and could not be produced through centralized distilleries.[14] Despite protests, there was a steady change in consumption habits in favor of factory-made liquor. The Bombay government also enacted the Mhowra Act in 1892, banning the collection and sale of mhowra flowers, which were used by Bombay's tribal population for food, cattle feed, and the brewing of alcohol.[15]

Criminal law was used to regulate alcohol only to the extent that revenues were hurt. The highest number of prosecutions dealt with cases of the manufacture and sale of illicit liquor. A prototypical case was that of Pestonji Barjorji, a distiller of spirits whose license had expired. He was arrested under the Abkari Act after the police found the copper utensils used for distillation in his possession.[16] Similarly, dealers or purchasers of mhowra flowers were also prosecuted.[17] The emphasis was to protect a major source of British government revenue.

In contrast, postcolonial India's alcohol policy consisted of determined demands for social reform and not revenue needs. Middle-class temperance movements the world over had viewed alcoholic beverages as a root of social evil, particularly for the working class. While sharing that sentiment, the Indian temperance movement stressed that drinking itself was alien to Indian culture.[18] Unlike in Britain, where liberal thought had criticized temperance projects as violations of individual liberty, temperance was almost a constitutive feature of Indian liberalism. This arose both from the belief that alcohol consumption was against Indian custom, which placed a premium on individual self-control and from the fact that the colonial government profited tremendously from alcohol.[19] The foreignness of alcohol is difficult to establish empirically, but it is clear that drinking practices—the kind of alcohol preferred, the quantities of alcohol drunk, and the sites of consumption—were transformed by the colonial state. Revenue policies encouraged the consumption of industrial-produced, low-quality alcohol over home-brewed liquors like toddy and mhowra. Licensing rules shifted drinking to the new liquor shops and bars far away from fields and villages.

Prohibition became a part of the Congress Party's "constructive program" in the mid-1920s, popularized by Mohandas Gandhi. This was a combination of three strategic reasons: the opportunity to hurt imperial revenues, the ability to forge a common platform between Hindus and Muslims, and the influence of the global temperance movement.[20] The differences between the nationalists and the colonial state were laid bare in the evidence submitted before the Bombay Prohibition Enquiry Committee, with the British members and liquor dealers supporting the status quo and the Indian representatives arguing for stricter regulation and Prohibition.

During civil disobedience movements on 1921 and 1930, Congress Party volunteers picketed liquor shops and sought to persuade drinkers to stop.

Temperance volunteers noted the people who frequented liquor shops and re-ported them to their families and caste organizations. In Bombay presidency (province), social pressure and threats of boycott were extremely successful in curbing drinking. Noting with alarm the success of picketing in Bombay, W. Dillion, the collector, warned that this would lead to large losses in excise revenue and upset civic budget estimates. Not only were liquor sales affected, there were fewer participants and paltrier bids in the auction of liquor li-censes.[21] The colonial officials saw the demand for Prohibition as a ploy to destabilize the colonial state and not tied to values of temperance.

However, central to Gandhi's imagination was his view of drinking as a for-eign custom that debilitated the body of the Indian worker and peasant and, by extension, the Indian body politic. The concept of *swaraj* implied freedom not just from foreign rule but also from foreign customs. Advocating total pro-hibition, he wrote that no country was "better fitted for immediate prohibition than India." First, drink was sapping the vitality of the working classes, "who had to be helped against themselves." Second, since the intellectual classes of India did not drink like those of Europe, there would be no referendum required.[22] In this brief essay he spells out what emerged as the nationalist consensus on prohibition: Drink was a practice and a problem for the poor, not part of the elite culture in India as in Europe or the United States. The poor therefore had to be saved from themselves through an intervention of the en-lightened classes. A drunkard was a diseased man, he wrote, "quite unable to help himself."[23]

Gandhi too recognized that temperance could not be achieved merely by giving speeches and through propaganda. "Why do people drink?" he asked. "They drink because they are suffocated living in pestilential dens."[24] Gandhi was empathetic toward poor drinkers, recognizing that for some it was the only way they could escape their wretched daily conditions. He urged volunteers to visit the homes of drinkers to educate them on the ills of liquor, to persuade liquor vendors to stop selling alcohol, and to picket liquor shops.

However, although the improvement of their conditions was essential, and persuasion was important, he emphasized that the prohibition of intoxicating liquor would ultimately have to be by law. Recognizing that the colonial state was unlikely to damage its revenue base, Gandhi stated that such a law would not come into being until "pressure from below is felt in no uncertain manner." He rejected the "specious argument" that India could not be made sober by compulsion and that those who wished to drink should have facilities pro-vided to them.[25] "The state does not cater to the vices of its people," he wrote.

"We do not regulate or license houses of ill fame. We do not provide facilities to thieves to indulge their propensity for thieving. I hold drink to be even more damnable than thieving and perhaps even prostitution. Is it not often the parent of both?"[26]

Addressing Congress Party workers at Bardoli in 1929, Gandhi highlighted that *swaraj* could not be established merely by "driving out the English." *Swaraj* did not mean "the freedom to live like pigs in a pigsty without help or hindrance from anyone."[27] Self-governance would therefore require Prohibition to create a healthy public. He famously reiterated, "If I were appointed dictator for one hour for all India, the first thing I would do would be to close without compensation all the liquor shops [and] destroy all the toddy palms such as I know them in Gujarat."[28]

The emphasis on social transformation through the will of the state was unusual for Gandhi, who had always urged that social reform must first come through the inner transformation of the people. He argued against the use of law and compulsion in all his other constructive projects, be it the emotive questions of cow protection and untouchability or developmental works such as the improvement of sanitation and hygiene. For Gandhi, constructive work and reform were necessary not just as a duty to the project of nation making but also to the self, to regain the power of action.[29] Drink more than anything else damaged the self and took away the power of action.

Elections in 1939 allowed the Congress Party to form the government in a number of provinces. The governments of Madras, Bihar, the Central Provinces, and Bombay introduced Prohibition in a phased manner. Gandhi praised the imposition of Prohibition on Bombay in 1939, stating appreciatively that the city of Bombay, with its "dirty chawls, overcrowded lanes, and uninhabitable hovels" will for the first time become truly beautiful when it goes dry. It was only with Prohibition and the removal of the temptation of drink from the laboring classes that the municipality of Bombay dealt with the problem of improving the conditions of the poor.[30] It is perhaps not surprising that Bombay, the quintessential modern Indian city, would become the site for experiments with Prohibition. As Gyan Prakash points out, an insistent demand of anticolonial nationalism was to establish a modernity of one's own.[31] What better way to transform Bombay's decadent modernity, with the hedonistic drinking of the rich and the squalid drunkenness of its workers, than through Prohibition? Prohibition was perceived as an easy solution to the problems of the urban poor, and its language of hygiene and morality blended with critiques of class and caste.

Although Gandhi mainstreamed and constantly urged the question of Prohibition, the issue itself enjoyed support from a wide cross-section of the party. Prohibition campaigns had been among the earliest activities involving the mass participation of women. The All India Women's Conference, a leading national women's organization, took up Prohibition as a major part of its agenda.[32] Along with economic analysis and moral opprobrium, scientific data was marshaled in support of Prohibition. Pamphlets and government reports heavily cited medical studies and chemical analyses that confirmed alcohol's damage to the body. In his introduction to a Congress Party pamphlet on Prohibition, Jawaharlal Nehru argued that if Prohibition were to triumph in India, it would do so not on religious grounds but because of the well-reasoned conviction that it was necessary for the well-being and economic progress of the nation.[33] Socioeconomic studies that tracked drinking's impact on family finances were commissioned and circulated.[34] Prohibition thus reflected the state's concern not just for the morals of its citizens but also for their social and economic well-being.

Undergirding the project of Prohibition was the notion of a strong state with a disciplined workforce. Prohibition became significant to the process of nation building initiated by the Congress Party. It was part of the Karachi Charter of Fundamental Rights and Economic Principles of 1931 and was included in the election manifestos in 1937. Crucial to the legitimacy of Prohibition was its introduction by an elected government. Though praising Bombay government efforts in 1939, Gandhi emphasized that Prohibition was not a superimposition, because it had been introduced by an elected government. It had been a plank in the "national program" since 1920 and therefore came in the "due fulfillment of the national will definitely expressed twenty years ago."[35] The conflation of the Congress Party's will with the national will was easily made. Deviations from the opinion were sharply criticized—Gandhi admonished Acharya Narendra Dev from omitting the prohibition of intoxicating liquor from the proposed constitution of the Congress Socialist Party, a subgroup of the Congress Party.[36]

Constitutionalizing Prohibition

In 1946 the Constituent Assembly spelled out the new state's aspirations in Part IV of the Constitution, Directive Principles of State Policy. Although these principles were not judicially enforceable, they were supposed to be guidelines for future governments.[37] Encompassing general commitments to social and economic justice and the reduction of disparities of income, the directive principles included specific commitments to create a system of social security, enact a uniform civil code for all communities, redistribute wealth, and ban cow slaughter. Most significant, for the subject of this chapter, Article 47 of the Constitution provided that the state "shall endeavor to bring about a prohibition of the consumption of intoxicating drinks and drugs that are injurious to health except for medicinal purposes."

The original draft brought to the Constituent Assembly by B. R. Ambedkar did not have a provision for Prohibition. The amendment first arose during a debate on the final draft of the Constitution, which some members alleged was alien to the Indian ethos and the goals of the freedom movement. Kengal Hanumanthaiya lamented, "We wanted the music of the veena or the sitar, but we have the music of an English band."[38] He attributed this to the fact that the members of the drafting committee, though able lawyers, were not associated with the freedom movement. He conceded that they might be "learned in the several laws and rules that were framed before we got independence," but that was insufficient for creating a constitution for India.

Kazi Syed Karimuddin, the Muslim member who sponsored the amendment to include Prohibition, expressed his astonishment that given Mahatma Gandhi's lifelong campaign for Prohibition, there was no mention of this in the Constitution. He pointed to the American precedent for incorporating Prohibition into the constitutional framework and warned the assembly that rejecting this clause would be "the rejection of the wishes of the Mahatma."[39] Karimuddin drew support from all sections of the house. Mohamed Ismail Sahib, a Muslim League member from Madras, emphasized that "Prohibition must find a place in the Constitution because there is absolutely . . . no difference of opinion in the matter."[40] Mahavir Tyagi, a Gandhian, reminded the house (to rousing applause) that Gandhi's foremost plank of constructive national work was Prohibition and that "we all stand pledged to this program we had pledged in front of Gandhi."[41] Prohibition thus became a plank that united the Hindu conservatives, the Gandhians, and the Muslim League. The ritual invocation of Gandhi's name six months after his assassination made opposition almost impossible.

The inclusion of the Prohibition clause played an important performative gesture in rehabilitating the Western-style constitution. The symbolic role of Prohibition emerged in Tyagi's powerful closing speech when he lamented the failure of the Constitution to meet many of the promises of the national movement, such as socialism and decentralized government. He stated the following:

> If we cannot accommodate even the idea of Prohibition in our Constitu-
> tion, then what else have we been sent here for? We have been talking of
> revolutions ... but if we cannot even have this small reform in our Constitu-
> tion, the book will not be even worth touching with a pair of tongs. I submit
> that if the Draft Constitution does not contain Prohibition, it does not
> contain Gandhi, because where there is liquor, Gandhi cannot be.

Prohibition thus linked the liberal document to Gandhi, making it modern and moral at the same time. A Bombay minister would later argue that "Prohibition was to be the foundation stone of reconstruction schemes [through which] we try to make a man sober, teach him the true value in terms of a standard living, eliminate waste, and create a wholesome atmosphere for both the family and the village."[42] Unlike decentralization, to village governments, or radical land redistribution, which would have led to a radical restructuring of the state, Prohibition could be implemented within the existing framework.

In an extraordinary speech to the Bombay Assembly, the Prohibition minister argued that "unrestrained free thinking and unlicensed individual liberty" were an ingenious idea introduced by the British to convince the traditionally abstemious Indians to drink.[43] The British education system had corrupted the minds of young Indians, who challenged religion, tradition, and the *shastras* (scriptures) and blindly aped the British, taking up drink because Englishmen drank. The minister suggested that both drink and the individualist civil liberty argument were poisoned British gifts that had to be resisted in an independent Indian republic.

The proponents of Prohibition were well aware of the policy's failure in the United States, but this did not deter them. As Morarji Desai rationalized, American cultural and social habits gave drinking social prestige, whereas Indian culture since time immemorial abhorred drink and drunkards.[44]

Creating Sober Citizens: Disciplining Drunkenness

As the Constituent Assembly met in Delhi in 1946, it envisioned a constitution that would empower the state to bring about the sweeping social and economic changes promised by the Congress Party–led political struggle. Individual rights were qualified.[45] Thus, the right to liberty granted in the Constitution was subject to permissible restrictions "in the interests of the sovereignty and integrity of India, the security of the state, friendly relations with foreign states, public order, decency or morality, or in relation to contempt of court, defamation, or incitement to an offense."[46]

The limited opposition to Prohibition was framed and articulated on four grounds: liberal cosmopolitanism, minority rights, economic loss, and sanctity of contract. It became almost unpatriotic to suggest, as Hemchandra (H. J.) Khandekar, did that Prohibition went against the grain of liberty. In his very first speech to the Constituent Assembly, Khandekar quoted Harold Laski's *Liberty in the Modern State* to argue that Prohibition militated against the development of personality, which must be the goal for Indian citizens. The real development of personality comes without suppression, taboos, and inhibitions, he added.[47] Yet the individualist argument got little traction in the assembly.

Khandekar attempted to humanize drinkers and present drinking as social ritual rather than a disease. He urged the house to remember that a majority (almost 90 percent) of drinkers were not drunkards and would be disproportionately inconvenienced, while the 1 percent who were drunkards would turn to illicit liquor, which is more dangerous. As a representative of the formerly untouchable (Dalit) caste, Khandekar was implicitly referring to the wide divergence in dietary practices between caste Hindus and others.

Khandekar also challenged the so-called unanimous consensus on Prohibition by pointing out that several Christians and Parsis, for whom drink was part of social life, were not in favor of Prohibition. Jaipal Singh Munda, a tribal representative, made the case for minority rights more vociferously, insisting that alcohol (particularly rice beer) was an essential part of tribal ceremonies. The amendment, he contended, was a "vicious one" that sought to interfere with his religious rights. Munda's radical assertions of tribal, or *abidbasi* (the term he preferred), autonomy were rebutted by paternalistic arguments on the benefits experienced by tribal peoples after they gave up liquor, whereas Christians and Jews were reassured that exceptions would be made for sacramental wine.[48] That the opposition to Prohibition came from the Dalit caste and from tribal members underlines the fact that the claims to the Indian culture of temperance were reproduction of certain caste norms and were not universally grounded.

Arguments focusing on the loss of excise revenue were rejected by assembly members who pointed out that excise revenue on alcohol also generated three times the social cost through increased crime, poor health, and lack of efficiency.[49] Others claimed democratic legitimacy by pointing to the experience of Madras, where despite the annual loss of nearly 170 million rupees, the party that had imposed Prohibition was brought back to power.[50] B. G. Kher was swift to brush aside these concerns, stating that "it was too late in the day to argue that the use of intoxicating drinks do not affect the moral sense of the person who uses them." Drinking extinguished "the lamp that showed the distinction between right and wrong," he said; thus drinkers were incapable of exercising moral choice, and their rights were "not a matter of individual liberty." The state was correct in curtailing the liberty of drinkers, Kher asserted, since there "could not be individual liberty to commit suicide."[51] L. M. Patil, Bombay's first Prohibition minister, was even clearer when he noted that "advocates of personal liberty forget that no state can allow civil liberty to ruin oneself." The concept of civil liberty thus had to be changed, he noted. The history of social legislation, he asserted, was a history of the curtailment of civil rights.[52]

Therefore, with an overwhelming majority, Article 47 was introduced to the Constitution of India, committing it to "raising the level of nutrition and standard of living and improve public health . . . and, in particular, . . . endeavour to bring about prohibition of the consumption, except for medicinal purposes, of intoxicating drinks and of drugs that are injurious to health."[53]

With independence, most states experimented with Prohibition (fig. 1.1). Bombay and Madras were the only two to introduce a system of complete prohibition, having had a long history of Prohibition activism. The leaders of both provinces were also committed to the idea of Prohibition. In the early 1950s, several states appointed committees to consider the effectiveness of Prohibition, and two recommended its repeal on the grounds that it had failed in 1951 and 1956, respectively. These two states did not return to the status quo but instead brought about a system of rationing in which an individual had to apply for a permit to drink alcohol. Almost all other states declared certain districts dry districts and monitored the sale of liquor closely. Despite this disparate approach among the provinces, the Prohibition Enquiry Committee (appointed by the Planning Commission in 1954) recommended that "nationwide prohibition" be completed by April 1, 1958.[54]

To this end, the state was urged to enact stricter laws; check illicit manufacturing; conduct public propaganda; ban drinking in hotels, bars, clubs, and parties; and make abstinence a rule for all government servants and defense forces. The Prohibition Enquiry Committee spelled out its requirements: the public should be more cooperative, the magistrates should be less lenient in

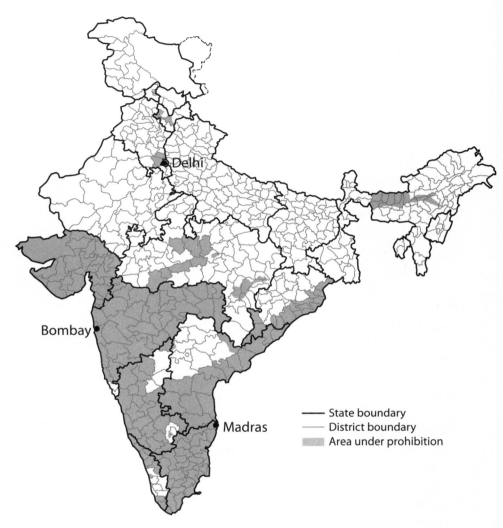

FIG 1.1. Districts with Prohibition in 1951. Redrawn from M. D. Bhansali (1951) Annexures.

convicting Prohibition offenders, and the police should be more vigilant. The language used against drinking was so strong that the dissenting member, P. Konada Rao, protested that "consumption may be an offense . . . but it seemed to be an unwarranted violence of language and sentiment to stigmatize consumption as moral turpitude, a vice, a sin!"[55]

Prohibition through law was an attempt to shape custom and morals. The Bombay Prohibition Act of 1949 reflected this expanded notion of state power and responsibility. The ten commandments of the bill (as they came to be known) were that no person should produce, manufacture, possess, export, import, transport, buy, sell, consume, or use liquor except under a permit issued by the government.[56] The BPA declared that possession, consumption, manufacturing, bottling, and export of liquor would be nonbailable offenses.[57] It held that anyone opening or patronizing a drinking house would be fined and that anyone found in a drinking house would be presumed to have been drinking.[58] Drunk or disorderly behavior on the street was punishable as well.[59] The act even criminalized commending the use of liquor or "encouraging or inciting any member of the public to do any act that might be in breach of prohibition laws."[60]

The BPA granted vast powers to the police and Prohibition officers. It empowered Prohibition officers and all police officers to "enter at any time, by day or by night, any warehouse, shop, house, building, vessel, vehicle, or enclosed place in which [they have] reason to believe [that] intoxicants or utensils, apparatus or implements used for manufacturing intoxicants are kept."[61] They could also open packages and confiscate goods that they suspected of containing illicit liquor. Warrants were not required for arrests for any of these offenses or for searching premises. The BPA provided that people believed to have committed an offense under the act could be detained without trial and have their movements restricted.[62] The Prohibition policy thus created a system that operated outside the penal code and the criminal procedure code that applied to most offenses.

The idea of exceptions also undergirded the permit system introduced under the act. The BPA enabled the government to issue permits to exempt certain categories of individuals from the purview of the act, such as military personnel, foreigners, and former princes. It also provided that addicts, whose health would suffer if they were deprived of alcohol, could be granted a permit after a medical diagnosis.

The new Prohibition regime greatly enhanced the police powers of the state to crack down on drinking. In its early days, the BPA created a "wholesome dread" of committing an offense under it, since it was punishable by fine and imprisonment.[63] In 1949, the year of the enactment of the BPA, 19,814 Prohibition offenses were recorded and 11,748 people were convicted, compared to 9,063 offenses recorded and 3,468 convicted in 1948. The number of people per million convicted for excise offenses increased by 240 percent.[64] The number of offenses involving the manufacture of illicit liquor dropped, but the crimes of possession and consumption rose steeply. To deal with the manpower shortage the government drafted special prohibition guards, who were nonofficial workers but were granted statutory powers.[65]

Police raids could take place almost anywhere and target anyone, as the ubiquitous Prohibition arrests section in the daily papers of Bombay showed.[66] Trains and railway stations were subject to sudden raids and searches, leading to the arrests of both passengers and staff. The police also followed tips about private parties and raided both elite and middle-class homes, arresting a range of people from the vice president of the Kandivili Municipality, the *sarpanch* (mayor) of the town of Dahisar, lawyers, doctors, and leading businessmen— all of whom were named and shamed in the papers. Nor were women exempt. Those targeted ranged from Catholic housewives in Thane found with cooking wine to Ameena Sultana, one of Bombay's leading courtesans. Women were seen as particularly complicit in both brewing illicit liquor and transporting it around cities. There was much excitement when one of the first female constables in Baroda arrested eight women on her first day who were said to be distributing illicit liquor to consumers.[67] Prohibition and its enforcement became part of the daily language of the province.

The idea of exceptional laws and procedures was not new to Indian law, but they had largely been applied in times of war (i.e., the Defense of India Regulations, 1914 and 1939), to cases of revolutionary terrorism (i.e., the Bengal Criminal Law Amendment, 1925) and in cases of dacoity (i.e., the Special Tribunal Act, 1942), an act of armed robbery committed by an Indian gang. Why did Prohibition offenders require a regime similar to those of terrorists and dacoits?

The answer lies in the way the postcolonial state viewed its relationship to its citizens. The dominant voices within the Congress Party believed that the state needed to ban intoxicating drugs and liquor that led to "ruin of the people." B. G. Kher, the premier of Bombay who had ushered in the Prohibition Act, defended the inclusion of Prohibition as a directive principle of state policy on the grounds that drinking was injurious to health of the individual and to that of the public because of an associated increase in crime and a decrease in efficiency and productivity of the worker.[68] The paternalism of the state ran through the debates: Shibban Lal Saxena defended the expected thirty-five-crore loss in revenue by arguing that this would lead to at least one-hundred-crore savings of income of the "families of drunkards, especially for the labor and Harijan families, where this vice is most prevalent."[69] The Harijan caste and laborers were more likely to spend their hard-earned money on drink, and given their lack of understanding of its ill effects, it was necessary for the state to intervene to protect them and their families.

The citizen was therefore perceived as a passive recipient of the government's program and not as a participant. Srirupa Roy observes that "Nehruvian India's most frequently invoked figure was that of the 'infantile citizen' requiring state tutelage and protection."[70] Two views of the drinker emerge. The first is that of someone incapable of making an informed choice, often a tribal member, a worker, a Harijan, or a member of the lower order who needed to be uplifted. Morarji Desai, Bombay's home minister, emphasized this inability of the lower classes to give up drink even though they were ashamed of it. He asserted that the poor people in Surat had told him, "How nice it would be if the liquor shops were closed once and for all! . . . We make up our minds to abstain, but when we pass by the liquor shops, the temptation is too great for us to resist and we succumb."[71]

The second image of drinkers to emerge is that of bad citizens, who, though aware of the loss of revenue sustained by the government, continued to persist in their selfish habits, doing damage to themselves and society. When confronted with the innovative ways that people continued to consume illicit liquor, a Bombay legislator labeled them as "mad men" and "subnormal,"[72] Defending the enhanced punishments under the amendments to the BPA, he argued that "it must be the object of government to see to the welfare of these people. They have to be looked after, and that is why we have jails or mental hospitals."[73]

In the postcolonial state's vision, there was unaminous support for Prohibition demonstrated through electoral victories and constitutional commitment. Those who wanted to drink were a minority who had to be protected from themselves and from damaging society at large. Given the importance of the goal (Prohibition) and the costs of deviation (illicit drinking), exceptional measures were necessary and could be justified under the constitutional dispensation.

The Fundamental Right to Drink:
Fram Nusserwanji Balsara v. State of Bombay

The first legal blow to the Prohibition regime was struck on April 13, 1950, when Fram Nusserwanji Balsara petitioned the Bombay High Court for a writ of mandamus against the state of Bombay in order that he be permitted to "exercise his right to possess and consumer foreign liquor." Legal challenges to Prohibition laws were by themselves not a novelty; the attempt by the Congress Party government to impose Prohibition in Bombay in 1939 had been crippled by a decision of the Bombay High Court as well. The high court had struck down attempts to impose Prohibition by amending an existing alcohol licensing law and "by a stroke of a pen, without any warning or compensation" to destroy businesses that had been build up in reliance of the continuation of this policy."[74] The experience of the earlier procedural challenge warned the government of the need to enact a law that explicitly imposed Prohibition, and it drew legitimacy both from the goal of Prohibition and the dilution of property rights by the Constitution in the name of "national interest."

Balsara's response also drew from the language of rights that was secured by the new Constitution. He argued that the BPA restricted his freedom of speech and action and that it violated his right to equal treatment. Moreover, the Constitution empowered him to approach the court for a writ of mandamus under Article 226, which significantly expanded the high court's power to issue writs for the violation of fundamental rights as well as for "any other purpose." Balsara himself was a new type of litigant, perhaps best described as a public-spirited citizen. He was a Parsi journalist who worked for several years with *Jam-e-Jamshed*, a Gujarati daily newspaper in Bombay. In the late 1950s he ran for parliament as an independent candidate from South Bombay.

Balsara launched a two-pronged attack on the BPA. He prayed for a writ of mandamus asking the government and the Prohibition commissioner to allow him to exercise his right to possess, consume, or otherwise use the prohibited items, including foreign liquor, eau de cologne, lavender water, medicines containing alcohol, and medicated wine. In the event that the court did not recognize his right of alcohol possession and consumption, he argued that the constitutional right to equality mandated an equal right to alcohol consumption and that the court must therefore strike down the permit system that provided for exceptions of various categories of people like soldiers and foreigners. Balsara asserted that his right to free speech was restricted by the section that criminalized the commending of drinking, and he protested that "encouraging or inciting any member of the public to do any act that might be in breach of Prohibition laws" might even be extended to cover his writ petition. Finally, he argued that the new federal division of powers did not give the province the power to interfere with interstate trade and commerce and thus restrict the import of foreign liquor into the province.[75] Given that the BPA was being assailed on several grounds, he also hoped that the Bombay High Court would declare the entire act unconstitutional.

Early in the hearing, the high court recognized that there was no question of striking down the entire Prohibition regime, because the Constitution made clear that drinking could be regulated by the state. Yet the court also declared it permissible to use the doctrine of severability: the power to declare certain sections ultra vires, beyond the power of the Constitution, while preserving the overall structure of the act.

Conceding that the state had the right to impose Prohibition and confiscate property, the Bombay High Court held that the legislature had the power to regulate only "alcoholic liquors" and not all "intoxicating liquors," as the BPA sought to do. Therefore, articles of everyday use that contained alcohol but were not ordinarily used as a beverage, such as eau de cologne or medicines, could not be proscribed under the act. Although the court recognized the possibility that such liquids could be used as a substitute for alcohol, the state could not prohibit their legitimate use, and in fact such a ban would violate Article 19, which included the right to acquire and hold property. Further restrictions on medicines and cosmetics would hurt the objectives of public health and social welfare promulgated by the state. Thus, although the court did not recognize a fundamental right to drink, it argued that the right to property conferred on citizens the right to possess liquids containing alcohol.[76]

Furthermore, the high court ruled that criminalizing incitement and encouragement would violate the freedom of speech under Article 19. C. P. Daphtary, the advocate general of Bombay, argued that the restriction was valid because it sought to regulate morals. The judges pointed out that this morality was subjective, since most of the neighboring provinces had not sought to regulate this. "How could the sentiments of common citizenship and equality in law be reconciled with different standards of morality in different places?" the chief justice asked.

The Bombay High Court took seriously the claim that the permit system denied the right to equality promised in the Constitution. Balsara had contended in his petition "that the system of granting permits under the act resulted in discrimination of one citizen from another and a citizen from a noncitizen."[77]

The exemption granted to the army was held to be arbitrary and without any reasonable basis. The judges rejected any attempt to show that the army should be treated differently from Indian citizens. Since India was not a military state, the judges ruled, the army was not entitled to special rights and privileges. The judges were particularly scathing toward attempts to distinguish the army from other categories of public servants. The maintenance of public order could not be said to be a higher order of responsibility, because a similar responsibility was conferred on the police, and they received no such exceptions. Nor did the judges agree that the armed forces were an all-India service; therefore, soldiers transferred to Bombay for a brief period should not be forced to live under Prohibition.

When the chief justice suggested that the armed forces were exempt in order to ensure the high morale that was required for the strenuous task of fighting, Balsara's lawyer countered by asking why the cultivator who worked in waist-deep water for hours at a time was not exempt, or miners in a deep mine. Noshirwan P. Engineer, Balsara's advocate, turned the logic of the government against it by asking the following: If drinking liquor at the end of the day rendered people unfit to perform their duties, how could the army be permitted to drink? In his judgment, the chief justice asked rather acerbically, "Why must the army be permitted to do something that is opposed to public welfare? Why should the army not conform to the standards of social reform laid down by the legislature as much as the civilian population?"[78] The Bombay High Court's challenge to a narrative of exceptionalism for the army was a break not only from the unchallenged position of the army in the colonial period but also from the privileges enjoyed by armed forces in other postcolonial states.

The high court also struck down the exemption for foreign tourists, stating that they had to be treated exactly like Indian visitors from other states. Noting that "before independence, we deeply resented any special treatment that was meted out to non-Indians," the judges expressed surprise that after independence the legislature continued the practice.

The court also challenged the system of granting exemptions to former princes, emphasizing the question of postcolonial sovereignty. The rulers of the princely states that had been absorbed in the Indian union had received several constitutional guarantees, such as social precedence, recognition of their titles, and continuation of their privy purses (i.e., payment of their private expenses with public revenue). Despite criticism, the government had thought it expedient to ensure the smooth integration of the princes' territories into India. The attorney general's argument that the government could not interfere with the "rights, privileges, and dignities of a ruler" did not impress the court.[79] Was this an admission that the right to drink was a personal right?

If princes had a right to drink, how could this right be withheld from other Indians?

The Bombay High Court came down strongly on provisions of the BPA that were akin to preventive detention—that is, detention without the safeguard of appearing before a magistrate within twenty-four hours, a right that is guaranteed in the Constitution.[80] Although the legislature was permitted to make laws for preventive detention, such provisions had to be for the maintenance of public order or the provision of essential supplies and services. The court ruled that since the Prohibition law did not deal with either of these two reasons, the laws that permitted a policeman to detain someone for fifteen days without a court hearing was void because they violated the constitutional right to move freely and reside in any part of the country. The judges decisively rejected the legislature's contention that these extraordinary powers were justified or that intemperance in Bombay had assumed such proportions that it was a threat to public order.

The Test Case for the New Republic

On August 23, 1950, the Bombay High Court unanimously ruled that the powers of the state legislature did not extend to the legitimate use of nonalcoholic beverages and medicinal preparations. The court struck down the system of permits that distinguished foreign visitors from Indian visitors, civilians from military personnel, and citizens from long-term foreign residents. The court also struck down the section that criminalized the commending of drinking and the publication of advertisements for liquor.[81] Furthermore, the judges issued a writ against the state to refrain from enforcing the provisions of the BPA that were void. Balsara was to be granted a liquor permit by the government without the ignominy of being classified as an addict, which the court found particularly objectionable because it carried a sense of moral obloquy. Furthermore, Balsara did not have to promise that he would do nothing that would frustrate or defeat the policy of Prohibition.

Compared to the effect of the high court judgments in the 1930s, which had effectively ended the Prohibition regime, the Bombay government initially believed that it had gotten off lightly. In fact, the cabinet resolved not to appeal the decision before the Supreme Court. However, the cancellation of permits for the army and foreigners caused a storm of protest from the Ministries of Defense and External Affairs as well as from army authorities.[82] The ability to create exceptions has always been held to be a norm of sovereignty, but by using the constitutional promise of equality, the court stripped the elected legislature of this power.

Furthermore, there was a sense that even this was a dangerous precedent. Sardar Patel, the deputy prime minister, wrote an urgent letter to B. G. Kher, the premier of Bombay, asking him to reconsider the decision of the cabinet not to appeal the judgment. Forwarding a memorandum by the attorney general that outlined a possible legal strategy for the Supreme Court, Kher warned, "Our Constitution is already *so much against us* that we should not accept any further encroachments by the judiciary, and in my opinion, any judgment of the High Court in constitutional matters that appears unsound should be appealed against."[83] Patel's reaction seems extreme, particularly given that he himself had mixed feelings about state-led Prohibition. In 1939 he had been horrified with the implementation of Prohibition policies in the provinces and had described it as an "utter fiasco" that in some states had led to drinking on a larger scale.[84]

Where did this sense of unease come from? The Prohibition policy had been hailed as critical to the refashioning of independent India; as necessary for social, economic, and moral progress; and as enjoying the unanimous support of the public. Even its coercive aspects were seen as part of a bitter medicine administered by a government that cared for its citizens' well-being, in contrast to the irresponsible colonial government that had sought to profit from alcohol revenues. Balsara's petition, however, shattered the assumption of public consensus. How could Prohibition reflect the promise of the postcolonial republic if it violated the principles of equality on which the republic was built? It was no coincidence that Balsara's arguments challenging the exemptions given to foreigners, soldiers, and princes got the greatest traction in the media, for it showed uncomfortable similarities between the colonial state and the republic. Discrimination in favor of foreigners had been one of the main complaints of the national movement. Apart from being representatives of an old feudal order, several princes had allied with the British and had crushed nationalist movements in their states. Finally, the most uncomfortable question was raised about the army that had been a colonial institution and that continued to have a Westernized officer core with a social life based on drinking.

The writ petition was framed in terms of an individual citizen's assertion of rights, but from its earliest stages the case was seen as being about the rights of all citizens. The newspapers began to refer to it as the "Prohibition test case," and this was even picked up by government functionaries such as Prohibition Commissioner Mausen D. Bhansali.[85] Balsara had clearly not petitioned the court for the sole purpose of enjoying a drink in the evening. A middle-class man with social connections, he could have easily acquired alcohol on the black market, bribed officials to look the other way, or even produced a medical permit for an addict from a compliant doctor. The decision to go to court and invoke the Constitution was a conscious one that he knew would have far-reaching implications.

The concept of test cases had been around in both England and India since the 1920s, but its use peaked in the late 1940s with the expansion of the state. The early cases centered on tax and commercial questions, but starting in the late 1940s these epithets were applied to cases that posed significant challenges to state policy. The test cases in the year preceding the *Balsara* decision indicate the kind of litigation strategies that were being adopted: the sweeper's case, in which a municipal sweeper who had participated in the Bombay sweepers' strike attempted to avoid prosecution under the new Essential Services Act of 1949;[86] the private-street case, in which a local landlord challenged the municipality's designation of several private thoroughfares as public streets;[87] and the tea vendor's case, in which a tea vendor challenged the requirement of licenses for tea stalls.[88] The test case helped predict the consequences of compliance to laws, determined litigation strategies and was strongly defended. Judicial restructuring at independence which had raised the pecuniary jurisdiction of the lowest civil courts of Bombay. Opponents was protested that this change was likely to limit the chances of test cases being decided by the High Court and thus having a lesser impact.[89]

How a case came to be described as a test case remained unclear. In some cases, the court identified the issue as a 'test case'. The *Kushaldas Advani* case, also in 1949, was treated as a 'test case' and given priority by the Bombay High Court since there were about 160 similar petitions before the court challenging the powers of the state government to requisition private residences for public purpose.[90] Similarly, in the milk powder case, the magistrate held that a coffee shop owner using powdered milk was not guilty of violating the rationing orders on milk, and he described it as a test case that would affect the decisions in three hundred cases pending before him.[91]

In other cases the test was being conducted by the government. In the moneylenders' test case, the government launched a prosecution against prominent businessman Maganlal Javerilal for unlicensed moneylending, in order to test the ability to enforce the Bombay Moneylenders Act of 1946.[92] Unlike these situations, in Balsara's case there was no flood of other petitions challenging the BPA, nor was the government particularly keen on putting its legal regime to the test. Unlike many of the plaintiffs in the previous test cases, Balsara had not been arrested or charged under the Prohibition laws. His petition was not one of hundreds of similar cases. Unlike contemporary constitutional cases, which arose from a situation in which the petitioner's liberty or property was being taken away, Balsara's petition was framed purely as a matter of principle. The test here was not only of the Prohibition policy but also of the possibilities offered by the Constitution.

Keeping this in mind, the courts were lenient in terms of procedural safeguards. Balsara had petitioned for a writ of mandamus, and his petition faced a preliminary challenge on the grounds that the writ was not the appropriate form of relief in this case. The advocates for Bombay argued that the writ of mandamus was not a remedial measure and that it could be used only to compel an authority to do something, not to force it to refrain from doing something. In the past, writ petitions had often failed for not asking for the right remedy; however, the Bombay High Court was almost gracious in allowing Balsara to amend his petition appropriately to ask for different forms of relief. One justice asked, "If a man goes to court and says, 'My rights are affected, give me a remedy,' can the court turn him away because he has not asked for a requisite remedy even if his grievance is real?"[93]

The role played by the Bombay High Court in admitting this petition was significant, especially because the neighboring Madhya Pradesh High Court had rejected a nearly identical petition for a writ of mandamus challenging the constitutionality of the BPA on simple procedural grounds. The petitioner, like Balsara, had not been arrested for an offense, nor had he had an application for exemption refused. The court ruled that since no legal right of the petitioner had been infringed, it could not issue a binding declaration.[94] The courts recognized their own role in advancing the rights of the citizens. In most civil cases, the losing party usually had to pay the legal costs of the victorious party. The attorney general of Bombay urged that since the petitioner had not succeeded in the entirety of his challenge, he should pay the costs. However, the court believed it could not overlook the fact that Balsara had succeeded in some important contentions. Since this was a result of tge extraordinary leniency of the court, there should be no order about costs.[95]

Justice Tendolkar, who was part of the Bombay High Court bench that ruled in Balsara's favor, eventually critiqued other aspects of the BPA. Addressing delegates at an international legal conference in New Delhi two years later, he contended that the BPA, which "enabled the police to raid a man's home, was a violation of the UN charter."[96] He argued that a legislative measure that made a man's home liable to be raided by the police for "finding out whether he was committing the heinous crime of having a drink in the evening" authorized interference with the privacy of the home and violated Article 12 of the UN Declaration of Human Rights. He asserted that the right of privacy was always recognized in the Indian tradition and that the home was regarded as "more sacred here than elsewhere." However, the "fanatical" and "fantastic" Prohibition law gave people no more privacy than "goldfish." There was a lack of proportionality in the fact that private premises could be raided in order to discover "not the secret den of anarchists plotting against the state or a gang of murderous thugs planning an armed dacoity, but whether a bottle contains a dram of whiskey or a tumbler emits the tainted smell of prohibited alcohol."[97]

Apart from the judicial enthusiasm in championing the cause of the individual, the *Balsara* case was also a celebrated public event. The courtroom was packed every day of the hearing, and the case and its proceedings received detailed coverage in both English-language and vernacular newspapers. On the first day, the papers reported, long before the court had assembled, "a large crowd clamored for admission to the courtroom, and when the doors were opened there was a scrambled for positions of vantage."[98] There were blow-by-blow accounts of the oral arguments between the parties and the interventions of the judges. The *Bombay Chronicle* noted that on the day of the judgment the street outside the high court was brimming with people. A crowd gathered at the Poona Railway Station, eagerly awaiting the evening newspapers from Bombay that would report on the decision. Newspaper offices were flooded with telephone inquiries regarding the outcome of the case, and it was the "topic of conversation on the street corners and in restaurants."[99] Thus the Prohibition case became a legal spectacle. In public imagination, it never was simply about Balsara's rights, it was an event in which everyone had a stake.

The case itself registered in the collective consciousness of Bombay's legal profession, which remembered the verbal jousting in court. Soli Sorabji, a former attorney general of India, reminisced visiting the Bombay High Court with his classmates from the Government Law College to witness the proceedings and recounted Noshirwan Engineer observing "that a republic without a pub is a relic." Ashok Desai, a former solicitor general and attorney general, remembered C. K. Daphtary (the advocate general of Bombay and the first solicitor general of India) wryly commenting that "the petitioner came for a bottle of whiskey but was returning with a vial of perfume."[100]

Balsara's case triggered at least one similar challenge in another state. In the neighboring state of Madhya Pradesh, a man named Sheoshankar applied for a writ of mandamus challenging the application of the Central Provinces and the Berar Prohibition Act of 1938.[101] Sheoshankar's arguments were virtually identical to those raised by Balsara, and he expressly relied on the *Balsara* decision. The Madhya Pradesh High Court also referenced the *Balsara* judgment in its scathing critique of the system of exemptions for non-Asians and members of armed forces. The legislature of Madhya Pradesh, which was in the process of enacting a new Prohibition law, took note of the *Balsara* judgment and amended the draft law to bring it into conformity with that decision.[102]

Immediately after the judgment, the liquor stocks of the area commander in Bombay were sealed.[103] However, the government by and large attempted to ignore the judgment and continued to issue permits to foreigners, servicemen, and ex-rulers for a few more weeks. On hearing of this, Balsara's attorney wrote to the director of Prohibition and the collector of Bombay seeking information on whether the government had continued to grant permits even after the High Court judgment. He also asked that his client be granted an interim permit until a permanent exemption ordered by the High Court could be issued to him.

The government solicitors politely recommended that Balsara follow the prescribed format for applying for the permit and stated that the other information he sought was not relevant to the orders in his favor, so the authorities could not be called upon to furnish it. Balsara reiterated that he was entitled to a permit under the High Court order and therefore must be given an interim permit without having to apply for it. He also pointed out that since no applications for a permit had been made by the ex-rulers, servicemen, and foreigners—whose earlier exemptions had been struck down by the High Court—to supply them with permits would amount to an act of discrimination. Furthermore, apart from being a petitioner, he was entitled as a citizen of the state to the information that he demanded, and he warned the government that if he did not receive a reply in a week, he would be forced to petition the High Court for an action of contempt.[104] Balsara made it quite clear that he was not satisfied with merely securing his individual right to drink and that he would continue to resist the Prohibition regime.

All this led to the government hastening to appeal the High Court's decision at the Supreme Court. The Supreme Court, located in distant Delhi, was not as spectacular a venue as the Bombay High Court. The Supreme Court had been newly constituted, and it sat in an unused chamber in the parliament building while the new courtroom was being constructed. Unlike the Bombay High Court with its crowded bustling corridors, the Supreme Court transacted few cases, had a small bar, and was largely empty.[105] Despite the less-charged atmosphere in Delhi, the stakes remained high. Motilal Setalvad, the attorney general of India, was asked by Sardar Patel to defend the state of Bombay. Setalvad was assisted by Daphtary as well as M. M. Desai and H. M. Seervai.[106] Balsara was defended by a veritable legal battery of Noshirwan Engineer assisted by G. N. Joshi, R. J. Kolah, and Nani Palkivalah.[107] Unlike the Bombay High Court, which deployed powerful rhetoric, the Supreme Court preferred to focus on the technical aspects of law, using the occasion to pronounce on the doctrine of pith and substance (a legal concept that determines under which branch of the central government has the power to legislate on a particular point) and on the commerce clause. The constitutional bench was quite anticlimactic, and it substantially reversed the judgment of the Bombay High Court, with one important exception.

The Supreme Court reversed the high court's finding that the permit system militated against equality, and it held that military servicemen and diplomats could be granted permits to drink alcohol.[108] It ruled that the armed forces could be treated as a class for certain purposes, because "they have their own traditions and modes of life, which maintain a high level of morale and those qualities that enable them to face dangers and perform unusual tasks of endurance and hardship."[109] Transient foreigners such as tourists and diplomats, Justice Fazl Ali argued, formed their own category of temporary residents.

The Supreme Court struck down all the restrictions on free speech and preventive detention. It upheld the contention that the legislature could not prohibit the legitimate use of a substance that was not ordinarily drunk merely because its use could be perverted for the purpose of defeating or frustrating the objectives of the BPA. The legislature could not deprive the general public of the legitimate use of personal property such as lavender water or eau de cologne.

Advocate General Seervai attempted to downplay the impact of the judgment, stating that "the petitioner had opened his mouth wide to drink intoxicating liquor and all he has been allowed to drink is medicated wine and denatured alcohol." Noting that the petitioner failed to get what he came for, he urged him to return "to the odorous cleanliness of which he says he has been deprived."[110] Yet the carving out of this exception eventually undermined the entire Prohibition regime.

Mausen D. Bhansali, the Prohibition commissioner who was a party in the *Balsara* case, authored a report on Prohibition in Bombay. He noted that the BPA had created a "wholesome dread" of committing an offense under it, since the punishment was an effective deterrent.[111] Immediately after the enactment of Prohibition, consumption fell, even in areas known for illicit liquor traffic. However, the high court judgment declaring certain sections of the act invalid and the subsequent Supreme Court appeal resulted in "intensifying the tendency for illicit consumption of liquor."[112] Why did the consumption of liquor increase even after the weak judgment of the Supreme Court? Was Bhansali suggesting that the judgments took the edge off the "wholesome dread" that the act had produced?

Smelling Like a State: Procedural Justice under the Law of Prohibition

Behram Khurshed Pesikaka, whose narrative began this chapter, was arrested for smelling of alcohol a month after the *Balsara* judgment by the Supreme Court. Pesikaka's defense rested on two grounds. First, he claimed that he had not consumed prohibited alcohol. He attributed the smell of alcohol to the consumption of BG Phos (a health tonic with 17 percent alcohol content). Second, he argued that the onus was on the prosecution to show that he had consumed illicit liquor and not, as he contended, alcohol prohibited by law (such as in medicines).[113] Both claims rested heavily on the gains of Balsara's case. The court had ruled in *Balsara* that the government could not ban all intoxicating liquids just because they could be misused; thus it legalized medicines and health tonics with alcohol content. The judgment had also launched the first assault on the special procedures that had been set up under the Prohibition regime.

Immediately after the *Balsara* decision, the newspapers carried front-page stories that after the judgment of the Supreme Court, perfumed spirits and toilet preparations containing alcohol could be freely sold in Bombay without a license.[114] Six months after the *Balsara* judgment the *Times of India* reported that there had been a sudden spurt in the sale of Tinctura Zingiberis Mitis (a weak tincture of ginger) in areas where the BPA applied. The tincture was being consumed on a considerable scale as a substitute for alcoholic beverages.[115] Its production increased from 36,000 pounds in 1949–1950 to 380,000 pounds in 1951–1952, just after the Balsara judgment.[116] Other tinctures and tonics also showed a steady growth. The production of the tonic Roma increased from 1,000 pounds in 1952 to 17,654 pounds in 1953, and Carminative increased from 341 to 1,476 BG (a unit of measure for medicines).[117] The Bombay government complained that these tinctures were sold everywhere—in hotels, restaurants, grocery stores, and barbershops.[118]

The newspapers were replete with advertisements for these tonics. BG Phos, which Pesikaka claimed to have consumed, began to be produced in the same period. Pesikaka, however, stated that he had begun to take the tonic when his health deteriorated during government service.[119] Pesikaka was employed by the transport officer. Until a month before his accident he had to tour districts all over Bombay province to supervise offenses under the Motor Vehicles Act. The constant strain of travel and the vagaries of his diet from village to village caused him to have digestive disorders and insomnia. This overwork and strain in the course of his duties as a public officer had led to his taking tonics, including BG Phos.

Pesikaka had been acquitted by the magistrate's (i.e., district) court. Given the importance of his defense, the state then petitioned the Bombay High Court on appeal.[120] Pesikaka's claims were rejected by the high court, however, which sentenced him to a month of rigorous imprisonment (i.e., prison with hard labor) with a fine of five hundred rupees. The high court was suspicious of the BG Phos explanation. The judges claimed it was "impossible that the doctor would ask him to take the tonic after dinner," since the instructions on the bottle said to take it before dinner.[121] Furthermore, they noted that when a bottle of BG Phos was produced before the court, the smell of alcohol was not prominent—the predominant smell was that of vitamin B. The court disregarded Pesikaka's written statement in its entirety and sentenced him. A worried Pesikaka petitioned the Supreme Court. His first appeal to it was dismissed by a majority of the judges, with one justice dissenting. The newspapers held that once the Supreme Court had made a pronouncement, it was futile to discuss the legal decision, but they rued the heavy burden that the onus of proof placed on the accused person. The evidence establishing consumption of alcohol was often very flimsy, the court had observed, being no more "than a hypersensitive nostril of an overzealous policeman." This would leave citizens vulnerable to harassment and blackmail by 'unscrupulous" people.[122]

Pesikaka persisted and, noting the differences of interpretation between the majority and the dissenting judgment, applied for a review by stating that the case raised important constitutional questions and should be heard before a constitutional bench. The judges were asked what the effect on the consumption of BG Phos would be of striking the clauses that criminalized the consumption of medicines, perfumes, and tonics. Pesikaka's conviction was entirely based a police statement that his breath smelled of alcohol and that he had therefore consumed alcohol in some form,[123]

His lawyers protested that no tests had been employed to ascertain the quantity or type of alcohol consumed. No mouth or stomach wash was taken, nor were blood or urine tests performed. The only "test" was the detected smell. The majority of the judges held that the smell of alcohol was a neutral fact, compatible with either innocence or guilt. It was thus the duty of the prosecution to establish that the alcohol whose smell was detected came from the category of prohibited alcohols and not the permitted ones.[124] The court referred to the *Balsara* case to highlight that not all liquids containing alcohol were proscribed.

The Supreme Court judgment raised the question of the status of convictions that had already taken place under the BPA. Would these convictions lapse automatically, or would separate legal proceedings have to be initiated? Since 1950, more than forty thousand people had been convicted in Bombay for consuming liquor without a permit.[125]

In all those cases the burden of proof had been placed on the accused. In several cases the accused had presented empty bottles of tinctures and other medicinal preparations as proof, but these had been rejected. However, much to the alarm of the Bombay government, the courts leaned toward applying the new defense and standard of proof in prosecutions.

In February 1954 the police arrested E. J. Saldanha, a resident of Bandra, after complaints that he was abusing a neighbor while drunk. A medical exam proved that he was under the influence of alcohol. Saldanha's defense was that he had consumed five ounces of Hall's Wine shortly before the police arrived, and he produced the empty bottle before the court. Hall's Wine was a patented restorative tonic considered rich in vitamins that had been invented by a nutritionist at the University College London. It was popular in Britain and the colonies and the subject of advertising through the 1930s. The magistrate had rejected Saldanha's defense on the grounds that there was no evidence to show that he had consumed Hall's Wine; the magistrate drew an adverse inference from the fact that the normal dose of Hall's Wine was only two ounces, not five. Saldanha was acquitted on appeal by the high court, which ruled that since Hall's wine was not ordinarily drunk in the presence of witnesses, there was no evidence that Saldanha could have provided. His statement on the quantity consumed was consistent with medical evidence, and the court had to take him at his word.[126] The Bombay High Court underlined the fact that the SC had held in *Balsara* that any restriction on consuming a medicinal preparation with alcohol was a violation of a citizen's rights.[127]

The shift in burden of proof began to be applied by magistrates in many everyday cases. For instance, Runga Bala Koli, a tribal fisherman in Bombay found with three bottles of illicit liquor and equipment to manufacture liquor, was acquitted of charges of illicit distillation on the grounds that there was no evidence that he had used the equipment. In a case involving another two Koli defendants, who were found with brewing equipment and empty containers with traces of liquor, the court ruled that all the items required for manufacturing liquor had not been found. These decisions caused a great deal of frustration for the administration, which described it as a miscarriage of justice.[128]

By 1963 the Planning Commission was protesting the number of tinctures available in India. It pointed out that the *British Pharmacopeia* had reduced the number of tinctures from thirty-four in 1932 to fourteen in 1963, but the *Indian Pharmacopeia* of 1955 listed forty-two different tinctures. After interviewing leading medical representatives, the Planning Commission came to the conclusion that there was hardly any medical use of tinctures, which were outmoded and being replaced by modern drugs that were not alcohol-based. Spot checks revealed that several tinctures on the market were actually spurious, consisting solely of alcohol and a suitable coloring agent. Other manufacturers were producing eardrops and eyedrops with a large percentage of alcohol. The frustrated Planning Commission suggested that tinctures be abandoned for more modern medicine and that industrially produced eyedrops and eardrops be replaced by prescriptions that could be made by pharmacists.[129]

Writ petitions continued to chip away at aspects of the Prohibition regime. Acquittals abounded, and new rules of procedure were formed. Since smell could no longer be the basis of an arrest, the police were instructed to take suspicious parties to be examined by a doctor. However, even here the Bombay High Court ruled that the police did not have the authority under the Police Act or the Evidence Act to compel a person to be taken for a medical test. The high court also acquitted the accused farmer of the charge of assaulting a policeman, holding that he was exercising his legitimate right of self defense.[130]

The possibility of determining the kind of liquor consumed through medical examinations was difficult. Doctors in hundreds of cases testified that prohibited spirits produced identical effects, reactions, and smells to those that were permitted. An association of doctors of all communities published an open letter in the press stating their opposition to Prohibition. They rejected the claims of the government that Prohibition was necessary on health grounds by pointing to its role in medicine.[131]

The rising acquittal rate created a sense of unease in the government. This was partly explained by government officials as a problem of detection. They recognized that innocent people were harassed and that the guilty managed to escape because of the "rough and ready" methods employed by the police to determine drunkenness.[132] These involved examining gait, speech, eyes, and behavior. Could a low-ranking police officer be trusted to make this assumption? Indirectly, the criticism in *Pesikaka* was that the conviction had been based on a reliance on the sense of smell of an overzealous policeman. Given the unreliability of medical testimony and the reluctance of any independent witnesses to come forward, the government moved toward a more scientific method for determining guilt.

The Prohibition commission settled on the breathalyzer after reviewing a wide range of tools for determining alcohol content that were easy to use, gave accurate results, and could be handled by people who were not experts in medicine or chemistry. Unlike chemical tests, the breathalyzer cost less and avoided delays because the result was instantaneous. The blood tests that the government was trying to rely on were frequently delayed. The deputy director of medical services in Bombay reported that in the first five months of 1963 at least 50,487 court-ordered blood reports were pending. Moreover, breathalyzer tests would make up for the lack of trustworthy oral evidence.[133]

Yet the commission remained wary of legal problems that could arise. It noted that the courts could question whether the breathalyzer test violated Article 20 of the Constitution, which included a defense against self-incrimination; whether taking samples from an unconscious victim violated his or her rights; whether the breathalyzer could be forced on an unwilling subject; and whether a refusal to take the test could be penalized. The commission consulted with lawyers and drew extensively on US precedents to evaluate whether these provisions would pass legal scrutiny. It was finally suggested that in order to avoid divergent views from the courts in India, breathalyzer tests should be given statutory recognition.[134] Unlike the self-confident regime of 1947, the government was now quite wary about courts and unsure about its ability to legislate problems away.

The Public Interest, Private Interests, and Parsi Interests

At first glance, Fram Balsara's petition (which started of this chain of events) appears to be a public-interest case that raises questions of individual liberty and equality. Balsara was a journalist, a prototypical public-spirited citizen whose petition could be seen as an extension of a principled journalistic crusade against Prohibition. Similarly, Pesikaka's case was that of an individual caught in the grip of Prohibition law who was testing various strategies to enable him to escape imprisonment. Was it then a mere coincidence that both men were Parsis? How do we situate claims of individual rights within the wider conceptions of status, class, and community?

Balsara died early and left few papers, so it is difficult to verify why exactly he went to court. However, given the expensive lawyers he hired, it is likely that he was not a solo actor. And given his journalistic background, one cannot ignore the fact that the press was particularly hard-hit during Prohibition because of the ban on liquor ads. The Planning Commission asserted that no serious reader could fail to note that the English-language press in particular had a strong bias against Prohibition. This leaning revealed itself in the extensive skeptical coverage of Prohibition, as well as the highlighting of Prohibition excesses in the *Times of India* and the *Bombay Chronicle*. Almost all the English-language newspapers cheered the liberalization of Prohibition in 1963, hailing it as "a victory of good sense over shiboleth" and a "belated return to reason and wisdom."[135] The Bombay-based *Times of India* greeted the news with "three cheers for good sense and boldness."[136]

Similarly, Pesikaka's role as a government servant was highlighted by both himself and the media, in different ways. Pesikaka referred constantly to his job, to the strains caused by public duty and contact with other government officials—such as the police commissioner, whom he met in the course of work on the day of the accident—in order to present himself as a responsible individual who was unlikely to violate the law.[137] His lawyers argued that a conviction would lead to his dismissal, a situation that would not have arisen had he been a person with a job in the private sector. The prosecution asked for maximum punishment because Pesikaka was a public servant and had therefore allegedly brought the Prohibition law into disrepute.[138] The press paid great attention to his case because he was a public servant; journalists reveled in stories of establishment figures who were caught violating Prohibition laws. When the health minister's butler was caught manufacturing illicit liquor in the minister's house, it was front-page news. Most columnists also gave ample space to the news that the author of the leading legal commentary on the BPA had been convicted of a Prohibition offense himself.[139]

Along with profession, community identity shaped both the legal strategy and the judicial and public responses to it. It is difficult to ignore the fact that both Balsara and Pesikaka were Parsis. In fact they identified themselves in their writ petitions as Parsi residents of the Fort of Bombay. Balsara worked as a journalist for many years with *Jam-e-Jamshed*, a Gujarati daily that had a largely Parsi readership.

Parsi businessmen had dominated the liquor trade in Bombay since its earliest days. The Parsis were Zoroastrians who had emigrated to India from Persia in the eighth century to avoid Muslim persecution. They were a close-knit and easily identifiable community that had grown economically under colonial rule.[140] An 1864 survey showed that Parsi liquor dealers accounted for 21 percent of all alcohol dealers in the province, despite the fact that Parsis constituted less than 5 percent of the city's population. Common Parsi surnames, such as Toddywalla, Ginwalla, and Daruwalla, indicated their intimate links with the liquor business. Parsi businesses were picketed, and during the 1921 Prince of Wales riots in Bombay, Parsis were attacked and their shops set on fire because of their supposed deviance from the national goals of the boycott of foreign-manufactured goods and Prohibition. Gandhi, though expressing dismay at the anti-Parsi violence, advised the Parsis to renounce the liquor trade themselves, suggesting that it was better to "break stones or even beg" than to sell liquor.[141] He periodically addressed Parsis, asking them to join the cause of Prohibition and not let the name of their community be defamed by their linkage with alcohol.[142] It was no coincidence that in 1939 the Congress Party government appointed a Parsi as the minister of health to implement Prohibition.

Organized opposition to Prohibition in the 1930s had largely come from castes and communities involved in the liquor industry. Although the Parsis were most prominent, the Bhandaris (who were categorized as a backward caste) and the Pasis (who were Dalits) were also involved.

The majority of Parsis saw Prohibition as an economic attack on their business and their way of life (fig. 1.2). Throughout the 1930s and 1940s they had appealed to the colonial state to protect them from the activities of the Prohibition activists. A petition from the Country Liquor, Foreign Liquor, and Toddy Merchants of Bombay, dominated by Parsi signatures, protested the agreement between the British and Gandhi to permit the peaceful picketing of liquor shops.[143] The Parsi Panchayat, the leading community organization,

Parsis are rather partial to toddy and many drink it daily.
That women also enjoy imbibing toddy is fairly obvious
from this picture.

FIG 1.2. Parsi women drinking. Homai Vyarawalla Collection,
Alkazi Foundation for the Arts, New Dehi.

passed a resolution declaring the Bombay government's experiments with Prohibition in 1939 to be a "serious and highly objectionable interference" with Parsi religious beliefs and a violation of Queen Victoria's proclamation of 1858 that safeguarded the interests of religious communities.[144]

However, independence changed the relationship between the Parsis and the state. With the introduction of a majoritarian democracy, the Parsis, as a minority community lost influence and access to state power.

During the early experiments with banning alcohol in the 1930s, the Parsis had petitioned the government and the Congress Party to revoke Prohibition.[145] In a lengthy memorandum of March 29, 1939, the Parsi Prohibition Protest Committee emphasized that although Prohibition affected all sections of society, it had a particular bearing on the religious, social, and economic life of the Parsis.[146] The largest demonstration of Parsi women in the history of Bombay was in opposition to the Congress Party's Prohibition policy in 1939, when they argued that this violated their civic rights to conduct the trade they had been carrying out for centuries and compared their erasure from the economic life of the city to the fate being faced by Jews in Germany.[147]

After detailing the uses of liquor in Parsi religious ceremonies backed by evidence from Zoroastrian scriptures, the committee emphasized that any restriction on the use of wine or liquor by Parsis in their religious or social lives was a direct interference with their religion and opposed to the principles enunciated by Queen Victoria's proclamation of 1858. Prohibition was thus an interference in minority religious beliefs. The Parsi Prohibition Protest Committee then argued that the Government of India Act of 1935 did not allow the state to acquire land or commercial undertakings for public purpose without compensating the owner. It pointed out that Prohibition had effectively shut established businesses, destroyed goodwill, and led to stock being taken over by the government or sold at a loss. Through licensing, the business of selling liquor had effectively been nationalized. The Parsi claims were backed by evidence of the group's disproportionate contribution to industry, charity, and the public life of the city.

Focusing the argument against Prohibition on freedom of religion and the right to property are not surprising, since these were possibly the only two rights protected in colonial India. Queen Victoria's proclamation of 1858, on the heels of the Indian revolt, had assured her Indian subjects that they would not be harassed for their religious faith and observance, for the state was to abstain from all interference in the religious belief or worship of the queen's subjects. This proclamation was constantly invoked as a guarantee for religious liberty in colonial India. Similarly, although there had always been some form of common-law protection of property, the Government of India Act of 1935 expressly provided for compensation in cases of state acquisition of property.[148]

However, both claims were difficult to sustain after independence. The right to religious freedom was subject to several limitations, including that of social reform, and the right to property was whittled away by a state that sought to nationalize industry and implement land reform. Moreover, whereas rights in colonial India were rooted in private identities (such as faith or personal property), in independent India the national interest was seen to trump private interests. Could the Parsis, a Westernized religious minority, put their private interests over the nation's need for Prohibition? The Parsis were hard-hit by the return of Prohibition in 1949, and Parsi trusts set up the Prohibition Relief Committee to secure ameliorative measures for those whose employment was terminated as a result.[149] Parsi political candidates promised the "death" of Prohibition.[150]

The 1939 Parsi Prohibition Protest Committee petition made two arguments that were carried over in Balsara's case—that is, they survived the postcolonial transition. The first was a fear that the preventive measures required to impose Prohibition would involve raiding and searching private homes, destroying the privacy of a citizen on mere suspicion. There was a concern that this would lead to harassment by police and the rise of a class of blackmailers. The petition was also acerbic on the distinction made in 1939 between Asians and non-Asians (to whom Prohibition did not apply). The petitioners pointed out that sustaining racial distinctions was an insult to Indians committed by the Congress Party government.

These arguments had limited traction in the 1930s; there was no general protection of life and liberty, and the Congress Party provincial government's powers were heavily circumscribed by the British governor, especially in acting against Europeans. Parsi attempts to seek similar exemptions as Europeans was categorically rejected by Congress Party leaders, who argued that they were "sons of the soil" and could not "clamor for a concession that *a majority of their countrymen* found immoral."[151] Gandhi himself had pointedly asked, "Must one hundred thousand Parsis hold up a social reform that brings a ray of light for a laboring population that far outnumbers the Parsi population?"[152]

After the *Pesikaka* case, the Council of the Parsi Central Association and the Parsi Political League appealed the Bombay government to appoint an independent committee to investigate all aspects of the Prohibition policy in the state.[153] The council expressed that it was watching with misgivings the Prohibition policy and the government's attempts to bolster it with legislative change. That the Parsis would turn to the courts was to be expected: not only had they lost privileged access to the state, as a community they also had a unique relationship with the Anglo-Indian legal system.[154] Mitra Sharafi suggests that because of a combination of factors, in the nineteenth century the Parsis began to use the legal system at a greater rate than other communities did, and they "de-Anglicized the law by sinking deeper into the colonial legal system."[155] Parsi litigants and Parsi lawyers had greater informational capital than other minority communities did when dealing with the legal system. Not only were the litigants Parsis, seven of the eight lawyers involved on each side of the *Balsara* case were Parsis, as was Naushir Bharucha, another lawyer and one of the few members of the state legislature to vote against the BPA. Thus, community identity played a major role in a case that was framed in terms of individual rights.

Finally, one could speculate that it was because Balsara was a Parsi that the case succeeded before the court. As a largely educated, philanthropic, and middle-class community, the Parsis were in some ways the ideal citizens of the Nehruvian state and furthest from the image of the drinker that was presented by the proponents of Prohibition.

A crude reading of interests would suggest that constitutional law was a tool that was used by Parsi economic interests to attack the Prohibition regime. Although the Parsis' community interests and identity definitely enabled certain forms of litigation and the choice of strategy, it did not necessarily give them the results they wanted. The actual victories were meager, and the large public liquor businesses either went bankrupt or operated outside the law. However, Parsi-led litigation for private interests opened up avenues for other less networked groups and provided an important way to critique the new state.

Prohibition, Law, and the Question of Postcolonial Sovereignty

Postcolonial sovereignty is based on a contradictory logic, straddling the bureaucratic methods of colonial rule and the claim to represent a free nation.[156] This becomes evident through the repeated sense of frustration expressed by the state every time its Prohibition policies were taken apart by litigation. The Bombay government attempted to repair the gaps in the Prohibition regime by repeated amendments and new executive notifications. After the judgment on medical tests, the Bombay government moved to amend the BPA to expressly empower Prohibition officers and the police to make a person suspected of drinking submit to a medical exam or have a blood sample collected to determine the percentage of alcohol.[157] If people resisted, it was lawful to use all means reasonably necessary to secure them, examine them physically, or take blood.[158] The government also inserted a provision creating a body of experts who would decide whether a certain alcoholic liquid was potable and thus proscribed.

A pessimistic reading of this process would make it appear that the legislature was able to undo the rights assertions of citizens. However, this does not take into account the sense of despondency the legislators expressed. Introducing the fourth set of amendments in four years to the BPA, Jivraj Mehta, the Prohibition minister, apologetically explained, "What is to be done? The moment one hole is patched up, something new appears on the market."[159] An exasperated legislator responded that he did not remember a single session of the house when the government did not give the public some form of Prohibition. It was a "pathetic confession" on the part of the government that in spite of its numerous attempts to tighten the law, public ingenuity continued to find alternative ways to circumvent prohibition regulations. Government helplessness came through when faced with the rising market in tinctures. In an attempt to reduce the production of tinctures, the government amended the Drugs Act of 1940 and the BPA to limit the production of ethyl alcohol in the state. But after the *Balsara* ruling on the limits of the state government to restrict interstate commerce, the government was powerless to impose the restrictions on ethyl alchohol and tinctures from other states. The police officers also expressed a feeling of frustration from the ineffectiveness of the Prohibition law in practice and the difficulties raised in its administration.[160]

On being asked what legal changes were required to implement Prohibition more effectively, the Bombay government blandly replied that *no legal change short of a constitutional amendment would work*. Fundamental rights and the wording of the directive principles had limited the power of the state to create strong legislation.[161]

The *Pesikaka* decision and the decisions that followed created a strange cycle. The government admitted that the *Pesikaka* case had made it very difficult to secure convictions in consumption cases.[162] Procedural legal challenges would make it easier to secure acquittals. A frustrated executive would tighten the laws to secure convictions, and these new amendments would again be watered down through legal challenges. Thus, a larger number of people were being charged with Prohibition offenses, but most could not be convicted; thus there was no effect on enforcement, yet it still cost the exchequer forty-five million rupees annually.[163] Examining the latest amendments to the BPA in 1959, an editorial noted with wry amusement that "the game of the lawyer picking holes in the legal armor of a moral law, the law courts exposing its seamy side, the legislature seeking to patch up the dilapidated fabric, with the lawyers and law courts at it again, has been played before."[164] The nationalist critique of the colonial state was often focused on the latter's failure to deliver justice and promise accountability. Prohibition was introduced through a popularly elected government to meet the goals laid down by a republican constitution. It was supposed to signify a break from the colonial state, but the successive constitutional cases brought attention back to the continuing lack of justice and accountability.

In the matter of Prohibition the government was finding itself at its wit's end. On New Year's Eve, 1963, Vasantrao Naik, the chief minister of Bombay, made a radical shift. He liberalized the issue of liquor permits to all people above the age of forty and permitted the free sale of beer and toddy with less than 3.5 percent alcohol to all people. Naik justified his actions as necessary to check the business of illicit liquor and the associated lawlessness. The main object was to "the people from ruining their health by drinking illicit liquor, which was in most cases worse than poison."[165] This step marked the beginning of the end of the early Indian Prohibition regime.

Although the government continued to assert that it was speaking for the majority of the populace, the legal defeats and enthusiastic exploitation of the lacunae by the public forced the government to consider that perhaps it did not represent the public will. The legitimacy of the Prohibition project was based on the argument that it received widespread public support. As the governor of Bombay pointed out, the one unanswerable argument for Prohibition was that it received the "unanimous support of every legislature in India."[166] Only one legislator of the three hundred or so in the Bombay Legislative Assembly had voted against the BPA. The will of the people was expressed through their representatives; otherwise, he said, democracy would become "a farce." A columnist remarked that it was a great shock to the government to discover that the public did not consider drinking a plight.[167] The Bombay government regretfully noted that the public had "learned to look upon the Prohibition officer as an outcast."[168]

Conversely, the petitioners and the court had to deal with the fact that the government in question was a popular government. Balsara, in a rare interview after his victory, noted that it was hard to be proud or joyful to have succeeded against the government, since this was a "popular government." However, when such a government "rode roughshod over the rights of citizens and disregarded public opinion," there was no other alternative than to approach the highest tribunal.[169] Furthermore, as a journalist Balsara held the judgment to be an achievement because the petition vindicated the rights of freedom of speech and expression.

Constitutional Law as an Arena of Politics

It would be easy to dismiss constitutional politics, as several scholars do, as products of liberal-bourgeois politics and thus not relevant to the wider populace. However, as the Prohibition cases indicate, constitutional cases became public spectacles consumed by a wide range of publics. Strategies against the state devised perhaps by the middle classes with access to legal resources and information were consumed and adapted by a larger populace. Furthermore, constitutional politics forced both private petitioners and the courts to see individual cases as representative of the needs of the people. Thus, Balsara's demand to get an individual permit became a case in the public interest, and the judiciary diluted the rules and procedures as a result.

There clearly was something different about the judicial space that had opened up. Reflecting upon the restructuring of the Prohibition laws by the Court, the Planning Commission report highlighted the essential distinction between the outlook of a legislator and that of a judge: the former "focuse[d] on the removal of a specific abuse, [whereas] the judge look[ed] upon a statute in the background of the entire legal system..[170] For instance, the commission mentioned the frustration felt by the executive in the inability to secure convictions because the courts tended to completely reject the evidence of *panchas*—respectable members of the local community whose presence was required at a police raid to ensure that the evidence recovered was admissible in court—on the grounds that most were stock witnesses. The report tried to explain the courts' position by attributing it to the courts' general experience that this testimony was unreliable. They remained unsympathetic to the police, who were rendered helpless because of the noncooperation of independent eyewitnesses. The courts' attitude was that in the absence of credible evidence, they had to give the accused the benefit of the doubt. This view led to an alarming rate of acquittals and, according to the Planning Commission, the demoralization of the prosecution agency. The high rate of acquittals also reflected an older distrust the judiciary had of the police.

The distinction between liberal-constitutional politics and street politics becomes further blunted if we compare the reaction of the Nehruvian elite to both processes. Opposition in the courts and on the streets was seen as challenging the legitimacy of a democratically elected government, and in the post-Nehruvian era the so-called democratic government hit back at both, suppressing people's movements, overturning judicial verdicts, and packing the courts. There was an idealization of apolitical behavior.[171]

The Constitution did make a difference, however. It created a space where the state's vision of social order could be contested, and it offered a neutral language to challenge the democratic legitimacy that was enjoyed by the state. Social histories of Prohibition have tended to emphasize and even valorize resistance to elite projects, largely through the persistence of subaltern culture. Although subaltern classes may resist co-optation into state projects, they are not always able to avoid state coercion.

Constitutional litigation highlights the possibility of engagement with state structures, which fractures the state's authority and coercive power. As a favorite project of Gandhi's, Prohibition gained a degree of moral sanctity after his death, which made it difficult to challenge the policy on the grounds of religious freedom or economic efficiency. Conventional critiques of the Prohibition policy had often been framed in terms of economic considerations, arguing that it led to significant revenue losses and had high administrative costs with few guaranteed results (fig. 1.3). Noted economist K. N. Raj even argued that given the nearly 1.5 billion-rupee revenue loss that the government lost to bootleggers each year, Prohibition should be considered a luxury good.[172] However, the economic argument received little political traction when faced with moral rhetoric. Nor did the attempt to describe the Prohibition supporters as faddists or puritans. Prohibition Minister Patil stated in response, "We do not mind being called puritans."[173]

The legal challenge allowed the debate to be carried out on two fronts. The first emphasized the antidemocratic character of Prohibition laws, and the second highlighted the consequences of a widespread failure of the state to ensure convictions under those laws. The language of constitutionalism and correct administrative procedure increasingly emerged as a means through which the state policy could be safely critiqued. An angry reader drew on Gandhi to

FIG 1.3. A power-drunk Morarji Desai demands more sacrifices for
Prohibition. *Film India*, January 1953.

challenge the expanded police powers of the state, stating, "The Mahatma was
against giving absolute powers to police because it constituted a negation of
true democracy. He always taught that the end did not justify the means. . . .
If prohibition cannot be gained except by the proposed bill, then clearly it
is an admission of the part of the government that the people are not behind it."[174]

Prohibition was seen as "police *raj*" (police rule), which was the very anti-
thesis of democracy. In an open letter, doctors opposed to Prohibition pointed
out that only 6 percent of the legislators had admitted to drinking; therefore
the law was being passed upon drinkers by a body composed of 94 percent
teetotalers. A law enacted by the brute majority on a minority that stood in
unanimous opposition to the minority was coercion and not democracy.[175]
The legislature had passed a law that concerned 6 percent of the population in
spite of the unanimous opposition of all the admitted drinkers. The question
of majority opinion came up more than once, beginning with H. J. Khandekar
in the Constituent Assembly. On discovering that the Congress Party opinion was overwhelmingly in favor of Prohibition, he reminded the assembly
that "there are things other than liquor that go to the head, and power is one.
Let not the majority party suffer from it."[176] This was echoed before the Bombay High Court in the *Balsara* case when the chief justice quipped that "power
is also an intoxicant," to which Balsara's lawyer added that it was the worst kind
of intoxicant."[177] As cartoons show (figs. 1.4, 1.5, and 1.6), people were receptive

FIG 1.4. The Congress Party High Command drunk on power.
Shankar's Weekly, August 12, 1962.

to the image of a government intoxicated with its own power and uncaring of its citizens.

Finally, the episode with Prohibition forced the Indian state to rethink the effectiveness of law. Justice Tek Chand admitted that it was not entirely correct to say that every law represents the will of the people.[178] If there were always unanimity, statutory amendments would have been unnecessary. Particularly in the case of social legislation, laws that cease to represent a consensus of support no longer remain effective. Recognizing the impact of human agency, Chand reflected that legislators and law courts cannot secure obedience to laws when the forces of disobedience and evasion are strongly entrenched. Congress Party President U. N. Debhar rather ineffectually attempted to argue that India was not like the United States and that the failure of the legal mechanism should not be seen indicative of the lack of support for Prohibition.[179] An increasing number of Prohibition arrests just underlined the absurdity of the Prohibition laws. Commenting on the fact that four hundred thousand people had been convicted of Prohibition offenses in just fourteen years, Chief Minister Naik was quoted as saying that unless he relaxed Prohibition, he would be ruling over a state of convicts.[180]

FIG. 1.5. Brahm Prakash Yadav, the minister for planning and development
from 1952–1955, warning that Prohibition will cause civil disobedience.
Shankar's Weekly, April 8, 1956.

FIG. 1.6. Prohibition and private enterprise. *Shankar's Weekly*, June 22, 1956.

A retired police officer wrote a series of articles for the tabloid press suggesting that the only way to rid Bombay of crime was to do away with Prohibition. Not only were policemen being forced to give priority to cases of drinking
over rape, murder, and robbery, they were also demoralized by not being allowed to relax with a drink themselves. Moreover, he argued, Prohibition begets
criminals in the form of smugglers and illicit distillers, who hire thugs to

protect themselves from the police and each other. The policemen who should have tackled this new menace were too busy searching for illegal alcohol.

The Planning Commission noted that several distinguished jurists had stated that a law that is not effectively enforced has the pernicious effect of bringing all laws to disrepute. Ineffective laws thus posed a serious challenge to the body politic. This admission was a sea change from the heady belief in law as an instrument of social transformation that had been expressed in the early years of independence. Given that the entire Prohibition regime was re-worked through the courts, it was quite ironic that one of the most common methods of liquor smuggling involved the smuggler dressing in a black robe like a Bombay advocate and concealing the tins of liquor in the advocate's briefcase.[181]

2

The Case of the Excess Baggage

COMMODITY CONTROLS, MARKET
GOVERNANCE, AND THE MAKING
OF ADMINISTRATIVE LAW

ON THE NIGHT of November 28, 1948, train number 197 of the Indian Railways was carrying hundreds of sleeping passengers eighty miles from Bombay to the industrial city of Kanpur. As the train trundled down the tracks, a telegraph message raced ahead on the wires warning the railway police in the town of Itarsi that the "Marwadi occupants in first- and second-class compartments were suspected of illegally transporting cotton cloth."[1] Preetam Singh, the subinspector of the railway police, stopped the train as it pulled into Itarsi around noon on November 29 and went on board to search the passengers.

In a first-class Lucknow compartment, Singh found a middle-age Marwadi couple, Harishankar and Gomtidevi Bagla, who were traveling with three of their servants. During a search of the compartment, he found two maunds (about 164 pounds) and thirty seers of cloth (about 60 pounds) concealed in the bathroom, thirteen seers underneath the mattress, twelve seers concealed inside the luggage, and two bundles of cloth tied up in the blanket of the servant Kedarnath. In total, the Baglas and their companions were found to be in possession of approximately 493 pounds of new cotton cloth and no valid permit to transport it from Bombay to Kanpur.[2] The cloth and the train tickets were seized, and charges were filed against the Baglas for committing an offense under the Essential Supplies Act (ESA) of 1946 and for violating the Cotton Textile Order of 1948.

What offense had the Baglas committed? The goods were neither illicit nor harmful. They were not evading taxes, nor had they taken goods illegally across a border. However, the mere act of moving cloth without a movement permit had placed them in breach of the system of economic controls that came to dominate the early decades of independent India. These controls were laws that restricted the manufacture, sale, price, or distribution of an economic commodity, including capital, foreign exchange, and finished commodities. They had been created by the colonial government during World War II to mobilize production for the war effort and to deal with shortages of consumer goods. Drafted as a draconian emergency legislation, the controls met few requirements of fair procedure and had been the subject of severe criticism by Gandhi and the nationalists. Nonetheless, after independence the same restrictions were adopted by the postcolonial government in the name of harnessing the national economy for development. The life of the ESA was extended several times, and in 1955 it was replaced by the more comprehensive Essential Commodities Act.

The Baglas were charged under the ESA, which contained a series of stringent provisions, such as placing the burden of proof on the accused and providing a summary trial with a limited number of appeals.[3] Most significantly, it provided that no order made in exercise of a power conferred by the ESA could be challenged in court.[4] The Baglas and their legal counsel must have understood that the evidence against them was overwhelming; they had been the subjects of police surveillance for months, and the state had built up considerable evidence against them.[5] Three months after the criminal trial began at a district magistrate's court in Hoshangabad, the Baglas first petitioned the Nagpur High Court and then the Supreme Court, challenging the constitutionality of the ESA. There were several grounds for this challenge; the two most relevant to this study are that the ESA infringed the Baglas' rights under Article 19 of the Constitution and that large parts of the ESA were void inasmuch as the legislature had delegated its powers to a nonlegislative body.[6]

In the course of the Baglas' constitutional litigation, it emerged that Article 19 challenges to the state's right to regulate economic life were difficult to argue; however, the charge of excessive delegation to a bureaucracy had better traction. The Baglas lost their appeal in the Supreme Court, but the decision in their case began an important debate over the role of the courts in curbing administrative action in the Indian republic. This chapter examines the litigation governing the circulation of commodities. It explores how those affected by the regime of commodity controls sought to challenge it through assertions of fair procedure and democratic values as standards to which economic legislation must conform.

The system of commodity controls exemplified the "permit-license-quota *raj*," an elaborate system of licenses and regulations required to run private businesses, that was established in independent India. Despite their centrality to both the economy and daily life, commodity-control operations have largely been neglected by historians and social scientists, except to the extent that they have identified such controls as areas of corruption and rent seeking. This absence in the accounts of postindependence India is curious, given that commodity controls had the greatest impact on the everyday life of the people, compared to, for instance, control over industry or imports, yet the latter two have been more prominent subjects of research.[7]

Noting the endemic corruption in the controlled economy, Paul Brass has argued that one must eschew laudatory concepts like the rule of law to describe postcolonial India. He has instead characterized it as a "corrupt bureaucratic state."[8] In contrast, I argue that judicial review of administrative action in India, the hallmark of a rule-of-law state, emerged from illegality (which itself developed from the misuse of emergency powers) and was rooted in a culture of corruption. Petty traders and merchants who were denied political legitimacy, such as those belonging to the Marwari community, began to claim their citizenship through the language of administrative law. State control of the economy was contested by critiquing the unregulated discretion exercised by low-ranking bureaucrats.

Administrative law had existed in a very limited form under the colonial regime in India. The emergence of administrative law through these postindependence rights challenges made commodity controls a prime focus for the legal academy and for bodies like the Ford Foundation, which were invested in building the rule of law in India. In this process the administrative law challenges were able to erase the distinction between "economic subjects of interests" and "subjects of rights," which Michel Foucault argues is characteristic of modern political economy.[9]

The commodity-control system is an important area to examine for the emergence, through law, of the economy as an object of governance in postcolonial India. Such an examination brings to the forefront the fact that the bazaar (the sum of the daily local circuits of production, consumption and retail) was a cause of anxiety to the postcolonial state. In response, the state, through law, began to penetrate economic activity at all levels. However, as administrative law challenges demonstrated, this brutal regulatory power of the state had to reconcile itself with the simultaneous constitution of citizens as free economic actors.[10]

The Constitution emerged as a means of contesting market governance, with bureaucrats, economists, and planners on one side, and petty merchants, traders, and retailers on the other. Research on the relationship between Indian capital and law has usually focused on the abstract notion of capital or has studied the role played by big business and industrialists. The challenges to commodity controls included local traders and corner-shop retailers as actors in the economy.[11] Using the Baglas' petition and its successive litigational challenges to the controls system, this chapter attempts to recount the ways in which the everyday life of the Indian market interacted with the world of constitutional law.

The Wartime System of Controls

The Baglas were arrested for violating the ESA and the Cotton Textile Order, both of which were products of wartime governance. The colonial state's goal had always been to control and subordinate India's economy to meet the government's needs, and to this end the state had intervened in industry and agriculture. However, the nature of this control was transformed by the outbreak of World War II.[12] Economic historians have long pointed out that the nature of modern war increases both the range and intensity of the state's control over daily life.[13] Beleaguered by the blitz in Britain, threatened with Japanese invasion on the eastern front, and facing noncooperation and internal rebellion led by Indian nationalists, the colonial state in 1942 was facing challenges on multiple fronts. These challenges to its authority prompted a massive expansion of the colonial state and a deeper penetration of Indian society and economy than before—through increased military recruitment, provisioning of the Allied armies, requisitioning, rationing, censorship, and detention.[14] The Congress Party's withdrawal from provincial ministries in 1939 and the mass detention of nationalist leaders in 1942 gave the colonial government space to govern unchecked by the constitutional safeguards provided in the Government of India Act of 1935.

As colonial India was mobilized for war, it became urgently necessary for a greater part of its productive activity to be geared toward the war effort and for the production of consumer goods to be limited to essential commodities. Under the original dispensation of the Government of India Act, commodity control was a power that was given exclusively to the provinces. The Central List contained a single entry (number 34), which encompassed "development of industries, where development under federal control is declared by federal law to be expedient in [the] public interest." The Provincial List, in contrast, included "trade and commerce within the province" and the "production, supply, and distribution of goods and development of industries."[15] The colonial government at Delhi seized control of the economy through the proclamation of a state of emergency under the Government of India Act.[16]

This was followed by the enactment of the Defense of India Act (DIA) of 1939. This conferred extensive powers on the central government, such as the right to make rules that "appear to be necessary to or expedient to securing the defense of British India, the public safety, the maintenance of public order, or the efficient prosecution of war[;] or to maintain supplies and services essential to the life of the community." The state was required to collect information and statistics with "a view to [the] rationing of any article essential to the life of the community." More specifically, the DIA rules empowered the government to regulate or prohibit the production, treatment, storage, movement, transport and distribution, acquisition, use, or consumption of any article. The government could prevent an article from being sold or force it to be sold. It could fix the price of any commodity.[17]

The DIA rules provided for the complete control of markets by the state. This intervention was initially limited to controlling the prices of necessities such as medical supplies, food, salt, cooking oil, and cotton cloth. The maximum price of these commodities was fixed according to a formula.[18] However, once Japan entered the war, controls were extended to other industrial commodities, like iron and steel. The Iron and Steel Order of 1943 ensured that no person could acquire or dispose of iron and steel without a license issued by the central government or a written order from the bureaucrat designated as the iron and steel controller.

Against the backdrop of chronic food shortages and famine conditions in Bengal, the Department of Food was created in 1942, and controls were imposed on all grains similar to those imposed on essential supplies and iron and steel. Finally, in 1943, faced with chronic shortages of consumer goods, the government set up the Department of Civil Supplies, which was tasked with creating a comprehensive system of controls over the production and distribution of almost all consumer goods and with the initiation of measures to eliminate hoarding and dealing on the black market.[19] By 1947 almost every commodity on the market, from ballpoint pens to nylon shirts, was controlled, and the two departments were combined. A provincial minister for the Food and Civil Supplies Department noted that given the interconnectedness of the market, controls tended to multiply rapidly:

Control over foodgrains led to control of fuel, then to sugar and jaggery and onto potatoes, and groundnuts, and then to tamarind, and from tamarind to chillies, and from chillies to onions. Every complaint about shortage or high price of any item brought an excuse for imposing control on that item. Seekers of permits and licenses crowded the multiplying offices and the lines got longer and longer.[20]

This large and proliferating system of controls gave the government untrammeled discretion over commodities. The administrative authorities controlled commodities through an elaborate system of licenses and permits to control production, distribution, sale, purchase, and storage. For instance, to plant rubber, a license had to be obtained from the Rubber Board under the Rubber Control and Production Order, 1946. Further permits would be required to sell the rubber in the market (only at the price fixed by the government), to store it without selling it, and to move it to another location.

The DIA rules provided for the appointment of a controller for each commodity at the provincial level, and the demands of the licensing system led to the creation of a massive economic bureaucracy.[21]

Although the powers of the officers varied, they all were able to impose significant restrictions on the trade and use of commodities. There was an absence of any standards or tests to control the exercise of executive discretion, as well as a lack of safeguards for the interests of those affected. There was little or no protection given to producers, dealers, and consumers against the misuse or improper exercise of power by the administrative officer.[22] Almost no criteria had been established for granting licenses, and most licenses could also be canceled at will. For instance, the textile commissioner, who issued licenses regulating the movement of raw cotton and cotton cloth, had the power to cancel or suspend a license if the license holder had given incorrect information on the application or had violated the conditions of the license—or "for any reason" the textile commissioner might have for believing that the licensee was not fit to hold the license.[23] The Foodgrains Order of 1946 specifically provided that the license could be canceled without giving any notice or reasons to the licensee.

There were no procedures for a licensee or an applicant for a license to challenge the decision to revoke or refuse a license. There were no limits placed on the licensing authority's powers to impose virtually any condition on the licensee, as well as to exempt any licensee from generally applicable conditions at the authority's discretion. But perhaps most significantly, these control orders declared that the decisions made by an administrative officer were final and could not be challenged before a higher authority.[24] This gave tremendous power to the administrators over traders, because they could effectively shut down a business while leaving no means of redress.

The DIA exemplified colonial legislation. It was a skeletal law that delegated broad rule-making powers to various administrative bodies and took discretion away from the legislatures. The DIA rules allowed various bureaucrats and levels of government to formulate orders to govern each commodity. Several critical commodities such as cotton were regulated by more than one order. The orders further conferred several rule-making powers on lower administrative authorities, such as the determination of license conditions.

Despite the enormous infrastructure for commodity controls, the system was unable to achieve most of its objectives. Because of the emphasis on meeting wartime production targets, the government was unable to control prices and was confronted with rapid food inflation. There was also widespread scarcity and a short supply of essential commodities. The system's most dramatic failure was its inability to prevent the Bengal famine of 1943, in which an estimated seven to ten million people died as a result of chronic food shortages.[25] The shortage of cotton cloth became the source of raging discontent, captured in the Bengali writer Nabendu Ghosh's visceral short story, "Bostrong Dehi" (Give Us Cloth), which charts the struggles and failure of an impoverished farmer to obtain a second sari for his wife, who only had one that was threadbare. The farmer's attempts to secure cloth through legitimate means failed, and he was caught in an attempt to steal; meanwhile, haunted by shame and guilt, his wife killed herself.

Reviewing the situation a decade later, Mahabir Prasad Jain pointed out that the policies intended to remedy scarcity were created belatedly, often after an item had already become scarce.[26] Policies were marked by an ad hoc mentality and were improvised without long-term planning. Price control, for instance, was started before controls on production and distribution had been established, leading to a rapid expansion of hoarding and the black market. A government committee examining the causes of the Bengal famine acknowledged that "the poor of Bengal fell victim to circumstances for which they were not themselves responsible . . . there had been an administrative breakdown."[27]

But it wasn't just poor policy design that led to the failure of the controls. Bureaucrats and academics both acknowledged that they were hampered by the widespread lack of public support and sympathy for the government.

Newspapers noted that the general public opinion was that the control of prices had mainly benefited the government in requisitioning stocks for the army and industrial production, whereas the public had been left to the mercy of the black market.[28] Prices rose astronomically. For instance, within six months in 1942, the price of tomatoes went up six times, and the price of mutton increased by 50 percent.[29] The rationing system did not necessarily guarantee a fairer distribution of goods. "Perplexed," a letter-writing resident of the small town of Dhulia, complained that in the absence of any rules or etiquette regarding lines, all shops witnessed a "great scramble" in which only the strong could get their allotted rations.[30]

A study by economists at Bombay University in 1943 identified that the psychological prerequisites for a successful policy of requisitioning supplies were lacking in the country. Requisitioning required "a people fully conscious of their rights and duties . . . but bearing inevitable hardship with cheer" and an administration that was "efficient, incorruptible, . . . and capable of getting its work done by evoking popular consent and support." However, this could be achieved only if there were confidence between the government and the governed. The breakdown of confidence was blamed pon the wide discretion allowed to local officers, who were proved "corrupt, oppressive, partial, and unaware of people's needs."[31]

That the controls policy had dubious legitimacy in the eyes of the population can be demonstrated from the numerous cases of evasion, exploitation, and noncompliance by ordinary citizens. Wartime controls were not unique to India, but the colonial state was unwilling and unable to give people a sense of being stakeholders in the system. In contrast, the US Office of Price Administration, which implemented very similar programs, was able to base them on a network of popular participation. US regulatory authorities were able to convince hundreds of thousands of householders to sign pledges not to buy goods on the black market and to act as vigilantes to check violations.[32]

People, understandably critical of a ration-and-control system that appeared to them unsuccessful in controlling scarcity or price inflation, subverted it with impunity. M. A. Sreenivasan, who oversaw the system of commodity controls in Mysore as the minister of Food and Civil Supplies, emphasized that people resorted to "ingenuity, inventiveness, and plain unvarnished mendacity" to evade the controls or to dull their edge.[33] The control system was not only manipulated by the citizens, it had also emerged as a major arena of governmental corruption.

Recent scholarship has suggested that this was the result of the peculiar structure of the commodity controls and the new hierarchy of administrative officers set up to execute them. Corruption became common because of the vast untrammeled discretion available to these petty bureaucrats, and it became public knowledge as a result of the temporary nature of their posts, which meant that they did not enjoy the same degree of immunity that permanent civil servants did.[34] This corruption was very visible, for commodity controls brought the state into the everyday lives of its citizens.

The strongest critique of commodity controls was articulated by Gandhi, who remained adamant that they would have to be dismantled in independent India. Gandhi's campaign against the controls took center stage immediately after independence, when he declared that his two immediate goals were to restore communal harmony in India and to launch a national campaign for the removal of food control and rationing.[35] Having consistently expressed deep skepticism about state control, he argued that controls imposed from above were "always bad" and made life unnatural. Discussing the subject of cloth control, he asserted that solutions could not be imposed from above but had to evolve from below.[36]

To his way of thinking, controls bred dependency. Gandhi argued that the country could become self-sufficient in food if not for the government policy that sought to wrap citizens up in "cottonwool" and did not train them to stand by themselves. Commodity controls, for Gandhi, were thus a shortsighted measure for the government of free India to adopt; a responsible government would seek to involve citizens in the crisis, improve transport, pay attention to small farmers, and improve agricultural yields.[37] Gandhi emphasized individual responsibility, suggesting that Indians combat the cloth shortage by taking up the spinning of *khadi* (homespun cotton).[38] The solution lay in the "public being true to themselves" and not putting the decision in the hands of a few members of the cabinet.[39]

Another line of Gandhi's critique was based on the observation that price control disproportionately hurt small farmers. Acknowledging that doing away with controls could lead to price rises, he argued that the government's efforts should be geared toward ensuring that any rise in prices benefited the small farmer and was not absorbed by middlemen. Gandhi believed in the necessity of daily reminders to the people that the urban populace had a duty to make sacrifices to help the poorer farmers.[40] Similarly, on being warned by an interlocutor that derationing could lead to discontent, Gandhi emphasized that it was an empirical fact that there was a cloth shortage. This shortage could not be resolved only through distribution; a sufficient and long-term solution lay either in nationalizing the textile industry and working it excessively, on the one hand, or in giving citizens the resources to spin their own cloth, on the other. He did not favor the former solution because it would not redress mass poverty in the way that spinning *khadi*, in his vision, would.[41]

The experience of controls for many Indians during the war is neatly summed up in an observation by Sreenivasan: "Controls begat hardship, hardship begat resentment, resentment begat evasion, evasion begat blackmarket, [and] blackmarket begat corruption. It was a dismal business."[42]

Controls and Freedom in the New Republic

Several countries had adopted some form of price control and rationing during World War II. However, in the United States and in western Europe these mechanisms were dismantled with surprising swiftness after the war. Given the general level of dissatisfaction with the existing system of controls and the vociferous opposition to it from the Gandhian wing of the Congress Party, one would imagine that commodity controls in India would have gone the same way. Within two months of independence, Rajendra Prasad, the food minister, grimly noted that "controls were becoming increasingly unpopular, in spite of their being administered by a popular government."[43] The Congress Party itself was deeply divided, with the leadership managing to defeat (by only ten votes) a resolution demanding the immediate abolition of controls.[44]

Contrary to the pattern in other countries, apart from a brief period of decontrol in 1948, commodity controls actually intensified in postcolonial India. Murarji J. Vaidya, the president of the Indian Merchants' Chamber, a business lobby that was very close to the Congress Party leadership, expressed his puzzlement that countries that were more directly involved in the war (like the UK), and those that had suffered severe ravages (like Germany and Japan), were devising ways to remove various economic controls, whereas India remained the "only free and democratic country" that sought to continue and even extend the controls in various spheres of activity.[45]

Extended in 1946 as a temporary measure in the face of a continuing economic crisis, commodity controls became established as the government's permanent practice with the enactment of the Essential Commodities Act of 1955 (also known simply as the Commodities Act). The wartime commodity-control system operated as an emergency measure. Accordingly, when the emergency was officially rescinded in April 1946, it might have been expected that all existing controls would lapse and that in the future the responsibility for commodity controls would reside only with the provinces. By this time, an interim government headed by Nehru held office in Delhi, and preparations for independence were under way.

The interim government asked the British Parliament to amend the Government of India Act to temporarily grant the central legislature the power to make laws concerning trade and commerce.[46] The central legislature went replaced the old controls with the Essential Supplies Act of 1946, under which Harishankar and Gomtidevi Bagla were charged. The operation of the ESA was time-bound: the power of the central government to regulate commodities was set to lapse in five years, by which time it was expected that the economic emergencies caused by high prices and chronic shortages would have been resolved. The ESA empowered the government to regulate or prohibit the production, supply, distribution, trade, and commerce of any commodity designated an "essential commodity" as much as was "necessary or expedient" to maintain supplies or secure their equitable distribution at fair prices.[47]

Mirroring the DIA (which it replaced), the ESA, through a system of licenses, allowed the central government to regulate the manufacture and production of any commodity and the expansion of cultivable land; to control prices; to regulate the storage, transport, supply, and distribution of essential commodities; to set limits on storage and stockpiling; to require the sale of goods to a particular category of people; and to prohibit any transactions that were, in the opinion of the central government or other authority under the ESA, detrimental to "public interest." Controllers were appointed for each essential commodity and vested with extensive powers and duties, including the responsibility of collecting information and statistics. Controllers under the ESA had the right to inspect the accounts, records, and receipts of individuals engaged in the production of or trade in essential commodities, as well as to search premises without a warrant.[48]

The government sought to protect the ESA from legal challenges. Thus the ESA provided that orders made under its section 3 had effect regardless of their inconsistency with any other law.[49] The government also sought to insulate such orders from judicial review by providing that no order made under the ESA could be called into question in any court.[50] Finally, the ESA bestowed immunity to legal proceedings on officers and the government for any damage that might be caused by actions in furtherance of an order under the ESA.[51] In effect, then, there was little incentive for administrators to take commercial or trading interests into account, for these administrators would not be liable even if a decision of theirs caused substantial economic loss.

The ESA was expected to lapse by the end of 1949, but the government used crises of shortages and inflation to periodically extend its life. The assumption persisted that the ESA and its commodity controls were merely a temporary solution. After several extensions, as the expiration date of the ESA approached, the government formed the Parliamentary Select Committee on Commodity Controls (known simply as the Commodity Controls Committee), headed by a member of parliament but composed entirely of bureaucrats, to examine the existing controls and streamline the system. Acknowledging the evidence that controls could and did cause harm, the committee argued that they should nevertheless be retained because they could be used for a positive purpose and maintained on an all-India basis. [52] Parliament acted on the advice of the committee, amended the Constitution, and enacted the Commodities Act in 1955, giving the central government the power to control all commodities through a comprehensive permanent law.[53]

How did an emergency wartime measure by a colonial government become a routine element of the postcolonial republic that opposed and then succeeded it? There is now a considerable body of scholarship that has identified the "state of exception" as a characteristic of the modern state that allows the government to expand its power over its citizens.[54] The Indian Constitution itself institutionalized emergency by incorporating provisions that explicitly authorized the use of extraordinary powers and the suspension of civil liberties during a designated period.[55] Controls in India assumed a different dimension not just because of their framing as a purely economic and politically neutral question but also because the emergency was seen as a permanent condition arising from an underdeveloped economy.

The Nehru government's enthusiasm for the retention of controls was the combined product of, on the one hand, modes of imagining the postcolonial state's relationship with its citizens and, on the other, the adoption of centralized economic planning as the main instrument for administering the economy. The Indian Constitution guaranteed economic justice to all its citizens.[56] On the eve of independence the governor-general reminded the members of the Constituent Assembly that it was their responsibility to ensure the happiness and prosperity of the people and to "provide against future scarcities of food, cloth, and essential commodities and to build up a balanced economy."[57] Nehru acknowledged that the first task before the assembly was "to free India through a new Constitution to feed the starving people and clothe the naked masses."[58] Another member suggested that the Constitution should ensure food and cloth for villagers, since a lack of these necessities had led to the demand for *swaraj*, or freedom from foreign rule and customs.[59]

These statements acknowledge that the independent republic, unlike its colonial predecessor, was expected to ensure that its citizens received the basic amenities of life. However, this was cast as a responsibility of the state rather than as a right (to food or clothing) vested in the citizens by the Constitution. The Constitution directed the state to make policies ensuring that the ownership and control of the material resources of the community were distributed to serve the common good. It also required the state to ensure that the "operation of the economic system" did not result in the concentration of wealth and means of production to the common detriment.[60] This arose from a concern over the provision of daily commodities. The original wording of the provision was that the state would ensure "that the *operation of competition* shall not be allowed to result in the concentration of ownership and control of *essential commodities*" (emphasis mine).[61] It was now the duty of the state to intervene in the quotidian life of markets.

However, the framing of the problem as a responsibility rather than a right meant that citizens were unable to make these claims through the Constitution.[62] Ananthasayanam Ayyangar complained as follows:

> Food and clothing are essentials of human existence. Where is a single word in the Constitution that a man shall be fed and clothed by the state? . . . We have not yet taken any lesson from the 35 lakhs of people who died in the Bengal famine? Is there a single word in the Constitution that imposes on future governments that nobody in India shall die of starvation? What is the good of saying that every man shall have political rights . . . and so forth, unless he has the wherewithal to live?"[63]

The expansion of the police powers of the state in order to meet an emergency was not exceptional among the constitutions of republics. What was unique to the postcolonial situation in India was the institution of these powers as a permanent instrument. The need to address the economy as an emergency was based on the national experience of the decade preceding independence, which had witnessed a devastating famine and chronic underdevelopment. The new government believed that the economic crisis could be managed only through the regulated circulation of goods and services.

The welfare state that would emerge as a result of this approach to economic governance was directed from the top and based on the perceived needs of the people rather than on their actual demands as expressed through their elected representatives or in other forums. As a result, economic controls did not need popular support to be continued. The Indian state acquired its representativeness not just through elected government but also by leading the nation to economic development through a process of economic planning. Thus, the sovereign powers of the state were directly connected to the economic well-being of its citizens.[64] What was good for the economic well-being of the people therefore outranked public preferences and could contradict and supersede the expression of these preferences through elections, the media, and the market.

In its first five-year plan, the Planning Commission argued that the free market was not a dependable mechanism for providing essential commodities in an economy that was likely to experience pressure from shortages and international fluctuations. Postcolonial India was imagined by its governing classes as a needy nation, permanently afflicted by an essential lack, in this case of consumer commodities.[65] This lack would be met only at some point in the distant future, and until that indeterminate date, extraordinary measures from the state would be required merely to manage it. Although the original justification for controls had been to ensure an equitable distribution of scarce commodities, the controls tended to perpetuate themselves even when scarcity ended. For instance, even when sugar production increased significantly, the control on sugar was retained on the grounds that it had to be exported to earn foreign exchange.[66]

The Commodity Controls Committee was convinced to retain controls in a permanent form by the ringing endorsement this measure received from the Planning Commission. The commission argued that controls provided a means by which the government could balance various sectional interests, control the limit of freedom of action on certain classes, and provide incentives to others.[67] It noted that the origins of the controls in wartime obscured the wider role they could play in a peacetime planned economy, such as "safeguarding the minimum consumption standards of poorer classes, preventing excessive or ostentatious consumption by the well-to-do, and facilitating the country's program of direct utilization of unemployment manpower for investment."[68] This argument resembled others that had been used to justify the continuation of various structures of the colonial government, such as the army and the police, in postcolonial India. It suggested that the institution in itself (in this case, economic controls), operated within a "rational universality" that had been misapplied in the colonial state but could now be utilized for development.[69]

For controls to be legitimate, they had to stand above sectional interests and the normal processes of politics and be directed by a neutral rational body of experts rather than by parliament. The noninvolvement of politicians, civil society, and community groups in the process of implementing controls was a a striking departure from the experiences of rationing and controls in other democracies, like the United States.[70] Even the opposition Socialist Party, which pointed out the people's loss of faith in the desirability and efficacy of the present system of controls, continued to advocate commodity controls. It attributed the public dissatisfaction to the centralized bureaucratic nature of the controls, which the Socialists promised to remedy by delegating authority from government departments to people's representative committees and associations.[71]

The Cotton Textile Order of 1948, under which the Baglas had been arrested and whose legality they challenged, provided a typical example of the byzantine systems of economic regulation. The Cotton Textile Order had been passed in the aftermath of the war, when certain parts of the country faced a severe shortage of cloth. The situation had grown so bad in the major cities that there were rumors of cloth being stolen from shrouds and coffins and a fear of cloth riots outside shops.[72]

The Cotton Textile Order sought to confer the power to regulate every phase of cotton cloth and yarn production on the office of the textile commissioner. The aim of the Cotton Textile Order was to ensure an adequate supply of yarn to the hand-loom industry by requiring manufacturers to sell yarn. It limited the installation of power looms, controlled the installation of power spindles, set the price of cloth, and ensured its distribution across the country. In order to prevent hoarding, the textile commissioner could set the maximum quantity of cloth and yarn that could be possessed by a producer or a dealer as well as the maximum time they could retain possession of it. To assist in the enforcement of these controls, the date of production was to be marked on all cloth and yarn. The country was divided into zones, and cotton cloth could be moved between zones only with a permit from the textile commissioner. The creation of a permit regime allowed new people who were able to secure the governmental permits to enter the cotton trade.[73] In some cases these new retailers were able to resell the licenses to those they had displaced, thus reducing the margin of profit. The entry of new participants meant that the dealers in older important centers of distribution—such as Bombay, Calcutta, Delhi, and Kanpur (the Baglas' base of operations)—lost their positions, and the trading networks they had built across the country collapsed.[74]

The complicated system of price and distribution controls, along with the displacement of normal trade channels, caused severe difficulties even for traders who had obtained licenses. A leading economist remarked that "the temptation of evading the control orders and the difficulty in comprehending them was so great" that there was hardly a trader who had not either knowingly or unknowingly evaded the controls.[75] For traders, abiding by the regulations would have meant acquiescing in the destruction of their business.

The complexity of the orders regime was such that even the parliamentary committee reviewing commodity controls had difficulty obtaining a list of all notifications issued under various orders. Several administrators admitted to parliament that even they were not sure of the latest position on the notifications governing the commodities they controlled. The Cotton Textile Order demanded an enormously increased burden of paperwork from traders. For instance, the mills in Bombay had to submit 577 forms a year to a variety of authorities, including the textile commissioner, the factory inspector, the labor minister, and the registrar of companies. The failure to submit accurate and timely returns was punishable by fine.[76]

The New Economic Criminal

The controls system created a new class of crimes in India that later came to be described as socioeconomic offenses.[77] The initial list of these offenses comprised hoarding, dealings on the black market, tax evasion, food adulteration, and illegal trading in licenses and permits. The novelty of these offenses is apparent from their absence in the Indian Penal Code, which as a model piece of utilitarian legislation had attempted to list all possible offenses in the mid-nineteenth century. The only economic offenses that appeared in treatises and commentaries before World War II were various types of betting and gambling, food adulteration, and counterfeiting of currency.

These new socioeconomic offenses consisted of acts calculated to prevent or obstruct the economic development of the country.[78] The victim of these offenses was the state and a segment of the consuming public. The crime was perpetrated by fraud and not by force. The Law Commission of India headed by Justice Gajendragadkar drew an analogy between the necessity of penalizing these offenses and the need to defend every inch of territory in war, stating that "in an economic crisis or in a massive effort to build up a healthy social structure, the purity of every grain had to be protected and every dot of evil wiped out." Recommending greater punishments for violating the Commodities Act, the Law Commission argued that offenses affecting the health of the entire community had to be crushed and that the legislative "armory" for fighting socioeconomic crimes needed "weapons" that were sharper and more effective than those used for ordinary crimes.[79]

The controls system was undergirded by an exceptional regime of criminal law. This framework arose from the belief that "socioeconomic" criminals would respond only to a stronger deterrence than fines and public shaming. Indeed, a socioeconomic offense was characterized as one that was not challenged by the "organized moral sentiments" of the community, because the crimes were often complex, and public agencies like the press were themselves controlled by businesses involved in violating these laws.[80]

Violating an order made under the ESA and the Commodities Act was punishable with imprisonment for three years, a fine, or both, and periodic amendments to the applicable law increased the punishments several times.[81] Property involved in such violations, like the bales of cloth found in the Baglas' carriage, could be forfeited. As Hiralal Sutwala, the Baglas' servant, found out, aiding and abetting such contraventions was also deemed punishable. In recognition of the likelihood that companies would attempt to violate the orders, the controls regime made all directors, managers, and officers of a corporate body liable for a contravention, unless they could prove that it took place without their knowledge or negligence.[82] In cases of a violation of control orders (in a deviation from the Indian Evidence Act of 1872), the burden of proof was shifted to the accused.[83]

Perhaps most ominous was that those charged with violating control orders would be subject to a summary trial under the Criminal Procedure Code of 1873.[84] Ordinarily a summary trial was mandated only for cases involving goods valued at less than two hundred rupees and in which the maximum punishment possible was imprisonment for two years. A summary trial was ordinarily provided for minor offenses, in which the interests of a speedy resolution and several procedural requirements could be ignored. The accused would, for instance, have only one opportunity to cross-examine witnesses and a limited or no right of appeal. An examination of just one of these debates illuminates the reasons for the state's conviction that extraordinary measures against such offenses were necessary.

The ESA was amended in 1949 to provide that imprisonment would be obligatory in cases arising from violations of orders involving grains and textiles, and exceptions could be made only if the judge provided a reason in writing. Furthermore, any vehicle or animal used for smuggling grains or textiles could be confiscated.[85]

The 1949 amendment to the ESA sought to remove all judicial discretion in sentencing. This change was a response to magistrates giving light sentences in most cases that involved controls infringement. Prabhu Dayal Himatsingka, a Marwari lawyer from Calcutta and one of the few opponents of the amendment in parliament, tried to convince the house that the reluctance of the courts to administer strict punishment indicated that public opinion in favor of the controls was weak. He failed.[86] Other members who criticized the amendment pointed out that the real cause of the violation of control orders was not criminal intent in the people but the shortage of goods. These shortages, coupled with the poor quality of available products (even in the ration shops), forced people to buy from the black market.[87] Could a father buying food for his children from the black market be considered a criminal?

The amendment to the ESA was passed by an overwhelming majority, thanks in part, perhaps, to a furious member of the Constituent Assembly reminding the house that other countries had even imposed the death penalty for violating economic controls. He urged the government to increase the period of compulsory imprisonment to seven years. Exasperated by the high incidence of violations, he concluded that these criminals were particularly amoral and unaffected by the threat of imprisonment. Because they evidently cared more about money than the prospect of serving time in prison, he said, the government should devise penalties involving the confiscation of their property.[88]

The provision for compulsory sentencing placed all violations of controls at the same level, so an industrialist who forgot to file a return, a small trader moving goods without a permit, and a buyer trying to obtain food from the black market would face equal terms of imprisonment. The voices dissenting from this amendment noted that in practice, penalties for violation of the controls were pursued mostly against "small dealers and helpless buyers" who did not have the capacity to bribe the police.[89] The law's desire to punish offenders would not end the black market but would merely drive it underground, forcing the public to take greater risks and to pay more for the same goods. Banarsi Prasad Jhunjhunwala, another Marwari member of Parliament, recounted how in Bihar the anti–black market officials arrested a poor widow who sold saris to women from her home rather than targeting the prominent dealers on the black market.[90] The president of the Rationing Employees Union in Uttar

Pradesh warned the house that in his experience the majority of people convicted of violations of the controls were poor peasants who were transporting small quantities of grain from one place to another.[91]

Despite the anecdotal and empirical evidence that controls were violated by various categories of people, both public and governmental imaginations envisioned a particular kind of villain: the hoarder and the black marketeer. A war propaganda advertisement described the legitimate market as consisting of three figures: the cultivator, the dealer, and the customer.[92] The ad asked people to cut out the sinister "fourth man," the hoarder, who was an "unscrupulous speculator . . . who hoards vast stocks of grains waiting for a further rise in prices in order to make huge profits" (fig. 2.1). While such ads cautioned individuals against buying and storing more than they needed, they

There are four men concerned with food.

FIRSTLY the cultivator. This year he is better off than usual; paying land revenues and buying necessities out of profits-keeping crops and feeding well. One can hardly begrudge him his good fortune.

SECONDLY the dealer. There are good dealers and bad. There are profiteers and honest men. Good or bad, he gets enough food for himself.

THIRDLY YOU, the customers. You, it is, who suffer. The 5% total shortage, which should be spread over the whole population, is largely borne by a tenth of the population.

FOURTHLY, there is the unscrupulous speculator-operating illegally outside the grain trade—who hoards vast stocks of grain waiting for a further rise in prices in order to make huge profits.

The Government is going to punish the fourth man ruthlessly.

But you must play your part. Buy only what you need. Think of the poor who buy day by day.

Leave the big hoarders to Government. But do not become a small hoarder yourself. So, in serving India, and India's poor, you will be serving yourself.

=the hoarder

ISSUED BY THE   NATIONAL WAR FRONT

FIG 2.1. "The Fourth Man," classified ad no. 4. *Times of India*, March 18, 1943.

also acted as reminders of the danger posed by the unscrupulous hoarder, usually depicted as a member of the trading classes.

Shopkeepers and traders, including those who worked at government ration shops, were seen as particularly corrupt. Some public advertisements reminded customers that they should keep all paper receipts obtained from ration shopkeepers for a month, which would allow the rationing inspector to check the shopkeepers' sale registers and prevent rationed goods from entering the black market. Others encouraged individuals to smash the black market by reporting unscrupulous traders to the police (fig. 2.2).

Despite the close links forged by some business houses with the Congress Party, merchants and traders in general were viewed with suspicion in independent India, by both the political elites and the general population. The public frustration with shortages and shoddy products was articulated against the retailer with whom the consumer came into daily contact rather than the big

FIG 2.2. Smashing the black market, classified ad no. 5. *Times of India*, January 19, 1945.

industrialist or corporate capital. Government documentaries of the period explicitly portrayed the shopkeeper as a bad citizen. The film *Citizens and Citizens*, released in 1952, opens by defining the good citizen as a family man who obeys the laws made by his elected representative and meets his obligations to other members of society with the same consideration that he expects to receive.[93] The film introduces a number of undesirable citizens, including a man named Chagganlal, who runs a government-licensed store and, having heard rumors of a shortage of oil, decides to hoard it. Chagganlal brusquely informs his young customer that all stocks of oil have been exhausted, but at night he is seen inside his secret storeroom gloating over all the oil he has hoarded (fig. 2.3). The voice-over wryly comments, "Chagganlal has just put a spoke in the wheel of progress, though such a suggestion would outrage him." Chagganlal Marwari happened to be the name of the villain in Nabendu Ghosh's short story "Bostrong Dehi"; he was a cloth trader from Rajasthan who exploited the cloth controls system and preyed on Bengali peasants.

The merchant's loyalty to the nation was subject to constant suspicion. In an effort to win goodwill, an Indian confectionary manufacturer put out an advertisement appealing to the commercial community to cooperate with the government (fig. 2.4). It was high time, said the ad, that traders realized that they now had their own government in independent India. Unless they wholeheartedly cooperated with this government, they would fail to get the benefits of a truly national government. Hoarding and dealing on the black market were depicted as a wrench thrown in the government machinery, leading to higher labor costs and more expensive raw materials. The supporters of the periodic amendments made to the control laws viewed every trader as a potential criminal, and the language against merchants grew more vitriolic. An amendment to the Commodities Act described hoarders as "these man-eaters" who were "playing hell with the lives of millions of people."[94]

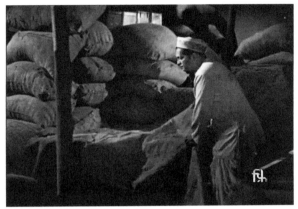

FIG. 2.3. "Oil stocks are exhausted," shopkeeper Chagganlal tells
a customer in *Citizens and Citizens* (1952), and then gloats over
his hoard in the storeroom.

Business had a poor rapport with the public, affecting its abilities to gain
representation in an elected government.[95] In colonial India, indigenous business interests had emerged as a legitimate interest group that was guaranteed
representation in the legislature. Chambers of commerce and merchants' associations formed electorates that sent members to legislative assemblies as
representatives of native commerce.[96] These interest groups were abolished
after independence; groups like the Indian Merchants' Chamber and the
Federation of Indian Chambers of Commerce and Industry lost ground to
planners and economists as spokespeople on market policies.[97] This is not to
suggest that traders and industrialists became powerless to influence policy.
However, their ability to act legitimately and publicly was greatly constrained.

INDIA
needs..

THE MERCHANTS' CO-OPERATION

It is high time the commercial community realised that it is now their own government. and that unless. they co-operated whole-heartedly t h e y would fail to reap the full benefits of a truly national government. Everytime a trader hoards goods, sells in the Black Market, or resorts to other forms of profiteering, he is throwing a spanner in the cogs of government machinery. Black Markets, rising costs of labour, high prices of raw materials—it's all a. vicious circle and the solution lies in co-operating with Government to stamp out these evils and thereby ensure a quicker return to prosperity.

★ INSERTED BY THE MAKERS OF

FIG. 2.4. Appeal to merchants, classified ad no. 7. Ministry of Information and Broadcasting, 1948.

Because of the distrust of business that permeated public culture, business interests attempted to make direct contact with the higher bureaucracy while staying out of the public eye.[98]

"The Marwari Occupants of the Lucknow Bogie": Caste, Criminality, and Constitutionalism

Traders, by virtue of their profession alone, were thus viewed as potential criminals by the postcolonial state. The Marwari had long been the image of the trader that inhabited both official discourses and popular folklore.[99] The Marwaris emerged as a particularly suspect community in postcolonial India.

The railway police officer who arrested the Baglas was alerted of their involvement in smuggling by a telegram that asked him to investigate the "Marwari occupants of the Lucknow Bogie." There were no names or seat numbers required—a Marwari's identity was considered sufficient for locating him in a crowded carriage. The Baglas explicitly identified themselves as Marwari on the police charge sheet, as did Hiralal Sutwala in his application before the Nagpur High Court.[100] This section will show how their caste identity was pivotal to the predicament in which they found themselves.

The name Marwari came to describe migrant merchant traders from Rajasthan who settled throughout the country. Once a heterogeneous group of merchants, consisting of both Hindu and Jain families, it grew into a more homogeneous community by forging networks of trade and credit.[101] Although they were always involved in trade, it was the particular circumstances of the nineteenth century colonial economy that led to the Marwaris emerging as a preeminent trading group. In the absence of a formal banking system, Marwari traders across the country became creditors and moneylenders. Drawing upon networks of trust within the community, the Marwaris were able to support a system of *hundis*, or indigenous bills of exchange. The late nineteenth century saw Marwaris migrating to prominent colonial cities and market centers as bankers and traders in agricultural commodities. Their involvement in commodity speculation helped them raise capital and emerge as financiers by World War I. Several Marwari families, such as the Birlas, the Dalmias, and the Ruias, emerged as preeminent industrial houses in late colonial India. However, a Marwari encountered by the typical Indian on an everyday basis was most likely to be the local grain merchant, cloth merchant, or moneylender.

It is not surprising that the Marwaris, acting as powerful economic intermediaries between the elites and the masses, were viewed with hostility and
suspicion by the local population. In her ethnography of Calcutta's Marwaris,
Anne Hardgrove compares the Marwaris to other middlemen minorities, such
as the Jews in Europe, the Chinese in Indonesia, or the Lebanese in West Africa, who also emerged through the globalization of capitalism.[102] Since the
late nineteenth century the Marwaris had often been criticized for being rapa-
cious and miserly and were accused of involvement in unethical business practices, including gambling, speculation on commodities, food adulteration, and
food hoarding. Anti-Marwari feelings were demonstrated most dramatically
during the Deccan Riots of 1875, during which thousands of peasants from rural
Maharashtra, mired in indebtedness, joined in attacks on Marwari
moneylenders.[103]

Despite the Marwaris' rise to prominence in the colonial economy, the public
and the government imagined Marwaris almost as premodern economic actors and not as the "homo economicus" required by modern capitalism. This
was in striking contrast to other commercial communities, like the Parsis, who
were viewed as modern, almost Western, subjects.[104] This anachronistic image
of Marwari business practices is captured neatly in Omkar Goswami's comparison of Burrabazar, the Marwari commercial district in Calcutta, with Dal-
housie Square, where most modern European firms were located:

> Burrabazar is the very antithesis of Dalhousie Square. In the place of the
> well laid-out roads were filthy, crooked, by-lanes and alleys; instead of pa-
> latial offices there were small, holes-in-the-wall-gaddis where the Marwaris
> conducted business worth millions of rupees in hard cash or against bills
> of exchanges (hundis) taken out from strong boxes; instead of maintaining
> audited accounts, the Marwaris made single entries in huge red clothbound
> ledgers which were undecipherable by anyone other than their family.[105]

The close kinship networks the Marwaris maintained across the nation,
along with their private business practices (like coded account books), granted
Marwari businesses a degree of opacity from governmental market discipline.
The state remained aware of this. In *Rights and Responsibilities*, a documentary
from 1952 that was aimed at educating citizens, the audience is first told that
not paying taxes will obstruct the state's functioning and is then reminded
that some people have made tax evasion a fine art. This is accompanied by the
image of a recognizably Marwari businessman, who, on being informed of a
visit by the tax department, hides his account books in a secret compartment
behind a bookshelf (fig. 2.5).

FIG. 2.5. Scenes from *Rights and Responsibilities* (1952): A
Marwari trader hides tax registers on a secret shelf; the
account books are concealed behind the bookcase.

Marwari prosperity and influence had developed because of the group's
ubiquitous presence throughout India, unlike other commercial groups like
the Parsis, Khojas, Gujaratis, and Chettiars, who operated primarily out of their
home bases.[106] However, it was their very cosmopolitanism that made them,
in the words of a contemporary political scientist, an "unusually sensitive political factor" in India in the 1950s.[107] The period after independence saw the
strengthening of regional identities and an increasing demand for the reorganization of the states on a linguistic basis. The Marwaris, by virtue of being the
dominant business community and perceived as outsiders, became a target for
political attacks, not just by the population that felt exploited but also by local
business groups that welcomed an easy way to harass the competition. Riots
over shortages of food or cloth often targeted Marwari traders: shops owned

by Marwaris were looted, and the traders were beaten and had their faces blackened.[108]

The Marwaris added fuel to the fire by publicly opposing the linguistic reorganization of the states.[109] Writing in the late 1950s, Selig Harrison documented quite extensively how Marwaris were portrayed as demons and Marwari politicians attacked with epithets based on their caste identity in areas as far apart as Bombay, Calcutta, Coimbatore, Bihar, Assam, and Kerala. Posters in Kerala during the first general election demanded, "Marwaris! Go home!"[110]

State propaganda was quite unsubtle in portraying the Marwari trader as a threat to the new state. In the 1948 film *The Case of Mr. Critic,* the audience is introduced to a number of fellow citizens who are cynical and who hinder the nation's progress. These include the middle-class employee who rejects the government's projected plans for growth, the radical student who is impatient with the pace of development, the superstitious farmer who is suspicious of modern technology, and a man named Sethji who is introduced as a shady character. Sethji appears as the stereotypical Marwari trader (fig. 2.6), with prominent caste marks and dressed in traditional Marwari garb that pulls tightly across his expansive girth. He lounges against a bolster from which he oversees obsequious clerks, the telephone the only necessary representative of modernity.

Sethji's morning reverie is broken by his clerk informing him that the government has imposed controls upon sugar. A furious Sethji shouts, "Satyanash ho sarkar ka!" (May this government be destroyed!) and complains that it should stick to governing and leave the selling of sugar to him. His clerk concurs that the government is useless. For the audience, which might have missed the message, the voice-over explains that Sethji considers the government his personal enemy because it is trying to check undue profiteering. At the conclusion of the movie, all the critics have been converted, except Sethji, who even grumbles in his sleep. Sethji is a figure to be both mocked and distrusted. Of all the dissident citizens, only the Marwari merchant, motivated by greed, remained irredeemable and permanently reluctant to join the national project.

Marwaris and the New Regulatory Order

The regulation of merchants and market practices by the state was not a new development. Since the late nineteenth century the Marwaris' customary economic practices had come into conflict with new market disciplinary ethics

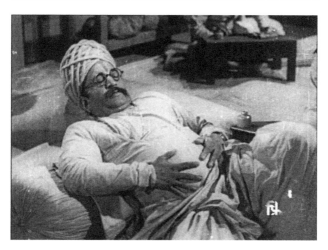

FIG. 2.6. Sethji, a shady character in *The Case of Mr. Critic* (1948); he is not happy to hear the news of sugar being controlled; he grumbles in his sleep.

and had been subject to criminal law. Ritu Birla has demonstrated that the Marwaris developed two complementary strategies to negotiate these new regulations. First, they resorted to the claim of cultural autonomy, coding commercial practices as culture and drawing on the colonial state's promise not to intervene in the cultural domain. Second, they sought to redefine and represent certain indigenous activities as legitimate and modern commercial activity.[111] However, the strategies that were developed against the colonial state had to be refashioned when dealing with the postcolonial state and with a democratic public.

It was difficult to argue for cultural autonomy from the state, given that the state now comprised Indians and was not external to the society it governed. Also, in an atmosphere in which the profession of trader was itself shrouded in suspicion, it became increasingly difficult to argue that certain business practices were legitimate indigenous practices.

The control system created many barriers for Marwari businesses. Marwaris played a disproportionate role in the commodity trade and controlled a significant part of the indigenous cotton cloth industry. Marwari associations, of course, opposed the controls. As soon as World War II ended, the Marwari Chamber of Commerce expressed its apprehension that the "crippling controls of wartime origin" were being perpetuated.[112] Marwari members of the Constituent Assembly, such as Prabhu Dayal Himatsingka and Banarsi Prasad Jhunjhunwala, were among the few critics of the ESA and its subsequent amendments.[113] Since 1940 almost every session of the Federation of Indian Chambers of Commerce and Industry had heard expressions of concern over state controls by the industrial and business communities. These demands went unheeded by the government. Rejecting a memorandum for the relaxation of controls, Rajendra Prasad pointed out to members of the Marwari Chamber of Commerce that it was not right for businessmen to set their minds on profit when the public at large was in distress.[114]

But when the formal channels of parliament and civil society proved ineffective in blocking the perpetuation of the controls system, traders had to develop various forms of accommodation with it. Several businessmen, including most of the prominent Marwari industrial houses, sought to achieve a modicum of cooperation with the Congress Party.[115] The controls system created several opportunities for rent seeking, which the larger players in the market were able to exploit, thus securing the required permits and licenses.

A majority of traders either simply disregarded the controls system or exploited its loopholes. For instance, the Cotton Textile Order limited the ration of cloth to fifteen yards a head for six months. Poorer consumers rarely used their entire allotment and thus sold the balance to illegal traders, who then resold it on the black market at a much higher price.[116] Others restamped the prices of cloth, forged permits, and attempted to move more cloth outside the controls regime into the black market. This was countered by the state toughening the system of system of surveillance and enforcement.

Newspapers reported the arrests of wealthy businessmen with glee. Four millionaire cloth dealers in Gaya were arrested for violating the ESA as a result of irregularities in their cloth registers. They were handcuffed and marched to the courtroom as thousands of jeering citizens lined up on either side of the road.[117] The sentencing of the richer merchants was often harsh; for instance, a Marwari cloth merchant from Bombay who was found selling cloth at 5.14 rupees per yard (the controlled price being 3.74 rupees) found himself fined 2 lakh rupees and sentenced to a year's rigorous imprisonment for violating the Cotton Textile Order.[118]

The Crime Branch and the Department of Civil Supplies organized periodic raids on suspected businesses. They had the power to search buildings and individuals without a warrant, so a Bombay constable who noticed strange lumps in a washerman's bundle was able to search it and recover four maunds of illicit sugar. Policemen noticed some people who frequently lined up before shops selling wristwatches and decided to search their houses.[119] Raids had also taken place in Harishankar Bagla's hometown of Cawnpore, where more than two hundred bales of cloth were found in the warehouses of well-known firms in boxes labeled "soap."[120]

The police set up elaborate plans for the entrapment of black-market traders. On receiving information about dealers who were selling cloth marked for export on the local black market, the police placed their firm under surveillance, tapping all their phone conversations and setting up decoy customers to entrap them.[121]

Bagla had also appeared on the police's list of people of interest who were placed under surveillance. Bombay was a major center of cotton textile production and thus had large stockpiles of cotton cloth. Since 1947 the police had been alert to cloth being smuggled out of Bombay on passenger trains, concealed in luggage and bedding.[122] As the record demonstrated, the Baglas and their contacts had been under investigation for some time by the Textiles Division of the Bombay police. The police were also able to trace and arrest Richard William Race, the superintendent at India United Mills in Bombay who had supplied Bagla with the black-market cloth.

By arresting Bagla, the authorities had netted a big fish and wanted to make an example of it. Bagla was involved in the management of a number of cotton textile mills in Kanpur. He had been elected president of the Uttar Pradesh Chamber of Commerce the preceding year and had dabbled in electoral politics, emerging as the runner-up representative of Indian Commerce in the 1946 Uttar Pradesh provincial assembly elections, and had also contested elections to the Central Legislative Assembly (a colonial body) as an independent.[123]

The world of Marwari-owned textile mills in Kanpur, of which Bagla was the prominent face, was mired in shadowy practices and now faced increased state surveillance. Other Marwari traders, including members of Bagla's extended family, had already faced arrest, and more would face it. His cousin, Harish Chandra Bagla, had been convicted in 1945 of selling cotton cloth for 14 rupees rather than at the approved rate of 13.46 rupees.[124] Prominent among the group of targeted Marwaris were the directors of the Swadeshi Cotton Mills, Mannu Lal Bagla and Sitaram Jaipuria, who were arrested for violating the ESA by stamping over the approved prices of dhotis and saris.[125]

Criminal Law and Constitutional Strategies

The Baglas were confronted with an overwhelming amount of evidence against them. Under the ESA, moreover, the burden of proof had been shifted to the defense. The Baglas faced mandatory imprisonment if convicted. Their original defense—that the cloth found on the train was for personal consumption—was not accepted by the magistrate.[126] In the second year of the prosecution, their lawyer, S. C. Dube, decided to move the case to another forum. He petitioned the Nagpur High Court on the grounds that the case raised substantial questions of law—namely, that the ESA was ultra vires the Constitution because it delegated excessive powers to the executive and that the extension of the ESA beyond its original expiration date through resolutions of parliament was impermissible. The initial arguments were tentative, and new decisions by the Supreme Court on delegated legislation led the lawyers to modify their petition and include additional grounds. They argued that the power given to the government under Section 3 of the ESA could not validly be delegated to a subordinate officer or authority.

Bagla retained Gopal Swarup Pathak, a leading lawyer from the Allahabad bar, to argue his case before the Nagpur High Court.[127] Pathak's presence was critical. Through the 1940s, several convictions under the ESA had been unsuccessfully challenged on the grounds of excessive delegation. The government lawyers raised a preliminary objection asking that this case be dismissed, following the precedents. However, Pathak successfully argued that since the previous applications had been made before the enactment of the Constitution, they could not be applied to the Bagla case.

Pathak confined his arguments solely to the question of whether the ESA was unconstitutional and suffered from the defect of excessive delegation; he chose not to argue the other procedural points raised in the petition. This decision was strategic, for the Supreme Court and high courts had already ruled on several of the technical contentions that Pathak was laying aside, also in cases involving Marwari traders.[128]

Pathak's primary argument was that essential legislative functions could not be delegated. These functions included the creation of policy and principles and the setting of standards that would restrict the actions of the authority to which power was being delegated. Pathak attacked the ESA for conferring unlimited arbitrary power without a policy to guide it. This arbitrary power included the conferral of subjective discretion on officials that could not be examined by a court, the power to select a delegate or an instrumentality, and the power to repeal an essential legislative function. Under Section 3 of the ESA, parliament made the central government the judge of the expediency of enacting an order. It provided no policy or standard to direct such judgment, and it conferred power of the widest latitude. Section 4 of the ESA left the choice of instrumentality and delegation to the government. Finally, Section 6 allowed the government to enact orders that were inconsistent with other laws enacted by parliament. The last provision virtually empowered executive authority to act inconsistently with the expressed desires of the legislature.

In particular, Pathak argued that the Cotton Textile Order had implicitly overruled the Indian Railways Act of 1890. Under Section 27 of the act, the railway authorities had a duty to provide all reasonable facilities for receiving, forwarding, and delivering traffic, and every citizen therefore had a corresponding right to transport by rail any goods of their choice. The Cotton Textile Order required anyone who wished to transport cloth, yarn, or apparel by rail to secure a permit from the textile commissioner. The effect of this requirement was virtually to abrogate the general right conferred on all citizens under the Railways Act and replace it with a considerably attenuated right. According to Pathak, by placing restrictions on the right of citizens to transport goods by rail, the Cotton Textile Order was partly repealing the Railways Act. The power to repeal a law could not be conferred upon an executive authority like the textile commissioner and had to be exercised by parliament. Therefore, Pathak contended, Section 6 of the ESA, which permitted the central government to make provisions under the ESA that were inconsistent with earlier laws, was invalid.

There was a curious irony underlying Pathak's distinction between executive and legislative authority. The Indian Railways Act—which the ESA was alleged to have partly repealed—was a colonial law enacted by the viceroy and his council, predating the reforms that allowed some Indian representation in the legislative process. The ESA, in contrast, which provided for delegation to executive authorities, was authored by the Constituent Assembly and administered by a Congress Party–led government. However, Pathak was conscious of the fact that the railways in India had always served as an arena in which relationships of power were defined and resisted. The railways were presented to India as an instrument of progress and a sign of modernity, and rail travel was seen as central to developing Indian national consciousness.[129] Thus, Pathak spelled out in legal terms what popular opinion had often expressed: commodity controls were transforming older conceptions of rights and privileges.

Separating Powers in the Indian Republic

The argument Pathak made in the *Bagla* case, on the unconstitutionality of excessive delegation, was not novel; however, its timing was critical. Similar arguments had been made in cases involving the ESA and the DIA rules before the enactment of the Constitution, and they had been dismissed. However, the Constitution allowed Pathak to develop several arguments drawing from American jurisprudence.

The earliest legal argument on the issue, arising from convictions for violations of controls during World War II, had asserted that the ESA's subject matter itself was beyond the jurisdiction of the colonial legislature. This argument was repeatedly dismissed by the courts.[130] The validity of several of the DIA rules had been challenged on the grounds that the rules were delegated legislation but had failed on every occasion. In the case of Meer Singh, a shopkeeper who refused to accept a valid currency note and was charged with undermining public confidence in the government, challenged the validity of the DIA rules on the grounds that the Indian legislature had no power to divest itself of legislative authority. The central legislature that had enacted the DIA derived its powers from the Government of India Act of 1935. Singh argued that the delegation of authority to the central government to make the DIA rules was tantamount to constituting the central government as a fresh legislative body. The court rejected this contention, noting that the legislature still retained the power to take back the authority it had delegated and destroy the agencies it had set up.[131] The decision in this case became the authoritative precedent for all challenges to the DIA rules until independence.[132]

Regardless of the determination, cases like this illustrated an important line of argument. Lawyers recognized that the powers of a legislature would be circumscribed by the Government of India Act, which was repeatedly referred to as the Constitution. This helped distinguish the Indian legislature from a Diceyan (an approach to separation of powers taken by the scholar A. V. Dicey) understanding of British parliamentary sovereignty. As the chief justice noted in another case involving detention under the DIA rules, "On account of the absolute sovereignty of parliament, no question of the constitutional invalidity of any parliamentary enactment can ever be raised in a court of law."[133] Although the courts in late colonial India began to recognize that there were limits to legislative power, they were initially uncomfortable enforcing them. In the *Meer Singh* case, the Allahabad High Court warned that when judging legislative propriety, the court must be careful not to "be led into a criticism of the constitutional propriety of that method, instead of confining our attention to its strictly legal aspect."[134] Acknowledging the debate about delegated powers that was emerging in Britain, the court nevertheless ruled that such questions were beside the point in India.

Lawyers continued to raise challenges to the Commodities Act and other commodities orders on the grounds of excessive delegation, saying that they were driven to this defense as a last resort because commodity control laws did not leave much room for the usual criminal defense based on the normal rules of evidence. Similar challenges were made to the ESA even after independence, such as by a Marwari trader in Bengal who was hoarding excess amounts of rice. The Calcutta High Court noted that there was no difference in principle between the rules made under the ESA and those made under the DIA.[135] This was echoed by several other high courts, which noted that parliament did not delegate its authority under the ESA but merely permitted the executive and its officers to carry out the policy stated in the act.[136]

Pathak, however, had been developing a more sophisticated version of the excessive-delegation argument. A year before he was retained by the Baglas, he had defended another Marwari trader, who had been arrested tampering with the stock registers at his kerosene shop.[137] Despite noting that the question of excessive delegation had been decided by the courts several times, the

Allahabad High Court agreed to consider the question again out of deference to Pathak's elaborate arguments, which drew on the work of several constitutional theorists.

Pathak's brief persuaded the court that with the enactment of the Constitution, parliamentary sovereignty in India had become transformed. Pathak quoted extensively from *American Administrative Law*, a recent treatise by Bernard Schwartz. A professor at the New York University law school, Schwartz had recently completed his doctorate at Cambridge University and was able to draw a clear distinction between the role of courts in the British and the American systems. Pathak quoted him, saying, "In Great Britain, excessive delegations of parliament are political concerns, while in the United States, they are primarily judicial."[138] He argued that as a nonsovereign parliament, the Indian legislature did not enjoy the immunities the British Parliament did. Pathak used Schwartz's work to contend that any delegation of power by a nonsovereign legislature must be a limited one and that the legislation enabling such delegation must contain a framework within which executive action must operate.[139] The Allahabad High Court was reminded of US Supreme Court Justice Benjamin Cardozo's words that the grant of authority must be "canalized within banks that keep it from overflowing."[140] Pathak directed a special attack on a proviso that allowed the delegated authority to create new offenses and prescribe punishments. He argued that, as in the United States, any penalties for violation of administrative rules and regulations must be fixed by the legislature itself.[141] The debates before the court highlight that there was no fixed conception of the constitutional order in India. Despite the extreme detail of the Constitution and long deliberations by the Constituent Assembly, arguments over quotidian acts could reshape how the Constitution was understood.

The Allahabad High Court responded extremely conservatively to Pathak's arguments, holding that the views of jurists and US courts were not binding on Indian legislatures. It ruled that it was not permitted for a court to throw out an enactment that was within the scope of the powers of the relevant legislature on the grounds of it being unreasonable, unnecessary, or improper or because it delegated excessive authority. The high court further held that the views of constitutionalists on what powers ought to be retained by the legislature and what could be conferred on other authorities were not binding in any way and could at best serve as a guideline that a legislature was free to ignore. The court held that it did not have the power to strike down an enactment on the basis of constitutional theory and foreign precedent. The court rejected

Pathak's arguments and upheld the prosecution on the grounds that the courts had no power to reject an act as ultra vires only because of the vice of excessive delegation.

The court preferred to follow nineteenth-century precedents from the colonial Privy Council to determine that the power to create penalties could be delegated to administrative authorities.[142] Recognizing that the American position on creating penalties was different, the court pointed out that even the US Congress could lay down policies and establish standards before leaving it to other authorities to fill in the details. The court upheld the DIA rules on the basis that they had been made by a legislature that was facing a serious emergency and could not immediately make laws to ensure public safety because it was short of time and was not cognizant of all the practical situations that might arise. The emergency was justification enough for the legislation to confer the rule-making powers on the central government. It was not for the judiciary to examine the question of the reasonableness or propriety of any enactment of even a nonsovereign legislature.

The decision in *Bagla* reflected two long-standing characteristics of Indian courts that would change with the commodity control cases. First, the courts exhibited a general deference to the executive, especially in political and security cases.[143] Scholars have suggested that it was this history of deference that made the expansion of the court's jurisdiction under the new Constitution uncontroversial.[144] Given their experience with the courts, the members of the Constituent Assembly assumed that their interventions in government policy would be rare.

Second, when considering foreign precedents, Indian courts relied largely on English decisions, and especially the decisions of the Privy Council. With the enactment of the Government of India Act in 1935 and the institution of the Federal Court, the courts began to pay attention to decisions from other dominions with constitutional government, particularly Australia and Canada. An inventory of the judges' library of the Federal Court revealed seven commentaries on the US Constitution, compared to more than thirty dealing with the constitutional law of Britain and of other dominions.[145]

However, with the enactment of the Constitution in 1950 and the incorporation of enforceable fundamental rights, both of these characteristics of the Indian courts began to change. Significantly for the Baglas' case, both phenomena came together in an advisory opinion of the Supreme Court in the case of *in re Delhi Laws Act*.

The *Delhi Laws Act* Problem

Given the importance of the *Delhi Laws Act* decision to Indian constitutional law, the origins of the case were surprisingly routine. The law in question authorized the executive to extend to the newly formed states the laws that were in force in the older states. The executive was also authorized to modify these laws to the extent that they did not affect policy. These laws were referred to the Supreme Court for its advisory opinion because of the increasing number of questions being raised about the delegation of executive power.[146] The judges of the Supreme Court responded in a lengthy decision with seven separate opinions. The majority of the court upheld two of the acts, following the nineteenth-century precedent of the Privy Council.[147] However, it struck down the third act, which authorized the executive to repeal or amend legislation using delegated powers.

Chief Justice Harilal Kania, writing for the majority, stated that with the enactment of the Constitution, the judges could not endorse the view that the Indian legislature had unlimited powers, like its British counterpart. After a careful reading of cases from Canada, Australia, and the United States, Kania ruled that although a legislature could confer powers to the executive to make rules and regulations for carrying out the objects of the act, it could not delegate "essential legislative functions" to the executive. He rejected the contention of the attorney general that India had adopted the English and not the American system of government and that the delegation of legislative function was valid as long as the legislature retained the final power to control the actions of the body to which it had delegated the function.[148] The Indian parliament was not sovereign but was restrained by the written Constitution.

The Baglas in Court

Pathak's gambit in the *Bagla* case was partly successful: the Nagpur High Court recognized that the *Delhi Laws Act* case had changed the law on the delegation of authority and, on that basis, overruled nine frequently cited precedents.[149] The Nagpur High Court further noted that the ESA conferred a wide power on the executive to make a law that might be inconsistent with preexisting laws and found it to be ultra vires the powers of parliament. However, to secure the acquittal of the Baglas it was necessary to establish that Section 3 of the ESA, under whose authority the Cotton Textile Order had been formulated, was also ultra vires.

Pathak had argued that the section was ultra vires because the ESA conferred power without guidelines to the Textile Commission under the Cotton Textile Order. The commissioner's powers were not guided by a policy, nor was there any provision limiting the use of such power. Pathak relied on the decision of the US Supreme Court in *Yick Wo v. Hopkins*.[150] The judges were unpersuaded that the analogy drawn from the American case would apply. They held that the power entrusted to the textile commissioner was guided by the policy laid down in the preamble to the ESA, which was to regulate the transport of cotton textiles in a manner that would ensure even distribution at a fair price to all. The high court held that the granting or refusal of permits under the Cotton Textile Order was governed by this policy, and the discretion given to the textile commissioner therefore limited.

Encouraged by the judicial application of the principle of excessive delegation, Pathak appealed to the Supreme Court. His primary contention was the reassertion that Section 3 of the ESA was unconstitutional and void because it delegated essential legislative functions to a nonlegislative body without setting any standards that would limit its discretion. In Pathak's argument, the subjective discretion given to the textile commissioner was not examinable by the court, and therefore the conferral of such discretion was tantamount to the conferral of an arbitrary power. The Supreme Court was receptive to this argument, unlike the Nagpur High Court, and pointed out that the broad aims of the ESA were merely illustrative of the matters for which orders could be enacted and did not exhaustively list the powers that were actually conferred. The textile commissioner continued to enjoy very wide latitude.

Pathak also argued that the powers conferred upon the Textile Commission interfered with the rights of citizens to dispose of property and carry on a trade and business. However, this argument was made last, in an almost formulaic fashion, and did not receive much attention in court. The courts were more receptive to claims about arbitrary bureaucratic power and proper procedure than assertion of rights.

The Supreme Court dismissed the Baglas' petition.[151] Although the judges reiterated the principles underlying the proscription of excessive delegation, they were unconvinced that Section 3 of the ESA, in particular, suffered from this defect. Since the Baglas had never applied for a permit to move cloth in the first place, the Supreme Court was reluctant to hold that the textile commissioner had been given an unregulated and arbitrary discretion to refuse or grant a permit. The court did concede that if the permit had been applied for and then refused, the Baglas might have had a stronger challenge to the law. The court's decision was carefully phrased, emphasizing judicial authority over the executive, but showing reluctance to let economic offenders benefit from it. It emphasized that the judiciary had the right to review legislation on the grounds of excessive delegation, and in the future it could review the discretion of bureaucrats like the textile commissioner. However, since the Baglas had failed to follow procedure in the first place and had never applied for the permit, they were not entitled to ask for procedural protection.

Little is known about what happened to Harishankar and Gomtidevi Bagla after the decision of the Supreme Court. The only record shows that their prosecution restarted in the district court at Hoshangabad.[152] However, the decision in the *Bagla* case would have a long afterlife.

The Arbitrary Administrator: The Shadow of the *Bagla* Case

Despite the final decision, the *Bagla* litigation demonstrated that the courts were receptive to arguments challenging excessive delegation of authority to the bureaucracy and were open to recognizing that British precedents in administrative law could not easily be applied to a constitutional republic. For instance, in the case of Dwarka Prasad Laxmi Narain, a firm of traders, the Supreme Court accepted the identical argument made (and ultimately rejected) in *Bagla* and struck down provisions of the Uttar Pradesh Coal Control Order of 1953.

The petitioners in *Messrs. Dwarka Prasad Laxmi Narain v. State of Uttar Pradesh* had been retailing coal in the town of Kanpur, the Baglas' hometown, and had had their licenses canceled. Under the Coal Control Order, the district magistrate of Kanpur and the district supply officer had been appointed as licensing authorities. Restrictions had frequently been imposed by the individual officers on the sale of various kinds of coal and soft coke, including fixed prices. In 1953 the district supply officer drastically reduced the prices of all commodities, effectively bringing down the profit margin by 50 percent. The prices were also fixed far lower than those set under the same Coal Control Order in other towns in Uttar Pradesh. The petitioner was found in noncompliance with the new directive, and the firm's license to sell coal was canceled. This left the firm incapable of disposing of the stocks of coal it already had and simultaneously made it liable to charges of hoarding, since holding on to coal stocks without a license was a criminal offense.[153]

The petitioners attacked the validity of the Uttar Pradesh Coal Control Order on the grounds that its provisions vested an "unfettered and unguided discretion" in the licensing authority on questions of granting and revoking licenses, fixing prices, and determining conditions of trade. The ability of the state coal controller to delegate licensing power to an unlimited number of subordinate authorities was also attacked. The ability of the licensing authority to exempt certain individuals from the general application of the Uttar Pradesh Coal Control Order was particularly targeted as an example of the arbitrary nature of the authority delegated. After a careful perusal of the facts, the Supreme Court reiterated that it was indisputable that "for ensuring equitable distribution of commodities considered essential to the community and their availability at fair prices, it is quite a reasonable thing to regulate sale of these commodities through licensed vendors to whom quotas are allotted in specified quantities and who are not permitted to sell them beyond the prices that are fixed by the controlling authorities."[154]

The Supreme Court also conceded that these powers had to be vested in public officials who would be required to exercise a certain amount of discretion. However, the judges argued that "mischief arises" when the power delegated is an arbitrary power unregulated by any rule or control by a higher authority. Keeping this in mind, they found the delegation of absolute power to grant licenses for the trade in coal, as well as the ability to exempt certain people from the licensing regime, prima facie unreasonable. In the absence of rules or directions to regulate the discretion of the licensing officer, the Coal Control Order committed to "the unrestrained will of a single individual" the power to grant, withhold, or cancel licenses in any way. Echoing the decision of the US Supreme Court in *Yick Wo v. Hopkins*, the judges pointed out that the action of an officer in this position could proceed from "enmity, prejudice, partisan zeal, animosity, favoritism, or other improper influences that were easy to conceal."[155]

The Supreme Court rejected the contention of the state of Uttar Pradesh that requiring controllers and other officers to record the reason for the granting or refusal of a license was a sufficient safeguard against the abuse of authority, on the grounds that there was no appeal to any authority on the decision to refuse a license. The Supreme Court struck down several clauses of the UP Coal Control Order on the grounds that it delegated excessive and arbitrary power to the executive and was an unreasonable restriction on fundamental rights. It also restored the coal trading license to the petitioners.

In an almost identical situation, Marwari grain traders from Jodhpur in Rajasthan successfully challenged the Rajasthan Foodgrain Controls Order of 1948.[156] The petitioners, licensed traders in *bajra* (pearl millet), had their stocks frozen and compulsorily acquired by the government at half the market price. The traders had challenged the clause that gave requisitioning powers to officers on the grounds that no principles had been laid down for freezing and requisitioning stocks. The Supreme Court rejected this contention, holding that the circumstances under which the stocks could be frozen had to be read along with Section 3 of the ESA. The requisitioning of stocks could be reasonably related to the object of the ESA. However, the court struck down as invalid the clause of the Rajasthan Foodgrain Controls Order that allowed the government to requisition and dispose of stock at any rate or price, on the grounds that this clause delegated unrestricted authority. As the court observed, this made it possible for the government to requisition the stocks at a price lower than the ceiling price, thus causing loss to the traders, while the government remained free to sell the same stocks at a higher price and make a profit.

The 1950s saw a plethora of cases challenging various aspects of commodity controls on the grounds that they conferred arbitrary powers on the designated officials. The success rates of these challenges varied. Toward the end of the decade, commentators observed that it was becoming extremely difficult to get relief from the judiciary except in cases involving licensing.[157] The judicial decisions differed widely and turned on the interpretation of specific facts, and the precedents set in both *Dwarka Prasad* and *State of Rajasthan v. Nathmal*, while never expressly overruled, were in many cases carefully distinguished on the basis of fact and not followed.[158]

However, the multitude of cases before the court kept governmental decision making in a state of complete flux. The uncertainty experienced by traders and consumers in the market at the onset of the controls regime was directed toward the government through the courts. The government took the litigation seriously, and the attorney general was asked by the central government to intervene in several cases in which it had not been prosecuted as a party.[159] Perhaps most significant is that the litigation was able to shift the focus of the commodity control question from the needs of a planned economy to a debate about the role of the administrator in a democracy.

The Rule of Law in a Planned Society:
Controls and the Birth of Administrative Law

The commodity controls regime had created an atmosphere that caused the noted economist Dhananjay R. Gadgil to observe that "the ordinary man on the street alleges today that the average administrator in India is neither efficient nor honest."[160] The effect of channeling litigation strategy to attack administrative discretion was that the figure of the dishonest (Marwari) trader produced by the state was effaced by the figure of the corrupt, power-hungry administrator. As Pathak's argument in the *Bagla* case indicated, the turning point in litigation over commodity controls had arrived with the introduction of administrative law arguments along with the discussion of American precedents.

This problem emerged at the forefront of legal academic research in India led by the Ford Foundation–funded Indian Law Institute in New Delhi.[161] India, with its modernist leadership and its adoption of liberal democratic principles, was identified as a critical site that contained both new markets and an environment in which democracy and rule of law could be strengthened. In 1952 the Ford Foundation began investing substantially in a rule-of-law project in India. Aiming to build the capacities of the legal profession in India, Ford sponsored exchanges of American law professors to India, arranged for Indian lawyers and judges to attend courses in the United States, hired experts to advise Indian law schools on structural and curriculum reform, and set up a legal research center modeled on the American Law Institute.[162] Although Ford's interest in developing a rule-of-law program in India and the initiatives it started have been noted by scholars, the content of the research it sponsored has not been examined.[163] Almost all the new research sponsored and published by the new Indian Law Institute and the scholars trained in the United States dealt with administrative law, and the dominant portion of it involved the study of administrative process in a planned economy.[164]

A. T. Markose, the Yale-educated founding director of the Indian Law Institute, authored the first treatise on judicial control of administrative action and produced a volume on cases and materials on administrative law, the only American-style casebook that was used in Indian law schools until the 1990s.[165] More than two-thirds of the studies commissioned by the Indian Law Institute in its first three years dealt with questions of administrative law, including a detailed study of the administrative process under the Essential Commodities Act.[166]

The focus on administrative law was prompted by the need to reconcile a planned economy with the rule of law. The Indian Law Institute casebook on administrative law excerpted extensively from Friedrich Hayek, the classical neoliberal economist, reminding law students that there was no justification for the belief that as long as power was conferred by democratic procedure it could not be arbitrary. This critique effectively challenged the rationale behind much of the Nehruvian regulatory state.

The new legal academy sought to emphasize a distinction between legality and the rule of law. To make the central direction of all economic activity possible, the government had to legalize what to all intents and purposes was arbitrary action. The legal academy recognized that national planning would involve public control and direction of economic and social activities, including control of basic industries, limits on land ownership, increased taxation, mobilization of labor, control of exports and imports, and slum clearance. However, by granting the government unlimited powers, the most arbitrary rule could now be made legal. The project of administrative law now became to reconcile national planning and administrative discretion with the greatest number of legal safeguards.[167]

Unlike the West, where systems of administrative law were shaped through legislative and bureaucratic action (such as the system of the *court administratif* in France or the enactment of the Administrative Procedure Act in the United States), India generated administrative law almost entirely through case law.[168] In postcolonial India, it was in the arena of public law rather than private law (torts, contracts, or *lex mercatoria* [merchant law]) that judge-created common law developed, often through ad hoc, tentative, and dynamic decisions. Upendra Baxi argues that this development created a dilemma because the state's need for "ruthless certitude" was much greater than the need for certitude between the individual orderings of social and economic relations.[169]

Given that the stakes had to be high before the ordinary citizen was motivated to initiate litigation, the majority of the cases that generated administrative law involved traders as litigants. The other two types of administrative law litigation—refugee resettlement and civil-service employment cases—received little research interest from the new legal academy.[170] Thus, litigation over commodity controls became the foundation for administrative law in India. The decisions in *Bagla* and *Dwarka Prasad* circulated through a variety of legal networks.

Writers of legal treatises and commentaries paired the *Bagla* and *Dwarka Prasad* decisions together, framing the strategy for most litigants. The first prong of the challenge would be procedural, attacking the regulation for delegating essential legislative function without a set of guidelines to guide the officials in performing such functions. If the court, as in *Bagla*, found for the existence of such guidelines, the lawyers would make a substantive challenge, arguing that the guidelines were not sufficient to regulate the discretion or to operate as a check on the injustice that might ensue from an improper exercise of discretion.

Despite Harishankar Bagla's conviction and the validation of the ESA, the Allahabad High Court read the *Bagla* and *Dwarka Prasad* decisions together and held that these judgments indicated that it was not up to the legislature to give arbitrary power to the state government unrestrained by discretion. In the absence of such guidelines the courts could annul the laws impugned for excessive delegation without limits or guidelines.[171] The Supreme Court, in a challenge to the powers of the Delhi Rent Control Authority, also read the two judgments together and set up a similar test.[172] In a narrow majority of the decisions, the challenges to administrative action were rejected. However, in many other decisions the courts could and did strike down the challenges.

A particularly effective example is the case of Amir Chand, a Marwari cloth trader in Uttar Pradesh who had a temporary license for storing cloth at his business premises. A month after the license had expired he was found selling a sari, and he was convicted and sentenced to three months of rigorous imprisonment for violating the Cotton Textile Order as well as the Uttar Pradesh Controlled Cotton Cloth and Yarn Dealers Licensing Order of 1948.[173] Chand challenged the constitutionality of certain clauses of the Cotton Textile Order, which had given the textile commissioner unrestricted power to refuse to grant a license without stating a reason. Chand also challenged the provisions that allowed the licensing authority the discretion to refuse to grant a license (even though it was required to provide a reason).

The Allahabad High Court considered the decisions in both *Bagla* and *Dwarka Prasad*. The *Bagla* decision had upheld the validity of other provisos of the Cotton Textile Order on the grounds that they sufficiently conformed with the stated policy of ensuring equal distribution of cotton textiles at a fair price to all. The court held that even though the same order was in question, the decision in *Bagla* could not be completely followed. The judges argued that the decision in *Bagla* had turned on the fact that the Baglas had never approached the authority in the first place, unlike Chand, who had originally held a license. The high court followed *Dwarka Prasad* in holding that even though the delegation of power was connected to the policy behind the

Cotton Textile Order, the fact that the decisions were made on the basis of the subjective satisfaction of a licensing authority, and provided no remedy to the affected party, counted against the legitimacy of the delegation. The validity of the delegation itself was not enough; the discretion granted to the authority could not be arbitrary and unfettered. Chand was accordingly acquitted of all charges.

The Trader as a Constitutional Actor

Why is the Baglas' brief journey through the courts, particularly in light of their eventual defeat, considered significant? First, it is an important early episode of an administrative challenge to the regime of commodity controls. The *Bagla* case would be followed by 568 reported cases of challenges to the ESA and nearly 4,000 reported challenges to its successor, the Commodities Act. Reported cases are only a small fraction of the litigation that appears before the high courts, and their number does not take into consideration the hundreds and thousands of unreported cases before the lower courts.

Second, *Bagla* was important doctrinally as precedent and was cited in 194 reported cases, 33 of them before the Supreme Court.[174] It allowed the courts to claim the authority to adjudicate the question of excessive delegation, thus empowering them to search for policy. It also set a broad pattern for administrative law in India in which the courts could uphold the validity of a delegation while also being critical of specific actions. Reviewing the developments in administrative law until the 1970s, a critical lawyer noted that courts in India had been more energetic in policing discretionary delegated powers than in challenging the validity of the delegation.[175]

It is tempting to see a parallel between the anxieties over administrative process in the United States after the New Deal and in Nehruvian India. Both settings saw the expansion of the administrative state and resistance from the judiciary. However, this comparison ignores the important differences in their respective legacies. Historians of US government emphasize that through the nineteenth century, in the absence of a large well-insulated bureaucracy, the courts and political parties provided the basic institutional structures of governance. This led to a conception of justice that was oriented to the individual and threatened both by codification and by the rise of the administrative state.[176] India, in contrast, had been governed by a large, centralized, and powerful bureaucracy since the late nineteenth century that was hailed as the iron frame of the state. Colonial India had a limited history of judicial intervention and had been the arena of several experiments with codification. [177] Therefore, creating a space for judicial contestation of the regulations was a significant achievement.

At first glance, the fact that traders were able to turn to the courts to challenge the commodity-control regime does not seem surprising. The law and courts have been critiqued as instruments of class control, and in its early years the Indian Supreme Court came under severe criticism for being a court of the "propertariat and not the proletariat."[178] A closer empirical investigation suggests a more complicated picture. A study of all reported Supreme Court decisions until 1970 revealed that business owners constituted the largest category of litigants against the government, about 22 percent. However, their success rate of 42 percent was only marginally higher than the 40 percent success rate of the average individual against the state and considerably lower than, for example, the success rate of government employees and trade unions, at 55 percent.[179]

This chapter has complicated the rather simplistic narrative of the Supreme Court favoring the propertied in two ways: by complicating the category of *business owner* and by focusing on the process of litigation rather than on the substantive outcome. Political scientists studying the postcolonial Indian state have argued that it was governed by compromise among the modernist professional elite, the capitalists, and the landed agrarian classes.[180] This analysis does not leave space for the bazaar, or the intermediate class of capitalists, which consisted of "small-scale, self-employed retailers and wholesalers (traders), manufacturers, service providers and farmers, lying between the bourgeoisie and the poor, laborer and rentier simultaneously."[181] These groups were often linked by kinship and community (like the Marwaris) and played the most direct role in the economic life of the average citizen.

Contrary to the popular adage that Nehruvian India was statist and anti-market, what we see is an attempt by the state to replace older forms of market regulation with newer, more productive forms of circulation. Rather than being anticapitalist, the state was privileging industrial capital over unproductive merchant and usury capital. This is mirrored in changes to company law and financial regulations as the Nehruvian state attempted social engineering in transforming mercantile business owners into industrial entrepreneurs.[182]

This chapter has shown that this bazaar class found itself excluded from the political dispensation of the new republic. As the commodity controls regime showed, this class was marked by the state as economic criminals, and their businesses faced a constant strain. These small-business traders and shopkeepers would later form the nucleus of support of the Bharatiya Janata Party (BJP), the chief opposition to the Congress Party, but it would gain electorally only in the 1980s. Thus, throughout the early decades of independence they found it almost impossible to make opposition to commodity controls an electoral issue. Most traders attempted to circumvent the control regime through various illegal practices, like cloth smuggling.

However, administrative law provided an alternative to the failed electoral route when these merchants' practices (like Bagla's) were exposed by state surveillance and the merchants were subjected to the criminal law regime. Arguing that the extent of administrative discretion that was permissible in a colonial state was unacceptable in a democratic republic governed by a written constitution, the litigants were able to replace the image of the wily trader with that of the neutral citizen. The growth of a Ford Foundation–aided administrative law project helped adapt the particular problems of traders to the new commodities regime as the more general experience of individuals in a regulatory welfare state. The debates over administrative law also threw into sharp relief the emergence of the Constitution as a critical arena for defining the relationship between the state and the market.

3

The Case of the Invisible Butchers

ECONOMIC RIGHTS AND RELIGIOUS RITES

The Constitution is not for the exclusive benefit of governments and states;
it is not only for lawyers and politicians and officials and those highly placed.
It also exists for the common man, for the poor and the humble, for those
who have businesses at stake, for the "butcher, the baker, and the candlestick
maker."

—JUSTICE VIVIAN BOSE, 1956[1]

IN 1957 SEVERAL PETITIONS were filed before the Supreme Court of India
challenging the constitutionality of newly enacted provincial laws banning
cow slaughter. These laws had been enacted to further the goals laid out in
Article 48 of the Constitution, which provided that "the State shall endeavor
to organize agriculture and animal husbandry on modern and scientific lines and
shall, in particular, take steps for preserving and improving the breeds, and
prohibiting the slaughter, of cows and calves and other milch and draught
cattle." The question of cow slaughter had been a matter of public debate, spo-
radic violence, and mass mobilization since the late nineteenth century, but
contemporary commentators noted that unlike in the past, in this case the proponents and opponents of the cow slaughter ban were strictly adhering to constitutional methods.[2] This amicable approach was lauded by Chief Justice
Sudhi R. Das, who in his judgment observed that

> the controversy concerning the slaughter of cows has been raging in this
> country for a number of years, and in the past it generated considerable ill

will among the two major communities, resulting even in riots and civil commotion in a number of places. We are, however, happy to note that several contentions of the parties to these proceedings have been urged before us without importing into them the heat of communal passion, and in a rational and objective way, as a matter involving constitutional issues should be.[3]

After hearing the arguments in *Mohd. Hanif Qureshi v. State of Bihar*, which lasted several months, the Supreme Court upheld a majority of the cow slaughter laws, ruling that a ban on cow slaughter did not restrict the freedom of religion or even the right to a trade or profession held by the petitioners. The court did rule, however, that such a ban could not be absolute and that some categories of cattle, such as aged bulls or unproductive cows, may be slaughtered.

The case is fertile terrain for exploring what it meant to "constitutionalize" an issue in independent India. Cow slaughter had been a volatile political subject on the subcontinent for centuries. How did independence and the enactment of the Constitution change the contours of the debate? Why did the proponents and opponents of the cow slaughter ban choose to operate through the constitutional field?

The *Hanif Qureshi* case gained nearly canonical status in constitutional law; it was repeatedly cited as a precedent for Article 25, which ensured freedom of religion.[4] The case has also been mourned by progressive scholars as an example of how Hindu majoritarian views were cloaked in the neutral guise of constitutional law and became a reference point in every legal debate over cow slaughter.[5] It was basically presented as a case in which the Hindu cow protectionists won and the Muslim petitioners lost. The decision, the longest judgment of the Supreme Court until then, had many remarkable features, including the admission of social science evidence and the appointment of one of the first amicus curiae ("friend of the court"). But the most remarkable feature of the case had remained hidden until a search for the case files led me to a dusty basement in the Supreme Court of India. I was aware that the decision in *Hanif Qureshi* had been given collectively in response to five different writ petitions. However, I was astonished to discover that these petitions had more than three thousand individually named petitioners, who had signed or put their thumbprint on the petition.[6] This fact has been missed by historians and lawyers, who have focused on the published decision of the court. All the petitioners were Muslims; close to 90 percent identified themselves as members of the Qureshi community who worked as butchers, hide traders, gut merchants, and leatherworkers. Thus the *Hanif Qureshi* case was possibly one of the earliest class-action cases in postindependent India. Not only were there more than three thousand petitioners, they hailed from at least ninety villages and towns throughout the states of Bombay, Madhya Pradesh, Uttar Pradesh, and Bihar. How had three thousand butchers come together? Why did they then disappear from the narrative?[7]

From the Queen Empress to the Gau Maharani: Cows, Community, and Sovereignty

To solve the mystery of the invisible butchers, one has to follow the journey through which the cow entered the constitutional domain. There is considerable debate over when and why the cow came to be considered holy for a large number of Hindus. There are documented cases of urban communal strife in north India, where the cow played a symbolic role, in the eighteenth and early nineteenth centuries.[8] These conflicts were often around the Muslim festival of Eid-ul-Adha, when Muslims practiced *qurbani*, the sacrifice of an animal, in memory of Abraham's willingness to sacrifice his son at God's command. Since beef was the least expensive meat and a cow provided more meat than other animals, it was the most common animal to be sacrificed. Eid-ul-Adha came to be locally known as Bakr-Eid (*bakr* is Arabic for "cow"). The nineteenth century saw a transformation in both the nature of the conflict and the way it was managed with the intrusion of the colonial state.[9]

In a society where food operated as a powerful semiotic device, condensing relations of production and exchange as well as regulating social contact, the fact that the British were a beef-eating people was very visible.[10] The reformulation of the cow question divided Hindus from Muslims (communities that had had a long experience with each other), upper-caste Hindus from the lower castes, and Hindus from Britons (communities that were relative strangers).[11] The colonial state came to be associated with beef consumption, and the British army became the largest buyers of beef. The colonial state had long been resistant to the idea of banning cow slaughter. Indian rulers who allied with the British and allowed them to station troops in their states often requested them not to slaughter cattle on their territories, but such requests were rejected as an "impossible requirement."[12] Western-educated Indians who were attempting to become modern and break caste taboos engaged in the public consumption of beef.

It is not surprising, then, that the cow emerged as a powerful anticolonial symbol and became the focus of both mobilization and violence through much of north India. In 1881 Arya Samaj, a popular Hindu reform movement based in Punjab, set up the Gorakshni Sabha (Cow Protection Society) to prevent the slaughter of cattle in India. Its founder, Swami Dayanand Saraswati, authored a pamphlet called *Gaukarunanidhi* that made the case for cow protection and presented an action plan for organizing through the establishment of local societies for the "protection of cow and agriculture." The stated aim was to prevent cattle from "passing under any circumstances into the hands of those who will either sacrifice them or slaughter them for food."[13]

The meetings were attended by thousands. People who breached the cow protection rules were subjected to social boycotts: no services were performed for them, their married daughters were sent back, and they faced economic ruin. There were cases of physical coercion as well, especially in the case of Muslims, and coercion could soon translate into violence. In 1893 alone, a hundred people were killed in communal violence over cow slaughter in towns as far apart as Junagadh, Oudh, and Rangoon.

The Gorakshni Sabha created tribunals that took cognizance of the offenses against cows, stepping in to create a parallel regulatory order. For instance, Sita Ram Ahir was found guilty of selling a cow to a low-caste butcher. The tribunal first ordered that he buy back the cow at a loss, which he did, and then found him guilty and fined him a further four rupees. His refusal to pay the fine was punished with twenty-four days of shunning and being subjected to a community boycott.[14] Mimicking the convention of state trials, which recorded criminal cases as offenses against the queen empress, the cases before the Gorakshni Sabha tribunals were recorded as offenses against the Gau Maharani, or Cow Empress.[15]

Although the Indian National Congress in this period never made cow protection an official goal, John McLane suggests that its demand for representative government, just when the cow protection movement demanded a legislative ban on cow slaughter, appeared to blur the distinction between the two groups.[16] Several congressmen were members of cow protection societies, and meetings held for the Gorakshni Sabha doubled as a forum for National Congress propaganda and vice versa. For instance, the Nagpur Gorakshni Sabha was allowed to hold its meeting in the National Congress pavilion, and government informants in Punjab reported that signatures were being collected for

National Congress petitions for legislative reforms on the pretext that it would end cow slaughter.[17] By 1882 reports had begun trickling in from various government officials that there was an attempt by the Gorakshni Sabha to prepare a "monster petition" for submission to the government, praying that kine killing be stopped.[18] The numbers of signatures were unprecedented; reports from Rajasthan suggested that a particular memorial had gathered 350,000 signatures, whereas other reports, from cities like Shimla, reported gatherings of 200 people where everyone had signed the petition.[19] The viceroy, Lord Lansdowne, noted that this involvement could turn the National Congress from "a foolish debating society to a real power."[20]

Why did cow protection become such a powerful political plank? The colonial state's ostensible religious neutrality underscored the impossibility of getting the state to protect the sacred cow.[21] This inability highlighted both the failure of the state to represent the interests of the nation and created a political role that a community could play, through petitions or direct action. The cow came to stand in for the community, as can be seen from the various images and pamphlets that were being circulated. A popular lithographic image depicted eighty-four major Hindu gods inside a cow that was being threatened by a dark man with a sword, and this image was widely distributed. The cow thus represented the greater Hindu community being threatened by a demon, which the government believed could represent Muslims or even the British.[22]

From the Streets to the Courts: Imperial Constitutionalism and Bovine Litigation

The cow protection movement seemed to be a classic case of political resistance; with the failure of the colonial state to meet their demands, Hindu cow protectionists sought to achieve results through street protests, violence, setting up a new regulatory order, and working to take control of the state through the demand of increased representation. However, if we shift focus from Hindu protectionists to Muslims, we see a continual engagement with the courts, for Muslims sought to establish a framework of rights within the colonial state that would continue to permit cow slaughter.

Archival sources show that since the late nineteenth century there had been an increase in litigation by Muslims asserting their right to slaughter the cow. This litigation came from a heightened sense of awareness of the right of religious expression that Muslims enjoyed under the British Crown. This wasn't a right that was graciously acknowledged by the administration; bureaucrats often expressed their exasperation at the insistence on rights when a compromise that would end the local practice of cow slaughter was likely to solve the law-and-order problem. Dennis Fitzpatrick, the lieutenant governor of Punjab, complained, "I have had one single Mussulman [Muslim] after me for months who quotes constitutional principles at me and wants to know why I won't upset an order of the District Magistrate refusing him leave to kill cows in a place where no one else wants them to be killed."[23]

So what options were available to a Muslim man who wanted legal recognition of a right that he believed he had by virtue of being a British imperial subject? First, he could make a claim of religious freedom, which was protected under Queen Victoria's proclamation of 1858. Second, he could argue the common-law right to property, which guaranteed that a man could enjoy his property provided he caused no nuisance to his neighbor. Finally, he could argue that cow killing was a customary practice protected by the promises of the British Crown. To meet these ends, he could rely on the newly enacted Civil Procedure Code and get the court to declare his particular right and thus protect it from encroachment.

A vocal group of Muslims believed that they had a right to practice their religion, which included the rite of cow sacrifice; however, in the absence of a written constitution and in the face of executive reluctance to enforce the right, this was difficult to achieve. The colonial government sought to establish rights claims through evidence of custom and local practice, which was often determined by local power dynamics.[24] The civil litigation process became the natural venue for the establishment of such rights. An intelligence officer noted, "People are asking themselves why should we not do this and why should our neighbors be allowed to do that, and they always find the pettifogging legal practitioners and professional agitators at their elbow to help them think out the question."[25]

These rights, including the right to enjoy one's property, were not different from the rights enshrined in classical liberal thought. They were not shared equally by all subjects but were confirmed by a particular set of circumstances and had to be proved in every individual case.

In the early cases the plaintiffs had to pray for the recognition of a customary right, but one plaintiff's success in getting a customary right to cow sacrifice recognized did not guarantee the rights of Muslims in the next village. Even when the courts recognized a more general right to slaughter cows, they held that no right could be claimed for a riotous demonstration activated by it or one that created animosities. They ruled that slaughter, even on one's own land, could not be done in an exposed way.[26]

The reliance on custom had its own pitfalls. In 1903 some Hindus in the United Provinces had petitioned the district magistrate to pass an order prohibiting the slaughter of cattle in the village. The magistrate noted in his order that Hindus outnumbered Muslims in the village and that cow slaughter was not a practice common to the area. Several Muslims, "feeling aggrieved at the prohibition of the exercise of what they conceived to be their legal rights," had instituted a civil suit.[27] The lower court initially admitted the suit, recognizing that there was a right of a substantial nature that was denied (as opposed to a right that affected mere dignity or privilege), but it dismissed the suit on the grounds that the Muslims had failed to establish that there was a custom of cow sacrifice in the village. In the appeal to the Allahabad High Court, the Muslim plaintiffs argued that regardless of custom, Muslims had a right to do all lawful acts upon their own property, so the killing of their own cows on their own land could not be unlawful.

The Allahabad High Court held that it was indisputable that under certain limitations the slaughtering of cattle by Muslims was legal. It located this view in the legal right of every person to make use of his or her own property provided that he or she did not cause injury to others or break the law. One could not limit this right because it offended the sensibilities of others. The court rejected the assumption that the burden of proof lay on Muslims to demonstrate the existence of a custom that allowed them to slaughter cattle. The Allahabad High Court decreed that the plaintiffs had the right to slaughter cows for daily consumption, for festivals and as sacrifices, provided that in the exercise of that right they did not create a nuisance. The court also passed an injunction restraining the Hindu defendants from interfering with these rights.

The possibility of litigation disrupted other forms of political mobilization. The compromise agreement had emerged as the political solution to keep order between communities in a locality and was often endorsed by the local administration. In Ghazipur in 1908, representatives of the local Hindus and Muslims signed a pact in which the Hindus agreed to stop playing musical instruments or blowing conches during festivals to avoid offending Muslims, and the Muslims agreed that there would be no dispute about the slaughter of cows. Several Muslims were persuaded to put their thumbprints on a document that stated they would not create any quarrel, disturbance, or litigation in connection with the sacrifice of cows.[28]

Although the Hindu district magistrate held that this document restrained the Muslims' right to litigate, the high court ruled that this was mere *nudum pactum* (a bare promise), with no legal force.[29] Plaintiffs often contended that the compromise document was not a representative agreement.[30] As a result, attempts by prominent men in the locality to resolve the issue, or coercion of community leaders into a compromise, could be disrupted through the litigation process. Through civil litigation, an alternative rights framework was articulated. Local dominance could no longer ensure control over the determination of customs or the use of public spaces.

The courts did not see Hindu objections to cow slaughter as a religious requirement, and thus integral to their rights as British subjects, but chose to understand it through the concept of nuisance, a category of private law.[31] For instance, the Allahabad High Court acquitted some Muslims from Pillibhit who had been arrested on the charge of creating a public nuisance by sacrificing a cow, on the grounds that the cows had been had been killed with a religious object, before sunrise, behind the walls of a compound, and with just one Hindu witness. The court warned, however, that anyone who willfully slaughtered cattle on a public street, "so that the 'groans and blood of a poor beast' were heard and seen by passersby," would be convicted under the laws of public nuisance.[32]

In another case, in which a Muslim had to slaughter a cow that broke its leg on a public highway, the court noted that the Hindu objection to cow slaughter was mere "religious feeling" rather than a nuisance, given that the complainant had said he had no objection to the Muslim slaughtering sheep or goats in the same area.[33] The slaughter of a cow on an "open veranda," in contrast, would lead to conviction.[34]

Thus, by 1947, groups of Muslim litigants had been able to establish a reinforced and certain right to religious practice rooted in common law, property rights, and imperial citizenship. However, this right would remain secure only as long as the executive chose not to get involved. With independence, partition, and the electoral dominance of the Congress Party, matters changed.

Constitutionalizing the Cow

From its earliest days, the mobilization for the Congress Party coincided with the mobilization for the cow protection movement. It was not surprising that with the increased popular reach of the Congress Party under Gandhi, cow protection had become a central part of the national agenda. Symbolically for

Gandhi, the protection of cows was equated with the protection of the weak, the dumb, and the powerless and was an essential quality to be cultivated for *swaraj*. He wrote that "the central fact of Hinduism is cow protection. Cow protection . . . takes the human being beyond his species. The cow to me means the entire subhuman world. Man, through the cow, is enjoined to realize his identity with all living beings. The cow is a poem of piety."[35]

During the Khilafat and the Noncooperation movements in 1921, Gandhi attempted to unite Hindus and Muslims with a common platform in which Hindus were encouraged to support Muslims on the caliphate question while Muslims were asked to refrain from cow slaughter. Each community thus respected the sentiments of the other.[36]

Gandhi himself was insistent that cow slaughter could not be stopped by law. Cow protection was a noble sentiment that he believed "must grow by patient toil and *tapasya* [meditation]. It cannot be imposed upon anyone."[37] Elsewhere he wrote, "Even in India, under *swaraj*, it would be unwise and improper for a Hindu majority to coerce by legislation a Mussulman minority into submission to statutory prohibition of cow slaughter."[38] At partition he was even more insistent on the question contrasting secular India to Pakistan. He argued that if cow slaughter could be prohibited in India on religious grounds, then why couldn't the Pakistani government prohibit idol worship on similar grounds? Just as sharia cannot be imposed on non-Muslims, he emphasized, Hindu law cannot be imposed on non-Hindus.

Because of the drafting committee's desire to define India as a secular republic, cow protection found no mention in the original draft of the Indian Constitution. The committee considered and rejected the clause pertaining to it on the grounds that it dealt with a matter of policy and not constitutional principle.[39] Indeed, the slogan of cow protection gained little traction with the modernist impulses of leaders like Jawaharlal Nehru and B. R. Ambedkar. However, on the eve of independence and impending partition, there was a vast popular outcry for a law on cow slaughter. Rajendra Prasad, the chairman of the Constituent Assembly, reported that he had received about fifty thousand postcards, almost thirty thousand letters, and many thousands of telegrams demanding the ban on cow slaughter.[40]

For those who had been involved in the cow protection movement for years, their moment had come: Indians could finally use the mechanisms of government to protect Gaumata (Cow Mother). An important marker of independence would be to protect the cow, something that the British colonial regime had failed to do and that the Muslim state of Pakistan was not going to do. This popular sentiment emboldened several Constituent Assembly members from north India to critique the draft Constitution. The cow protection lobby initially proposed an amendment that would have made cow protection a fundamental right that could be judicially enforced. To critics who argued that fundamental rights could be enjoyed only by human beings, Raghunath V. Dhulekar forcefully replied as follows:

> Suppose it is a question of saving your mother or protecting your mother. Whose fundamental right is it? Is it the fundamental right of the mother? No. It is my fundamental right to protect my mother, to protect my wife, my children, and my country. In the Fundamental Rights [section] you have said that you will give justice, equity, and all these things. Why? Because you say "it is your fundamental right to have justice." What does that justice mean? It means that we shall be protected, our families shall be protected. And our Hindu society, or our Indian society, has included the cow in our fold. It is just like our mother. In fact, it is more than our mother.[41]

Ambedkar persuaded the group to offer the amendment as a directive principle of state policy instead. Unlike the earlier amendments that absolutely banned cow slaughter, the amendment proposed by Thakur Das Bhargava justified the ban in terms of economic interests. The proposed Article 38-A would be added to Article 38, which in the draft Constitution provided that "the state shall regard the raising of the level of nutrition and the standard of living of its people and the improvement of public health as its primary duties." To this Bhargava proposed adding the following: "Article 38-A: The State shall endeavor to organize agriculture and animal husbandry on modern scientific lines and shall in particular take steps for preserving and improving the breeds of cattle and prohibit the slaughter of cow and other useful cattle, specially milch and draught cattle and their young stock." Bhargava argued that without this amendment, Article 38, which dealt with nutrition, standard of living, and public health, would be meaningless, "a body without a soul."[42]

The amendment consisted of three parts: the improvement of agriculture along scientific and modern lines, the improvement of cattle breeds, and the ban on cow slaughter. The reference to the economic value of the cow to justify a ban on cow slaughter was not new. Pamphlets by the cow protection movement in the late nineteenth century had emphasized the centrality of the cow to Indian agriculture and of milk to the human diet. This economic argument grew more prominent in the 1930s as economists, scientists, and planners waxed eloquent on the economic benefits of dairy products, cow dung, and cow urine and stressed the need to protect cattle wealth as a national resource.[43]

After independence arguments shifted from economics to the value to the national economy. Several members noted with alarm a decrease in India's cattle population during World War II, making the ban on slaughter an urgent question.[44] It was a shame, Bhargava declaimed, that India had to import food from abroad when it could be self-sufficient.[45] He portrayed cattle as a national resource that was being mismanaged because of indiscriminate slaughter. He drew an analogy between cattle slaughter and the other great project of Nehruvian modernity, the building of dams. To utilize water properly, the state had to construct dams and change the course of some rivers. Similarly, to improve the health of humans and cattle, it was essential to check cow slaughter.

The idea of cattle as a scarce resource that had to be managed with care was reinforced through the use of economic and statistical data. In 1947, a few months after independence, the Ministry of Agriculture set up the Cattle Preservation and Development Committee to consider the question of prohibiting cow slaughter by legislation and to recommend a comprehensive plan of action that could be put into effect to preserve the cattle wealth of the nation. The committee found itself handicapped in arriving at a decision on the prevention of cow slaughter because of "the want of complete and accurate statistics."[46] The collation of statistics about cattle made the abstraction suddenly legible. Cattle, like citizens, were counted in the national census; their declining population and poor health were made a cause of concern, and proposals were made for camps where old and abandoned cattle could be looked after.

Appeals to cultural homogeneity and majoritarianism went hand in hand with the economic arguments. Shibban Lal Saxena asserted that the Constituent Assembly should not leave out something "that thirty crores of the population" want incorporated merely because it also had a religious aspect.[47] Perhaps the most powerful claim was made in the name of a national culture that would separate the Indian republic from the colonial state. Seth Govind Das linked cow protection to the question of the name of the country, the national language, the national script, and the national anthem. "Unless the Constituent Assembly decides these questions according to the wishes of the people of the country," he asserted "*swarajya* would have no meaning to them."[48]

Bhargava refused requests from south Indian members to address the house in English, insisting that he wanted to "speak in Hindi, which is his own language about the cow." Dhulekar pointed out that independence was not for the "loaves and fishes" of office, "for ambassadorships, premierships, minister-ships, or wealth" but for India to declare "that today the whole human world and the animal world is free and will be protected."[49] Independence for a vocal group of Hindus meant the protection of national wealth, the righting of his-torical wrongs, the embrace of a unique civilization ethos, and a break from a foreign regime that aided or was at best indifferent to cow slaughter.

The economic reasoning had proven powerful and led to the Constituent Assembly preferring Bhargava's amendment, which protected useful cattle (i.e., "milch cattle, cattle of childbearing age, young stocks, and draught cattle"), to Das's broader definition, which included "all cows, bulls, bullocks, and young stock of the genus cow."[50] However, the national-economy angle changed the debate. As long as cow protection was demanded as a religious right of Hindus, it could be countered by the assertion of the equal religious obligation of Mus-lims to sacrifice the cow. These rights could then be negotiated in the local context through the courts, as they had been during the colonial period. How-ever, by incorporating the amendment into the Constitution, the question of cow protection was now to be decided on the national scale, and it was linked to the question of the national economy. The entire arena for the debate had therefore changed, and the old system of locally won rights could now be transformed.

The position of Muslim representatives in the postpartition Constituent As-sembly was fraught with tension, and there was considerable pressure to as-similate. Muslims made up about 10 percent of the assembly, and the Congress Party's chief opposition consisted of twenty-eight members of the Muslim League who had not emigrated to Pakistan. The Muslim members' loyalty to the new state was constantly questioned.[51] Despite this, the Muslim League members challenged the ambiguous rationale behind the ban.[52]

Scholars are divided over whether to read the use of economic arguments as merely strategic, utilized to blend with Hindu majoritarian impulses.[53] The discursive intent behind the arguments is important, of course, but this chap-ter focuses on the impact these had on the people who now had to live under the regulatory regimes they legitimized. Therefore, regardless of whether the economic argument was strategic or inextricable from the religious, it would have serious consequences.

Framing the cow slaughter ban in economic terms caused significant confu-sion for Muslims. Before independence the understanding was that Queen Victoria's proclamation of 1858 had guaranteed them the right of religious free-dom, that "none be in anywise favored, none molested or disquieted by reason of their religious faith and observances." For decades Muslims had believed that cow sacrifice on Eid was a right, and now they were not clear what the new order entailed. Zairul Hasan Lari insisted that the assembly make the provision clearer and remove "all ambiguity or doubt" that the Constitution would absolutely ban cow slaughter: "Let it be prohibited in clear, definite and unambiguous word." This was because Indian Muslims were "under the impression that they can, without violence to the principles which govern the State, sacrifice cows and other animals on the occasion of Bakrid." Lari appealed to the assembly to "let there not linger an idea in the mind of the Muslim public that they can do one thing, though in fact they are not expected to that."[54] The indeterminate wording of the amendment left open the possibility that economically useless cows could still be slaughtered, but public sentiment and that of the amendment's movers would clearly object to that.

Thinking Nationally, Acting Locally: Municipal Management of Cow Slaughter

The cow protection amendment finally found its place as a directive principle of state policy, under Article 48 of the republican Constitution. However, the central government, headed by Nehru, made it very clear that it would not enact a national law banning cow slaughter. The official reason given was that the central government was not competent to legislate on cow slaughter; both agriculture and animal husbandry were state subjects under the new Constitution. However, much of the pushback came from Nehru, who in 1955 threatened to resign if a private member's bill banning cow slaughter was enacted (figs. 3.1 and 3.2).[55]

Although both his supporters and his detractors identified Nehru's vision of secularism as his motivation, nowhere does secularism or minority rights appear in his speeches against the cow slaughter ban. The chief argument he made was that a national ban would not achieve the objective of preserving the cattle wealth of the country, because aging and economically unprofitable cattle would be expensive to maintain, would reduce the quality of the breed, and would damage agricultural land.[56]

It is questionable to what extent Nehru's beliefs extended to the state and district Congress Party machinery.[57] Purushottam Das Tandon, the president of the All India Cow Protection Society, was elected president of the Indian National Congress in 1950. Most strikingly, the Congress Party's election

FIG. 3.1. Nehru as Lord Krishna charming the cow protection lobby.
Shankar's Weekly, September 6, 1953.

symbol was of a cow suckling her calf, completing the linkage of the figure of the cow, the nation-state, and the ruling party.

In their manifestos, the main opposition parties had all made a commitment to ban cow slaughter and castigated the Congress Party as "cow killers."[58] The right-wing Jan Sangh (fig. 3.3) manifesto accused Nehru of sacrificing national interests and "encouraging" Muslims.[59] The Socialists, led by Jaiprakash Narayan, announced that banning cow slaughter was itself an affirmation of a great human value.[60] In 1955 even the Communists joined hands with orthodox Hindu leaders: trade union leaders and factory workers carrying hammer-and-sickle banners marched with Hindu priests in a procession in New Delhi shouting slogans for a complete ban.[61] As the *New York Times* commented, most Western-educated Indians who opposed the ban conceded that if put to the test, most Indians would enthusiastically vote to ban cow slaughter.[62] There were repeated public demonstrations in favor of the ban. In 1951 Ahmedabad activist Arjun Bhagat fasted to death outside the local slaughterhouse, demanding that cow slaughter be banned. Bhagat was supported by thirty-three thousand millworkers who went on strike in support of his cause, virtually shutting down the economy of the textile town.[63]

In the context of this public opinion, the number of cattle slaughtered in the United Provinces declined from a high of 142,237 in 1937 to 2,708 in 1951;

FIG. 3.2. Nehru chases away the cow protectionists. *Shankar's Weekly*, April 10, 1955.

a sharp drop after 1947 was the result of the trend in public opinion.[64] How did cattle slaughter drop sharply in the absence of statewide legislation? In most cases, elected local government bodies such as municipal boards, district boards, and notified town area committees passed bylaws banning slaughter of the cow and its progeny. This was an old tactic by the cow protection movement going back to the late nineteenth century. This had been difficult to achieve in many areas, since most local government bodies had a significant number of official (i.e., nominated by the British) and Muslim members. However, independence and partition had changed the composition of local politics by ensuring a dominant Hindu electoral majority. With the central government refusing to enact a cow slaughter ban, the state and local arenas became the focus of political contestations.

A month after the coming into force of the new Constitution, Mangru Meya, a Muslim beef-shop owner in Budge Budge, near Calcutta, received a letter from the chairman of the Budge Budge municipality stating that in order "to increase the supply of milk and cattle wealth," his license for the sale of beef or buffalo meat would be canceled, effective immediately. Meya and his family had been running beef stalls in the neighborhood for more than a hundred years and had at all times held licenses from the municipality. The neighborhood near Trunk Road was a predominantly poor Muslim area, and the demand for beef was high enough to have led to two other shops

FIG. 3.3. The Congress Party silences the Jan Sangh by enacting a ban on cow slaughter. *Shankar's Weekly*, May 22, 1955.

opening in the 1920s. Meya had not contravened the only grounds for cancellation of a municipal license: becoming a cause of annoyance or offense or a danger to people residing in the neighborhood.

The main material change had been the election of Pandit Ram Chandra Awasthi as chairman of the municipality. Awasthi, a north Indian Hindu Brahmin, was instrumental in passing a resolution in February 1950 stating that "in view of the fact that due to indiscriminate slaughter there has been a depletion of cattle wealth—the backbone of this country . . . and inasmuch as an acute shortage of draft animals and a paucity in the milk supply has brought in their wake woes and miseries in building up a strong nation of healthy and happy inhabitants, be it resolved that with a view to increasing the yield of milk and cattle for the general economic uplifting of the masses," the municipality would close its slaughterhouse, and no licenses would be granted for the slaughter or sale of beef. [65]

The municipality allowed for exceptions made on bona fide religious festivals and ceremonial occasions, which is perhaps why Meya's petition to the president of the District Minority Board and the chairman of the Minority Commission of West Bengal went unheeded. Since the Budge Budge municipality had made exceptions for cow sacrifice on Eid, the ban on cow slaughter could no longer be said to prevent Muslims from practicing their religious beliefs. This, however, hurt the business of shopkeepers like Meya and deprived poor Muslims of a staple commodity in their diet. Meya and the two other stallholders took the only option they had and went to court.

Litigating against the cancellation of a municipal license was not new; however, litigating over the cancellation of a license because of cow protection was rare and not very successful. In one of the few reported cases, a hide merchant named Madran Kassab challenged the cancellation of his license after he was arrested and convicted for carrying on his trade without a license. Kassab's license had come up for renewal the day the vice chairman of the municipality passed a resolution that all existing slaughterhouses be closed and no new licenses granted "in view of the fact that our country is suffering great loss and innumerable miseries by the indiscriminate slaughter of cows."[66] The resolution was a contentious one, and Kassab's application for renewal was rejected by a margin of one vote on the council. Kassab unsuccessfully appealed to the additional deputy commissioner and the district magistrate to reverse this decision using their powers under Section 383 of the Bihar and Orissa Municipalities Act on the grounds that the resolution caused serious injury to the public or a class of people. Kassab then decided to flout the cancellation of his license; he continued with his business and was arrested. During his trial he attempted to challenge the cancellation of his license on the grounds that no reason had been specified and that the real motive was to prevent cattle slaughter. The courts, while sympathetic to the loss of his business, said they could not query the reason behind the decision of the municipality, thus continuing the trend of the colonial courts, which had been reluctant to exercise administrative review, particularly over an elected municipal board.

In Meya's case, administrative review was never an option. The municipality's reason was clearly specified, and the other state agencies were in broad sympathy with it; however, Meya was empowered by the new Constitution to challenge the municipal resolution and the cancellation of his license on the grounds that it violated his fundamental rights. He filed an application at the Calcutta High Court under Article 226 of the Constitution for a writ of mandamus directing the municipality to cancel the notice served to him and to order the cancellation of the resolution. Meya's lawyer, an upper-caste Bengali Hindu, contended that the only grounds on which his license could have been canceled were if the business caused "annoyance, offense, or danger to people in their immediate neighborhood."[67]

The municipality's lawyers argued that Budge Budge was merely carrying out its obligation under Article 48 of the Constitution, which stated that the "state shall endeavour . . . to prohibit slaughter of cows and cattle" and that the state would include local authorities such as the Budge Budge municipality. The court rejected such an argument, noting that Article 48 was only a directive principle of state policy and not enforceable in the courts. In the absence of a law forbidding the sale of beef, the municipalities law continued to be in force, and the commissioners were required to "act within the four corners of the statute, and they could not travel beyond to take shelter under Article 48 of the Constitution."[68] The resolution of the municipality and the notice to the petitioners were both canceled by the courts, and the municipality was asked to reconsider the license renewal within the parameters of the act.

The Calcutta High Court emphasized that the remedy of appealing to the elected government did not debar the jurisdiction of the courts. The municipality did not take cover behind Article 48 but instead made the technical argument that the high court could not cancel the resolution passed by the municipality. The majority of the high court judges agreed with the municipality but asked it to reconsider Meya's license within the limits of the statute.[69] However, in a particularly sharp dissent, Justice Sudhi Ranjan Dasgupta affirmed the powers of the court to issue such an order and noted that the resolution also interfered with Meya's fundamental rights as a citizen of India: he was for all time prevented from carrying on his occupation, trade, or business as a butcher or a seller of beef. The resolution was not merely words; it was given effect by canceling licenses. Litigation finally allowed Meya to reapply for his license, which could not be rejected on the grounds of cow protection.

Similar attempts were made by butchers in Allahabad, in Uttar Pradesh, in 1952. Haji Ahmad Raza and two others filed a lawsuit under Order 1, Rule 8, of the Civil Procedure Code representing the butchers and hide merchants in the city of Allahabad who were seeking a permanent injunction against the new municipal bylaw banning cow slaughter.[70] In another case, a butcher named Buddhu filed an application for a writ of mandamus under Article 226 of the Constitution against the Allahabad municipality contending that the bylaw was an infringement of his fundamental right to a trade and a profession guaranteed by the Constitution and was in violation of Article14 (the right to equality) because it made a distinction between those who slaughtered goats and sheep and those who slaughtered cows.[71] Both petitions asserted that the municipality overreached its power by attempting to ban cattle slaughter.

Raza's civil suit failed. First, it had not met the requirement for giving adequate notice to the government. Under the Uttar Pradesh Municipalities Act of 1916, no lawsuits could be initiated against the board or its members until two months after notice in writing had been given.[72] The provision was typical of most statutory authorities in colonial India, which sought to minimize litigation against themselves. Second, the Allahabad High Court rejected Raza's argument that there was a violation of an implied contract between the butchers and hide merchants and the city that there would be no interference in their trade or profession. Third, Raza's main contention that the notice period would have defeated the purpose of the suit was rejected. The delay of two months, the court held, would inconvenience the petitioners, but the objective of the suit, which was to restrain the municipality from prohibiting cattle slaughter, could still be attained. The court did not consider the impact of two months of economic unemployment.

Finally, the court was not convinced of the merits of the representative suit. The petitioners had argued that the numbers of butchers and hide merchants was "so large that it would be difficult for each of them to bring a suit of damages against the municipal board." The court examined witnesses and came to the conclusion that there were as many as three hundred families of butchers in Allahabad and saw ' "no insuperable difficulty in 300 bringing separate suits for damages if the bylaws are found ultra vires."[73] The judges pointed to the thousands of writ petitions filed in response to the Zamindari Abolition Act (a land reform act), not noting the difference between petty traders like the butchers of Allahabad and the dispossessed aristocrats who challenged land reform.

Buddhu's writ petition was also unsuccessful: the majority of the Allahabad High Court ruled against him. The court reiterated the old English precedent that there should be a presumption of constitutionality when considering by-laws of representative body.[74] Two judges, constituting the majority of the court, found the bylaw a reasonable restriction on the petitioner's fundamental rights under Article 19 to practice his trade and profession. They highlighted the fact that the government of the state of Uttar Pradesh had expressed concern about the declining cattle wealth of the country, an unlike the High Court of Calcutta they were convinced that the municipality was acting in furtherance of Article 48 of the Constitution. The state, as defined by Article 12 of the Constitution, included local authorities, and the directive principles cast a duty on the state to raise the level of nutrition, improve public health, and prohibit cow slaughter.

Justice B. B. Prasad's sympathies with the ban became clear when he stated that it was common knowledge that the price of milk was high and that grains were scarce. The ban was an attempt to correct this situation. The judges also countered the petitioner's allegations that there was no reason to prohibit the slaughter of old and infirm cattle by referring to a number of veterinary authorities that suggested that there is no fixed age after which a cow becomes useless.[75] The court noted that "there is no data to determine what is the percentage of the so-called useless cows, bulls, and bullocks. It is possible that by exempting such cattle from protection, there may be danger to even useful cows, cattle, and bullocks."[76]

Buddhu's writ petition got a more robust hearing than Raza's civil suit did. The court observed that the terms of Article 226 were very broad and thus enabled the court to issue all manner of writs for the enforcement of rights. Justice Prasad wrote the following:

> The fact that the Constituent Assembly has vested this court with vast powers imposes a heavy responsibility upon it to use them with circumspection. We must not be understood to suggest that in a suitable case this court will be hesitant in issuing an appropriate writ , order, or direction, nor must be understood to lay down that there is any universal or general principle which governs the grant and refusal of writs or directions.[77]

There was no requirement of notice to the government in the case of a writ petition, and the petitioner did not have to justify urgency. All three judges agreed that the preliminary procedural objections to Buddhu's suit should be dismissed. Moreover, in his dissent Justice Raghuveer Dayal invalidated the bylaw on the grounds that it was beyond the competence of a municipality.[78] He rejected the claim that the municipality was implementing directive principles, stating that the municipality could only implement these principles within its existing powers. Municipalities were given limited powers for a purpose, he argued, and did not have any general power to control people. The Uttar Pradesh Municipalities Act provided that municipalities could regulate cow slaughter, but the power to regulate did not imply the power to prohibit completely. The municipality was within its powers in closing slaughterhouses, but it could not prohibit a person from slaughtering cattle in any other place in the municipality.[79] Moreover, he held that a bylaw was a valid restriction of a fundamental right only if it were for the purpose of promoting or maintaining the health and safety of the inhabitants of the municipality. The connection between the bylaw and the purpose had to be immediate. Justice Dayal held that the municipality had been unable to demonstrate that the prohibition of cattle slaughter affected the safety or health of the inhabitants of the municipality in any direct way that was different from the slaughter of other animals. Buddhu was unsuccessful in his case, but the possibility of a legal victory over municipal regulations had been presented.

Dayal's minority judgment seemed along the lines of that taken in the few reported cases on bylaw violations in Uttar Pradesh. Challenging the bylaw prohibiting cow slaughter as ultra vires, the Uttar Pradesh Municipalities Act appeared to become a common strategy for people arrested for violating the ban. In a case from Meerut, ten Muslim butchers who were arrested for slaughtering a buffalo and selling its meat urged that the bylaw be declared void.[80] The Uttar Pradesh High Court found that the town committee had passed a resolution prohibiting cattle slaughter because the majority of inhabitants belonged to the Vaish Jains, the Vaish Agarwal, and Brahman communities that did not eat meat and found cow slaughter objectionable. The high court found that the local authorities, such as the town committee, were set up to provide better sanitation and lighting and to improve living conditions. Local authorities were not competent to frame bylaws merely to satisfy the sentiments of local people.[81]

Moreover, the court conceded that under special circumstances, the prohibition of cow slaughter might become necessary for the purpose of regulation, but in general, the power to regulate did not include the power to prohibit. The state could prohibit a trade or profession only if it was illegal, immoral, or injurious to the health of the public. Justice Vidhyadhar Govind Oak held that the profession of a butcher might be objectionable to some people, but it could not be said to be illegal or inherently immoral. The impugned bylaw was invalidated, the ten butchers from Meerut were acquitted, and their fines were refunded.

The high court's striking down of the bylaw was remarkable, given that the Town Area Committee Act expressly provided that "orders of the committee under sections 26 and 27," under which the bylaw was purportedly enacted, "shall be final and shall not be called into question in any court."[82]

Therefore, attempts at local regulation were upset through low-intensity litigation by butchers. Although the arguments made by the state differed in each of the cases, the arguments made by the butchers were largely consistent. In almost every case they initially claimed that the municipality had no power to prohibit slaughter through a bylaw, which they said violated of Article 19 of the Constitution.

Several butchers dealt with the new regulations by just ignoring them. In 1952 the Gosamvardhan Committee discovered forty-five unlicensed slaughterhouses in just nine districts of Uttar Pradesh.[83] Much of this illegal activity was carried out in the butchers' residences or in rural areas where effective policing was limited. Arrests were occasionally made for violating the bylaws, but convictions were hard to secure.

Within the scheme of legal orders, constitutional rights are largely located in national (and now supranational) statutes and are experienced by citizens as part of their national or supranational citizenship.[84] Ordinarily, the police powers of the liberal state tend to remain under the political radar, in part because they are largely exercised locally—and often by individuals who are regarded not as part of the coercive apparatus of state but rather as protectors of health, safety, and welfare. Since the 1920s, local and municipal governments had regulated cow slaughter, which was determined by custom, local rights, and license agreements. However, through invoking constitutional principles in the challenges to municipal orders, the butchers were able to create a dialogue between the two orders and to make constitutional rights local.

The Shield of Legislation: Cow Protection in the Provincial Assembly

As it became clear that local regulation was not sufficient to prevent cow slaughter, cow protection activists began pressuring the newly elected central and state governments to pass legislation. The Cattle Preservation and Development Committee passed a resolution urging that cow slaughter be prohibited by law because the "prosperity of India depends on its cattle and the soul of the country can be satisfied only if cattle slaughter is banned completely."[85]

The challenge for legislation was threefold: the law could not be framed in majoritarian religious terms, it had to meet concerns about the economy, and it had to be designed to be effective. The central government circulated a piece of model legislation recommending that the slaughter of cows be prohibited, with exceptions made for animals over fifteen years old and those that were unable to work or breed. It also provided that all unlicensed slaughter be made a cognizable offense under the law.[86] On the advice of the Ministry of Commerce and Industry, the central government warned against the indiscriminate stopping of slaughter because of the effect it would have on the leather industry. The proposed regulatory system provided that any cow that was to be slaughtered had to have a certificate from the veterinary officer (an appointed municipal government official) and the president of the municipality, stating that the cow was fit for slaughter. These individuals were supposed to represent local political authority and technical expertise.

The design of the legislation appeared ineffective. State bureaucrats noted that it would be difficult to apply in practice and might not even address the problem, since it prohibited slaughter without a certificate in writing by *both* the president of the concerned municipality and the veterinary officer.[87] The bill provided that if there was a difference of opinion between the two officials, the cow would not be slaughtered. This implied that the act would not cover rural areas and would merely lead to a relocation of cattle outside municipal limits. The chief commissioner of Bhopal, a town with a significant Muslim population, doubted the practicability of a joint certificate from two officials, who would be influenced by their respective community identities. When they were from two different communities, there would be a perpetual difference of opinion, leading to frequent appeals to the provincial government and subsequent embarrassment.[88]

The passivity of the central government and Nehru's resistance shifted the focus of attention onto the state legislatures. The system of patchy local regulations also found disfavor with the cow protection lobby. Between 1949 and 1955, nine of the fourteen Indian states enacted strict laws banning cow slaughter. An issue that had once been settled through local custom and administrative orders, cow slaughter in independent India came to be settled through statutory law.

The most comprehensive and controversial pieces of legislation came from Uttar Pradesh, India's largest province and the center of the cow protection movement for more than a century. It also had the largest cattle population: at least 32,763,327 cows.[89] Leading members of the cow protection lobby in the Constituent Assembly, like Seth Govind Das and Shibban Lal Saxena, had been elected by the provincial legislature. The Congress Party in Uttar Pradesh differed widely from the Nehruvian vision of secularism.[90] Purushottam Das Tandon, Congress Party president and Speaker of the Uttar Pradesh Legislative Assembly, told the All India Cow Protection Society that the country had been divided so that Muslims would have a homeland of their own where they were free to live their according to their religion, and Hindus could do likewise in India.[91]

Until partition Uttar Pradesh had been a power center for the Muslim League, and even though many of the Muslim League leaders had left for Pakistan, a substantial Muslim population remained in the state. After partition, Uttar Pradesh's Muslim political elite were anxious to integrate with the new order, and several Muslim League leaders joined the Congress Party and were eager to fall in line. In 1953 the Uttar Pradesh Legislative Assembly set up the Gosamvardhan Committee to study the situation and make recommendations to the government. The committee, which consisted of a number of legislators, police officers, academics, and bureaucrats, investigated the trends of cattle population, examined the issue of preservation of the cow in light of available nutrition, developed methods to address the problem of stray and wild cattle, provided for better economic utilization of old and decrepit cattle, improved cattle breeds, ensured purity in dairy products, and reviewed existing regulations on cow slaughter.[92] The committee functioned through its own secretariat and met regularly; it went on investigative field trips, toured several districts, and collected evidence from a wide range of stakeholders.[93] The committee examined the nutritional value of cow's milk and the chemical composition of cow dung and cow urine, calculated the contribution of the leather industry to the national economy, and made the question of cattle slaughter commensurable.

Rejecting the central law enacting a partial ban on cow slaughter, the committee resolved that "apart from the deep-rooted religious sentiments of a very large number of the residents of Uttar Pradesh, it is not only desirable but imperative in the interests of national economy, national health, and national goodwill to save, protect, and improve the cow and her progeny . . . that cow slaughter should be totally banned." The Gosamvardhan Committee, which recommended statewide legislation banning cow slaughter in Uttar Pradesh, noted that when local bodies had different regulations it led to a "perpetual and festering sore in the body politic." Enacting a statewide ban would be a "bold and decisive step" in the interest of "national harmony and national wealth."[94]

With relatively little resistance, the assembly enacted the Prevention of Cow SlaughterAct in 1955. It provided that no person should slaughter a cow or cause a cow to be a slaughtered anwhere in Uttar Pradesh. The only exceptions were cows that were suffering from contagious diseases or animals required for medical and public health research.[95] Most striking was that the offense of cow slaughter was made both cognizable and nonbailable. A cognizable offense meant that an accused person could be arrested without a warrant and would have to apply for bail before a court.

This legislation became the model for laws in other states. The Bihar assembly was originally considering a ban on cows below three years of age, but following the Uttar Pradesh legislation, it widened the scope of the Bihari statute to provide for an absolute ban on cow slaughter.[96] Similarly, the state of Madhya Pradesh enacted significant amendments in the Central Provinces, and the Berar Animal Preservation Act of 1951 brought about an absolute ban on cow slaughter.

The constitutionality of the Uttar Pradesh Prevention of Cow Slaughter Act was of some concern to the central government. The governor of Uttar Pradesh reserved the bill for the consideration of the president on the grounds that it violated the Criminal Procedure Code.[97] H. R. Krishnan, the joint secretary of the Ministry of Law, expressed doubt from a "purely legal point of view" that the Supreme Court would approve a law completely banning cow slaughter. Such a law, he argued, would be an infringement of the right to property as guaranteed under Article 19 of the Constitution.[98] The right to property could be restricted only by reasonable limitations in the interest of the general public, something that was "objectively ascertainable." In order for the law to be held valid, Krishnan suggested, it should categorize different types of cattle and provide that certain kinds (such as those that provide milk or draft power) should not be killed. He recommended that some kind of authority be set up to certify cattle that were outside the protected category. Alternatively, restrictions could be used to ensure that the manner of killing did not hurt religious sentiments. He was emphatic that the fifth clause was poorly phrased; for instance, if beef was imported from outside the state, there could be no objection to its sale. The legislature did not have the power to ban the consumption of beef.

Krishnan was backed by his immediate superior, K. Y. Bhandarkar, the law secretary. Bhandarkar emphasized that the Ministry of Law interpreted Article 48 of the Constitution as prohibiting the slaughter of only useful cattle. Bhandarkar insisted that a person who owns an economically unprofitable cow had a substantial right to kill it or "dispose of it through slaughter" and that this right was protected as part of the right to property in the Constitution. The provisions the bill made for establishing institutions for economically unprofitable cows required fees to be paid by the owners. There was no provision that would allow the owner to sell the economically unprofitable cow to the government; thus the law was forcing the burden of an economically unprofitable cow on the owner. Bhandarkar warned that this restriction was likely to be struck down by the courts as unreasonable restrictions and not in the interest of the general public. He recommended that the president be advised to return the bill for reconsideration with the suggestions made by Krishnan incorporated. If the bill was to be accepted, the government of Uttar Pradesh should be warned about the constitutional difficulties it would cause.

The advice of the two bureaucrats in the Ministry of Law was overruled by the law minister, H. V. Pataskar, who insisted that the bill was merely an attempt to carry out the goals set in Article 48 and that no "reasonable court" can regard this as a violation of a fundamental right. The president was advised to sign the bill.[99]

Taking Cows to the Supreme Court

We have examined how butchers utilized the Supreme Court. By 1955 their early experience with litigation had made two things clear to the butchers: they had to show that they were affected as a class and not just as individuals, and piecemeal litigation took too much time and caused uncertainty. In early 1956, twelve writ petitions were filed before the Supreme Court challenging the constitutionality of the Uttar Pradesh Prevention of Cow Slaughter Act of 1955, the Bihar Preservation and Improvement of Animals Act of 1955, and the Berar Animal Preservation Act 1949. The petitioners were three thousand Muslim men from more than a hundred villages in the states of Bombay, Madhya Pradesh, Uttar Pradesh, and Bihar.

In the petitions, submitted to the Supreme Court, which were presented collectively and contained similar language, the petitioners "respectfully sheweth" that they were "members of the Quresh community and . . . also citizens of India." They identified the Qureshi community as numerous and as "an important segment of the Muslims of this country." The petitions then listed the various professions the members of the community were engaged in, such as butchering and its subsidiary undertakings, like supplying, tanning, and curing hides, glue making, gut merchants, and blood dehydrating.[100] The Supreme Court, however, identified the petitioners as "citizens of India, and Muslims by religion, mostly belong to the Quraishi community and generally engaged in the butcher's trade." The reversal of the order was crucial: the court saw the petitioners as Muslims first and Qureshis incidentally, whereas for the petitioners it was their Qureshi identity and their profession that were most significant. Their reference to their faith was only to emphasize their dominant role among Indian Muslims.

The Qureshis were a caste of South Asian Muslims who were engaged in the meat trade. They were known by slightly different names across north India and in certain districts where their members were concentrated. In Bihar, for instance, an anthropological survey identified them as Kassab, a class of Sunni Muslim butchers who deal with slaughtered cattle, and as a subgroup of Qureshis. Etymologically, Kassabs were those who slaughtered a cow or a buffalo, whereas those who slaughtered goats or chickens were known as *chiks* or *chikwas*. In Uttar Pradesh they were known as Kasais and were engaged in the slaughter of big animals like buffaloes and cows.[101]

It is significant that the legal challenge to the cow slaughter laws came from the Qureshis and not other Muslim groups. Although applications to intervene in the case were put forward by Hindu groups like the Bharat Go Sevak Sangh (Indian Cow Service Society), the All India Anti–Cow Slaughter Movement Committee (different from the All India Cow Protection Society), the Sarvadeshik Arya Pratinidhi Sabha (International Aryan Representative Organization), and the Gorakshan Sangh (Cow Protection Society), no petitions were filed by other Muslim groups. The absence of religious scholars and Muslim politicians was telling. Moreover, as the respondents stated in their counterpetition, the three Muslim members of the Gosamvardhan Committee—the Nawab of Chattri, Akhtar Hussein, and Professor Mohammed Habib, all leading members of the Uttar Pradesh Muslim community—had come out in favor of the absolute ban on cow slaughter.[102]

The petitioners made four constitutional claims. They alleged that an absolute ban on cow slaughter infringed on their fundamental rights under Article 19 of the Constitution to carry on their respective trades as butchers, hide curers, bone and gut dealers, and cattle exporters. A total prohibition on their trades was not a reasonable restriction in the interest of the general public as contemplated under the Constitution. They argued that the law violated the equality clause under Article 14 because it discriminated between butchers who slaughtered cows and butchers who slaughtered other animals. They argued that it forbade them to carry on their legitimate trade or business, thus depriving them of their property without compensation and violating Article 31 of the Constitution. Finally, they argued that the total ban violated the fundamental rights guaranteed to the petitioners under Article 25 of the Constitution, which promised "freedom of belief," by not permitting the sacrifice of a cow on the holiday of Eid-ul-Fitr.[103]

The ban on cow slaughter on Eid was inconvenient for poor Muslims and humiliating to Muslims in general, but given the changed political dynamics in north India, traditional Muslim representatives were being accommodating. The Qureshis, however, did not have such luxury. The ban on cow slaughter hit them most directly. When cow slaughter was banned in the Central Provinces, more than two hundred butchers were left without jobs. One butcher facing economic ruin reportedly killed himself by jumping into a well; others demanded alternative employment from the government.[104]

There was a great diversity among the litigants who went to court to challenge cow slaughter bans in colonial India. However, in almost every case filed after independence, the petitioners self-identified as butchers, were marked by their names as Qureshis, were found slaughtering the cow for food, or were in the possession of beef.

Religion versus Profession

The first two challenges, based on the right to trade and the right to equality, relatively new legal gambits, had been attempted with a limited degree of success in the cases involving municipal regulations. The argument rooted in religious freedom was possibly the most successful strategy and dated back almost a century. Muslims believed that they enjoyed freedom of religion under the British Crown. Article 25 of the Constitution provided that "subject to public order, morality, and health, all persons are equally entitled to freedom of conscience and the right to freely profess, practice, and propagate religion," which included the right to sacrifice a cow on Eid.[105] It was always expected that a challenge to cow slaughter would come from Muslims, because it affected their religious practices.

However, the Qureshis, the petitioners in the case, considered this argument relatively unimportant. The Qureshis were uninterested in getting permission to sacrifice a cow once a year on Eid; they wanted to ensure the continuation of their livelihood. Freedom of religion was the last of the four challenges in the petition and took up a single paragraph. There was little attempt made by the petitioners to substantiate this claim in the petition or before the court. However, this was apparently not obvious to the contemporary actors, nor has it struck later commentators. Despite the Qureshi butchers' lack of interest in making a claim as Muslims, the court tended to see their claims through this lens. Chief Justice Das expressed his exasperation at the absence of material before the court to substantiate the claim that it was the religious practice of the petitioner's community to sacrifice a cow:

> No affidavit has been filed by any person specially competent to expound the relevant tenets of Islam. No reference is made in the petition to any particular surah of the Holy Quran which, in terms, requires the sacrifice of a cow. All that was placed before us during the argument were surah 22, verses 28 and 33. What the Holy Book enjoins is that people should pray unto the Lord and make sacrifice. We have no affidavit before us by any Maulana [learned Muslim scholar] explaining the implications of those verses or throwing any light on this problem.[106]

In the absence of expert evidence, the Supreme Court magnanimously delved into Islamic law relying on Charles Hamilton's commentary on the Hedaya and noted that the hadiths held that it was the duty of every free adult Muslim to sacrifice on Eid. The sacrifice established could be a goat per person or, alternatively, a cow or a camel for a group of seven. The court interpreted this to mean that Muslims had the option of sacrificing seven goats or a camel instead of a cow. Since there was an option, the sacrifice of a cow could not be said to be obligatory. The court recognized that a household of seven members might be able to afford to sacrifice a cow but not seven goats; however, this would be an economic compulsion and not a religious compulsion and was therefore not protected by the Constitution. The Uttar Pradesh state government, represented by the Department of Animal Husbandry, stated that many Muslims sacrificed other four-legged animals, such as sheep, goats, and rams.[107]

Furthermore, the Gosamvardhan Committee, which had recommended the absolute ban on cow slaughter, had three eminent Muslim representatives who did not see a violation of religious practice by banning cow slaughter. The court accepted that there was a widespread divergence of practice in sacrificing and noted that several Indian Muslim rulers (e.g., Mughal Emperors Akbar and Jahangir, the Bahmani Sultan Ahmad Shah, and Nawab Hyder Ali of Mysore) had all prohibited cow slaughter in their realms.

The court held that Article 25 of the Constitution protected only the "essential features" of a religion and that cow sacrifice could not be said to be an essential feature of Islam. Supreme Court doctrine had established that even though the state could not interfere with the essential practices of a religion, it could restrict "extraneous factors."[108] That the courts, rather than those who practiced the faith, were the final authority in determining the essential features of a religion was a colonial inheritance dating back to the implementation of religious laws by a secular judiciary.

In an attempt to determine the reasonableness of the restrictions on the trade of the petitioners, the court very comfortably engaged in examining Hindu religious texts as well. Article 19 of the Constitution protected laws that imposed a restriction in the "interest of the general public" on the right to trade and occupation guaranteed under the article. The Supreme Court had previously held that the test for reasonableness of the restriction had "no abstract standard or general pattern" and required "the purpose of restrictions imposed, the extent and urgency of the evil sought to be remedied, and the prevailing conditions of the time." The court recognized that it was "inevitable that the social philosophy and scale of value of the judges would play an important part," but this had to be limited by the " 'sobering reflection that the Constitution is meant not only for people of their way of thinking but for all, and the majority of the elected representatives of the people have, in authorizing these restrictions, deemed them to be reasonable."[109] The court then proceeded to investigate the origins of the appreciation of cows, noting that early Vedic texts contain evidence of the prevalence of cow slaughter. In their narrative, the cow came to acquire a special sanctity with a shift from pastoralism to a predominantly agrarian society. The court quoted hymns from the Vedas, such as the tenth hymn of the Artharva Veda in a rapturous glorification of the cow:

> The cow is heaven, the cow is earth, the cow is Vishnu, Lord of Life,
> the Sadhyas and Vayus have drunk the outpourings of the cow.
> Both gods and mortal men depend for life and being on the cow
> She hath become the Universe, all that the sun surveys is she.

The court used such hymns to argue that even though there had been cow killing in ancient India, only barren cows were killed, and the custom was soon abolished. Finally, the court held that "there can be no gainsaying the fact that the Hindus in general hold the cow in great reverence, the idea of the slaughter of cows for food is repugnant to their notions, and this sentiment has even led to communal riots."[110] The judges emphasized that constitutional questions could not be decided on the grounds of mere sentiment. However, they acknowledged that sentiment had to be taken into consideration as one of the many elements in determining the reasonableness of restrictions.

There is little evidence to suggest that the submissions regarding the Hindu belief in the sanctity of the cow were made by the respondents. Indeed, the only possible allusion the state made in its affidavit was the assertion that the statutes had been enacted by a democratic body. Some of the arguments might have come from the intervener, Thakur Das Bhargava, whose submissions have not been preserved. However, it is much more likely that these were the interventions of the judges themselves. New histories of lawyering have revealed ways in which non-European lawyers and judges in the colonies often functioned as "cultural translators and ethnographic intermediaries," using their authority as "natives" to make legible cultural and religious practices.[111]

In its early years, the Supreme Court shared the modernizing nationalist impulses of the Nehruvian state and sought to rationalize religion. All six judges on the bench were upper-caste Hindus, and at least two were noted Sanskrit scholars.[112] Justice P. B. Gajendragatkar, one of the judges joining Chief Justice Das in his concurrence, had a long history of engaging in personal reform projects from the bench.[113] That the judges were insiders to Hinduism and outsiders to Islam is clear from their use of sources. To examine Islamic law the judges turned to the *Hedaya*, a four-volume text whose authority was the result of the pruning and simplification of Islamic law through British colonial courts over a century. This text was pared down in the 1870 edition in the interests of cost and utility, and the portions "more interesting to the antiquarian . . . than useful to the practitioner" were expunged.[114] In contrast, when considering Hindu law apart from references to original Sanskrit sources, the court chose to rely on Abinas Das's study of Rig Vedic culture and Pāṇḍuraṅga Kāṇe's work on the Dharmasastras.[115] Both were nationalist scholars who had delved into ancient Indian history, motivated in part to recapture the glory of a lost civilization.

The dominant theme in the decision was framed around the question of denying that Muslims were required to sacrifice a cow on Eid and recognizing Hindu sentiments. This was emphasized in contemporary commentaries in both the legal sphere and the general media. Bombay lawyer Rafiq Zakaria wrote in his legal column in the English daily, the *Times of India*, that in "one of the bulkiest judgments" ever delivered, the Supreme Court "said that the sacrifice of the cow is not an obligatory overt act for a Musselman to exhibit his religious belief and ideas" and that the ban on cow slaughter was therefore not a denial of Muslims' rights to "freely profess, practice, and propagate religion."[116] The popular law reporter asserted that the judgment was remarkable in many ways for its breadth and did not infringe on the fundamental rights of Muslims. Much of the progressive critique of the judgment has also centered on the theme, arguing that the judgment cloaked majoritarian impulses and did not accommodate minority religious identity. In a contemporary review, Upendra Baxi critiqued the judgment for its lazy assumption that the Hindu reverence for cows was an "indubitable fact" and sarcastically suggested that the only drawback in the case was that the Muslims had not agitated sufficiently for "judicial cognition of their sentiment."[117]

Economy versus Identity

The *Hanif Qureshi* decision has been interpreted through the traditional lens of Hindu-Muslim conflict in which Muslims have been deemed to have lost a significant right that they enjoyed in colonial India. Empirically this might well be true, but what is often missed is that the three thousand petitioners in the case were not invested in basing their argument on freedom of religion. This difference is clear if we compare how the petitioners presented themselves in the writ petition with how the Supreme Court recognized them.

In the petition the Qureshis identified themselves by their individual trades and also demonstrated a range of economic uses of the cow. They mostly spoke

Bhojpuri, a dialect of Hindi. The Qureshis were *ajlafs*, or of common birth, unlike most Muslim political leaders, who belonged to the *ashraf* (aristocratic) classes and spoke Urdu. As a group they always had a poor literacy rate and limited access to state services like education, health care, drinking water, and financial services.[118] By the 1990s they were identified as part of the Other Backward Classes, a category that benefits from government affirmative action policies.[119]

The Qureshis might not have been represented in the hierarchy of the mainstream political parties, but they were very well organized. As the anthropological survey noted in Bihar, they were a close-knit body and had their own elected *anjuman* (village council) that determined internal matters. Its decisions could be appealed to a *chourasi*, which comprised the *anjumans* of the neighboring districts. The Qureshis had also constituted themselves into a registered organization called the All India Jamiatul Quresh, founded in 1926 by Qureshis from Meerut and Delhi to improve the position of the community. It was similar to other community-based organizations that were set up around the time, but it was unlike other caste or communal organizations—the Qureshi linkage of caste identity and livelihood was very strong, making the group active interveners in questions about the meat industry.

The twelve writ petitions filed by the Qureshis were clearly influenced by the Jamiat; indeed, the organization is mentioned in the first paragraph of each petitions as a body that looks after the interests and welfare of the community. Several officeholders of the state Jamiat appeared as individual petitioners. A year before the petition, during the course of the debates over the Uttar Pradesh Cow Protection Act, the twenty-ninth All India Jamiatul Quresh conference had been held in Bombay. The lead speaker, M. N. Lakhanpaul, the president of the All India Guts Manufacturers Association had addressed the seven hundred delegates on the need to redress their grievances through persuasion and a "spirit of understanding and friendliness." [120] This was despite the provocation caused by members of the All India Hindu Raj Party who had barged into the conference shouting slogans and demanding the stoppage of cow slaughter. The Qureshis also underscored their "backward" status. In his presidential address Haji Akhtar Hussein said that the community deserved preferential treatment, including reserved seats in the legislatures and educational institutions to speed up their progress. He appealed to the state governments to think twice before imposing legislative restrictions on the Qureshis' profession.

Clearly, the desire to "redress their grievances through persuasion," coupled with the Qureshis' extraordinarily effective organization, was instrumental in getting three thousand petitioners to file before the Supreme Court at Delhi within months of a national meeting and with wide geographic representation. The petitions invoked the court's jurisdiction under Article 32 and marked the event as a national campaign, which would not have been the case if the petitions had been filed before the high courts of each state. Writ petitions were filed by individuals to meet their individual grievances. In Balsara's case (see chapter 1), for instance, the direct remedy sought was an individual license to drink. Attempts at a representative's suit by butchers under Order 1, Rule 8, of the Civil Procedure Code had already been struck down by the Allahabad High Court in Ahmad Raza's case.[121] Therefore, to make a case for the harm the ban caused to the community, the Qureshis had to appear in a substantial number before the Supreme Court.

The first half of their petition explained their business positions and role in the economy, asserting that the Qureshis were a very important feature of the country's economic and social life and played a crucial role in the people's food supply. As the petition from Rampur noted, the butchers among the petitioners used to slaughter around 150 cattle a month before the ban came into force. These animals, they emphasized, were buffaloes, bullocks (castrated bulls), old bulls, and heifers. The average price of these animals ranged from thirty to fifty rupees. It was rare for a fertile milk cow to be slaughtered, for its price ranged from three hundred to five hundred rupees. They outlined the interconnectedness of transactions by noting that while the meat was sold to Muslims, the guts and hides were sold to gut and hide merchants, respectively. Haji Amjad Ali, a hide merchant, explained that after buying the hides from butchers and curing them, he would export them to the cities of Bombay and Madras, where they would be tanned, demonstrating an economic chain across India. The Qureshis submitted that the absolute ban on cow slaughter was a "hostile and discriminatory piece of legislation" directed against the Muslim community, in particular the Qureshis.

The Qureshis argued that there were more than two million of them across the country, and they depended solely on the buying, selling, and slaughter of cattle. The petitioners argued that if the sale of cattle for slaughter was prohibited, they would have to acquire seven goats or sheep to make up for each cow or buffalo they would have slaughtered, and statistics produced before the court indicated that goats and sheep were not available in such numbers.[122] This meat would be more expensive than beef and out of reach of most poor people, consequently reducing the market for meat and the Qureshis' incomes. Furthermore, goat and sheep hides and guts could not be used as effectively for the manufacture of secondary products.

Conceding that the Constitution permitted the state to impose reasonable restrictions on the right to a trade or a profession in the interest of the general public, the Qureshis argued that this could not extend to total prohibition. This argument was very similar to the one successfully made in Buddhu's case and in Meya's case challenging the municipality's ability to prohibit an activity that it had the power to regulate.

The argument did not work as successfully here, for the court was unable to understand who the Qureshis were. The judges argued that the dictionary definition of *butcher* was the "slaughter of animals; a dealer in meat." It was a familiar occupation, the judges reminded the public, memorably included in the "homey phrase 'the butcher, the baker, the candlestick maker.'"[123] Chief Justice Das drew an analogy to the retailers of clothing: Some may sell indigenous cloth, whereas others may import clothing from England or Japan. However, they are all clothing merchants. A hypothetical piece of legislation to protect the indigenous textile industry by stopping the import of foreign cloth would not prevent clothing merchants from carrying out their business but would merely require them to sell other items. Similarly, he continued, if the state sought to encourage *khadi* (homespun cotton) and banned the sale of fine muslin, it could not be said to prohibit the retail clothing business. The analogy of cloth was particularly powerful, given that a campaign against foreign cloth and the production of *khadi* had been central to the Gandhian project and the national movement, seeking to produce economic self-reliance and nationalist pride.[124]

Chief Justice Das then turned to the acts in contention and examined what they really prohibited. In Uttar Pradesh the petitioners could slaughter buffaloes, goats, and sheep, so there was no prohibition on their occupation. In Madhya Pradesh the act permitted the slaughter of some buffaloes under certain conditions. In Bihar there was a total ban on slaughtering cattle, but butchers were still allowed to slaughter goats and sheep and sell mutton. Therefore, there was no total prohibition of the right of butchers to carry on their trade and occupation.

In this line of argument, the court did not seek to understand caste differences among the Qureshis: the *kasais*, who slaughtered big animals, and the *chikwas*, who slaughtered chickens and goats. The judges echoed the government affidavit that the hide merchants could continue their trade with hides obtained from cattle that died of natural causes. The Qureshis had stated in their petition that cultural taboos prevented them from touching the carcasses or skin of animals that had not been slaughtered according to halal rules. They pointed out that the collection of hides from fallen animals was usually done by untouchable Hindu groups.

The court chose to treat the category of butcher as an independent economic agent who was free to adapt his methods according to the shifting contours of regulation. The court was caste-blind and ignored the limits placed by the economy and the community, which circumscribed the Qureshis' ability to branch out to other slaughter other animals.

Making Economic Policy in the Supreme Court

Although the court seemed to have disposed of the question of fundamental rights fairly neatly, the cow slaughter laws continued to pose a significant cause of concern for the judges. This unease arose not from the fundamental-rights challenges made by the Qureshis but from questions of policy. The Qureshis turned to the wording of Article 48 in the Constitution and argued that it consisted of three different directives. The directive that sought to prohibit the "slaughter of cows, calves, and milch and draught cattle" was subordinate and ancillary to the provisions that came before it—namely, "organizing agriculture and animal husbandry on modern and scientific lines" and "preserving and improving the breeds of cattle." The Qureshis argued that a complete ban on cow slaughter would be wasteful. To this end, they quoted the following from a circular issued by the central government:

> A compulsory ban on cow slaughter would lead to a lower standard of cattle life in the country. Nearly 40 million cattle in the country do not give milk and are a drain on available fodder and other cattle food. Their maintenance entails enormous expenditure, making it impossible to provide the care and nourishment to productive cattle that is required to improve their milk capacity and traction power. The result is that even productive cattle gradually deteriorate and cease to be productive.[125]

The petitions attempted to rob the state legislation of some of its democratic sheen by pointing out that the national parliament had overwhelmingly rejected the bill proposed by Seth Govind Das that advocated a complete ban on cow slaughter.

In order to demonstrate that this restriction was not in the interest of the general public, the Qureshis pointed out that it deprived many people of a cheap source of food—beef—and that these people had suffered loss and hardship as a result of the disappearance of essential an essential part of their diet. They argued that the measure was economically faulty, given that a considerable portion of cattle had no economic value and were a drain on the food supply for animals. Attacking the arguments that linked cattle to milk supply, they pointed out that an increase in cattle between 1945 and 1951 because of a reduction in cow slaughter had not led to a significant increase in milk supply.

The modernization of agriculture and the introduction of tractors, an aspect of many development policies, was reducing the usefulness of cattle in agriculture. A total ban on slaughter would also damage the leather trade, given that the hide obtained from already-dead animals was not suitable for high-quality leather goods. Furthermore, the ban would effectively end industries like gut making, glue making, and blood dehydrating, which were dependent on cattle by-products.

Finally, Mohammed Siddiq of Rampur, who identified himself as a cultivator, alleged that he was having considerable difficulty protecting his crops from the ravages of hordes of abandoned cattle that were roaming the countryside, "unclaimed by anyone and which could be destroyed by no one."[126] He complained that he now had to make arrangements to keep watch over his fields day and night, and he pointed to several crops that had been damaged by rampaging cattle.

The Supreme Court was placed in a quandary over how to evaluate these claims. Unlike a district court or even a high court, the Supreme Court was never a court of first instance. It did not have the power to take evidence, listen to witnesses, or allow for cross-examination. The petitioners for the state of Uttar Pradesh challenged all the contentions of the Qureshis by referring to the findings of the *Gosamvardhan Enquiry Committee Report*. It insisted that the question of whether an absolute ban on cow slaughter hurt the quality of cattle had been settled by the Gosamvardhan Committee, which had observed that "the absence of the ban on cow slaughter had been tried for years past with no appreciable results on the improvement of the cows, nor have uneconomic cattle been lessened with the freedom to kill."[127] The committee had noted that bans to prevent the killing of economically profitable cattle during World War II did not yield satisfactory results. The committee had also warned that the loophole for killing economically unprofitable cows left open the possibility that healthy cows would be maimed to attract mercy or pity. An absolute ban was thus considered the best way of reaching a final decision. Faced with competing claims, Chief Justice Das expressed his frustration, stating "that it was difficult to find one's way out of this labyrinth of figures, and it will be futile for us to attempt to come to a figure of unserviceable animals that may even be approximately correct."[128]

The court did not allow petitions from partisan groups like the Bharat Go Sevak Samaj, the All India Anti–Cow Slaughter Movement Committee, the Sarvedeshik Arya Pratinidhi Sabha, and the Madhya Pradesh Gorakshan Saminit, on the grounds that Order 41, Rule 2, of the Supreme Court permitted only the attorney general of India or the advocate general of the states to intervene in a case involving other parties; the only exception was when the third party was already involved in a similar case before another court. The Supreme Court decided to exercise its inherent powers and invite Thakur Das Bhargava to intervene as amicus curiae, given the "importance of questions involved." (An amicus curiae, or friend of the court, is not a party to a case but volunteers to assist the court in deciding the matter before it; he or she usually submits a legal brief containing information not provided by the parties.)

Bhargava was a successful lawyer based in Hissar, East Punjab, and was a member of the Indian parliament. As a member of the Constituent Assembly, he had authored Article 48, which brought cow protection into the Constitution as a directive principle. Over the past few years, as a legislator and as a member of the Grow-More-Food Enquiry Committee, Bhargava had campaigned and written on the subject of cow slaughter.

The court relied on Bhargava as a guide and turned to investigating the impact of the total ban on cow slaughter on the national economy. The judges turned to a number of reports by central and state governments, chambers of commerce, scientists, and agricultural economists to distill the truth. These included the *Report on the Marketing of Cattle in India* (1946), the *Report of the Cattle Preservation and Development Committee* (1949), the *Gosamvardhan Enquiry Committee Report* (1955), the first and second five-year plans issued by the Planning Commission, publicity documents of the governments of Uttar Pradesh and Bihar, a memorandum prepared by the Nutrition Advisory Committee of the Indian Council of Medical Research, and a report by the Indian Council of Agricultural Research. With the exception of the Gosamvardhan Committee report, all the other reports were prepared by bureaucrats. Shiv Visvanathan has argued that the bureaucratic report is one of the great literary forms of the twentieth century, which in the Indian context performs the role of the detective novel, interrogating both individuals and a system.[129]

This investigation brought up some uncomfortable facts. Drawing on the *Report on the Marketing of Cattle in India*, issued by the Ministry of Food and Agriculture, the court discovered that even though India had the largest number of cattle in the world, it ranked among the lowest in milk production. The data produced by the five-year plans showed that the average yield of milk per cow in India was 413 pounds, the lowest in the world.[130]

The report also confirmed the truth of the allegation made by the Qureshis that buffaloes provided more milk than cows and that their milk was richer in fat. The memorandum of the Nutrition Advisory Committee noted that from an economic point of view, there was no justification for maintaining a cow that yielded less than two pounds of milk. This would eliminate 90 percent of all Indian cows, and if milk yield were the only criterion, the comparatively smaller number of buffaloes that produced 54 percent of the milk should be given preferential treatment.

Cow protectionists had struggled with the obvious economic advantage the buffalo had over the cow. The Gosamvardhan Committee had to grapple with the view that it was wasteful to, and beyond the means of, farmers with small holdings to retain two species of domestic animals when one could meet the demands of both milk and draft. The committee attempted to explain the buffalo's advantage of a greater yield of milk by citing the higher butterfat content and a better use of coarse fodder, but the committee said it was unfair to compare the pampered buffalo with the neglected cow.[131] The committee quoted Gandhi, who observed that "we have a weakness, in a way it is common to all mankind, but it is a special trait of the Indian character that we readily take to things that are easy to get and give up things that are difficult. In *khadi*, people seek cheapness and convenience. People relish buffalo's milk because it is sweet and cheap."[132]

By comparing buffalo with foreign-spun cloth (the other scourge of the Indian nation), Gandhi invested protecting the economically unprofitable cow as a national moral duty. Gandhi even suggested that buffalo breeding be given up and that the buffalo be "liberated from human bondage."[133]

Bhargava played a pivotal role by convincing the court that the cow was useful for meeting the power requirements in agricultural production. Based on their long-term experience, most Indian farmers preferred cattle bullocks to male buffaloes. Bhargava even attempted to justify the fact that cattle were more numerous than buffaloes in the census as a result of evolutionary natural selection.

The court spent considerable time discussing the utility of cattle dung, the one output that was prolific even among old and dry cows. The court approvingly cited the first five-year plan, which recorded that eight hundred million tons of dung were available per year and utilized as both fuel and manure. Cattle urine was rich in nitrogen, phosphates, and potash and was good for the fertility of the field. Bhargava, as amicus curiae, claimed that cow dung contributed 630 million rupees a year to the national income.

The court had been able to reconcile its position with the fact that the ban would in practice cause considerable inconvenience and expense to the Qureshis. There were already precedents for the state blocking avenues of livelihood for hundreds of citizens without any compensation, as in the case of bus transport nationalization.[134] But the court could not deny that beef or buffalo meat was an important food item for a large number of people. The *Report on the Marketing of Cattle in India* showed that contrary to the government's claim that beef was not consumed, the annual demand for cattle for food included 1,893,000 cows and 6,900,000 buffaloes.[135] The court noted that beef was a common part of the diet of poorer Muslims, Christians, and members of the Scheduled Castes and Tribes. Here the cow scored higher than the buffalo because buffalo flesh is coarser and tougher than beef.

Beef was also considerably cheaper than goat and mutton; for instance, in 1950 the price of beef in Bombay was 0.12 rupees a pound, compared to 1.30 rupees a pound for mutton and goat meat. The counsel for the Qureshis pointed out that in the case of several boarding schools, beef was the only meat the school authorities could afford to supply to meet the needs of growing children. If the ban were enforced, it would preclude them from having even this little bit of nourishment. The court noted that the memorandum of the Nutrition Advisory Committee recommended meat as a necessity rather than a luxury, particularly for people who were too poor to afford fruit or clarified butter.

The court confirmed the Qureshi claim that the presence of a large number of nonproductive cattle was a burden on the scarce fodder and animal-food resources of the nation.[136] The judges took seriously Mohammed Nasim's complaint about rampaging hordes of wild cattle. Given the shortfall in feed and the lack of economic benefits from old cows, it was not surprising that several cows were abandoned by their owners. The court noted that "these old and useless animals roaming about at pleasure are a nuisance, a source of danger to the countryside. And a menace to crop production."[137]

The government's proposed solutions were deemed unsatisfactory. The Gosamvardhan Committee had suggested licensing cattle in urban areas and establishing centers for captured wild cattle.[138] The central government had proposed a scheme in which owners could leave their old and economically unprofitable cattle in a camp to be maintained at state expense. The Supreme Court pointed out that the proposed cost for setting up and running such a camp had been estimated at around forty-five thousand rupees a year in 1949, whereas the camp could hope to recoup only around five thousand rupees through the sale of cow products.[139]

More recent studies suggested that taking into account the land required to produce the fodder (i.e., four thousand acres of land for every two thousand cattle), the present cost to the state exchequer of maintaining economically unprofitable cattle would be 12.50 rupees per head. In order to set up the ninety-one camps that the state of Uttar Pradesh required, it would cost the state nineteen rupees per head. The court declared that it would be shocking to spend that amount to preserve economically useless cattle, especially since the total national expenditure on education was four rupees per person. In the absence of finances and fodder, sending cattle to a camp would leave them to a fate of slow death.

Moreover, the court sarcastically noted, the scheme for such a camp relied on cattle owners donating their cows. For unwanted and economically unprofitable cows to be effectively saved from slaughter, "the responsibility had to be shared by the individual and the local community, and not merely within the exclusive means and competence of the state." Such an expectation was "wishful thinking" when farmers, regardless of their religion, were guided by profit. The court noted approvingly that the states of Assam, Bombay, West Bengal, Hyderabad, and Travancore-Cochin placed only a partial ban on cattle slaughter.[140]

The court categorically stated that maintaining economically useless cattle deprived the economically useful cattle of nourishment, led to the deterioration of the breed of cattle, and drained the nation's cattle feed. Furthermore, the judges noted that such a ban would cause a serious problem for *kasais* and hide merchants and deprive a larger number of people of their staple food and source of cheap protein.

Thus the court held that whereas a total ban on the slaughter of cows and calves was reasonable, a total ban on the slaughter of female buffaloes, bulls, and male cows after they ceased to be productive could not be supported in the interest of the general public. Testing each act on this basis, they found that the Bihar Preservation and Improvement of Animals Act, insofar as it prohibited the slaughter of female buffaloes, bulls, and working bullocks (cattle and buffalo), infringed upon the fundamental rights of the petitioners and was therefore be invalid. The Uttar Pradesh and the Madhya Pradesh acts were held to be invalid insofar as they totally prohibited the slaughter of breeding bulls and working bullocks without prescribing any test or requirement of age or economic usefulness.

The New Bovine Order

The majority of the laws were upheld, and all the fundamental-rights claims were rejected. Thus the *Hanif Qureshi* decision was immediately viewed as a victory for the cow protection forces. A Canadian newspaper noted that "Indian rationalists suffered a severe setback from a decision from the Supreme Court to uphold the validity of a cow slaughter ban."[141] A Florida newpaper noted that the group of butchers, merchants, and cattle dealers lost their appeal and the court held that "the ban on cow slaughter preserves the nation's cattle health."[142] Later commentaries by politicians, lawyers, and social scientists continued to identify the Qureshis as the losers in the judgment.[143]

Yet even a cursory examination of the situation after the judgment shows a very different sort of regulatory order than the one imagined. For the cow slaughter bans to continue to stay valid, the states of Uttar Pradesh, Madhya Pradesh, and Bihar were required to amend their laws to introduce a test to determine economically useful livestock. In almost identical moves the state governments amended the laws to provide an exception for cattle over a certain age to be slaughtered only in concurrence with local government officials. The Bihar Preservation and Improvement of Animals (Amendment) Act of 1958 provided that cattle over twenty-five years old may be slaughtered. Rule 3 of the Bihar Preservation and Improvement of Animal Rules of 1960 required that a certificate designating an animal fit for slaughter could be granted only with the concurrence of the veterinary office and the chairman of the local government body—that is, both technical and political representation. The Uttar Pradesh Prevention of Cow Slaughter (Amendment) Act of 1958 provided that only cattle over twenty years old could be slaughtered, with a similar process of certification and the added precaution of a twenty-day gap between the issue of the certificate and the actual slaughter of the animal. It gave the right of appeal to any person who challenged the grant of the certificate. The Madhya Pradesh Agricultural Cattle Preservation Act of 1958 also required the animal to be at least twenty years of age and provided a ten-day appeal period after the grant of the certificate.[144]

In a well-orchestrated move, the Qureshis challenged all three amendments and were represented by the same set of lawyers as in the previous case.[145] Once again the Qureshis identified themselves as nationals and citizens of India and listed their professions in their petitions.[146] They pointed out that the various amendments in the pieces of legislations infringed on their fundamental rights and placed a total ban on the slaughter of female buffaloes, bulls, and bullocks even after they had ceased to be economically useful. It was pointed out, with reference to scientific authorities, that cattle seldom live beyond fifteen or sixteen years, and even breeding bulls cease to be productive after twelve years. The practical effect of allowing the animals to be slaughtered at twenty or twenty-five years old was that no animals could be slaughtered. The attendant regulations were arbitrary and restrictive because they prohibited or destroyed the petitioners' right to a trade or profession.

The respective state governments attempted to argue that cattle were living longer because of an improvement in feeding and management and a better control of diseases. The court agreed with the Qureshis that these were arbitrary exercises of power and violated the fundamental rights of the petitioners. The court held that the ban on the slaughter of cattle under the age of twenty was not a reasonable restriction in the interest of the general public, and its utility was offset by the cost of upkeep. The judges struck down the requirement that the cow had to be infirm as well as old. Finally, the judges found the rules of slaughter invalid because they imposed disproportionate restrictions on the rights of the petitioners, in effect putting a total ban on slaughter and the ability of an aggrieved party to appeal the ban.

In practice the state governments found the cow slaughter ban difficult to enforce. Cow slaughter went underground and occurred in unlicensed slaughterhouses. Furthermore, apprehended offenders were hard to convict. In a case from Uttar Pradesh, a Hindu police officer raided the house of a Muslim in Badaun and apprehended four men who were cutting up the carcass of a cow while others divided the large pieces into smaller ones.[147] Medical evidence established that the animal was killed recently and was a healthy cow. The

accused were convicted and sentenced to eighteen months of rigorous imprisonment by the local magistrate without any reason given for the sentence. On
appeal, the question of the severity of the sentence was raised before the high
court.

Reviewing this case, Justice Basil James of the Allahabad High Court noted
that the court was concerned about the punishment the lower courts had been
"thoughtlessly inflicting" on people found guilty of breaching the cow slaughter act. Justice James drew precedents from cases involving acts that breached
state objectives but were dealt with leniently, including convictions in cases of
black marketing, abusing police constables, picketing liquor shops, and producing illicit liquor.[148] Noticeably, all were clearly offenses against state legislation but were often expressions of a different morality, such as in the case of a
Gandhian protester picketing a liquor shop or nationalists abusing police constables working for the British. Since there was no evidence to suggest that the
accused were repeat offenders, the only question to be determined was
whether slaughtering a cow could be considered a heinous offense.

The court said it was aware that much of the community deified the cow
but that a close reading of the act showed that the objective was viewed exclusively as an economic proposition, ignoring the religious and sentimental
aspects of the subject. The court noted the act prohibited cow slaughter only,
not the possession or eating of beef. Similarly, while the sale of beef was prohibited, a gift of beef was not. Moreover, the court highlighted that the act was
a very recent piece of legislation and that beef remained the staple meat for
many of India's poor, thus making it unlikely that the act of cow slaughter was
one that involved moral turpitude. The judges noted approvingly that the ap-
plicants did not commit slaughter to hurt the religious feelings of their fellow
citizens (Hindus); they did not take the cow on a procession, slaughter it in
public, or expose its flesh and blood to public gaze. The killing was done dis-
creetly and for food. The court held that sentences for cow slaughter had to be
moderate, at the most a fine of fifty rupees (the price of a cow). It also acquitted the accused on the grounds that there was no evidence they had actually
killed the cow.

In 1961 the Allahabad High Court drew up a list of principles to limit the
discretion of the lower judiciary in mandating sentences in cow slaughter cases.
It held that the ban was enacted primarily to prevent a supply of milk, bullock
power, and cow dung to the economy. Thus the punishment should vary with
the economic value of the animal killed. The burden of proving that the animal
was an old one, however, lay upon the accused. The question of offending

religious sentiments of the Hindu community was not a relevant consideration unless there was a deliberate attempt to inflame communal passions.[149]

To dismiss the *Hanif Qureshi* judgment merely as a victory for Hindu majoritarianism would be shortsighted. It heralded a regime in which economically unprofitable cattle of various kinds could be slaughtered with state sanction. When older and useless cows were slaughtered in violation of the law, the courts were prepared to give moderate sentences. Unlike the litigation in colonial India, the litigation in postcolonial India did not center on the right to cow sacrifice. The need to kill cows was linked to livelihood. The cow was not just an important political symbol, it was also a commodity tied to a network of production, consumption, and retail. The Qureshis were able to provide evidence of the economic value of a dead cow, not just in terms of food but also of the other industries it supported. For instance, hide was used for leather goods, tallow for soap, bones for crockery, blood to make iron tablets, and entrails for making surgical thread.[150]

The litigation on cow protection also revealed the tensions between the different levels of government. Independence and the enactment of the Constitution created a new political geography. Nehru had attempted to defuse the political crisis of cow slaughter by referring it to the states, but the Qureshis chose to bring their challenges directly to Delhi to return the question to the national level. The Qureshis were a minority within a minority in independent India. They were a socially and educationally "backward" class of Muslims who were marginalized within mainstream political leadership.

After independence they were faced with a new moral regulatory regime that threatened to strangle their livelihood. Although they had some moral support from Nehru and the central government, they were faced with overwhelming opposition in both the state and local arenas. The Qureshis were based in north India, which had recently witnessed widespread communal violence during the partition and seen a mass exodus of Muslims. Consequently, they had limited ability to maneuver using public demonstrations or through electoral politics.

It was not surprising that their leadership called for restraint; faced with violent intimidation and moral opprobrium, they had few other options apart from going to court. Not only could they pool their resources and win a more comprehensive victory, they could also present themselves as a national community and not a local group. The question of caste was rendered invisible in the litigation before the Supreme Court. It was uncritically assumed that all Hindus venerated the cow, ignoring the practices of Hindus for whom beef was an ordinary part of the diet. In addition, caste was not recognized for Muslims, and the Qureshi self-presentation as a distinct community was ignored.

The Qureshis learned important lessons from their early experiences of litigating against municipal orders. They were able to make fundamental rights superior to directive principles of state policy, to bring the language of rights to the table, and to continually frame the question in terms of the limits of governmental power. They argued that municipal governments were not empowered by their legislations to impose prohibitions on cow slaughter and that state governments did not have the resources to provide fodder or run homes for economically unprofitable cows.

The cow protection lobby was aware of the shortcomings and continued to push for a national ban on cow slaughter and an absolute ban on cow slaughter in the states. The Qureshi judgment was printed in pamphlet form by the Gohatya Nirodh Samiti (Stop Cow Slaughter Committee) and circulated among cow protectionists, including the Congress Party. The judgment was not circulated appreciatively. Lala Hardev Sahai, the president of the committee, fulminated against both the Supreme Court and Western-educated animal experts for accepting only a partial ban. He attacked the idea that economically unproductive cows could be killed on two levels. First, he challenged the credentials of the animal husbandry experts who claimed that cows became unproductive after a particular age, pointing again to the benefits of dung. Second, he argued that to sell cattle that worked tirelessly "to fill our stomachs" to "any Musla" (a derogatory term for Muslims) was against Indian tradition and sense of obligation. Dubbing the partial ban a betrayal that would ensure that healthy cows continued to be killed, he appealed to those who cared about national interest to not rely on the Supreme Court decision but to lead an agitation.[151]

Since the nineteenth century, cow protectionists had been able to create a tremendous popular enthusiasm for a ban on cow slaughter and had generated a large variety of popular practices. However, the constitutional framework of developmentalism and secularism was a tighter constraint than people have imagined. The cow protection lobby had to perform rhetorical cartwheels to continually show why the cow was economically important. Finally, it was this economic argument that led them to lose the battle to secure an absolute ban on cow slaughter. In the course of time, twenty-three of twenty-eight Indian states achieved bans on cow slaughter, but the Qureshi judgment ensured that that despite the cow being sacralized in the Constitution, and cow slaughter being banned in 90 percent of Indian states, India continued to produce and consume more beef than chicken or mutton.[152]

In the 1960s the cow protectionists turned to unconstitutional means—violent demonstrations, coercion, and hunger strikes—but found they had limited traction. Their efforts then focused on litigation to change the judicial definition of the economic value of the cow, until the Supreme Court in 2005 interpreted the Qureshi judgment to allow for the possibility of an absolute ban. With this step we see the Qureshis engaging in more public action, taking to the streets and threatening a withdrawal of all meat products. As this episode proves, constitutional law is not removed from street politics but actually complements and restraints it.[153]

4

The Case of the Honest Prostitute

SEX, WORK, AND FREEDOM
IN THE INDIAN CONSTITUTION

THE ALLAHABAD HIGH COURT exercises jurisdiction over Uttar Pradesh, the largest state in India. Housed in an elegant nineteenth-century neo-Romanesque building, the court has always been a hive of activity. However, even frequent visitors would agree that on May 1, 1958, an unusually large crowd had gathered in the courtroom of Justice Jagdish Sahai. The crowd was drawn there by the rare presence of a young female petitioner in the over-whelmingly masculine courtroom.

Adding to the notoriety of the case, the petitioner, a twenty-four-year-old Muslim woman, Husna Bai, had openly stated that her profession was prostitution. Bai's writ petition, filed under Article 226 of the Constitution, challenged the validity of the recently enforced Suppression of Immoral Traffic in Women and Girls Act of 1956 (known simply as the Suppression of Immoral Traffic Act, or SITA). Husna Bai demanded that the new law, enacted to meet the constitutional promise to ban trafficking in human beings, be declared ultra vires because it violated her fundamental right to practice her profession as a prostitute, which was guaranteed to her under Article 19 of the Constitution. She argued that by striking at her means of livelihood, SITA "frustrated the purpose of the welfare state established by the Constitution in the country."[1]

Husna Bai's petition compelled attention throughout India quite out of proportion to the legal or practical significance of her case, despite the fact that her petition was dismissed within a month on technical grounds.[2] The case was covered extensively by newspapers in Delhi, Bombay, and Calcutta. The newly

formed Allahabad Dancing Girls Union came out in support of it, as did prostitutes' associations as far away as Calcutta. Most significantly, her petition
generated a series of anxious communications between bureaucrats and politicians in Delhi that left behind a voluminous paper trail.[3] The existence of extensive correspondence about a minor petition in a provincial high court is
very surprising, because even Supreme Court cases, which had a greater
effect on the government's fortunes, did not generate this volume of bureaucratic correspondence. Both the Ministry of Home Affairs and police
officials expressed their concern over the implications of such a petition, but
the strongest condemnation came from female parliamentarians and social
workers who had been leading the campaign for legislation against immoral
traffic.

These critics of Husna Bai's petition were particularly aghast at the invocation of constitutional principles by prostitutes, especially since this was followed by similar petitions by other prostitutes before the Delhi and Bombay
High Courts. The fundamental-rights implications of the fight against prostitution had been brought home to legislators a few years before. In September
1954, almost four years before the first petition, Durgabai Deshmukh, the chairwoman of the Central Social Welfare Board and one of India's first female
lawyers, had written to Prime Minister Nehru with some dismay about the
findings of a survey of "social and moral hygiene" in India, noting, "It was painful to social workers to hear an attempt made to invoke fundamental rights in
an argument to uphold the right to carry on prostitution or the business of
brothel keeping . . . the Constitution must be reworded and our notions of freedom undergo a change."[4]

As a member of the Constituent Assembly and as a campaigner against
prostitution for more than two decades, Deshmukh had been instrumental in
having prohibitions enacted on human trafficking and forced labor. An advocate for greater civil liberties, she had played an active role in drafting the
fundamental-rights clauses.[5] For Deshmukh and her colleagues, the Constitution represented an opportunity for women to take their place as equal citizens
in a free India. This would be achieved both through the institution of equal
fundamental rights and a constitutional commitment to social reform. Article
23 of the Constitution, which formally abolished trafficking in human beings,
was to these campaigners the symbol and instrument of their success.

Husna Bai's petition and the similar petitions that followed it were seen as
an attack on the progressive agenda of the new republic. It was unimaginable
to the authors of Article 23 that the very women whom the Constitutional

Assembly sought to free from the profession of prostitution would assert a fundamental right to ply it as their trade and continue a "life of degradation." It particularly astonished the commentators that poor Muslim prostitutes, a group believed to be exploited several times over, would not only choose to continue their vocation in light of the remarkable progress offered by the new Constitution but would also use the same constitutional system to accomplish their aim.[6]

This forgotten episode challenges the "commonplace knowledge" that the everyday practices of citizenship in India excluded prostitutes from the domain of civil society.[7] The extensive body of scholarship on prostitution in India has focused on the colonial period, dominated by (the often disproportionate) concerns about the health of British soldiers or the traffic in European prostitutes or by the reformist concerns of early nationalists and feminists.[8] What happens to the question of prostitution when questions of racial health or miscegenation become less important? What happens when nationalists and feminists control the state? These are questions that Husna Bai's petition will help answer.

What did it mean to be a woman in republican India? Scholars of citizenship have largely focused on two sets of state interventions: legislative reform in Hindu family law, and the state-led recovery of women abducted during the partition violence.[9] Both concern fixing the place of women in the patriarchal household. Bai's petition forces us to look at the women on the street.

Constituting Women in the New Republic

In 1950 the hundreds of thousands of Indians who flocked to the cinema every week were treated to a compulsory screening of a state-produced documentary before the start of any feature film.[10] These films, produced by the Films Division of India, were part of the state's pedagogic project to train its citizens. Moviegoers in early 1950 would have watched *Our Constitution*, which sought to explain to the "common man of India what the words of the constitution signified." The anglicized voice-over in the film outlined, with accompanying visuals, the new rights that the Constitution conferred upon citizens. However, moments after a shot of a policeman arresting a burglar (an illustration of the protection of life and liberty), the camera panned to a visual of an expensively dressed young woman, eyes downcast, leaning against a pillar (fig. 4.1) while the voice-over announced that the state had abolished trafficking in human beings.

FIG. 4.1. A scene from *Our Constitution*
(1950, Films Division of India).

The abolition of trafficking and the emancipation of prostitutes was central to the imagination of freedom under the new Constitution. This becomes evident in the film as the image of the prostitute is succeeded by images of a worker in a coal mine and a man being refused entrance to a temple—representing the other two categories of abolished forms of oppression: forced labor and untouchability. Freedom was to be achieved not merely through self-rule by Indians but also by ensuring freedom to specific unfree populations: prostitutes, untouchables, and bonded labor. Thus the Constitution was an emancipation edict for millions of its citizens.

Although questions of slavery (in the form of forced labor) had arisen during moments of constitution making in other countries, the inclusion of prostitutes as a category is fairly unique to the framing of the Indian Constitution.[11] Unlike the prohibition of alcohol, the abolition of untouchability, the abolition of cow slaughter, or the imposition of economic planning, the regulation of prostitution was not a central plank of the Congress Party's agenda. Yet Article 23 enshrined the ban on human trafficking as a fundamental right, whereas prohibition, cow slaughter, and planning were included only as directive principles of state policy. How did the prostitute make the journey into the heart of the Constitution?

To understand this, we need to recognize that the prostitute in India was entirely a creation of colonial law. Although both ancient Indian texts and medieval sources referred to a class of prostitutes, the term became invested with legal consequences under the colonial state. Through the nineteenth century, women—ranging from temple dancers, aristocratic concubines, courtesans, classical musicians, and dancers to widows, vagrant women, and sex workers found in the town bazaars—came to be categorized as prostitutes and were thus subject to state regulation and violence and marked as sources of immorality and disease.[12] For both the colonial state and the new Indian elite, sexuality could be accepted only within a heterosexual household. For the colonial state, the prostitute became the focus of concerns about venereal disease and racial mixing, whereas for Indian nationalists she appeared as a threat to a national culture based on the ideal of middle-class domesticity.

The nineteenth and early twentieth centuries witnessed three phases of legal engagement with prostitution: regulationist (late nineteenth century), antitrafficking (early twentieth century) and abolitionist (1920s and 1930s).[13] In the regulationist phase, laws were enacted on the basis of concern over the spread of venereal disease among soldiers, and the goal was to closely monitor brothels and supervise military prostitutes. In the antitrafficking phase, the state was driven by internationalist anxieties of white slavery and miscegenation and therefore focused on the presence of European prostitutes in the colony. The abolitionist phase was a product of the growing influence of Indian reformers and nationalists who saw prostitution as a threat to respectable public morals. Common to all three phases was a concern with the effect of prostitution on the public, and not with the prostitute herself.

What changed in the Constituent Assembly? Prostitution became a constitutional issue because of the significant presence of female members in the assembly (fig. 4.2), many of whom had more than two decades of experience in organizing.[14] Well before the proceedings of the Constituent Assembly began, its female members seized the initiative to present a comprehensive plan for women in the Indian republic. In December 1945 All India Women's Conference (AIWC) President Hansa Mehta reminded the members that for Indian women, postwar reconstruction was a question not just of mere adjustments here and there but of the reconstruction of "our entire national life."[15] Members were instructed to collect the relevant clauses dealing with women's rights from various constitutions.[16]

In 1946 the AIWC adopted the Charter of Rights of and Duties for Indian Women and forwarded it to the central and provincial governments, strongly urging that the fundamental-rights and economic and social directives embodied in it form "an integral part of the Constitution."[17] The AWIC charter argued for complete civil and political equality, sought to expand the welfare

FIG. 4.2. Female members of the Constituent Assembly. Hansa Mehta, the president of the All India Women's Conference, is seated second from left. Courtesy of Meera Velayudhan.

functions of the state, and promoted the economic rights of women. It recognized that in order to achieve these goals, a total mobilization of the nation's human and material resources was necessary, which could be achieved only through a network of specialized social service ministries. These ministries would be required to mobilize all available human resources to supplement the existing health, education, and welfare services, and to this end they would train teachers, doctors, nurses, and social workers.[18]

Thus, in the vision of the AIWC, state instrumentalities would be harnessed for the purpose of social welfare to ensure the Indian woman's rightful place in society. Conversely, social welfare would also be cast as a special responsibility of women. Purnima Banerjee complained of the replacement of female members of the Constituent Assembly, on their death or resignation, by men; she pointed out that "since the entire basis of the state has changed and it is no longer a police state, certain social functions such as education and health now feature among the major items of the state's development, which made the association of women in the field of politics indispensable."[19]

Freedom thus held a distinct meaning for the women in the Constituent Assembly. Freedom, in their view, would not only mean formal equality between men and women but would also include the active duty of the state to intervene to bring about substantive equality. Article 15 of the Constitution, which prohibited discrimination on the grounds of sex, race, caste, religion, or place of birth, stipulated that this would not restrain the state from making special provisions for women and children. Action in the area protected by this proviso would require the creation of a welfare-state apparatus directed toward the needs of women. It was natural in these circumstances that the state would feel impelled to intervene significantly to emancipate prostitutes. A prominent leader of a nationalist women's organization stated, "Democratic India, which upholds the highest spiritual and moral values and looks at its women as the symbol of purity and unselfish love, cannot go on tolerating a segment of its daughters being exploited and degraded through prostitution." The goal of women's organizations after independence was to "end such exploitation and to restore to the victims of such exploitation an honorable place as useful citizens with dignity and self-confidence as the women and workers of a free India."[20]

The regulation of prostitution and the prevention of trafficking were pressing concerns for the female members of the Constituent Assembly and formed a significant part of their agenda. Article 6 of the AIWC charter had highlighted the role of women in maintaining moral standards. It had also noted with concern that poor social conditions and economic distress had led to helpless and destitute women being enticed into immoral activities, and it emphasized the need for laws to prevent trafficking. The AIWC demanded an equal moral standard for men and women and suggested that the roles of men in prostitution (as buyers and sellers) also be criminalized. Moreover, they wanted rescue homes to be established for the women, which would be closely supervised by a government agency.[21] This new approach to prostitution was dominated by the question, How did women become prostitutes? Studies were commissioned by women's organizations that focused on poverty, oppression within existing family systems, and disruption caused by the violence of partition as the leading causes.[22] Thus, the major focus of women's organizations—reform of family law, provision of economic opportunities, and the recovery and rehabilitation of abducted women—were all framed by the concern with prostitution. Prostitution was seen as a product of external circumstances and not as a choice that someone excerising agency would ever make.

As briefly discussed at the beginning of this chapter, the Constituent Assembly addressed the problem of prostitution through Article 23, which prohibited trafficking in human beings and *begar* (forced labor). Even though all the members of the assembly agreed that prostitution was a "social evil," "a heinous practice," and degrading to women, some were wary about including it in the constitutional domain. T. T. Krishnamachari, the finance minister, cautioned against social reform questions being "imported into fundamental rights."[23] In the eyes of this segment of the assembly, prostitution in particular was a practice that would gradually disappear through legislation over the course of time, whereas incorporating it permanently into the Constitution would put "a blot on the fair name of India." Several members rose to counter Krishnamachari, and Bishwanath Das asked the assembly not to be "prudish" and to "admit that there existed a traffic in women for which men are responsible." The members of the assembly made it clear that prostitution had no place in the new republic.[24] Although the inclusion of the provision was relatively uncontroversial, it would take another six years before the women's lobby would convince the central government to enact a law enforcing it.

How do we read the incorporation of Article 23 into the Constitution, especially given that it came into operation only with the enactment of SITA in 1956 and that it was clearly unsuccessful in eradicating trafficking and emancipating prostitutes? The suppression of prostitution in postcolonial India was framed in terms of granting freedom to female citizens. But as Gyan Prakash reminds us, freedom is never an innate human condition, only created through a range of historical practices. The common prostitute, like the bonded laborer of Prakash's study, emerged in the nineteenth century through the reconstitution of a variety of women who fell outside the heterosexual family.[25] In his work on the emancipation of Japanese prostitutes, Daniel Botsman has persuasively argued that freedom should be understood as "an idea that has in modern times been used to reorder social relationships and constitute new frameworks for their management."[26] In making this argument, Botsman builds on the idea of freedom as an integral part of the "reorganizing project of modern power."[27] The inclusion of Article 23 in the Constitution may be understood as facilitating the democratic state's regulation of the sexuality of marginal women, the reimagining of prostitution as an economic problem central to the nation's development, the replacement of the discourse of penalization with that of rehabilitation, and the legitimization of the role of welfare agencies and female social workers in the process.

The Birth of SITA: The Making of a Postcolonial Prostitution Law

The Suppression of Immoral Traffic Act, which Husna Bai challenged, was enacted in 1956 but came into force only in 1958, several years after the commitment to end trafficking had been enshrined in the Constitution as a fundamental right. Unlike in the case of cow slaughter, in which the lack of governmental enthusiasm arose from Nehru's commitment to secularism and political compulsions, the delay in acting on Article 23 reflected the political uninterest of the central government. Prevention of cow slaughter was only a directive principle of state policy, but abolition of trafficking was in the fundamental rights section, and the Constitution gave the central government power to enforce Article 23 with legislation.[28] The traditional narrative of SITA states that it was enacted to meet India's international legal obligations under the New York convention for the suppression of immoral traffic.[29] SITA was actually the product of sustained lobbying by women's organizations and female politicians and reflected new conceptions of the state and social welfare.[30] Leading figures of the Indian women's movement were able to forge new alliances and utilize existing networks to place the issue on the national agenda.

As a member of the Planning Commission, Durgabai Deshmukh designated funds for setting up the Central Social Welfare Board, which funded women's groups and commissioned a national survey on social and moral hygiene that became the basis for SITA.[31] This survey was carried out by the Association for Social and Moral Hygiene (ASMH), a leading abolitionist organization in London that had emerged in 1914 from British abolitionist efforts to repeal the Contagious Diseases Act.[32] Led in India by Meliscent Shepherd, an Englishwoman, the ASMH achieved some success, beginning in 1928, in closing down military and public brothels.[33] It focused on generating pressure from London on the colonial administration and building better linkages with colonial officers—thus it was viewed with suspicion by nationalist organizations.

However, the ASMH completely transformed after independence, when it was led by Rameshwari Nehru, a prominent Gandhian social worker and legislator who was also the prime minister's aunt.[34] The postcolonial ASMH began an active membership drive and established a presence in all states and in more than 140 districts. Institutionally, it moved from being funded from London to being supported by the government through the Planning Commission. The promotion of welfare services was no longer the sole concern of unregulated private philanthropy but was a chief concern of the welfare state.[35] The second five-year plan addressed the abolition of prostitution as a question of national economic importance. Frustrated by the government's reluctance to enact a national law to enforce the constitutional provisions, the ASMH reached out to female members of parliament and formed a cross-party caucus comprising Congress Party and Communist Party members. They introduced private bills in both houses of parliament, castigated the government for its failure to legislate, and made frequent visits to the prime minister and the home minister, leading to SITA being enacted in 1956.[36]

Why did the suppression of trafficking require a national law? The key was uniformity. Surveying the range of existing provincial legislations, the ASMH expressed concern that the individual freedom of movement guaranteed in the Constitution complicated the state's plans, and the mobility of people across jurisdictions rendered the province powerless to deal with problems like trafficking.[37] Moreover, although several of the provinces had some form of legislation against trafficking, these laws were rarely implemented or enforced.[38]

The activists advised the government that while the law must be harsh on prostitution, "it must show a concern—nay, a tenderness—to the prostitute."[39] Rather than targeting women, the law should aim at closing the entrances to prostitution and opening several exits from it. A special committee of the ASMH noted that in the course of its survey, many people expressed the belief that prostitution could not be legislated against because the Constitution of India recognized the fundamental right of a person to practice any profession. However, the ASMH committee argued that by destroying the machinery that sustained prostitution— the network of procurers, pimps, and brothel keepers; rent laws; and the regulation of public spaces—prostitution could be eradicated.

The committee was critical of fines and imprisonment as punishments, but this disagreement with the existing penalties was not motivated by any notion of the prostitute's rights. Their report argued that detention for women in shelters would be more effective in helping them than a short term in prison would be (after which they would just return to their old lives). In their report the ASMH accordingly recommended that the courts should deny bail in most circumstances, on the assumption that the people bailing out the woman were likely to be their pimps or others involved in the sex trade. They proposed a new criminal system that would place the burden of proof on the accused and that would provide for a speedy trial on camera. According to the report, this modified legal process would be more humane to the woman arrested and ensure her cooperation with the police, enabling them to capture the others involved in the case. Detention in a shelter would be compulsory for a woman found guilty, and only hardened cases that were likely to be considered an evil influence would be given a prison sentence.

The ASMH committee's approach to legislation differed from the existing laws addressing prostitution in two significant ways: it placed equal emphasis on rescue and rehabilitation, and it demanded that the state create a special bureaucracy that would be staffed by specialists and female social workers to deal with the problem.

The goal of feminizing the state set apart the ASMH and its associates from their contemporaries in the West. In her study of American reformers dealing with "fallen women," Regina Kuenzel argues that the professionalization of social work involved the "masculinization" of an older ethic of female values. American social workers in the 1920s and 1930s sought to encourage a greater male presence in positions of authority dealing with unmarried women, so they specifically invited male speakers to conferences and appointed male advisors to shelters to reduce the female influence in the program.[40] The Indian reformers, in contrast, were suspicious of male functionaries and campaigned for a greater deployment of women at every level of administration, from the police to the judiciary. The emphasis here was not on feminine qualities but on representation: the belief that women would better represent women and understand women's needs. With independence, women's activists had moved from being advocates of reform to actually implementing it.

Unlike the existing provincial antitrafficking acts that were concerned with the regulation of proscribed acts and the punishment of offenses, SITA provided an elaborate government program for the rescue and rehabilitation of prostitutes, attempted to set up safeguards against police excesses, and laid the basis for a bureaucracy of social welfare staffed by women. SITA had three broad sections, dealing with restrictive and punitive measures, executive and procedural questions, and reform and rehabilitation. SITA did not seek to ban the practice of prostitution by an individual woman, but it sought to suppress activities connected with prostitution, particularly brothel keeping, pimping, and kidnapping. The first set of penal provisions made it an offense to maintain a brothel or to live off a woman's earnings from prostitution, and the second set prohibited the kidnapping and detention of women or inducing a woman to take up prostitution.

Though not prohibiting prostitution outright, SITA made it a criminal offense to practice prostitution within two hundred yards of a place of religious worship, an educational institution, a hotel, a hospital, a nursing home, or any other area determined by the police or a magistrate.[41] It also criminalized public soliciting for sex, defined as a person in a public place or within sight of a public place, through the use of words, gesture, or "willful exposure of her person."[42]

The procedural sections of SITA authorized the court to detain a person convicted under this statute in a shelter for a period of two to five years.[43] The courts did not have the discretion to release such an offender on probation. SITA empowered magistrates to evict women from their homes if they violated the two-hundred-yard rule, and it granted the magistrate wide powers to expel from his district any woman whom the magistrate considered a danger to public morals.

The ASMH was convinced that the problem of prostitution could not be addressed through routine police administration, and it successfully lobbied for the appointment of a special police officer by the state government. This officer would be assisted by policewomen and a nonofficial advisory body comprising leading social welfare workers, preferably women. The special officer would have the power to arrest without a warrant. He could also search the premises without a warrant if he suspected the site was being used for an offense. However, he had to be accompanied by two respectable witnesses, at least one of whom was a woman.

Finally, SITA provided that the state would establish shelters under the statute. It also provided that no other authority, including charitable organizations, could maintain such a shelter unless licensed for the purpose by the state. SITA was accompanied by the Women and Children's Institutions (Licensing) Act of 1956, drafted by ASMH member Seeta Parmanand, which laid down extensive guidelines for the state licensing of private institutions. It was the rehabilitative approach that really set the 1956 SITA apart from its provincial predecessors.

A Representative Prostitute: Husna Bai and Subaltern Legal Mobilization

SITA finally took effect on May 1, 1958. Husna Bai petitioned the Allahabad High Court on the same day. Her petition was unusual both in its timing and in the fact that SITA had not yet been applied against her. Previous challenges by prostitutes to the legality of antitrafficking laws and municipal regulations had been made only after the issue had been forced on them—that is, they had been arrested or had found themselves evicted from their homes.[44] Therefore, their encounter with the courts was the result of an initial intervention by the police or the municipal government.

Husna Bai's petition was a radical departure from this pattern. It reveals her awareness of the implications of the legislation well before it had come into force, and Husna Bai had the resources and strategy to attempt to counter it.

Her petition, in view of the surrounding circumstances, is similar to Fram Nusserwanji Balsara's petition in the case of Prohibition, even though hers was not described as a test case. Rather, it was an individual petition filed to challenge a law on behalf of a larger group.

The press gave wide coverage to the enactment of SITA and the debates leading up to it. The police and social workers, the two groups that prostitutes would come into contact with, had been involved in drafting the law. The ASMH survey had interviewed a number of prostitutes about the conditions of their profession and found that SITA had created fear in the minds of prostitutes. Mary, a prostitute interviewed in 1965, recalled that she left Delhi for Agra in 1958, where she had plied her trade on GB Road, because she was terribly worried about the police raids that were expected with the enforcement of SITA.[45] Prostitutes, particularly in Uttar Pradesh, faced a harder time in the 1950s under Congress Party rule. Prostitutes interviewed in the city of Kanpur reported that the number of their customers had declined after the departure of American troops, the abolition of the zamindari (the landed aristocracy whose property was redistributed as part of land reform), and the emigration of many rich patrons at partition.[46] SITA was the last straw.

Clearly, those involved in the sex trade were aware of the implications of SITA. Funds were collected from customers and local merchants on GB Road and at the Kath Bazaar in order to fight the statute in the courts.[47] The day before SITA came into effect, seventy-five women claiming to be members of the Professional Singers and Dancers Association staged a silent demonstration outside parliament. They spent the day on the grounds near its northern gates and presented a memorandum stating that the suppression of their profession would lead to its spread to respectable areas.[48]

Meanwhile, on the day that Husna Bai filed her petition in Allahabad, about 450 singers, dancing girls, and women of "ill fame" in the city formed a union to fight SITA. The Allahabad Dancing Girls Union announced that it would hold demonstrations in protest of the enforcement of the law and would take legal steps for its nullification because "it was a clear encroachment on the right to carry on any profession guaranteed by the Constitution."[49] Simultaneously, a group of prostitutes in Calcutta's red-light district threatened to go on a hunger strike if the government did not provide them with an alternative means of livelihood. Brojobala Dassi, a representative of the Calcutta organization, convened a press conference and noted that the law would reduce thirteen thousand prostitutes to penury.[50]

Within a week of Husna Bai filing her petition, Mahroo and Ram Pyari, two prostitutes from Delhi, filed a petition almost identical to Husna Bai's before the Punjab High Court. The Delhi petition challenged SITA for violating the rights guaranteed under Articles 14 and 19 of the Constitution, and it applied for an interim stay against the state and against eviction of the petitioners by their landlords.[51] The government was clearly expecting such a challenge. The Ministry of Home Affairs, which had authored SITA, noted about Bai's petition that "*as was expected*, a prostitute of Allahabad filed a writ petition before the High Court challenging the validity of SITA."[52]

The circumstances thus suggest that Husna Bai's petition was not an isolated individual act but part of a concerted set of actions by groups of prostitutes in north India to resist SITA. The scale of these activities led to an editorial decrying "demonstrations, moves to form trade unions, and threats of civil disobedience that have accompanied the promulgation of SITA."[53]

How do we read Husna Bai's petition? Looking closely, it becomes clear that this is not an individual heroic act of resistance but rather one part of a collective action by a loosely organized group engaged in the sex trade throughout India. It is clear that this new law added to the pressures that those engaged in the sex trade were already facing and threatened to upset long-standing practices. However, to understand the really radical nature of the challenge posed by Husna Bai's petition, it is useful to examine what other alternatives existed for prostitutes to deal with an intrusive state.

Living with Regulations:
Alternatives to Constitutional Litigation

Prostitutes had learned to live with repressive legislation before SITA. There were several methods they used, often simultaneously; these included practices that evaded the law altogether, like bribing policemen and escaping physical surveillance, as well as practices that sought to engage with the legal system, like petitioning through political networks and evading legal categorization. That antiprostitution laws generate economies of corruption is well documented.[54] Before the enactment of SITA, prostitutes in India bought protection from policemen and state officials by paying bribes in cash or in kind. Evidence of this practice dates back to the nineteenth century, when the

Indian Contagious Diseases Act was passed in 1868. Prostitutes are known to have paid bribes to evade the medical examination mandated by this statute.[55]

Evasion of the existing laws through bribery was a practice that continued well after independence. A 1962 social science study of the red-light district of Bombay noted that a majority of prostitutes described their relations with the police as very good, in large part because of cash bribes. The amount paid as a weekly bribe, or *hafta*, varied between two and five rupees a week and was often in return for concessions by the police. As a result of purchasing official favor with money, only 22 of the 350 women interviewed had been arrested, and in a remarkably candid admission, the only respondent who had had multiple arrests stated that this was because she had persistently refused to bribe a local policeman. Economic efficiency supported a culture of bribery, given that prostitutes could be fined amounts up to ten rupees or imprisoned upon arrest.[56]

The enactment of colonial antiprostitution laws and increased surveillance after various episodes of moral panic led to several prostitutes trying to evade the gaze of the state. The recorded number of prostitutes dropped with the enactment of repressive legislation like the Indian Contagious Diseases Act and increased upon its repeal.[57] While such legislation was in effect, women were less willing to identify themselves as prostitutes and went into hiding to avoid the attention of the state. A report by the deputy registrar general of the census of India in 1953 noted that the number of prostitutes fell from fifty-four thousand in 1931 to twenty-eight thousand in 1951. He added a word of caution that the census recorded as prostitutes only the women who practiced this profession openly; it did not account for the larger number of "clandestine" prostitutes. He opined that several women who stated their profession as dancing, and were accordingly classified as dancers, were actually prostitutes.[58]

Other women evaded the coercive apparatus of the state by physically removing themselves from its attention. The state's toleration of red-light districts meant that such areas and their occupants were well-known to the police. In cities like Bombay and Calcutta, the police were able to maintain extensive registers of prostitutes that documented fairly intimate details, such as age, address, and history of venereal disease. Stricter antiprostitution laws and moral panic led to periods of more intrusive policing, causing several women to move out of the red-light districts and away from police information networks.

The authors of SITA were dismayed by these unintended consequences. re-doubtable Rameshwari Nehru, the president of the ASMH and the moving force behind SITA, wrote to the home minister six months after the implementation of SITA noting that the new legislation had "put fright into the heart of prostitutes" and that by clearing the red-light district of Delhi, like GB Road and Kath Bazaar, had served "some useful purpose."[59] However, the frequent prosecutions under SITA only made prostitutes leave their homes in panic to seek shelter in other parts of the city. Ironically, as long as the women lived in the red-light district, which was known to the police, they could be prosecuted and punished for solicitation, but once they had spread throughout the city it was difficult for the police to trace them. Rameshwari Nehru noted with some alarm that since they had no other means of subsistence and knew no other trade, they were bound to stick to their old profession and would "exert themselves all the more" to attract new customers. This complaint was echoed by the law minister, Ashoke Sen, who noted the complaints by residents of respectable localities in Calcutta that prostitutes were moving into their neighborhoods after the implementation of SITA, thus frustrating the very aims of the act and bringing residential neighborhoods into disrepute.[60]

Writer Ghulam Abbas foresaw that prostitution would not only evade regulation but also have generative powers. In his short story, prostitutes who were expelled by the municipal board move to an area far from town; however, the traffic of customers led to shopkeepers, restaurant owners, musicians, and popular religious figures moving to the region. As a result, brothels formed the heart of a new township.

Prostitutes achieved limited success in making direct appeals to the government; however, these were framed as demands for benevolence or exemption rather than as assertions of rights. In the nineteenth and early twentieth centuries, these demands were mostly in the form of petitions by individual prostitutes to government authorities asking for an exception to be made in their favor on the grounds of hardship.[61] Ironically, since colonial franchise was granted according to tax and property qualifications, prostitutes were one of the few groups of women who could vote. Residing in segregated neighborhoods in some cities, like Lucknow, they emerged as an influential political constituency and were able to access certain political channels. However, these channels began to narrow with the Gandhian phase of the national movement, which emphasized the need to recruit respectable women to the struggle and urged them to maintain modesty and decorum.[62]

Reclassification as Resistance

Whereas some prostitutes tried to minimize their physical presence and be invisible to the state, others contested the logic of enforcement and attempted to become irrelevant to the state by denying that they fit the definition of a prostitute. In the nineteenth century, prostitutes in Bombay sought to evade registration by the state by claiming to be married.[63] More than four hundred women engaged in prostitution got married within days of the Indian Contagious Diseases Act being enforced in Bombay. Similarly, when the Delhi municipality began evicting prostitutes from the red-light district in the 1920s, several women claimed that even though they did exchange sexual favors for money, they were not public prostitutes as defined by the statute.[64] The key term here was *public* (or *common*) prostitute.

These claims of existing and making a living outside the law's definition of prostitution reached the civil courts and enjoyed mixed success there. The Lahore High Court ruled that women could earn a living by selling their bodies and would be exempt from the antiprostitution law unless it was proved that they were public prostitutes—that is, they were "available at any time to the public at large."[65] Six women residing in Delhi had contested a notice of the municipality that sought to evict them for being public prostitutes. They lost their case before the district judge but found the high court more amenable to their reading of the facts. A woman named Mussamat Bandi Jan, for instance, was living with a man named Chandu Lal as his mistress and was being paid 220 rupees a month for her maintenance. The court found that the fact that she remained content with one man for several years suggested that she did not fall within the definition of a public prostitute, which would imply that she was renting her body out to all visitors. Even though it was proved that she had lived with different lovers, it was clear that she was with only one man at a time. The court held that she was a prostitute but said it was doubtful whether she could be called a public prostitute.

The category of dancers created a certain ambiguity for the law, arising from the difficulties caused by transplanting the European idea of a prostitute to colonial India. As a result, most women who were outside the patriarchal household were labeled prostitutes. These included courtesans, *nautch* (dancers), and temple dancers, all of whom played important social roles in performing and maintaining artistic traditions but also engaged in select sexual relations with patrons.[66] Dancers were a difficult category for Indian nationalists. To nationalists and reformers these women represented the decadent old order that had to be cleansed from modern India, but singing and dancing as occupations came to enjoy a new respectability. Indian music and dance were cast as part of the nationalist project, with the discovery of "classical" traditions, and posed a challenge to the West's claim to cultural superiority.[67] Several women from courtesan backgrounds, such as Gauhar Jaan and Madurai S. Subbulakshmi, emerged as national cultural figures.[68]

In independent India, classical traditions of music and dance were cast as integral elements of national culture. The decision made by the prostitutes of Allahabad to name their union the Dancing Girls Union in the aftermath of SITA in the 1950s was a strategic one. For decades the courts had been holding that the profession of singer or dancer does not necessarily connote the business of prostitution.[69] The case of *Parbatti Dassi v. King Emperor* was prominently featured in the commentaries and legal guides on the Bombay Prevention of Prostitution Act of 1923, the Bengal Suppression of Immoral Traffic Act of 1923, and finally SITA. Thus, a lawyer advising a client facing prosecution under any of these laws would turn to the textbook and find the *Parbatti Dassi* decision prominently featured.[70]

However, recognition as a dancer, distinct from a prostitute, depended entirely on the worldview of the judge in question. The decision of the Allahabad High Court in *Municipal Board, Etah v. Asghari Jaan and Mt. Bismillah* was cited as a strong precedent that a woman who was a professional musician or dancer, yet engaged in sexual intimacy in exchange for favors with one or two men, could not be presumed to be a public prostitute.[71]

Yet a closer look at the *Asghari Jaan* case reveals the evidentiary perils a woman had to negotiate if she tried to argue that she was a dancer and not a prostitute. In December 1927 Asghari Jaan, a fifteen-year-old who identified herself as "belonging to the prostitute caste," was served with a notice from the newly elected municipal board of Etah, directing her to cease practicing her occupation as a prostitute at her place of residence or face legal action. The notice stated that she was in violation of the municipal bylaw that prohibited prostitutes from carrying on their occupation in houses near major roads. This information had been proclaimed to the public with the beat of a drum.[72]

Asghari Jaan (with her mother) argued that the bylaw was not applicable to her, since she was a singer and a dancer and not a public prostitute. At the initiation of her suit, Asghari Jaan claimed that she was a virgin and produced several witnesses who had approached her mother to purchase her sexual favors but had been refused. Her statement was challenged by witnesses produced by the municipal board, who stated in their depositions that they "were

on terms of intimacy with the plaintiff and had sexual connection with her."
Asghari Jaan refused to submit to a medical examination of her hymen by a
female doctor on the grounds that during the litigation she had lost her virgin-
ity to a patron whose mistress she had become. The case went through three
levels of trial and appeal, and each court arrived at a different determination
of Asghari Jaan's occupation.[73]

The lowest court noted that Asghari Jaan had identified herself as belonging
to a caste of prostitutes. Asghari Jaan's mother had admitted to being a public
prostitute in the past, and most of Asghari Jaan's aunts also carried on the
profession. The court noted that in India, prostitutes who habitually allowed
"the use of their person for sexual intercourse in lieu of hire" also cultivated
the arts of singing and dancing "for gain and as an additional attraction." Just
because some of the women earned more from music and dancing, the district
court ruled, this did not place them in a different category from public
prostitutes.

On appeal, the court found that the case hinged on whether Jaan's chief
business was public prostitution or singing and dancing. The municipality
acknowledged that Asghari Jaan could sing and dance but argued that it was
not her chief profession, whereas her lawyer argued that she practiced an art.
In order to determine this, the court bizarrely sought to appoint an expert,
paid for by Asghari Jaan, who would watch her perform and then give evidence
in court. A. A. Jilani, a local lawyer, volunteered as the expert and organized a
performance of music by Asghari Jaan. She had to perform for four hours, till
1:30 a.m., before an audience of the "best educated singers in the city," who
would hear her singing and assist Jilani as evaluators. Jilani deposed in court
that Asghari Jaan was a tolerably fair singer, that she was clearly trained in the
arts, and that he could identify seven special characteristics of her performance.
He added that a girl who is habituated to promiscuous sex as a public prostitute could not possibly "possess a melodious and sustained voice" like Asghari
Jaan's.[74]

Jilani's claims to expertise were dubious. He stated that even though he
wasn't trained in music himself, he had been watching performances by dancers for twelve years. He had also been appointed by the municipal board of
Aligarh to survey the houses of prostitutes to assess their value. His claim was
that this made him familiar with the lifestyles of several public prostitutes, who
rarely had arrangments for professional singing. The high court was horrified
that the powers provided by the Civil Procedure Code for the establishment
of a commission to examine accounts or to hold a local examination had been

used to direct a man to listen to a woman sing and then not only report on her skill as a singer but also deduce her occupation from her musical talent.

The Allahabad High Court attempted to disregard Jilani's evidence and drew instead on the common understanding of a public prostitute. According to the high court, a public prostitute was "a woman who usually and generally offers her person to sexual intercourse for hire and who openly advertises and acknowledges her occupation by word of mouth, deportment, or conduct." The court noted that such a woman usually exhibited herself on a balcony or on the street to attract people. The high court ruled that it would need evidence of a great degree of moral degradation before a woman could be evicted from her house, where her family might live or in which she might have invested her money. It even took account of Asghari Jaan's patron and noted that an exclusive patron suggested that the intimacy might assume the form of a "more lasting alliance." Thus, there was no presumption that she was a public prostitute.[75]

Asghari Jaan's case underscores that even though it was possible to escape being hit by the laws targeting public prostitutes, the escape route was available only to women with certain resources. Civil litigation remained a lengthy and expensive process and had significant barriers to access. The Delhi litigation took five years, and the decision in *Asghari Jaan* took four years. Only comparatively affluent women could sustain such litigation.

The maneuver of taking to the courts to contest categorization as a prostitute was often successful. However this strategy was based on an implicit *class differentiation* of prostitutes. For a woman to escape regulations targeting public prostitutes, she would have to demonstrate that she was sexually exclusive or attached to a single man as a mistress or a "kept woman" at the relevant time. The courts privileged a certain kind of sexual commerce over others, reflecting a need to prevent the urban government from interfering with the sexual lives of upper-class men, who were the patrons of the more exclusive prostitutes.

As the high court decision in Asghari Jaan's case demonstrates, the court was reluctant to interfere with individual property rights, including the right to a home in which a woman might have invested her fortune, unless the municipality could show some extreme level of moral degradation. These categorizations allowed only wealthier prostitutes and those who belonged to established prostitute clans to evade the regulations. The pattern of the courts' interpretations of the law reinforced hierarchies and allowed the rights of one set of female sexual laborers to be won at the expense of another, while also protecting the male desire for sexual entertainment.[76]

The Prostitute as a Citizen: Disrupting Older Narratives

Many of the older methods of negotiation might have been available to Husna Bai or her lawyers, but she chose to radically break with them. Prostitutes had usually dealt with repressive laws by evading the state's gaze; Husna Bai, in contrast, put herself firmly in the state's line of sight. The act of filing a writ petition was an extremely public one, which is evident from the extensive coverage of Husna Bai's petition in the national media. Husna Bai (with her cousin, Shama Bai) named five respondents before the Allahabad High Court: the central government, the state government of Uttar Pradesh, the district magistrate of Allahabad, and Husna Bai's landlords, two private individuals. The court proceedings therefore alerted the Ministry of Home Affairs in Delhi, the state government under whose authority the police operated, and Husna Bai's local municipality.

In addition to being publicly defiant, Husna Bai departed from the prevalent strategies of her peers by taking advantage of the constitutional discourse, which allowed her to challenge the very fundamentals of the law. The previous history of litigation focused on women who argued that the categories criminalized by the state did not apply to them as individuals, whereas Husna Bai's petition sought to contest the categories themselves. Husna Bai claimed her right to a trade and a profession, guaranteed to her under the Constitution, by stating that prostitution was her hereditary trade and her only means of livelihood. She claimed freedom for her entire class rather than asking for an individual exemption from the law.

Husna Bai's open declaration of her profession was no accident and was backed by sound legal advice. The courts had made it impossible for women who tried to evade being classified as prostitutes to challenge the constitutionality of antiprostitution laws. In 1956 several women living in Agra were served notices of eviction by the municipal board under a bylaw that sought to keep public prostitutes out of certain neighborhoods, and then they faced criminal proceedings for not complying. In the criminal case the women contended that they were singers and not public prostitutes, and their lawyer simultaneously filed a writ petition before the Allahabad High Court under Article 226 challenging the constitutionality of the bylaw on the grounds that it infringed his clients' rights to freedom of trade and profession. The Allahabad High Court dismissed the petition on the grounds that if the women stated they were not public prostitutes, then they had no standing to challenge the bylaw in court. That is, you couldn't deny being a prostitute in a criminal case but then challenge the constitutionality of legislation for infringing on your right to be a prostitute.[77] Thus, for Husna Bai to challenge the antiprostitution law, she had to declare herself a prostitute.

Furthermore, contrary to the official discourse of prostitution as unproductive labor, Husna Bai presented herself as a laboring citizen claiming economic rights. She represented herself as the breadwinner in her household: her female cousin and two younger brothers were wholly dependent on her earnings. Acknowledging that she had no other source of livelihood than prostitution and was unlikely to have marriage prospects, she contended that SITA would render both her and her family destitute and therefore defeat the goal of the welfare state laid out in the Constitution. She pointed out that it was the law that rendered her an unproductive citizen and a burden on the state, and she challenged the state's narrative of prostitution as unproductive employment.[78]

Husna Bai's self-representation as a prostitute challenged the presumptions that framed the debates over prostitution, especially the argument that the prostitute was a victim coerced by men or economic circumstances.[79] We should exercise caution in reading her petition as a representation of her reality; nevertheless, it was a powerful discursive act, forcing the state to deal with the apparently willing sex worker. It was possibly the first such articulation in the Indian public sphere, predating the radical feminist position by several decades.

Finally, the writ petition Husna Bai filed required a minimal, fixed court fee, unlike the expenses that would have been incurred in a civil suit. Husna Bai's petition was heard directly by the Allahabad High Court and disposed of within two weeks, unlike a civil suit, which took an average of five to six years. In contrast, the writ petitions by prostitutes, even ones that went through several stages of appeals to the Supreme Court, were disposed of within a year at most.[80] The potential effectiveness of the remedy and the availability of multiple forums in which to pursue it caused a degree of panic within the bureaucracy and social organizations.

Husna Bai's lawyers made a two-pronged claim. First, they argued that various sections of SITA were an unreasonable restriction of her right to practice a trade and a profession. Second, they targeted Section 20 of SITA, which gave the magistrate wide powers to expel a woman who was suspected of being a prostitute—that is, remove her from the area under his jurisdiction. These claims are examined separately in the next two sections.

The Right to Practice the "World's Oldest Profession"

Husna Bai's first claim, and the one that caused the greatest amount of anxiety, was that SITA had violated her constitutional right to practice her trade and profession. The ASMH committee had been alerted to the understanding that since the Constitution recognized the fundamental right of a person to practice a profession, no authority could prohibit the act of prostitution without denying this right.[81] The drafters of SITA had tried to get around this by allowing an individual woman to be a prostitute, provided she did not create a public nuisance, while criminalizing acts that supported organized prostitution, such as brothel keeping.

Husna Bai claimed that SITA, in effect, illegally prohibited her from carrying on her trade by imposing unreasonable and illegal restrictions on it. The Allahabad High Court first had to consider whether prostitution could be considered a profession. Justice Jagdish Sahai reflected that the profession of prostitution had existed in all known nations from the earliest times. This reference to the ancient origins of prostitution was a feature common to most writings of prostitutes in this period; it established that the prostitute had always played a deplorable but an important social role.[82] The strongest challenge to this school of thought came from women's activists, like Kamaladevi Chattopadhyaya, who argued that prostitution arose "from old habits of degrading customs, outmoded rotting vestiges of the past that cling to present social modes and need to be swept away."[83] However, both narratives suggested that the existence of prostitution as a social fact had very little to do with the exercise of choice by the woman involved.

In contrast, it was evident that a large number of prostitutes saw themselves as professionals and sex as their work. It has been noted that the colloquial terms for prostitution in vernacular languages—including *kaam*, *dhanda*, and *pesha*—translate as "work," not as anything related to pleasure. The Advisory Committee on Social and Moral Hygiene found that two large categories of prostitutes saw no shame in their profession and viewed it as a legitimate activity. The first category consisted of hereditary prostitutes, or women who came from communities in which daughters traditionally took up sex work to maintain the family while the men were employed as pimps or musicians. Such communities included the Gomantak Maratha and Kolatis in Bombay and Goa, the Basavi and Koyi in Madras, and the Nutts and Bedias in north India.[84] The other category were *devadasis*, women who had been dedicated to temples as young girls and were sexually available to local gentry.

For many of these women, sex work was simply part of their larger reper-toire of skills. The ASMH committee interviewed a number of women in a north Indian brothel and was taken aback when, at the conclusion of the in-terview, the women pleaded with the members of the Committee to stay longer and watch them sing and dance. What should one make of this insistence? Perhaps after a detailed examination by the ASMH on the subject of their entry to the profession, the conditions they lived in, and whether they desired to leave, the women thought it was important to communicate this aspect of their work. Studies showed that a large number of prostitutes entered the profession as a result of being born in a particular family or community; for instance, 54 percent of prostitutes in Kanpur belonged to prostitute families.[85]

For judges and other state actors, it was easier to reconcile oneself with the idea of singers and dancers as professionals—after all, several had received rig-orous musical training and supported large households. Claims to professional status made by women found in lower-class brothels, who had little exposure to artistic training, were much harder for state authorities and women's orga-nizations to comprehend. Lady Rama Rau, who chaired the ASMH commit-tee, presented a vignette in which three prostitutes who could not sing or dance and who had no education told the ASMH that they preferred their lives in brothels to the conditions in the underdeveloped villages they had come from. Rama Rau described it as follows:

> There were three young lovely girls protected by three elderly, hideously ugly women, whom they claimed as their mothers; we asked questions and were told that these young women were very happy in town, for in the village they lived in the darkness, worked hard in the fields, ground corn on *chakkis* [millstones], which blistered their hands, were never able to buy new clothes, had no new entertainments such as cinema, motor drive, and parties. They were never able to earn more than a few annas a day, but since they had moved to their city their income had gone up to 1,000 rupees a month between them, and they had to work only from 8 to 11 p.m., leaving them free to do what they liked the rest of the day. One of the girls told us that she had four young brothers in the villages whom she could now afford to send to school, and in time she would like to buy her family more land in the village.[86]

With remarkable candor, Lady Rama Rau concluded, "the [ASMH] could not find an adequate answer to their arguments." Contemporary surveys of prostitutes give us a sense of their earnings as well as their class differentiation. In the Kamathipura area of Bombay, the ASMH committee's findings showed that two-thirds of the women earned between fifty-one to one hundred rupees a month after paying a cut to the middleman.[87] Another study from the interior industrial city of Kanpur revealed that 53 percent of the prostitutes earned less than fifty rupees a month, and another 33 percent earned between fifty and one hundred. Thus, the average income for a prostitute would be sixty-eight rupees a month, comparable to that of a junior government clerk.

Justice Sahai settled the debate by declaring that the state could not deny that prostitution was a trade for the purposes of Article 19(1)(g) of the Constitution, since SITA itself referred to prostitution as a trade on several occasions.[88] Finally, he ruled that the use of the word *any* in Article 19 of the Constitution, in "any profession, or to carry on any occupation, trade, or business," clearly indicated that normally a citizen is free to carry on *any* trade. He noted that even under the Indian Penal Code, prostitution itself was not a crime; the code prohibited only the sale or employment of a minor for the purpose of prostitution or illicit intercourse.[89]

Reasonable restriction of the right to freedom of trade and profession had been permitted by the courts in the general public interest.[90] However, multiple cases had established that if the restrictive legislation *totally prevented* a citizen from carrying on a trade, business, or profession, such a restriction would be unreasonable and void.[91] Justice Sahai reiterated that the key question was whether the restrictions imposed on the trade of prostitution under SITA *were reasonable* in the interest of the general public and if they did, in effect, completely restrict the practice of prostitution.

Husna Bai's lawyer highlighted two major provisions of SITA that indirectly limited her ability to practice prostitution even as an independent profession. These provisions defined brothels and criminalized living on the earnings of prostitution.

SITA was aimed at destroying organized prostitution; therefore, one of its chief aims was the closure of brothels. Section 2(A) of SITA defined a brothel as a house, a room, a place, or any portion of the same that was used for the purpose of prostitution for the gain of another person or for the mutual gain of two or more prostitutes. Thus, in effect, wherever more than one prostitute resided would be defined as a brothel. Women living in a brothel could be evicted by a magistrate and be expelled from a district.[92]

Husna Bai, however, lived with her extended family at 54-A Mohammad Ali Park. This included her cousin and copetitioner Shama, who was also a prostitute, which under SITA automatically designated her home as a brothel. The petition by Mahroo and Ram Pyari, the prostitutes from Delhi, also pointed out that the definition of a brothel was so broad that it prohibited any kind of association between prostitutes and prohibited their relations with their friends and families. It also prevented them from living with their adult children. More than half the prostitutes surveyed in Kanpur shared a single room with two or three other women. Several prostitutes who shared premises attempted to evade the law by putting up partitions in their tiny rooms so that each woman would have her own residence, and thus the dwelling could avoid being classified as a brothel.[93]

The realities of a prostitute's life were also hit by Section 4(2)(a) of SITA, which criminalized living on the earnings of prostitution. This provided that any person over the age of eighteen who knowingly lived on the earnings of the prostitution of a woman or a girl would be subject to imprisonment for up to two years and a fine of one thousand rupees. The provision also identified certain categories of people who were presumed to be living on the earnings of prostitutes, unless it was proven otherwise. These included pimps, those exercising control and influence over a prostitute's movements, and "any person" living with or habitually in the company of a prostitute. These provisions were put in place to penalize pimps, brothel keepers, and others who exploit women for prostitution. However, the phrase "any person" covered a wide range of people, including the parents and siblings of prostitutes. If a prostitute was living with her family or friends, an automatic presumption would be drawn against them.

The original governmental draft of SITA had exempted the mother of the prostitute, if she was infirm or over the age of sixty, and children under the age of twenty-one. However, Lady Rama Rau persuaded the Ministry of Home Affairs that the exemption for the mother should be removed and that for children lowered to eighteen years of age.[94] In an explanatory note, the AIWC explained that a mother, as an adult, is supposed to know better and be more responsible. Furthermore, the women's conference believed that this would create an incentive for a prostitute to leave the trade, to shield her parents from prosecution.[95] During its visits to brothels, the ASMH committee had noted the presence of several elderly women who posed as relatives and friends of the prostitutes, taking care of them when they were ill, accompanying them to doctors, and lending them money.[96] The committee, however, viewed these older women with suspicion and were convinced that they were brothel mad-ams who were living off the prostitutes like parasites.

Prostitution is often seen as an activity located outside the familial space of the home. However, Ashwini Tambe points out the strong similarities be-tween families and brothels in their structures of affection, obligation, and domination.[97] The empirical reality of prostitution, which challenged the sep-arateness of the domestic sphere in the abstract, was that many women who engaged in prostitution lived with their extended families. Most prostitutes not only supported their children and maintained their family establishments in the cities where they worked, they also sent remittances back to their families in villages. The Bombay survey showed that more than one-third of prostitutes sent home ten to twenty rupees every month. The organization of prostitution was diverse, but SITA treated all prostitutes the same. For instance, only 36 percent of the prostitutes interviewed in Kamathipura in Bombay admitted giving a commission to the brothel keeper that usually amounted to half their income.[98]

Justice Sahai was quite persuaded by the claim that Section 4(2)(a) was an unreasonable restriction on Husna Bai's ability to practice her profession. He noted that, unlike in other countries, in India it was common for family mem-bers to live together as adults. He agreed with the petitioner's contention that there must be hundreds of prostitutes whose parents and other family mem-bers lived with them and shared household expenses but were not encourag-ing, abetting, or helping them as prostitutes. Unless it was specifically proved that such family members were living off the prostitute's income or encourag-ing her profession, Justice Sahai ruled, it would be "extremely risky and not free from danger" to place the burden of presumption on them. This SITA subsection, it was accordingly held, was not reasonable and had no sufficiently close connection with the object of suppressing immoral traffic in women and girls.

This portion of the judgment generated some anxiety back in Delhi. The law minister expressed concern that the court had declared that prostitution was "a profession, or at least a trade," and that it could therefore not be banned, only reasonably restricted. He wrote to his advisors asking whether the gov-ernment could make a distinction between trades that could be legitimately followed and trades that might not amount to a crime but were opposed to public policy. He drew an analogy to telling a lie, which was not a legal offense but could not be considered legitimate or proper.[99]

The Geography of Freedom:
Eviction and the Freedom of Movement

Husna Bai's second major challenge was to Section 20 of SITA. A contemporary legal expert described it as "section 20 finishes the entire business of prostitution."[100] It gave the magistrate the power to remove any woman or girl from the limits of his jurisdiction upon receiving information that she was a prostitute. If the woman failed to comply with the court's order, both she and any party that harbored or concealed her were liable to steep fines. This was in addition to the restriction instituted by Section 7 of SITA, which prevented prostitution from being carried out within two hundred yards of a place of public religious worship, an educational institution, a hospital, or a nursing home.

Since the nineteenth century the movement of prostitutes had come under the intense scrutiny of the state, linked to its concern with the spread of venereal disease. Several scholars have demonstrated that colonial intervention in public health and hygiene was spatial, through the creation and monitoring of new geographies.[101] The Cantonment Acts of 1864 and 1889 and the Indian Contagious Diseases Act of 1868 were enacted over concerns about the rising rate of venereal disease among British soldiers; they sought the compulsory registration of brothels and prostitutes, regular medical exams, and the mandatory treatment of infected women. Women who refused to comply with the regulations were expelled from cantonments and regimental bazaars, where prostitution had led to the creation of segregated red-light districts in Indian cities.[102]

Military authorities remained concerned about the presence of women outside the cantonment who were not within the scope of the Cantonment Act. Rather than extend military powers to cities, the colonial government suggested that the problem be resolved through the use of municipal laws. Since the entire town could not be declared out of bounds for soldiers, municipalities drew on both common-law principles and new powers to segregate prostitutes. New municipal and police laws gave the city authorities the power to evict prostitutes and keepers of brothels and to punish women for soliciting in a public place. The state did not use these powers to abolish prostitution, only to push prostitutes into tolerated zones. Specific red-light districts, like Grant Road and Kamathipura in Bombay, GB Road in Delhi, and Sonagachi in Calcutta, emerged after this shift in law and policing.

Despite the colonial origins of the municipal administration system, the political reforms of 1909 and 1919 brought about greater Indian involvement—and thus changes—in municipal governance. For instance, the Delhi Municipal Corporation received an increasing number of petitions from citizens in Delhi demanding the eviction of prostitutes from specific commercial areas. As municipal governments came to be dominated by elected representatives, abolitionist campaigns were launched against red-light districts. For instance, in the *Asghari Jaan* case the chief complainant was Pundit Shiva Datt, the vice chairman of the municipal board of Etah, and the chief witnesses for the prosecution included a servant of the chairman of the municipal board and the cousins of a municipal contractor.[103]

With independence, popularly elected municipalities began to exercise greater vigilance and challenged the very geography of toleration that they had previously created, forcing prostitutes and brothel keepers to grapple with this shift in governance. In a case from Calcutta, a brothel keeper attempted to contest a prosecution for nuisance on the grounds that the brothel was in a recognized red-light district and next to several other brothels that had not been charged. This argument was rejected by the court, which ruled that the test for immoral activity was the normative standards of the society, not the standards of the judge or of "those advancing new sociology or advanced moral philosophy."[104] The emergence of a new public morality with the growth of democratic municipal governance was making itself felt with the extension of the franchise in the 1930s.

Urdu writer Ghulam Hussain's 1938 short story "Aanandi" (Delightful One) focused on the municipal council's attempts to expel the *zanan-e-bazaari* (women of the marketplace) from the heart of the city. These attempts were complicated by the fact that many of the prostitutes were wealthy and actually owned their homes and the brothels they worked in. The women resisted, paid fines, and even endured jail sentences by refusing to obey the expulsion orders, but ultimately the council prevailed. Hussain's short story was adapted as Shyam Benegal's film *Mandi* (The Marketplace) in 1983, in which the all-male municipal board was enlivened by the presence of Shanti Devi, a female social worker-turned-politician who made the expulsion of prostitutes a personal crusade (fig. 4.3). When the women in the brothel respond to her demands that they give up prostitution by asking what they should eat, she retorted that food is not everything. Hussain's story and the film both depict a milieu in which newly empowered legislative bodies embarked on moral crusades in neighborhoods.

Under the new constitutional order, even long-standing sovereign guarantees could be overturned. The municipality served notices of eviction to several

FIG. 4.3. A scene from *Mandi* (1983) showing Shanti Devi, a social worker
and elected municipality member, demonstrating for the closure
of a brothel while being heckled by its prostitutes.

women belonging to the Kanchan community who resided in the prostitute
quarters in the old city of Malerkotla. The women had been granted permission in 1913 to reside in the Sunami Gate area. However, the high court held
that the decision of a former sovereign could not bind the rights of a sovereign
legislature.[105]

Common to all sets of regulations, whether in the segregationist or abolitionist phase, was a lack of interest in the prostitute and her well-being. The
governing principle behind tolerating and evicting prostitutes was a concern
with disease, public health, and morals. The prostitute herself was treated according to the prevalent logic of the government. Section 20 of SITA elevated
the power of local government and granted it uniformly to magistrates across
the country. However, the provision did exist rather discordantly within legislation that was seeking to rescue and rehabilitate the prostitute rather than
maintain public order.

Husna Bai's petition attacked Section 20 of SITA on three grounds. First,
the section infringed on her right to move freely through the territory of India
and her right to reside and settle in any part of India as guaranteed by the

Constitution. Second, it infringed on her right to equality under Article 14 of the Constitution, inasmusch as it conferred unrestricted powers on the magistrate and provided no reasonable basis for classifying prostitutes. Third, these powers were not a reasonable restriction on her right to practice her trade and business as contemplated under Article19(6) of the Constitution.

Husna Bai's concern about eviction becomes clear through the list of respondents. Two of them were Abdul Hameed and Abdul Hameed Khan. Abdul Hameed, a wealthy businessman and the proprietor of Lal Biri Works at Allahabad was the owner of 54-A Mohammad Ali Park, where Husna Bai resided. Abdul Hameed Khan was the tenant from whom Bai had subleased her room. She prayed that the two men would be restrained from taking any action for her forcible eviction from the premises.

Justice Sahai was quite emphatic that there was some merit in the objection to the constitutionality of Section 20 of SITA on the grounds that it violated a citizen's right to move freely and settle in any part of the territory of India. He noted that under this provision the magistrate had the power to remove a prostitute from a place for *all time*. There was no fixed amount of time for which she could be removed or prohibited from reentering. The court noted that this could not be seen as a reasonable restriction because it seemed to have no connection with the goal of suppressing human trafficking and exploitation. Evicting a prostitute from a locality merely prevented prostitution in that particular locality and shifted the activity to another location; it did not liberate any woman from the profession, nor did it allow the possibility for reform.

There was already a precedent for a ruling like Justice Sahai's. In 1950 the Bombay High Court had struck down an analogous provision of the Bombay Prevention of Prostitution Act of 1923 on the grounds that freedom of residence and movement was guaranteed under the Constitution. In Shantabai Rani Benoor's case, the petitioner had been served an order by the additional district magistrate of Poona directing her to remove herself within a month from Poona City to a place beyond a radius of five miles. The high court noted that "the dominion of India was very vast" and that there seemed to be no way to enforce the order or for the police to know where the woman would go.[106] Whereas only 16 women had approached the high court, the judgment invalidated the notices issued to 340 women in Poona, emphasizing the connection between individual writs and their larger effects.[107]

Both Justice Sahai's response to Husna Bai and the Bombay High Court's response to Shantabai Benoor relied on a decision of the Bombay High Court in a case involving expulsion orders under the Bombay Public Security

Measures Act of 1947.[108] The petitioner in this case had been evicted from the city limits of Ahmedabad in 1948 because of his political activities. On the enactment of the Constitution, he challenged the orders and the law as a violation of his rights of residence and movement. The court rejected the contention that such a restriction was reasonable because it permitted the citizen to be anywhere in the vast territory of India except the city of Ahmedabad. The state conception of populations that could be moved around as required was profoundly challenged through the Constitution. As Durgabai Deshmukh had presciently warned Nehru, "The individual freedom of movement that the Constitution guaranteed complicated the state's plans. The state was powerless to check the flow of people."[109]

Justice Sahai took seriously Husna Bai's claim that Section 20 was arbitrary and conferred wide discretion on the magistrate in deciding which prostitute to remove from his jurisdiction. He noted, "It is left to the sweet will of the magistrate to remove one prostitute and not another, though her case may be quite similar to the case of one who is being removed." There were no guidelines to determine in which cases "it became necessary in the interest of the general public" that a woman would be required to remove herself.[110]

It's worth considering why Husna Bai's lawyer chose to frame his argument in terms of the Constitution even though the idea of rational classification and equality of treatment within the same class had been prevalent in cases involving prostitutes before the Constitution. In 1931 several challenges were made to bylaws enacted by municipalities under the Uttar Pradesh Municipalities Act, which prohibited prostitutes from residing in certain areas or, conversely, limited them to certain localities.

In one case, Chanchal, a prostitute in Hathras, was arrested and fined for violating a bylaw that listed thirteen streets and localities where no public prostitute was permitted to reside. This prohibition exempted all prostitutes who already owned homes or resided in these areas at the end of 1925. The Allahabad High Court acquitted Chanchal and struck down the bylaw as ultra vires the act, for it amounted not to the prohibition of public prostitutes but merely to the prohibition of an arbitrary class of prostitutes. Justice Shah Sulaiman ruled that this arbitrariness created an "invidious distinction" that benefited one class of prostitutes and injured another. The court ruled that it was illegal for the municipal board to single out a particular prostitute or group of prostitutes and prohibit her or them from residing in a particular area. Such discrimination would defeat the point of framing such a bylaw and would not meet the requirements of the "maintenance of health, safety, and convenience of the inhabitants of the town," the grounds on which the municipality was delegated this power.[111]

The Allahabad High Court also struck down similar bylaws that were enacted by the municipality of Agra, holding that a prohibition must be general and of universal application and that the court could not make an exception for a particular group.[112] Although there was an older precedent of the Allahabad High Court that required equal treatment within a class to meet the purpose of the legislation, Husna Bai's lawyers chose to draw upon new constitutional jurisprudence under Article 14.

The Supreme Court of India had held in 1952 that the principle of equal protection under the law permitted reasonable classification for the purpose of legislation. However, for a law to pass the test of valid classification, it must be founded on an intelligible difference (which distinguishes those affected from those not), and such classification must have a rational nexus with the law's objective.[113]

According to Justice Sahai in Husna Bai's case, Section 20 of SITA failed to meet this test of valid classification. He pointed out that SITA provided no guiding principles a magistrate could use to determine whether a prostitute should be removed. The preamble to SITA noted only that the act was "in pursuance of the International Convention signed in New York on May 9, 1950, for the suppression of immoral traffic in women and girls." The magistrate was given "a naked and arbitrary power," in Justice Sahai's words, and a law that gave uncontrolled authority to discriminate violated Article 14 of the Constitution. Justice Sahai approvingly quoted a decision of the US Supreme Court on the Equal Protection Clause, holding that "if a statute does not disclose a definite policy or objective and confers authority on an administrative body to make the selection at its pleasure, the statute would be held to be discriminatory irrespective of how it is applied."[114]

Critical to his judgment was his identification of the magistrate's office as an executive authority. The magistrate in colonial India was a civil servant appointed by the government who exercised a wide range of powers. Nationalists had argued that this made magistrates less likely to be neutral when serving in a judicial capacity and had campaigned for the complete separation of the judiciary from the executive. Article 50 of the Constitution required the state to achieve complete separation of the judiciary from the executive in the public services of the state. However, administrative reforms were slow, and the complete separation would not be achieved until the 1970s.[115]

The striking down of Section 20 of SITA caused considerable consternation among the bureaucrats at the Ministry of Home Affairs. The drafters of this statute believed they had been careful in avoiding charges of arbitrariness. They had learned from the experience of the Bombay government in Benoor's case, in which the court had declared void the clause conferring the power to expel under the Bombay Prevention of Prostitution Act because it did not give the affected person an opportunity to be heard.[116] Taking this into consideration, Section 20 of SITA explicitly required the magistrate to give the girl or woman in question an opportunity to provide evidence before determining that she was a prostitute and should be removed from the area.[117] The law minister asserted that this clause was sufficient to meet the test for arbitrary classification.[118]

The debate over Section 20 of SITA and the power to expel reflected the tension between an older colonial ethics of government and a new vision of governance that was made possible through the Constitution. For the Home Ministry bureaucrats, the powers of the magistrate under Section 20 were not unusual; as one of them said, "Such discretion was often vested with judicial officers."[119] However, the argument made by Husna Bai relied on a new standard of citizens' rights echoed in a series of court decisions, all of which reflected Justice Vivian Bose's belief that the test for arbitrariness was whether

> the collective conscience of a sovereign democratic republic as reflected in the views of fair-minded, reasonable, unbiased men, who are not swayed by emotion or prejudice, can consider the impugned laws as reasonable, just and fair and regard them as that equal treatment and protection in the defense of liberties which is expected of a sovereign democratic republic in the conditions which obtain in India today.[120]

It was therefore not surprising that Bai chose to rely on the new constitutional jurisprudence on equality rather than on the older Allahabad cases that dealt with rational classification. The decisions in *Mt. Chanchal v. King Emperor* and *Mt. Naziran v. King Emperor* had struck down the impugned bylaws on the grounds that they discriminated between different types of prostitutes and defeated the purpose, which was to end prostitution. Although both women were acquitted and excused from paying the fine, the court's recommendation to the municipality was to redraft the bylaw to make the prohibition general and not "leave other prostitutes free to ply their trade."[121] The central motivation of the constitutional jurisprudence was not the efficacy of the laws but the restrictions on the rights of the citizens. The courts conceded that rights could be restricted, but such restrictions were to be strictly scrutinized.

From Husna Bai to Kaushalya Devi: The Legacy of a Court Decision

Despite the excitement raised by Husna Bai's petition and the contentions that were accepted by the court, Justice Sahai's final decision was mild. While noting that he found "some substance in the submissions of the petition" that Sections 4 and 20 of SITA were unconstitutional, he declined to express any further opinion. Since Husna Bai's rights had not yet been infringed on, he held, the petition had been filed prematurely and could not be entertained.[122] Husna Bai argued that there was a real possibility that her landlords might threaten her with legal proceedings, but she could provide no tangible evidence of it. Therefore, the judge's determination—that prostitutes had the fundamental right to carry out their trade and that the definition of the brothel and Section 4(2)(a) of SITA were unconstitutional—did not have legal force and was only in the nature of an obiter dictum (an incidental and nonbinding opinion expressed by a judge).

The newspaper headlines portrayed this as Husna Bai's defeat, declaring that the SITA was held valid and the woman's pleas failed.[123] Although the court had noted that several sections of SITA were unconstitutional, what remained, after the dismissal of the petition on technical grounds, were nonbinding observations of a single judge of the Allahabad High Court. Thus, in the ordinary course of events this should not have been a cause of concern for the government.

The Ministry of Home Affairs, which had jurisdiction over SITA, had followed Bai's petition closely. After the decision the home minister asked the law minister for a detailed opinion on the possible impact of the amendment. After three months of consultations the law minister was able to assure the home minister that the comments made by Justice Sahai were nonbinding; thus there was no serious risk of the provisions being struck down as unconstitutional, and no immediate action was therefore required.[124]

Nevertheless, the decision in Husna Bai's case began to take on a life of its own. As one of the earliest cases challenging SITA (decided within just two weeks of the act coming into effect), the decision was reproduced in all leading commentaries on the act. Mazhar Hussein's popular commentary on SITA in 1958 reproduced a newspaper article that described Justice Sahai's decision, because the case had not yet been published in any law journal. In his introduction Hussein noted that Justice Sahai had observed that Sections 4 and 20 of SITA placed unreasonable restrictions and were invalidated by Articles 15 and 19 of the Constitution. Hussein, a lawyer based in Lucknow, was the author of several treatises. His commentary on SITA remains the leading textbook for practitioners, and until 1960 it was the only work on the subject. The possible impact of the Constitution's fundamental rights on SITA had troubled both the government and women's groups for a few years, and Justice Sahai's decision provided the road map for lawyers.

SITA cases rarely went to the appellate courts and have therefore left few traces in the judicial record. One of the small number of reported high court decisions under SITA was a complaint before the Bombay High Court against a prostitute living in the Radhabai building in Bombay. She faced proceedings under SITA for practicing her profession near schools, temples, and hospitals. The woman admitted to being a prostitute but denied soliciting customers in public. The high court dismissed the complaint, holding that a woman's right to practice her profession could be restricted only "in the interest of the general public," and since the residents of the locality had not complained about the woman and did not mind if she carried on the profession inside her room, no case could be made under SITA.[125]

The older municipal regulations that sought to regulate prostitution also faced constitutional challenges, and although the courts differed in their decisions, some did consider the arguments for reasonable classification and arbitrariness laid down in Justice Sahai's decision. For instance, the sessions court (the criminal court in a jurisdiction where the district court is only a civil court) of Malerkotla acquitted thirteen people who had been charged with violating the municipal prohibition on practicing prostitution in the old city of Malerkotla. The judge expressed the view that the municipal resolution was not a reasonable restriction on the practice of trade and occupation guaranteed in the Constitution. Although this acquittal was reversed by the high court, it was because of evidence that the municipality had targeted several areas, including Satta Bazaar, Quila Rehmatganj, the railway station, and the area outside the walled city. The courts accepted that restrictions on prostitution could not be absolute.[126]

Similarly, Kamla China, a prostitute residing on GB Road in Delhi's notorious red-light district, was expelled from the neighborhood and contested her conviction in court. The judge acquitted her, explicitly citing Justice Sahai's assessment of the constitutionality of Section 20 of SITA.[127] The next few years saw repeated contestation of SITA before the high courts, usually arising from the criminal cases of women arrested for prostitution or for refusing to heed an eviction order. The Bombay and Uttar Pradesh High Courts struck down Section 20 of SITA as unconstitutional, whereas the Andhra Pradesh High Court upheld the law. Not only did all the courts address Justice Sahai's decision, the women's lawyers in these cases made complex arguments on the relationship between prostitution and the new postcolonial state.

Begum Kalawat, a prostitute living in the town of Barsi in Bombay state, was served with a notice by a magistrate to remove herself from the city and go to Osmanabad within three days. He made the order after receiving several complaints that she was carrying on her profession within eighty feet of the municipal school, that her behavior was indecent, that young girls had to go past her house to go to school, and that she often advertised herself by standing on the public road. Prima facie, the magistrate found that she fit the category of prostitutes who ought to be removed in the interest of the general public.

Kalawat petitioned the Bombay High Court and argued based that Section 20 violated the rights to equality, freedom of trade, and freedom of movement. In striking down Section 20 as unconstitutional, the high court noted that in order to determine whether the restrictions on fundamental rights were reasonable in the interest of the general public, "one must remember that women do not choose their vocation because they like it. It has been recognized that in a large measure they are forced into this vocation by social conditions and most often against their will. One may not, therefore, judge these cases with any amount of harshness."[128]

The high court, however, refused to accept the contention that the law violated Kalawat's right to practice her trade and profession under Article 19. Her lawyer conceded that the restriction of that right had to be read with Article 23, which prohibited traffic in human beings. Moreover, in a case involving the auctioning of alcohol licenses, the Supreme Court had observed "that it could not be denied that the state has the power to prohibit trades that are illegal or immoral or injurious to the health of the public . . . laws prohibiting trades in noxious or dangerous goods or trafficking in women cannot be held to be unconstitutional because they enact a complete prohibition."[129]

Reflecting on the *In re Shantabai Rani Benoor* decision, in which the Bombay Prevention of Prostitution Act was struck down as unconstitutional, the ASMH committee expressed apprehension that similar challenges under

Article 19 might be raised against any effort to regulate prostitution unless the article was made subject to some restrictions in the interests of public decency, public morality, and public health.[130]

The Allahabad High Court too refused to accept that SITA encroached on a woman's right to carry out her trade and profession. Noting that the women rested their claim on the nonbinding observations made by Justice Sahai in Husna Bai's case, the high court ruled that prostitution, like gambling and other "inherently immoral" occupations, could not be put on par with normal respectable professions.[131] The words "any profession" found in Article 19(1)(g) could not, in the court's view, be interpreted as any kind of activity that a citizen might adopt, regardless of the effect on public interest.[132]

However, the court found that the petitioners, six prostitutes from Kanpur who faced an expulsion order, were on surer ground when they relied on the constitutional right to freely move throughout the country. Justice William Broome highlighted the fact that Section 20 sought to control the movement and residence of prostitutes rather than bring prostitution to an end. It did not require the prostitute to give up her trade, only to remove herself from the limits of the local jurisdiction. This, the court held, was not a reasonable restriction on the petitioner's right of movement. In determining whether a restriction was reasonable, the Supreme Court had recently held it would take into account the "nature of evil that was sought to be remedied, the ratio of harm caused to individual citizens, and the beneficial effect reasonably expected to result for the general public."[133] Following this, Justice Broome found that a woman proceeded against under Section 20 did not have the option to cease to be a prostitute and continue to reside in the neighborhood.[134] A woman's history as a prostitute could even be used in the present as grounds for expulsion, and there was no time limit on the period of expulsion.

The court carefully distinguished the case at hand from a recent Supreme Court decision on the Bombay Police Act, which had upheld the power to expel dangerous thugs from the district on the grounds that the state could put fetters on an individual's freedom in the larger interests of society.[135] Broome distinguished the threats that thugs and prostitutes posed to the community: thugs were likely to commit violence and therefore posed a greater threat to the community, justifying drastic measures limiting their rights; prostitutes, in contrast, presented only a threat of the contamination of morals, at worst.

Justice Broome echoed the reasoning in Husna Bai's case, attacking the "unguided and unfettered power" delegated to the subordinate magistrate, by pointing out that in the absence of guidelines he could make the determination of abridging fundamental rights at his own sweet will and that this decision was not subject to the scrutiny of a higher authority.[136] Central to Justice Broome's objection was the exercise of this power of determination by an executive authority. Even the lawyer for the state of Uttar Pradesh conceded that if Section 20 were to be construed as conferring powers on the executive, it must held to be unconstitutional. The court rejected the contention that the magistrate's powers under Section 20 were in his judicial capacity, observing that the procedure described in SITA, given the absence of cross-examination or the requirement for a reasoned decision, could not be equated with a judicial trial before a court of law by "any stretch of imagination."[137] The court accordingly declared Section 20 of SITA unconstitutional and quashed the proceedings against the six women.

The Andhra Pradesh High Court adopted a divergent view, upholding the constitutionality of Section 20.[138] There were two important points of difference between the Andhra Pradesh decision and the cases before the Allahabad and Bombay High Courts discussed above. First, the Andhra Pradesh High Court emphasized that SITA had been passed long after the Constitution, was necessary to enforce Article 23 of the Constitution, and thus enjoyed a greater presumption of constitutionality. The judge disagreed with the decisions in Bai's and Kalawat's cases by holding that the restrictions imposed by Section 20 were reasonable in light of the objective. He defended the absence of any limit on the duration of expulsion on the grounds that it was difficult for a magistrate to "divine at the time of the order how long it would take for the woman to be rid of such tendencies as are likely to pollute the atmosphere."[139]

Second, the judge held that the magistrate did not have unchecked discretion or arbitrary powers under the act. He went through the procedure step-by-step to demonstrate that the process described was a judicial one. However, the empirical distinction between Andhra Pradesh and the states of Uttar Pradesh and Bombay was that in Andhra Pradesh, postindependence reforms had been successful in separating the judiciary from the executive at the magistrate level. The court ruled that the discretion exercised by a magistrate in a state where there is a separation of the judiciary from the executive cannot be deemed to be the exercise of discretion by an executive authority. The discretion that would be disallowed in an administrative or executive authority would be permitted in a judicial body.

Whether the courts upheld the constitutionality of SITA or chose to strike it down, the debate gradually shifted emphasis from the rights of a prostitute to the process that the state must follow. The decisions increasingly turned on the question of discretion given to a magistrate, a figure who came to be viewed differently as the postcolonial state sought to separate the judiciary from the executive.

Faced with conflicting decisions across the country, the Supreme Court accepted the Uttar Pradesh government appeal of the case of Kaushalya Devi. After hearing heated arguments from both sides, the court ruled to uphold the validity of Section 20 and expressly overruled the decisions in Husna Bai's and Begum Kalawat's cases.[140] The court went through the procedure laid down under Section 20 and noted that it approximated the process of a judicial inquiry. The fact that the state had given Kaushalya Devi an opportunity to be heard on the charges against her indicated her right to a public inquiry. She could engage an advocate, ask for examination of the informant, cross-examine witnesses, and cite her own evidence. Furthermore, the Supreme Court settled the question of the magistrate's role, holding that it was a judicial one and therefore subject to revisions by the lower courts.

Kaushalya Devi's lawyers had argued that Section 20 violated the principle of reasonable classification required by Article 14 on the grounds that it allowed the magistrate to discriminate between different types of prostitutes who lived in the jurisdiction. Chief Justice Koka Subbarao held that the reasonable-classification test was founded on the idea of an intelligible difference that had a rational nexus with the law's objective. The court held that there was an obvious difference between a prostitute who practiced her trade secretly or lived in a sparsely populated area of the town and one who lived in a busy locality within easy reach of religious, educational, and other public institutions. Chief Justice Subbarao explained as follows:

> Though both sell their bodies, the latter is far more dangerous to the public, particularly to the younger generation during the emotional stage of their life. Their freedom of uncontrolled movement in a crowded locality or in the vicinity of public institutions not only helps to demoralize the public morals, but, what is worse, to spread diseases not only affecting the present generation but also the future ones. Such trade in public may also lead to scandals and unseemly broils.[141]

The Supreme Court accepted the claim that a prostitute has the fundamental right to move freely and reside throughout the territory of India, and Section 20 of SITA was clearly a restriction of this right. However, the court also held that the reasonableness of such a restriction depended upon the "values of life in a society . . . and the degree and urgency of the evil sought to be controlled." Departing from the earlier, more neutral descriptions of prostitution, the court noted that the magnitude of the evil and the urgency of the reform might require drastic remedies, like deporting the worst prostitutes from their areas of operation. The prostitutes' contention that this would lead to a situation in which they were forced to wander around the country through consecutive orders of various magistrates was rejected by the Supreme Court as "bordering on a fantasy." The court continued that if the presence of a prostitute in a locality had a demoralizing influence on the public (with regard to the density of the population and the existence of schools, and other public institutions), the deportation order was necessary to curb the evil of prostitution and to improve public morals.

With the decision of the Supreme Court in *State of Uttar Pradesh v. Kaushalya Devi*, the constitutionality of SITA was settled, and no further constitutional challenges would arise for the next fifty years.[142] However, can we write off this entire process of litigation as a complete victory for the state? What does the litigation reveal about the changing vocabulary of prostitutes and ways of organizing? How did the Constitution come to matter in the lives of prostitutes?

Conclusion

Even a depraved woman cannot be deprived of her rights except for good reasons.

— CHIEF JUSTICE KOKA SUBBARAO[143]

The enactment of the Constitution transformed the everyday regulation of prostitution in India. First, by abolishing trafficking through the Constitution, the authors sought to create conditions of freedom for prostitutes (from individual exploiters) while also providing a legitimate basis for the state to regulate the daily lives of these newly freed subjects. This process of abolition and rescue by the bureaucracy of social welfare, in contrast to its colonial predecessor, became marked as an arena where women could play a role in public life. Second, a prostitute who filed a lawsuit in the Indian republic was able to represent herself as an economic actor asserting her rights in a public space. Central to such prostitutes' claims was the redefinition of the idea of the productive citizen, challenging claims made by elite women that prostitution was unproductive work.

How does one evaluate the process of litigation that began with Husna Bai's petition? What insights does it offer into the relationship between women and a postcolonial constitutional republic? If one adopts a doctrinal approach, the process of litigation initiated by Husna Bai stands defeated in the Supreme Court's decision in Kaushalya Devi's case. The Supreme Court declared SITA to be constitutionally sound and held that the rights of prostitutes could be restricted in the interest of the general public. This reading echoed the views of Indian feminists, who have argued that law is a hegemonic project of patriarchy and modernity that legitimizes only particular ways of being and doing, and that rights lose their transformative potential when institutionalized by law.[144] Such a reading would also find favor with American critics of the rights revolution, who have argued that courts have limited power to create social change and that the costs of litigation are not worth the small judicial victories that can be achieved.[145] Prabha Kottiswaran, a legal ethnographer of the contemporary sex industry in India, argues that sex workers are unlikely to participate in bourgeois civil society mechanisms like litigation, winning greater victories through their participation in political society.[146]

This skepticism toward the law is a valuable corrective to triumphant accounts of legal liberalism. However, viewing the success or failure of legal mobilization purely in terms of a judicial verdict severely limits our understanding of the role of law in society.

Legal practices and rights discourses develop lives outside formal state institutions.[147] It is remarkable that before Husna Bai's petition, there existed in the popular imagination of prostitutes the belief that the right to work in the Constitution meant that the state could not abolish prostitution. This argument was made several times to the ASMH membersAdvisory Committee of Social and Moral Hygiene , so they had to recognize the fact at the beginning of their report. Prostitutes talked back to middle-class women's groups in the language of rights. A bemused Rameshwari Nehru recounted that a number of prostitutes marched to her house "to claim the freedom given to them by the Constitution to ply their trade unharrassed by police for earning their livelihood."[148]

Any interpretation of these cases must begin by acknowledging the significance of both the number of prostitutes who became litigants and the confident assertion of their rights. This challenges us to rethink the belief that the courts in India were the exclusive domain of the bourgeoisie. Muslim prostitutes like Husna Bai faced several degrees of marginalization and do not fit easily with other oppressed groups whose presence in the colonial courtroom has recently been studied. Nita Verma Prasad and Mitra Sharafi attribute the legal successes forged by Hindu widows and Muslim wives to "liberal judges" and "chivalric imperialism," respectively.[149] But destitute widows and abandoned wives were easier objects of sympathy than prostitutes, whose disruptive presence was recognized even by judges who gave favorable hearings.

I would argue that the presence of prostitutes in courts and their legal consciousness are both products of their marginalization. Prostitutes became subject of intense state scrutiny and regulation since the mid-nineteenth century. Their lives and movements were often circumscribed by regulations, the breach of which subjected them to harassment from state authorities. Prostitutes had multiple points of contact with state agencies, ranging from policemen and doctors to social workers. Their experience with the criminal justice system would bring them into contact with lawyers. Thus, they would have greater awareness of the laws that affected them than middle-class or elite women, who had little direct contact with the state.

Direct evidence for this hypothesis exists in fragments. Mary, a prostitute based in Agra, noted in a 1958 interview that "the brothel keeper and the inmates knew that SITA would soon be implemented in Delhi . . . they had good knowledge of the provisions of the law and they were very clear the act forbade commercialized prostitution but not prostitution itself."[150] Prostitutes were one of the few groups of women who owned property and appeared as taxpayers in colonial registers, exercising some of the basic requirements for citizenship. Ghulam Abbas's Aanandi offers a powerful insight into the ability of sex work to evade regulation. The prostitutes are expelled by the municipal council from the heart of the city; they sell their houses and eventually buy land many miles out of town. However, the presence of the prostitutes draws both customers and a range of service providers to the remote location, leading to the establishment of another township with brothels at the core.

More significantly, prostitutes rarely acted alone. Almost all the cases that appeared before court had multiple petitioners, and even in Husna Bai's case it becomes clear that her petition was being supported by other prostitutes in the city. The role of associations in supporting legal mobilization has also been emphasized.[151] Living in geographically restricted areas and linked to each other with kinship and caste ties, prostitutes began forming organizations in the 1950s. The Allahabad Dancing Girls Union and the Calcutta organizations had already been discussed.

As professional associations, these organizations were distinct from charitable groups that worked with prostitutes. A study of the Bombay red-light district contrasted the Gomantak Maratha Samaj, an organization led by middle-class men who sought to prevent the dedication of girls of the Naik community, and the activities of the Association of Tawaifs and Deredars, a prostitutes' society that ostensibly promoted music and provided facilities for its members to train in music and dance. Although the first organization was praised for its success in providing matrimonial opportunities to Naik girls, the second was described as a "shield to protect the unscrupulous from law-enforcing activities."[152]

The role of caste in this process cannot be overemphasized; it provided a resource for organizing, and the existence of a hereditary group of prostitutes complicated the narrative framed by trafficking. Despite the efforts of colonial law to homogenize all nonconformist sexual practices as prostitution, the courts were able draw upon the cultural memory of categories such as courtesans. It is striking that no other common-law jurisdiction recognized or sustained arguments defending the right to practice prostitution as a profession. It is this recognition of cultural categories that has allowed for the Supreme Courts of India, Pakistan, and Bangladesh to recognize rights of sexual autonomy for *hijras* and *kwajasarahs* (traditional transgender communities) while rejecting claims by gay men and lesbians.[153]

Studies of legal mobilization emphasize that every culture offers only a limited stock of resources and practices from which citizens draw to construct meaning and negotiate social interactions.[154] The enactment of the Constitution created a powerful new resource and added to this stock. The ability of prostitutes to mobilize the resources was limited by the biases the figure of the prostitute evoked in the judicial system. This interplay becomes clear when we notice what arguments have greater legal traction. Husna Bai's claim that SITA restricted her freedom to practice her profession is more easily dismissed than her complaint that the powers of expulsion granted to the magistrate were arbitrary and violated her right of free movement. The prostitutes were successful to the extent that they were able to show that SITA adversely affected society at large, such as by granting unregulated powers to a magistrate. Michael McCann observed, "To take advantage of contradictions, to open up silences, to turn the rules against the rulers, to work for change within existing cultural traditions—these generally are the most effective strategies available to traditionally oppressed and marginal groups."[155]

This recognition by the court was not insignificant, and till the decision in *Kaushalya Devi*, it operated as a precedent in almost all cases. Even after the decision in *Kaushalya Devi*, the judgments for Husna Bai and Begum Kalawat circulated in legal textbooks and commentaries and continue to be used by lawyers.

Litigation was also one of those rare instances in which a subaltern would *appear* to speak. This remained its most discomfiting feature, particularly for female leaders who had carved a role for themselves within the postcolonial state by speaking on behalf of these marginalized women. This form of speech also manifested itself in petitions of habeas corpus brought by women who were confined to rehabilitation and shelters and were seeking to free themselves from the state's interference. These moves drove one editorial to sarcastically remark that "the primary assumption behind the rescue of fallen women now being systematically undertaken in the country in obedience to SITA is that the fallen women are anxious to be rescued"; however, the escape of women from shelters and their challenges to their confinement should compel sociologists and psychologists to address themselves to the "mystery of certain women's prejudice against respectability."[156] I am not suggesting that this was the authentic voice of the prostitutes, but the Constitution did allow for a voice that represented the prostitute to become visible in a public domain.

Women's groups were extremely critical of representations by prostitutes as authentic and unmediated speech. In its report to the government, the ASMH committee warned that "if every adult woman must be taken at her word, and her statement in court while [she is] still under the influence of her pimp must be accepted as incontrovertible, no charge can be driven home in a court of law."[157] Durgabai Deshmukh stated that she was "deeply concerned to hear that the beggar and the prostitute have asserted their right under our Constitution to carry out their ancient professions."[158] The solution, to her and her contemporaries, lay in having the courage to amend the freedoms in the Constitution and "not sacrifice the welfare of the community as a whole to the vagaries of a dissolute few."[159]

The ASMH's response to the court's findings was even stronger. Rameshwari Nehru argued that there should be a total abolition of prostitution, which would require even individual and voluntary prostitution by adult women to be made illegal. In order to further this goal, she argued that the Constitution should be amended to abrogate the freedom to a trade and a profession. Despite judicial victories, the experience of litigation brought a degree of wariness to the state, which can be seen in the demands for greater clarity in the law to prevent people from resorting to court on "frivolous grounds." She lamented that "the uncertainty of law" deterred social work.[160]

Since the early 1990s scholars and activists have increasingly being paying attention to sex-worker mobilization in India and other developing countries for decriminalization and access to welfare. However, this is held to be catalyzed by the rise of transnational NGOs and the concerns over HIV and AIDs, which led to a greater engagement with the needs of sex workers.[161] The argument that sex can be work is a radical position that emerged in the West in the 1980s. Husna Bai's case revealed a long history of sex workers organizing in India and a rights narrative shaped by engagements with the Indian Constitution, contrary to the vision of the Indian women's movement. Despite judicial pronouncements, the belief that the right to work in the Indian Constitution guarantees the right to exchange sex for money continues to be asserted by prostitutes' organizations. In 2012, four decades after *Kaushalya Devi*, the Darbar Mahila Samanwaya Committee, a prostitutes' union in Calcutta, distributed pamphlets to its members that open with Articles 19 and 21 of the Indian Constitution, asserting the right to a trade and a profession, as well as to life and liberty.

Epilogue

THE EVE OF INDIAN INDEPENDENCE was marked by joyous celebrations as thousands of ordinary Indians flooded the formerly inaccessible government buildings to witness the rituals of the transfer of power. Cheering crowds occupied every inch of the central government in Delhi and blocked the viceregal cavalcade, forcing Jawaharlal Nehru to lean out from the Constituent Assembly terrace and cajole the crowd into letting the viceroy move. In Calcutta, boisterous crowds invaded the governor's palace, jumped on the four-poster beds, ran the bathtub faucets, and even knocked off the departing English governor's hat. The world had momentarily turned upside down—the people and the state had merged. Yet this moment was short-lived; as Nehru announced Indian independence, mounted policemen pushed back the crowds with sticks, and in the following week the rituals of state took over. The people were put back in their place, permitted to emerge only when an election was held. This book has argued that it was the promulgation of the republican constitution in 1950 that made the people a constant presence for the government.

Let us return to Mohammed Yasin, the vegetable seller from Jalalabad, to answer the two original questions raised in this book: Did the Indian Constitution matter, and to whom did it matter? Yasin emerged victorious in his bid to sell vegetables. The Supreme Court ruled that the Jalalabad municipality did not have the authority to impose a license fee and that this was an unreasonable restriction on Yasin's fundamental right to carry out a trade or business.

Yasin was not a wealthy man. Local tax records show that his father, Niamatullah, had asked to be excused from paying taxes because it was difficult to support his family of eight on an income of 150 rupees a month. Yasin's decision to go to court was a calculated risk, influenced by the fact that the municipal regulation effectively shut down his business and that other people in neighboring towns had been successful in bringing similar action before the courts. Yasin's petition refers to two previous cases, before the high court and the Supreme Court, that involved Muslim vegetable sellers suing municipalities within the same district. The fact that both cases had been successful encouraged Yasin to take his chances in court.[1]

Yasin's story mirrors that of dozens of others, making the case that the Indian Constitution *mattered* in the everyday lives of its citizens in significant ways. The first decade after independence saw constitutional law emerge as a field in which the postcolonial state and other authorities (e.g., religious, community, or political, or market logic) would interact and a new postcolonial governmentality would take shape. This was not a process that was strategized by a set of individuals or an organization with an agenda; it arose through the actions of thousands of Indians who learned from one another.[2] This marks a departure from other postcolonial narratives of constitutionalism in which the foundations were laid by either a heroic judge or a well-resourced, often internationally funded organization.[3] For such a phenomenon to exist, there had to emerge a shared popular understanding of the role of constitutional law as distinct from ordinary law. As the rate of civil litigation fell, that of litigation against the state rose.

These claims are more significant than they might appear at first glance. Scholars writing about law and society in the West have not needed to be apologetic about legal histories. American historians, for instance, have held law and legal practices to be intrinsic to American life. Hendrik Hartog states, "Americans had law, they made law, they inherited law, they used law, and they were subject to law."[4] However, this was not as apparent in India. Under colonial rule India was portrayed as a place without law, thus justifying British governance. Therefore, many of the laws that existed until 1947 were neither made nor inherited by Indians. Whether Indians used law or were actually subject to law in colonial India has been debated, with a significant number of scholars arguing that the law and the state was external to the imagination of a majority of Indians. Gandhi himself launched a blistering critique of the colonial legal system, encouraged both ordinary Indians and nationalist lawyers to boycott courts, and encouraged the development of indigenous systems of arbitration and mediation.

The constitutional litigation challenges the above narrative, for various groups and individuals showed a great awareness of the law and engaged the legal system quite skillfully. In fact, it is the government that often found itself frustrated and underprepared before the courts. In Yasin's case, the municipality of Jalalabad found itself begging the Supreme Court for an extension of its deadline to file a response; it had no budget for litigation expenses because it had never had to deal with legal challenges in Delhi before.[5] Litigation was an expense not just for the ordinary citizen but also for the state, and the bureaucrats began to note with alarm the exorbitant fees commanded by the government's own lawyers. For instance, a lawyer who was prosecuting men accused of treason in Kashmir was billing 1,750 rupees a day, with a total bill of 301,850 rupees. In more ordinary cases involving government promotions, the lawyer billed 600 rupees per hearing.[6]

This uncertainty about the results of a case and the novelty of constitutional law made possible a widespread investment in constitutional litigation. Writ petitions were new not just to litigants but also to lawyers and judges. Shanti Bhushan, a leading constitutional lawyer and a former law minister, recounts in his memoirs how he got out of a traffic ticket by filing a writ petition and educating a rather bemused judge about his new powers. Justice Mehr Chand Mahajan of the Supreme Court of India reminisced that he knew little of constitutional law when appointed to the bench, and he spent his first couple of years on the Supreme Court reading American constitutional treatises. Entrepreneurial law publishers sent agents to different cities to ask lawyers what books they needed and began to commission textbooks and treatises on constitutional and administrative law.[7] This was a period of experimentation, flux, and creativity, when anything, much to the horror of the state, was possible.

Talking the State's Language

Critics of the Indian Constitution have repeatedly pointed out that it reflected a certain bourgeois nationalist vision of the state rather than popular constitutionalism. This concern was shared by B. R. Ambedkar, the chairman of the drafting committee; he warned the Constituent Assembly, "Constitutional morality is not a natural sentiment. It has to be cultivated. We must realize that our people have yet to learn it."[8] To its authors, the Constitution was a state project that had to be disseminated among the masses, through school textbooks, pamphlets, public exhibition, and documentaries.[9]

The availability of judicial remedies, however, made the Constitution a two-way process. This point was noted by Zairul Hassan Lari, a renegade Muslim League member of the Constituent Assembly, who left for Pakistan midway through the deliberations. Lari agreed with Ambedkar that "constitutional

FIG. 5.1. "Battle of Wits." *Shankar's Weekly,* March 20, 1955.

morality . . . had to be cultivated," but he perceptively noted that not only people *but governments* had to learn it.[10] The Constitution by itself was neither emancipatory nor repressive but merely provided a language in which the citizen could communicate with the state. Upendra Baxi has argued that the power of judicial discourse in India was the capacity to raise awkward questions about the intention, competence, and wisdom of the executive.[11] This awkwardness frustrated the executive, delayed and forced policy changes, and caused significant expenses. A newspaper cartoon (fig. 5.1) conveys some of this frustration; it shows Nehru patching up holes in the Constitution while lawyers are digging new ones.

Those who had made successful interventions in the process of constitution making now demanded that the Constitution be amended or transformed. Bombay ministers finally held that no solution except a constitutional amendment could successfully implement Prohibition.[12] After the *Hanif Qureshi* judgment, the cow protection lobby despaired of any solution under the present Constitution.[13] Poignantly, a liberal lawyer like Durgabai Deshmukh, on being confronted by prostitutes asserting their right to their profession, argued that the solution lay in having the courage to amend the freedoms in the Constitution.[14]

Although the constitutional strategy was often used as a tactical tool, it also began to operate as an organizational assumption for citizens and as a background threat for the state.[15] Despite frequent denials of their rights by the state, Muslims in colonial India continued to assert that they could sacrifice cows based on a right rooted in their status as British subjects. Similarly, sex workers continued to assert that they had a right to practice their profession even after Supreme Court judgments to the contrary. This is slightly different from American constitutional rights consciousness, which Hartog defines as "a faith that the received meanings of constitutional texts will change when confronted with the legitimate aspirations of autonomous citizens and groups."[16]

This faith survived even when these aspirations, such as those of blacks, women, and gays, ran contrary to the current doctrines of constitutional law. However, implicit in this aspiration was the idea that the state would endorse such faith at some point in the future. In the Indian context, such faith seemed to exist without necessarily requiring or seeking state endorsement, and it remains a puzzle for further inquiry. It is tempting to suggest that Indians began to believe in the Constitution or that they were internally transformed by it, but it is impossible to prove this. What is definite is that Indians from a wide range of groups came to see the Constitution as a check on executive power and a powerful way to frame their claims.

Concurrently, state authorities began to become more cautious about law. In the Prohibition case, after multiple legal challenges, the government spent considerable time and energy trying to make the system of investigation and administration of Prohibition offenses conform to legal standards.[17] Experts hired by the government drew widely on knowledge of comparative law and experiences in other jurisdictions, particularly the United States.[18] Legal experts in the Ministry of Law at Delhi struggled to bring wayward state legislation in conformity with the Supreme Court decisions in the Qureshis' cases.[19] Similarly, the problems of prosecuting sex workers led to significant rounds of consultations between police officers and social workers.[20] Therefore, it was a constitutionalism from below that made the postcolonial state attempt to discipline itself.

What emerges is not a story of simple resistance to state authority. The process of pushing back through the Constitution brought citizens into closer engagement with the state and reaffirmed its right to exist.

Procedure over Substance

It is evident that all arguments did not gain an equal level of traction before the courts. Substantive rights claims that were more likely to capture public imagination had less success. The answer lay partly in the nature of rights themselves. As noted earlier, fundamental rights in the Indian Constitution could be circumscribed on a variety of grounds, and the list of grounds was expanded through amendments.[21] Moreover, because the drafters feared litigation, the Constitution expressly provided that the rights could be limited by a procedure established through law rather than the more substantive due process of law.[22] The courts were hesitant in the early years to strike down legislative initiatives even when they had concerns about the policy implications. Therefore, the courts found that the ban on cow slaughter and the imposition of commodity controls were reasonable restrictions on the right to a trade and a profession, the eviction of prostitutes was a reasonable restriction of their right to freedom of movement, and the imposition of Prohibition was a reasonable restriction on property. The courts remained conscious of the fact that these laws had been enacted by a popularly elected government that enjoyed both democratic legitimacy and popular authority, so they were careful about what they struck down.

However, it was precisely in the cases involving the more procedural aspect that the courts emerged as strict taskmasters. They came down heavily on what they perceived as bureaucratic arbitrariness. In the Prohibition cases, expanded police powers and the unfair burden of proof was challenged. In the commodity control cases, excessive delegation of authority to bureaucrats drew judicial ire. In the prostitution cases, the arbitrary powers of a local magistrate to evict any woman from the neighborhood became the area of contestation.

Independence created the conditions for such claims to resonate strongly. The state was being reconstituted, more than five hundred territories were being absorbed, the administration had rapidly expanded, and government was entering new arenas. This raised the question of defining jurisdictions. Federalism and the separation of the judiciary from the executive both became productive sites of litigation. With a strong centralized government for the first time, the local, provincial, and national arenas of politics began to interact more closely. Shared competences and diverging policies, in the case of Prohibition and cow slaughter, provided many loopholes that could be exploited. The centralizing tendencies of the Indian state were activated not just by state functionaries, who saw a patchwork of state laws as loopholes for those seeking to engage in illegal traffic (of women, alcohol, cows, or commodities), but also by electoral minorities who petitioned the Supreme Court or the newly empowered high courts over local authorities. The Qureshis organized nationally and petitioned the Supreme Court directly; information networks of prostitutes saw simultaneous action in Bombay, Allahabad, Punjab, and Bengal.

FIG. 5.2. The Congress Party government in Bombay was reluctant to create
an independent lower judiciary, separate from the executive branch.
Shankar's Weekly, July 5, 1953.

Yet despite the constitutional mandate, the separation of the judiciary from
the executive was a slow process (fig. 5.2).[23] The high courts, staffed largely by
judges drawn from the bar, were suspicious of the district magistrates, who
were drawn from the civil service and also served executive functions. The
judges remained unconvinced that members of the administration could play
an independent judicial role. In the prostitution cases, this is most clearly evident in the contrast between the decisions of the Allahabad and Andhra
Pradesh High Courts on Section 20 of SITA. In Allahabad, where the separation of the judiciary from the executive had not yet taken place, the clause was
struck down on the grounds that it permitted the magistrate to exercise power
arbitrarily, but in Andhra Pradesh, which was one of the first states to separate
the judiciary, the court upheld its constitutionality.

Karen Orren narrates an account of American constitutional development
through the lens of conflict between the older notions of the rights of officeholders and those of private citizens, with the Supreme Court frequently siding
with the former.[24] India did not have a long common-law history of officeholders, and the 1950s placed the offices that had evolved under colonial rule
in a state of flux. As a representative democratic state, India did not hesitate to
intervene with authorities (princes, landlords, priests, or husbands) that the
colonial state had at least publicly appeared to grant neutrality. Similarly, the
great office of the colonial district magistrate was also being redefined through
these constitutional challenges.

Critical legal scholars have observed with some regret the transformation of a heated rights question into a debate over procedure. Upendra Baxi lamented how the crucial grassroots issue of agrarian reform was converted into a "superstructural issue" of the limits of judicial power and the plenary power over amendments.[25] The translation of politics into law has consequences. We are cautioned that the growing centrality of legal norms in people's attempts to resist governmental authority is changing the modes of resistance and submission. It reduces the pluralism of the "weapons of the weak" and replaces, to some degree, the many other forms of circumventing, subverting, and conforming to authority.[26]

However, as this book has demonstrated, the consequences of this transformation can be beneficial to subaltern litigants. The four sets of litigants in this book represent groups that are marginal and have limited social capital amid a wider public. All were vilified in public discourse—as the pro-British Parsis, the corrupt and venal Marwari traders, the seductive and immoral prostitutes, and the brutal and cruel Muslim butchers—and had few allies outside their own groups. They stood outside the consensus of what a good Indian citizen should be.

Therefore, an argument rooted in their rights as prostitutes, traders, or butchers would not find popular resonance outside their groups. However, by framing their problem as one of procedure, these litigants were able to deflect attention from themselves and generalize the problem to the broader public. This was an interesting contrast to colonial India, where emphasizing particular rights was more profitable, but all of them were rooted in custom and religion.

Constitutionalism from the Margins

This book has shown that constitutional litigation was not limited to elites but was accessed by a cross-section of people. I would even suggest that the constitutional culture of the 1950s was shaped predominantly by the interventions of certain marginal groups. The institution of electoral democracy generated a particular form of subalternity: minorities that were unable to succeed electorally increasingly turned to the courts. Although this is not unusual in most democracies, the situation was complicated in India because electoral minorities are not just members of a socioeconomic class or followers of a certain ideology but are inextricably linked to ascriptive identities.

As I started looking for cases involving transformative legislation, I did not expect that every set of legal challenges would be dominated by members of a particular community. Although cow slaughter was more easily an identity issue, I had not imagined that commodity controls, Prohibition, and prostitution would also have a preponderance of cases filed by certain electoral minorities. Conversely, all electoral minorities were not able to gain access to the courts. So what determined the ability to successfully litigate?

As this book has shown, it was often groups that faced the greatest degree of state oppression that were the most able to litigate. Butchers, liquor sellers, and sex workers all dealt with multiple sets of regulation and faced the intrusive presence of state officials (health inspectors, policemen, social workers, or municipal officers). They all experienced multiple points of contact with the state and gained familiarity with the rules and regulations.[27] The level of awareness demonstrated by illiterate sex workers about the intricacies of zoning regulations, for instance, is often surprising. Traders, often operating outside the gaze of the state, suddenly found themselves under surveillance during World War II, and this surveillance became institutionalized after independence.

The groups that exhibited greater legal consciousness and access were those with strong community associations. These included formal institutions like the Bombay Parsi Panchayat and the Marwari-dominated Federation of Indian Chambers of Commerce and Industry, more hybrid associations like the All India Jamiatul Quresh Action Committee, and the newly set-up Allahabad Dancing Girls Union. Groups that doubled as professional associations and caste or community organizations were instrumental in legal mobilizing, lobbying, circulating knowledge, and supporting litigation. The existence of these associational forms complicates the divide between the categories of civil society and political society. It also challenges traditional accounts of liberal politics and suggests that liberty, property, and community are inextricably linked in India. Although liberal theory has carefully distinguished individual rights and groups rights, it is clear that in India the claims for individual rights were organized, funded, and supported by a group seeking to protect its own practices.

Group rights, particularly minority rights in India, have largely centered on questions of culture (language, religion, and status). This is despite Ambedkar's memorandum on minority rights, which noted that the "connection between individual liberty and the shape and form of the economic structure of the society may not be apparent to everyone . . . nonetheless the connection is real."[28] In a society build on caste, ascriptive identities and the structure of the economy were closely interlinked, and the Nehruvian state's attempts to reengineer the economy were resisted through networks of caste. This challenges the widely held belief that the vernacularization of Indian politics and the deepening of its electoral democracy happened in the 1970s and that this was when politics of caste, region, and religion erased an earlier vocabulary of class interests and capitalism. Claims for liberal rights in the 1950s arose from an economic world that was structured by caste. For instance, Yasin's case followed similar attempts by Muslim vegetable sellers in other towns in the province of Uttar Pradesh. This was not a coincidence. Much of the vegetable trade in north India is dominated by Arians, a Muslim subcaste of market gardeners, and it is likely that Yasin's petition was part of a coordinated action, or at least a result of networked information sharing.[29]

This book has therefore built on the argument that the introduction of liberal democratic processes in India, whether elections or judicial review, have not eradicated caste but have been mediated by it. It is now widely acknowledged that the poorest and most vulnerable populations in India are perhaps the most active participants in electoral politics, and it is through their participation that the "democratic process has in some ways detached itself from the institutional infirmities that surround it and acquired an autonomy of its own."[30] Contrary to conventional belief, similar processes, I have shown, are at play with constitutionalism.

This is not to suggest that all castes and groups could participate in these processes in the 1950s. Landless peasants do not appear in these narratives, and Dalits and tribals remain underrepresented, except when they were arrested by the police. The majority of the groups appearing in the archive are able to participate in the bazaar economy. However, scholars have demonstrated that in recent years, both Dalits and tribal groups have drawn upon the Constitution to make assertive claims in the courts and outside.[31]

A Constitution for Butchers? Markets, Circulation, and the Origin of Rights

In 1978 the Supreme Court of India admitted a petition from a poor mason, Moti Ram, who was asking for his bail order to be modified. The local magistrate had set the bail surety at ten thousand rupees and required the sureties from the same district, rejecting the suretyship of the petitioner's brother because his assets were in another jurisdiction. Justice Krishna Iyer ruled in Ram's favor, holding that there was a need for "liberal interpretation in areas of social justice, individual freedom, and indigent rights." He thundered from the bench that it shocked one's conscience to ask a mason like the petitioner to furnish sureties for ten thousand rupees. He reminded the court and the errant magistrate that "our Constitution, enacted by 'We the People of India,' is meant for the butcher, the baker, and the candlestick maker—shall we add the bonded laborer and the pavement dweller?"[32]

Justice Iyer's exhortation was a conscious reference to a statement made by Justice Vivian Bose in 1956. Expressing exasperation at procedural delays in getting relief for a petitioner, Justice Bose declaimed "that the Constitution is not for the exclusive benefit of governments and states; it is not only for lawyers and politicians and officials and those highly placed. It also exists for the common man, for the poor and the humble, for those who have businesses at stake, for the butcher, the baker, and the candlestick maker."[33] Justice Iyer's inclusion of the pavement dweller and the bonded laborer to this list, marks the beginning of public-interest litigation in the narrative of constitutional law in India.

Upendra Baxi argues that the elevation of Justice Iyer reinforced the tendency of the court to judicial populism, for he "unrelentingly insisted that the law is meant for the people, and not the people for the law, and as a neo-Marxist, he meant by people, mainly the proletariat and not the propertariat."[34] As Baxi states, this marked the beginning of a phase that led the Supreme Court of India to become the Supreme Court of Indians. This implies that the Supreme Court in the period this book covers was not a court for all Indians when it was only the court for butchers, bakers, and candlestick makers. Baxi echoes a criticism often made by Nehru and others in government that constitutional litigation was led by vested or special interests, unlike the state, which represented national interest. I argue that these value-loaded terms mischaracterize a natural consequence of the policies of the Nehruvian state.

Where did claims for rights emerge from in the 1950s? A common thread running through the cases in this book is a concern about the practice of a trade and profession and the free movement of people, goods and services. Although the butchers and the commodity traders directly fall into this category, it also exposes the commercial interests that lay behind the civil liberty challenges to prohibition. The cases brought by the sex workers were about harassment and equality but also fundamentally about the right to earn their livelihood. Therefore, a significant proportion of everyday rights cases in Nehruvian India emerged through the market.

The easiest explanation, of course, is that people would incur costs to go to court only if there was something substantial at stake. However, this also sets up a new template for thinking about the Nehruvian state in India. The Nehruvian state, with its instrumentalities of planning, nationalizing of key industries, and state-directed development projects, has been described as antimarket. The multitude of new legislation examined in this book suggests that instead of being crudely antimarket, the new state was attempting to create a new set of market norms and reshape networks of circulation, whether of goods (alcohol, beef, and cotton), capital, or bodies. The vision laid out in the Directive Principles of State Policy imagined a new governing logic for state and society. This transformation did not take place overnight, and the roots of this were laid in the late 1920s and 1930s with increasing electoral representation in municipal and provincial governments. Municipalities in the 1920s sought to expel prostitutes, whereas the first elected provincial governments in 1939 attempted to bring about prohibition.

The rights claims before the judiciary in the 1950s, unlike the rights claims today, were claims not for new rights but for continuing older practices that were now being challenged or forbidden by the new government. Therefore, the contest was not just between a totalitarian state imagination and an individual, or even the majority and a minority, although both of these were factors, but between the virtuous citizen (who practiced austerity, was sexually abstinent, didn't drink alcohol or consume beef, and didn't waste time or money) and those who fell outside this definition; the latter created a new kind of ethical agent, the litigious citizen. This book has pointed out, that although a claim of cultural autonomy to protect lifestyles could be made against a colonial state, it was harder to sustain in a democratic republic. The overrepresentation of minorities in litigation shows that they took seriously the promise of equality and the state's obligation to protect their rights. Despite minority rights in India having been largely understood through the realm of identity and culture, the claims made by minorities were for economic rights: the need to protect minority-owned businesses (Parsi liquor interests and Muslim butchers), to feed the poor (prostitutes' claims to welfare), or to reduce bureaucratic arbitrariness.

Constitutional law thus became the field in which citizens marked as deviant in the new order could recast themselves as virtuous constitutional actors. These citizens differed in the extent of their marginality—for instance, Marwari petty merchants were better placed than prostitutes and vegetable vendors. However, all their cases carved out rules and norms that benefited a larger populace.

Making themselves subject to the Constitution did not necessarily bind enterprising citizens to the hegemony of courts and judges. To return to the vegetable vendor, Mohammed Yasin, even before the Supreme Court arrived at a decision, Yasin and his friends hired Nanu, the local Dalit town crier, to beat his drum and announce across the town of Jalalabad that there was a case between the public and the town, and the public had won and the town had lost. The town committee was outraged and wrote to the Supreme Court urging that Yasin be charged with contempt, both for conflating his petition with the public and for putting out a false story. The judges just filed away the complaint. Clearly, as early as 1950, a popular language existed which would cause an individual's claim against the state to be translated as a public claim against the state. It starkly demonstrates that jurisgenesis, or the creation of legal meaning, is not only in the hands of legal elites.[35] Regardless of the court's judgments, people created and disseminated their own meanings of the Constitution, which may even be a successful insurgent and displace the elite conception of the law.[36] As citizens, historians, and lawyers, we should listen for Nanu's drumming as we look at the Constitution, reminding ourselves that constitutional narratives are forged both inside and outside courtrooms.

ACKNOWLEDGMENTS

IN THE WINTER OF 2004 I experienced my first admissions day in the Supreme Court of India as a law student interning in the judges' chambers, when
more than a hundred lawyers sought to make two-minute arguments to get
their clients' cases admitted for hearing before the Supreme Court. My four
years in law school had cultivated the belief that going to court and asserting
constitutional claims for redress were natural reactions for most people; however, a few months at the court made it evident how remarkable it was that
Indians continued to engage with the legal system that often delivered little at
a very high cost. The seeds of this book were planted in those months as I was
jostled between lawyers, and they germinated in the next decade as I moved
across three continents and various institutions. In the process I have incurred
intellectual, material, and emotional debts to several people and institutions,
to whom I remain I deeply grateful.

This research was possible only because Justice K. G. Balakrishnan, then the
chief justice of India, graciously granted permission to consult the records at
the Supreme Court of India. I am grateful to Dinesh Gulati, Sidharth Chauhan,
and the staff of the Supreme Court Record Room and Museum for making my
time at the Supreme Court so rewarding. I would like to thank the staff of the
National Archives of India, particularly Jaya Raman; the Nehru Memorial Museum and Library and the Indian Law Institute in Delhi; the Punjab State
Archives in Chandigarh; the Maharashtra State Archives, the Forum for Free
Enterprise, and the Films Division of India in Mumbai; the Centre for South
Asian Studies at Cambridge University; the Asian and African Studies Collection at the British Library in London; and the Rockerfeller Foundation Archive
in New York. Bipin Aspatwar, Menaka Guruswamy, Arundhati Katju, Arjun
Krishnan, and Jawahar Raja cheerfully accepted the role of native informants
on appellate litigation that I thrust upon them, and they patiently answered my
questions on procedure, filing, and judicial politics. I am particularly grateful

to the staff of Firestone Library at Princeton University and the Sterling Memorial Library at Yale University for their extraordinary efforts to procure materials through interlibrary loan. One of the pleasures of working on postcolonial India was the ability to talk to those who had lived through and participated in the events I study. I feel privileged to have learned from Upendra Baxi, Rajeev Dhavan, George Gadbois, Marc Galanter, Brenda Gelhot, Kapila Hingorani, Nirmal Hingorani, Imran Khan, B. B. Majumdar, A. G. Noorani, Jehangir Patel, Raju Ramachandran, Barry Sen, and Krishan Wadhwa.

I would like to thank Yamuna Shankar for permission to reproduce the cartoons of her father, K. Shankar Pillai, from *Shankar's Weekly*; Meera Velayudhan for permission to reproduce her mother's photograph; and the Homai Vyarawalla Collection, Alkazi Collection of Photography. I am grateful to Prashant Reddy for his advice on copyright.

I am grateful to the editors of the Histories of Economic Life series for encouraging me to think of the constitutive relationship of the law and the economy. I am deeply indebted to Gautam Bhatia, Karuna Mantena, Peter Perdue, Mrinalini Sinha, Anupama Rao, and the two anonymous reviewers for Princeton University Press for reading and engaging vigorously with the manuscript. Ritu Birla, Binyamin Blum, Joya Chatterji, Rahul De, David Gilmartin, Manu Goswami, Iza Hussin, Niraja Jayal, Mary E. John, Sunil Khilnani, Prabha Kottiswaran, Nivedita Menon, Thomas Metcalf, Durba Mitra, Ajay Skaria, Nandini Sundar, Robert Travers, V. Umakanth, and Barbara Welke all read portions of the manuscript and gave me invaluable feedback. It was a privilege to have worked with Brigitta van Rheinberg and Amanda Peery on this manuscript, and I am thankful for their careful engagement with this manuscript. I am grateful to Sumati Dwivedi, Amberle Sherman, and Audra Wolfe for their editorial assistance.

I've benefited from being able to present parts of this book to perceptive and knowledgeable audiences at numerous venues: the Hurst Summer Institute in Legal History; the Center for History and Economics at Harvard University; the Centre for South Asian Studies at Cambridge University; the King's India Institute in London; the Recalling Democracy Workshop at the University of Michigan in Ann Arbor; the School of Oriental and African Studies in London; the South Asian History Seminar at St. Anthony's College in Oxford; the Comparative Political Thought Seminar at Oxford University; the University of Virginia Law School; the Legal History Colloquium at the New York University School of Law; the Daniel Jacobson Legal History and Comparative Law Workshop at the Hebrew University Law School in Jerusalem; the

Critical Analysis of Law Workshop at the University of Toronto Law School; the Department of History at the University of Delhi; the Department of Sociology at South Asia University; the Dirty History Seminar at the University of Georgia; the Centre for Asian Legal Studies at the National University of Singapore's Faculty of Law; the Center for Democracy, Development, and Rule of Law in Stanford, California; the British Institute for East Africa in Nairobi; the National Institute for Advanced Studies in Bangalore, India, and the annual meetings of the Law and Society Association; the American Society for Legal History; the annual South Asian Studies Conference in Madison, Wisconsin; and the Law and Social Sciences Research Network of Jawaharlal Nehru University in Delhi. The labor of writing was made possible by committed and generous members of writing groups in New Haven, Princeton, and Cambridge (UK); I am grateful to Rosie Bsheer, Franziska Exeler, Rotem Geva, Kasturi Gupta, Radha Kumar, Eleanor Newbigin, Poornima Paidypati, Norbert Peabody, Ornit Shani, and Nurfadzilah Yahaya.

At Princeton University I was fortunate to have both Gyan Prakash and Hendrik Hartog as my PhD advisors, to whom I owe a great intellectual debt for guiding me through the shores of South Asian history and legal history. Through their writing they demonstrated how to ask big theoretical questions while writing about the narratives of ordinary lives, and through practice they showed how to build and sustain an intellectually committed and socially engaged community of scholars. I am immensely grateful to Gyan for helping me to articulate what postcolonial freedom entailed and to Dirk for pushing me to take legal forms more seriously even as I remained skeptical of their claims. Gyan and Dirk have my deepest admiration and gratitude.

Bhavani Raman has been an inspirational teacher and scholar, and my arguments have developed over the course of many conversations with her. I owe a tremendous debt of gratitude to Kim Lane Scheppele, who introduced me to law and society scholarship and who built a cosmopolitan field of constitutional law. My decision to become a legal historian came from a chance meeting with Mitra Sharafi over dinner. Through her generosity with her time and advice, her infectious enthusiasm for her subject that fosters a community of scholars on South Asian legal history, and her courage and cheerfulness in times of adversity, Mitra sets the gold standard for the kind of academic I aspire to be. I am particularly thankful to her for reading and commenting on several drafts of this manuscript.

I am grateful to Carol Greenhouse, Partha Chatterjee, and Bruce Ackerman for being inspiring teachers and generous interlocutors and showing me how to approach the subject of law and society. I am particularly grateful to V. S. Elizabeth and Sitaramam Karkarla for nourishing the social sciences, enabling critical thinking, and being ethical voices at the National Law School in Bangalore. I was fortunate to have encountered the dynamic Chitra Srinivas in middle school, who made history exciting and meaningful despite the limitations of a state-mandated, exam-focused syllabus.

A postdoctoral fellowship at the Centre for History and Economics at Cambridge University has made this book possible. I am deeply grateful to Emma Rothschild for her encouragement, support, and incisive comments, particularly about the quotidian lives of law. I was fortunate to find generous and thoughtful interlocutors in Sunil Amrith, Tim Harper, William O'Reilly, and Fei-Hsien Wang. Julia Stephens's friendship and intellectual camaraderie has shaped my work over a decade, as we navigated new jobs together.

At Yale University I found a home in the Department of History, the law school, and the South Asian Studies Council, and my work has benefited tremendously from the intellectual generosity of my colleagues and friends. I am thankful to Jennifer Allen, Sergei Antonov, Piyali Bhattacharya, Daniel Botsman, Carolyn Dean, Fabian Drixler, Alejandra Dubcovsky, Marcella Eccheveri, Paul Freedman, Beverly Gage, Inderpal Grewal, Denise Ho, Benedict Keirnan, Naomi Lamoureaux, Louisa Lombard, Daniel Magaziner, Daniel Markovits, Joanne Meyerowitz, Alan Mikhail, Samuel Moyn, Isaac Nakhimovsky, Peter Perdue, Steve Pincus, Chitra Ramalingam, Terence Renaud, Paul Sabin, K. Sivaramakrishnan, Tariq Thachil, Francesca Trivellato, Jennifer van Vleck, Steven Wilkinson, and John Witt. Karuna Mantena and Rosie Bsheer have been towering pillars of support.

The research was made possible by the generosity of several institutions. My travel to archives and libraries in Europe and Asia was generously supported by the Graduate School, the Department of History, and the Law and Public Affairs Program at Princeton University; the Princeton Institute for International and Regional Studies; the Centre for History and Economics at Cambridge University; and the Macmillan Center for International and Area Studies at Yale University. The Department of History at Yale provided a year of research leave to complete this book. The Frederick W. Hilles Fund at Yale supported this manuscript. I am grateful to some wonderful and committed administrators, particularly Judith Hanson, Kristy Novak, Reagan Maraghy, Dana Lee, Denise Scott, Mary Rose Cheadle, Caryn Carson, Ammaar Al-Hayder, and Lina Chan for their efficiency and kindness. I am particularly grateful to Liza Joyner and Inga Huld Markan, whose prompt action and empathetic support helped me work my way through the immigration bureaucracies in the United Kingdom and the United States.

A decade ago, South Asian legal history and postcolonial Indian history were understudied fields, and I feel privileged to be part of a growing community of scholars who are charting the terrain. Their friendship, camaraderie, and conversations have greatly enriched the process of writing and thinking. I am grateful to Zarine Ahmad, J. Aniruddha, Pratiksha Bakshi, Aparna Balachandran, Yael Berda, Rachel Berger, Mohsin Bhat, Udit Bhatia, Debjani Bhattacharya, Anuj Bhuwania, Fahad Bishara, Arudra Burra, Sandipto Dasgupta, Arvind Elangovan, Shahana Ghosh, William Gould, Rebecca Grapevine, Tarunabh Khaitan, Elizabeth Kolsky, Jayant Krishnan, Harshan Kumarsingham, Stephen Legg, Lawrence Liang, Martin Mattsson, Arvind Narrain, Pooja Parmar, Jahnavi Phalkey, Jeff Redding, Nicholas Robinson, Ornit Shani, Taylor Sherman, Arun Kumar Thiruvengadam, and Namita Wahi. I combated archival dust and historiography demons with Tariq Omar Ali, Rotem Geva, Arunabh Ghosh, Riyad Koya, Radha Kumar, Johan Mathew, Nikhil Menon, Durba Mitra, Kalyani Ramnath, Uditi Sen, Julia Stephens, and Benjamin Siegel as they provided inspiration with their own work.

Friends and colleagues across three continents have filled my days with happiness and sustained this project in many ways I cannot adequately acknowledge. Thank you to Anthony Acciavati, Sare Aricanli, Aditya Balasubramian, Nimisha Barton, Rachel Berger, Ritwik Bhattacharjo, Debjani Bhattacharya, Omar Cheta, Shinjini Das, Rohan Debroy, William Deringer, Catherine Evans, Joppan George, Nabaparna Ghosh, Matthew Grohowski, Jitendra Kanodia, Radha Kumar, Kyril Kunakhovich, Jebro Lit Lay, Nayanika Mathur, Nikhil Menon, Sarah Milov, Kanta Murali, Darren Pais, Ninad Pandit, Dinyar Patel, Farah Peterson, James Pickett, Ronny Regev, Mishka Sinha Roy, Padraic Scanlan, Margaret Schotte, Vinay Sitapati, John Slight, Avani Mehta Sood, Molly Wright Steeson, and Alden Young. I want to thank Rohit Lamba, Arijeet Pal, and Nurfadzilah Yahaya for bringing a sense of balance in turbulent times and a sense of turbulence in dull ones. Mitra Sharafi, Kaveri Gill, and Kriti Kapila have provided constant encouragement and a sympathetic year to the travails of research and writing. Anubhuti Agrawal, Ashwin Bishnoi, Sundip Biswas, Sumona Bose, Ashvin Iyengar, Chandra Iyengar, Neha Kaul, Aditya Sarkar, Devottam Sengupta, and Faiz Tajuddin generously opened their homes to me, playing host in New York, London, and Mumbai.

I have been blessed with a preponderance of aunts (and a few uncles) who made the process of research and writing much easier. Suparna, Debabrata,

Deepa, and Mala Sarkar welcomed me into their home with love and affection, making the transition from India to the United States much easier. I would not have been able to complete this book or even be in this country without their quiet presence and constant support. I am grateful to Arup and Swapna Roy for their encouragement. In Delhi, Mohua Mitra and Ella Dutta remain a bedrock of support and through their own work have demonstrated the importance of good writing. Sanjukta Dutta helped me appreciate academic rigor as well as the importance of cultivating a sense of the ridiculous. My deepest gratitude goes to my family. My grandparents, Himadri Shekhar Day and Protima Mitra, both saw me leave India to begin this project and are not here to see me finish it. I hope my work will redeem their faith in me. I am lucky to have grown up with a brother like Rahul De, and I often take his support and affirmation for granted. His love for teaching and his impatience with what he considers trendy research make me strive to be a better scholar and teacher. I am grateful for him and Neeraja Sundaram for their love and support.

Surabhi Ranganathan and I began our academic journeys together at the age of seventeen. She has been a constant companion throughout the process (although she will remind me that she finished her PhD and her book several years before I finished mine). It is almost impossible to list the many ways in which her friendship sustains me and my work.

My parents, Anuradha De and Ranjan De, have been my foundation, sustaining me with their love and confidence. They inculcated me with a love of books at an early age, without which I would have been neither a lawyer nor a historian. It is because of their hard work, sacrifice, and commitment that I had the luxury to do what I love. Without my mother's periodic reminders to stop dillydallying and get on with writing, this book would not have been completed. My *amma*, Jyotsna Day, was a beacon of unstinted love and comfort, and I feel her loss deeply. Having being present at the birth of the Indian republic, she embodied the optimism, honesty, and clarity of her generation. To her and my parents, I dedicate this book with love and gratitude.

NOTES

Introduction

1. For more on Yasin's story, see Rohit De, "Beyond the Social Contract," *Seminar* (special issue on sixty years of the Indian Constitution), November 2010.

2. *Virendra Singh* v. *State of Uttar Pradesh* (1955) 1 SCR 415 (Justice Vivian Bose).

3. This absence is perhaps most keenly felt in the burgeoning field of comparative constitutional law. For instance, Asia is entirely ignored in Christopher Thornhill, *A Sociology of Constitutions: Constitutions and State Legitimacy in a Historico-Sociological Perspective* (Cambridge, UK: Cambridge University Press, 2011), a sociological account of the reasons modern societies seek constitutions and constitutional norms. A suggestive chapter, titled "Postwar Transformations," deals with socialist constitutions in Eastern Europe rather than postcolonial constitutions. Tvsi Kahana and Richard Bauman, eds., *The Least Examined Branch: The Role of the Legislature in a Constitutional State* (Cambridge, UK: Cambridge University Press, 2006) examines the dialogic role of legislatures with constitutions and the implication for democratic theory, yet it leaves out the world's largest democracy, which has a history of strong contestation between the legislature and the judiciary.

4. Granville Austin, *The Indian Constitution: Cornerstone of a Nation* (New Delhi: Oxford University Press, 1964), a study of constitution making in the 1960s, remains the standard text on the subject. More recent scholarship continues to draw heavily upon Austin's account. See, e.g., Ramachandra Guha, *India after Gandhi: The History of the World's Largest Democracy* (New Delhi: HarperCollins, 2007), 115–36; and Sarbani Sen, *The Constitution of India: Popular Sovereignty and Democratic Transformations* (New Delhi: Oxford University Press, 2008). An original and important departure from this tradition is Arun Kumar Thiruvengadam, *The Constitution of India: Contextual Analysis* (London: Bloomsbury, 2017).

5. This correspondence has been largely ignored, with the exception of Ornit Shani, *How India Became Democratic: Citizenship and the Making of Universal Franchise* (Cambridge, UK: Cambridge University Press, 2018), a study of those involved in the making of the franchise provisions.

6. File 1/5/54, Foreigners Branch, Ministry of Home Affairs Files, National Archives of India (NAI), New Delhi; File 71/3/54, 1954, Ministry of External Affairs Files, NAI.

7. *Sudhir Chandra Neogy* v. *Calcutta Tramways*; AIR 1960 Cal 396.

8. *Kailash Chand Garg* v. *Regional Passport Officer*, Bombay, Civil Appeal 513 of 1959, cited in Kailash Chand, *Mother's Son*, South Asia Pamphlet Collection 30, Library of Congress.

9. Pratap Bhanu Mehta, "What Is Constitutional Morality?", *Seminar*, November 2010. In recent years there has been a renewed interest in the prehistory of the Indian Constitution. See, e.g., Rohit De, " Constitutional Antecedents," *The Oxford Handbook to the Indian Constitution*, ed. Sujit Choudhary, Madhav Khosla, and Pratap Bhanu Mehta (New York: Oxford University Press, 2015), 23–46; Eleanor Newbigin, Ornit Shani, and Stephen Legg, "Constitutionalism and the Evolution of Democracy in India," *Comparative Studies of South Asia, Africa, and the Middle East [CSSAAME]* 36, no. 1 (2017): 42–43; Arvind Elangovan, "Provincial Autonomy, Sir Benegal Narsing Rau, and an Improbable Imagination of Constitutionalism in India, 1935–38," in *CSSAAME* 36, no. 1 (2017): 66–82; and Stephen Legg, " Dyarchy: Democracy, Autocracy, and the Scalar Sovereignty of Interwar India," *CSSAAME* 36, no. 1 (2017): 44–65.

10. S. P. Sathe, *Judicial Activism in India: Transgressing Borders and Enforcing Limits* (New Delhi: Oxford University Press, 2002), 249; Peter Waldman, "Jurist's Prudence: India's Supreme Court Makes Rule of Law a Way of Governing," *Wall Street Journal*, May 6, 1996.

11. Pratap Bhanu Mehta, "India's Judiciary: The Promise of Uncertainty," in *India's Public Institutions*, ed. Pratap Mehta and Devesh Kapur (New Delhi: Oxford University Press, 2005), 159. See also Nicholas Robinson, "Expanding Judiciaries: India and the Rise of the Good Governance Court," *Washington University Global Studies Law Review* 8, no. 1 (2009): 1–70.

12. Priya Ranjan Sahu, "The Constitution Set in Stone: Adivsasis in Jharkhand are using an old tradition as a novel protest" , *Scroll*, https://scroll.in/article/878468/the-constitution-set-in-stone-adivasis-in-jharkhand-are-using-an-old-tradition-as-a-novel-protest; Nandini Sundar, "Pathalgadi is Nothing But Constitutional Messianism So Why is the BJP Afraid of It", *The Wire*, 15 May 2018, https://thewire.in/rights/pathalgadi-is-nothing-but-constitutional-messianism-so-why-is-the-bjp-afraid-of-it.

13. Jean Comaroff and John Comaroff, eds., *Law and Disorder in the Postcolony* (Chicago: University of Chicago Press, 2006), 1–56.

14. It has been observed that it would take three centuries to clear the backlog of pending cases before Indian courts. "Courts Will Take 320 Years to Clear Backlog Cases: Justice Rao," *Hindustan Times*, March 6, 2010, http://articles.timesofindia.indiatimes.com/2010-03-06/india/28143242_1_high-court-judges-literacy-rate-backlog.

15. Marc Galanter, "To the Listed Field: The Myth of Civil Litigiousness in India," *Jindal Global Law Review* 1, no. 1 (2009): 65–78.

16. Jean Comaroff and John Comaroff, "Reflections on the Anthropology of Law, Governance, and Sovereignty," in *Rules of Law and Laws of Ruling: On the Governance of Law*, ed. Franz von Benda-Beckmann, Keebet von Benda-Beckmann, and Julia Eckert (Surrey, UK: Ashgate, 2009), 31.

17. Ran Hirschl, *Towards Juristocracy: The Origins and Functions of New Constitutionalism* (Cambridge, MA: Harvard University Press, 2007).

18. This period is marked by the collapse of communist regimes in Eastern Europe and Central Asia. Jeremy Gould, "Strong Bar, Weak State: Lawyers, Liberalism, and State Formation in Zambia," *Development and Change* 37, no. 4 (2006): 921–41; Julia Eckert, Brian Donaho, Christian Strümpel, and Zerrin Özlem Biner, eds., *Law against the State: Ethnographic Forays into Law's Transformations* (Cambridge, UK: Cambridge University Press, 2012); Javier Couso, Alexandra Huneeus, and Rachel Sieder, *Cultures of Legality: Judicialization and Political Activism in Latin America* (Cambridge, UK: Cambridge University Press, 2010); Hirschl, *Towards Juristocracy*.

19. Similar arguments are made about India's legal trajectory. Mayur Suresh and Siddharth Narrain, eds., *The Shifting Scales of Justice: The Supreme Court in the 1990s* (Telangana: Orient Blackswa,: 2014); Oishik Sircar, "Spectacles of Emancipation: Reading Rights Differently in India's Legal Discourse," *Osgood Hall Law Journal* 49, no. 3 (2012): 527–75; Radha D'Souza, "The 'Third World' and Socio-Legal Studies: Neo-Liberalism and Lessons from India's Legal Innovations," *Social and Legal Studies* 14, no. 4 (2005): 487–513.

20. Robert Cover, "The Supreme Court, 1982 Term—Foreword: Nomos and Narrative," *Harvard Law Review* 97, no. 4 (1983): 7.

21. *Virendra Singh v. State of Uttar Pradesh* (1955) 1 SCR 415 (Justice Vivian Bose).

22. Bruce Ackerman, "The Rise of World Constitutionalism," *Virginia Law Review* (1997): 771–97; Sen, *Constitution of India*.

23. Rajeev Bhargava, ed., *Politics and Ethics of the Indian Constitution* (New Delhi: Oxford University Press, 2008), 2.

24. Ibid. This volume remains the most important work dealing with several aspects of the Constitution. The bulk of the intellectual history of modern India, however, remains concerned with the leading figures in the preindependence period. See also Rochona Bajpai, *Debating Difference: Groups Rights and Liberal Democracy in India* (New Delhi: Oxford University Press, 2011); Pratap Bhanu Mehta, *The Burden of Democracy* (New Delhi: Penguin, 2003); Udit Bhatia, ed., *The Indian Constituent Assembly: Deliberations on Democracy* (New Delhi: Routledge, 2017).

25. Shani, *How India Became Democratic*.

26. A very small segment of propertied Indian men were enfranchised for municipal elections in the late nineteenth century. The Indian Councils Act in 1909 provided for some elected representatives in legislative councils. Elected legislators remained a minority and had few powers. For a history of franchise in India, see Sumit Sarkar, "Indian Democracy: The Historical Inheritance," in *The Success of India's Democracy*, ed. Atul Kohli (Cambridge, UK: Cambridge University Press, 1991), 23–46. On women's franchise, see Geraldine Forbes, "Votes for Women: The Demand for Women's Franchise in India, 1917–1937," in *Symbols of Power: Studies on the Political Status of Women in India*, ed. Vina Mazumdar (Bombay: Allied, 1979), 3–23.

27. Sunil Khilnani, *The Idea of India* (New Delhi: Penguin, 2004), 17. See also Gyan Prakash, "Anxious Constitution Making," in *The Postcolonial Moment in South and Southeast Asia*, ed. Gyan Prakash, Nikhil Menon, and Michael Laffan (London: Bloomsbury, 2018), 141–62.

28. Articles 36–51, Constitution of India, 1950.

29. B. R. Ambedkar, *Constituent Assembly Debates*, November 19, 1948.

30. Kalyani Ramnath, "We the People: Seamless Webs and Social Revolution in the Indian Constituent Assembly Debates," *South Asia Research* 32 (2012): 57. See also "K. M. Munshi's Note and Draft Articles on Fundamental Rights," March 17, 1947, in B. Shiva Rao, *The Framing of India's Constitution: A Study* (Nashik: Government of India Press, 1968) 69–80; "The Fundamental Rights Resolution: Nationalism, Internationalism, and Cosmopolitanism in an Interwar Moment," *CSSAAME* 37, no. 2 (2017): 213–19.

31. Javed Majeed, "'A Nation on the Move': The Indian Constitution, Life Writing, and Cosmopolitanism," *Life Writing* 13, no. 2 (2016): 237–53.

32. Uday Singh Mehta, "The Social Question and the Absolutism of Politics," in *Seminar*, November 2010. For the original argument on which this is based, see Hannah Arendt, *On Revolution* (London: Penguin Books, 1990), 112.

33. Khilnani, *Idea of India*.

34. Ananya Vajpeyi, *Righteous Republic: The Political Foundations of Modern India* (Cambridge, MA: Harvard University Press, 2012); Ramachandra Guha, *The Makers of Modern India* (Cambridge, MA: Harvard University Press, 2011). See also Ackerman, "Rise of World Constitutionalism."

35. Upendra Baxi, *The Indian Supreme Court and Politics* (New Delhi: Eastern Book, 1980); Granville Austin, *Working a Democratic Constitution: A History of the Indian Experience* (New York: Oxford University Press, 2003).

36. Saadat Hasan Manto, "The New Constitution," in *Bitter Fruit: The Very Best of Saadat Hasan Manto*, ed. Khalid Hasan (New Delhi: Penguin Books, 2008), 206–15. There is a growing body of work on Manto and his literary contributions. See, e.g., Ayesha Jalal, *The Pity of Partition: Manto's Life, Time, and Work across the India-Pakistan Divide* (Princeton, NJ: Princeton University Press, 2013).

37. Sircar, "Spectacles of Emancipation," 530.

38. Aamir R. Mufti, "A Greater Story-Writer Than God: Genre, Gender, and Minority in Late Colonial India," in *Community, Gender and Violence: Subaltern Studies XI*, ed. Partha Chatterjee and Pradeep Jeganathan (New York: Columbia University Press, 2000), 21.

39. Upendra Baxi, "The Little Done, the Vast Undone: Reflections on Reading Granville Austin's 'The Indian Constitution,'" *Journal of the Indian Law Institute* 9 (1967): 323–430.

40. Anil Kalhan, "Constitution and Extra Constitution: Emergency Powers in Postcolonial Pakistan and India," in *Emergency Powers in Asia: Exploring the Limits of Legality*, ed. Victor Ramraj and Arun V. Thiruvengadam (Cambridge, UK: Cambridge University Press, 2010); Perry Anderson, "After Nehru," *London Review of Books*, August 2, 2012.

41. Articles 352–360, Constitution of India, 1950.

42. Article 19:2–6, Constitution of India, 1953.

43. Somnath Lahiri, *Constituent Assembly Debates*, April 29, 1947.

44. Article 368, Constitution of India, 1950.

45. In contrast, the US Constitution has been amended twenty-two times in more than two hundred years. The conflict between the Supreme Court and the parliament of India over the question of amendments has dominated the literature on Indian constitutional law. The question achieved a certain resolution in *Kesavananda Bharti* v. *State of Kerala*, AIR 1973 SC 1461, in which the Supreme Court held that certain constitutional principles were inviolable and could not be amended by parliament, thus subjecting all constitutional amendments to judicial review. See Sudhir Krishnaswamy, *Democracy and Constitutionalism in India: A Study of the Basic Structure* (New Delhi: Oxford University Press, 2009).

46. This reflects an older debate over the question of legal transplants dating back to Savigny. The debate at its crudest is between scholars who believe that a certain autonomy of law and can easily be transferred and those who argue that law is deeply embedded in society and can only survive a transfer if it matches the social and economic conditions of the new society. For a detailed review, see Assaf Likhovski and Ron Harris, eds, *Theme Issue: Histories of Legal Transplantations, Theoretical Inquiries in Law*, 10.2 (2009).

47. Damodar Swarup Seth, *Constituent Assembly Debates*, November 5, 1948. The term "slavish imitation" gained some currency among critics in the Constituent Assembly and was used a few times. See also Raj Bahadur, *Constituent Assembly Debates*, November 9, 1948; and B. Pocker Sahib Bahadur, *Constituent Assembly Debates*, November 9, 1948.

48. K. Hamumanthaiya, *Constituent Assembly Debates*, November 17, 1949.

49. B. R. Ambedkar, *Constituent Assembly Debates*, November 25, 1949.

50. Sandipto Dasgupta, "A Language Which Is Foreign to Us: Continuities and Anxieties in the Making of the Indian Constitution." *CSSAAME* 34, no. 2 (2014): 228–42.

51. "Fortnightly Reports from Hyderabad," File 17 (7) H/51, 1951, Ministry of States Files, NAI.

52. Upendra Baxi, "Outline of a 'Theory of Practice' of Indian Constitutionalism," in *Politics and Ethics of the Indian Constitution*, ed. Rajeev Bhargava (New Delhi: Oxford University Press, 2008), 101.

53. Article 32, Constitution of India, 1950.

54. Article 226, Constitution of India, 1950.

55. Galanter, "To the Listed Field."

56. Law Commission of India, *14th Report: Reform of Judicial Administration* (New Delhi, 1958).

57. Rajeev Dhavan, *The Supreme Court of India: A Socio-Legal Critique of its Juristic Techniques* (Bombay: N. M. Tripathi, 1977), 16.

58. Kim Lane Scheppele, "Constitutional Ethnography: An Introduction," *Law and Society Review* 38, no. 3 (2004): 389–406.

59. Maya Dodd, "Archives of Democracy: Technologies of Witness in Literatures on Indian Democracy since 1975," unpublished manuscript, 2006.

60. Rohit De, "The Federal Court and Civil Liberties in Late Colonial India," in *Fates of Political Liberalism in the British Post-Colony: The Politics of the Legal Complex*, ed. Terence Halliday, Lucien Karpik, and Malcolm Feeley (Cambridge, UK: Cambridge University Press, 2012), 59–90.

61. Article 50, Constitution of India, 1950.

62. Lauren Benton, "Colonial Law and Cultural Difference: Jurisdictional Politics and the Formation of the Colonial State," *Comparative Studies in Society and History* 41, no. 3 (2000): 563–88; Robert Travers, *Ideology and Empire in Eighteenth-Century India* (Cambridge, UK: Cambridge University Press, 2007).

63. Mithi Mukherjee, *India in the Shadows of the Empire: A Legal and Political History (1774–1950)* (New Delhi: Oxford University Press, 2010).

64. A. T. Markose, *Judicial Control of Administrative Action in India* (Madras: Madras Law Journal, 1956), 88–91.

65. *In re Benoarilal Roy*, (1944) 48 CWN 766.

66. Nasser Hussain, *The Jurisprudence of Emergency* (Ann Arbor: University of Michigan Press, 2003), 75.

67. See, e.g., S.270, Government of India Act, 1950; S.197, Criminal Procedure Code, 1898; and S.16, Defense of India Act, 1914 and 1939.

68. According to the Nehru Report, there were five attempts in the 1920s to set up a new Federal Court. The Indian Reforms Commission of 1919 made no mention of the judiciary. The Simon Commission of 1930 justified its noninterference in the judiciary by citing the legitimacy of colonial courts in India, which were used by large number of "natives."

69. B. R. Ambedkar, *Constituent Assembly Debates*, September 8, 1949.

70. Alladi Krishnaswami Ayyar, *Constituent Assembly Debates*, September 8, 1949.

71. Rajeev Dhavan, ed., *Nehru and the Constitution* (Bombay: N. M. Tripathi, 1992), xxxi.

72. "Ad Hoc Committee of the Supreme Court of India," Rajendra Prasad Papers, NAI.

73. Robinson, "Expanding Judiciaries," 14–15.

74. I received permission from Justice Konakuppakatil (K. G.) Balakrishnan, the chief justice of India, to access the Supreme Court Record Room and Museum, neither of which has been accessed as an archive before. I spent nine months in 2009–2010 working through the original petitions and documents of constitutional cases from the 1950s.

75. I discuss the conventional political cases in some detail in Rohit De, "Rebellion, Dacoity, and Equality: The Emergence of the Constitutional Field in Postcolonial India," *CSSAAME* 34, no. 2 (2014): 260–78. On the right to property, see Namita Wahi, *The Right to Property and Economic Development in India*, PhD dissertation, Harvard University, 2014. On speech, see Gautam Bhatia, *Offend, Shock, or Disturb: Free Speech under the Indian Constitution* (Delhi: Oxford University Press, 2016); Abhinav Chandrachud, *Republic of rhetoric: Free Speech and the Constitution of India* (New Delhi: Penguin, 2017); and Rajeev Dhavan, *Only the Good News: Law of Press in India* (New Delhi: Manohar, 1987). On religion, see Ronojoy Sen, *Articles of Faith: Religion, Secularism, and the Supreme Court* (New Delhi: Oxford University Press, 2012).

76. K. L. Gauba, *Famous Trials for Love and Murder* (Bombay: Hind Pocket Books, 1967); K. L. Gauba, *Famous and Historic Trials* (Lahore: Lions Press, 1946); Kailash Nath Katju, *Sherlock Holmes in India* (Calcutta: printed by author, 1956).

77. Arthur Berriedale Keith, *A Constitutional History of India* (New York: Barnes and Noble, 1969); M. V. Pylee, *Constitutional History of India* (London: Asia, 1967).

78. Inga Markovits, *Imperfect Justice: An East-West German Diary* (Oxford, UK: Clarendon Press, 1995), 204.

79. Stanford Levinson, *Constitutional Faith* (Princeton. NJ: Princeton University Press, 1987). He describes this as the contrast between Catholic (top-down) and Protestant (democratic) readings of the Constitution. Since Catholics and Protestants have different ways of reading the Bible, Levinson analogizes that to ways of reading the Constitution.

80. Arvind Elangovan, "The Making of the Indian Constitution: A Case for a Non-Nationalist Approach," *History Compass* 12, no. 1 (2014): 1–10; Baxi, "Outline of a 'Theory of Practice,'" 92–118; Partha Chatterjee, "Introduction Postcolonial Legalism," *CSSAME* 34, no. 2 (2014): 224–27.

81. Ramachandra Guha, "The Challenge of Contemporary History," *Economic and Political Weekly*, June 28, 2008.

82. Dinyar Patel, "Repairing the Damage at India's National Archives," *India Ink*, March 22, 2011, http://india.blogs.nytimes.com/2012/03/21/repairing-the-damage-at-indias-national-archives/. During my research I found that regular file transfers from central ministries ceased in 1953 or 1954. The Ministry of States and the Ministry of Refugees and Rehabilitation remain important exceptions. The coverage in state archives remains patchy and arbitrary.

83. Rajni Kothari, "Political Consensus in India: Decline and Reconstruction," *Economic and Political Weekly*, October 11, 1969; David Arnold, ed., *Burton Stein's A History of India*, 2, 2nd edn., (London: Wiley Blackwell, 2010), 399–400.

84. Sudipta Kaviraj, *The Enchantment of Indian Democracy* (New Delhi: Permanent Black, 2010).

85. An important exception to this is the large body of work on the partition of India, which takes the idea of the everyday experiential state or local setting more seriously. For recent works

that reevaluate the impact of partition on the making of the Indian state, see Vazira Fazilah-Yacoobali Zamindar, *The Long Partition and the Making of Modern South Asia: Refugees, Boundaries, Histories* (New York: Columbia University, 2007); Yashmin Khan, *The Great Partition: The Making of India and Pakistan* (New Haven, CT: Yale University Press, 2007); Joya Chatterjee, *The Spoils of Partition: Bengal and India, 1947–1967* (Cambridge, UK: Cambridge University, 2007); Rotem Geva, "The Scramble for Houses: Violence, A Factionalized State, and Informal Economy in Postpartition Delhi," *Modern Asian Studies* 51, no. 3 (2017): 769–824; and Uditi Sen, *Citizen Refugee: Forging the Indian Nation after Pakistan* (Cambridge, UK: Cambridge University Press, 2018).

86. Benjamin R. Seigel, *Hungry Nation: Food Famine and the Making of Modern India* (Cambridge, UK: Cambridge University Press, 2018); Nikhil Menon, "Planned Democracy: Citizenship, Development, and the Practices of Planning in Independent India, c. 1947–1966," PhD dissertation, Princeton University, 2017; Taylor C. Sherman, *Muslim Belonging in Secular India: Negotiating Citizenship in Postcolonial Hyderabad* (Cambridge, UK: Cambridge University Press, 2015); Shani, *How India Became Democratic*; Sen, *Citizen Refugee*.

87. A combination of poor archiving practices and neglect has made the Supreme Court records the only records on many of these questions. Even in cases in which the state was a party, the corresponding files were not transferred by the Ministry of Law to the archive. The official and private papers of lawyers have rarely been preserved.

88. Thomas Hansen, *States of Imagination: Ethnographic Explorations of the Postcolonial State* (Durham, NC: Duke University Press, 2001), 6–7.

89. Srirupa Roy, *Beyond Belief: India and the Politics of Postcolonial Nationalism* (Durham, NC: Duke University Press, 2007), vii; Benjamin Zachariah, *Developing India: An Intellectual and Social History, c.1930–50* (New Delhi: Oxford University Press, 2005); Gyanesh Kudasiya, *A Republic in the Making: India in the 1950s* (Oxford, UK: Oxford University Press, 2018).

90. Khilnani, *Idea of India*, 39.

91. Partha Chatterjee, *The Nation and Its Fragments* (New Delhi: Oxford University Press, 1993), 14.

92. *Civil Court Manual, Madras Law Journal,, and the All India Minor Criminal Acts*, 6 vols. (Allahabad: Law, 1957).

93. I. P. Massey, *Administrative Law*, 7th ed. (Lucknow: Eastern Book, 2008), 14.

94. Dhavan, *Nehru and the Constitution*, 45–62.

95. There is a considerable body of the work on partition, but the bureaucratic violence narrative is best explained in Vazira Zamindar, *The Long Partition and the Making of Modern South Asia: Refugees, Boundaries, Histories* (New York: Columbia University, 2007). For the refugee agency argument, see Joya Chatterji, "South Asian Histories of Citizenship, 1946–1970." *Historical Journal* 55, no. 4 (2012): 1049–71.

96. For a study of the interaction of the refugees, minorities, and the postcolonial state in the creation of evacuee property law, see Rohit De, "Taming the Custodian: Evacuee Property and the Management of Economic Life in Postcolonial India," in *The Postcolonial Moment in South and Southeast Asia*, ed. Gyan Prakash, Michael Laffan, and Nikhil Menon (London: Bloomsbury, 2018).

97. Law Commission of India, *14th Report: Reform of Judicial Administration* (New Delhi, 1958), 673.

98. *Ram Jawaya Kapur v. State of Punjab*, AIR 1955 SC 549.

99. *State of Bombay v. Bombay Education Society and Others*, AIR 1954 SC 561.

100. *Union of India v. Shirinbai Aspandier Irani*, Civil Appeal No. 154 of 1953.

101. *Narasu Appa Mali v. State of Bombay*, AIR 1952 Bom 84.

102. *Romesh Thapar v. State of Madras*, [1950] SCR 549.

103. Michel de Certeau, *The Practice of Everyday Life*, trans. Steven Rendall (Los Angeles: University of California Press, 1984), xiii.

104. George Gadbois, "Indian Judicial Behavior," *Economic and Political Weekly*, January 1, 1970.

105. Kim Lane Scheppele, "Legal Theory and Social Theory," *Annual Review of Sociology* 20 (1994): 383–406.

106. S. P. Sathe, *Judicial Activism in India* (New York: Oxford University Press, 2002); Upendra Baxi, *Courage, Craft, and Contention: The Indian Supreme Court in the Eighties* (Bombay: N. M. Tripathi, 1986); Krishnaswamy, *Democracy and Constitutionalism*.

107. Kim Lane Scheppele, "Constitutional Ethnography: An Introduction," *Law and Society Review* 38, no. 3 (2004): 390–91.There is surprisingly little work on the actual routines of constitutional courts. For a rare example of an appellate court ethnography, see Kalyankrishnan Sivaramakrishnan, "Environment, Law, and Democracy in India," *Journal of Asian Studies* 70, no. 4 (2011): 90528.

108. Chatterjee, *Spoils of Partition*, 57.

109. The actual number is hard to estimate, but this figure comes from All India Bar Committee, *Report* (Delhi: Manager of Publications, 1953), 72–73, which shows the total number of the different classes of legal practitioners as of March 31, 1952.

110. Christopher Bayly, *Recovering Liberties: Indian Thought in the Age of Liberalism and Empire* (Cambridge, UK: Cambridge University Press, 2012).

111. Sukanya Banerjee, *Becoming Imperial Citizens: Indians in the Late Victorian Empire* (Durham, NC: Duke University Press, 2010).

112. Mukherjee, *India in the Shadows*.

113. Bayly *Recovering Liberties*, 8; see also Banerjee, *Becoming Imperial Citizens*, 10.

114. Bayly, *Recovering Liberties*, 32.

115. Chatterjee, *Nation and Its Fragments*, 1–14.

116. See Tanika Sarkar, "A Pre-History of Rights: The Age of Consent Debates in Colonial India," *Feminist Studies* 26, no. 3 (Autumn 2000): 601–22; Rachel Sturman, *The Government of Social Life in Colonial India: Liberalism, Religious Law, and Women's Rights* (Cambridge, UK: Cambridge University Press, 2012).

117. Tanika Sarkar, "Something Like Rights? Faith, Law, and Widow Immolation Debates in Bengal," *Indian Economic and Social History Review* 49, no. 3 (2012): 295–320.

118. Neeraja Jayal, *Citizenship and Its Discontents: An Indian History* (Cambridge, MA: Harvard University Press, 2013).

119. Article 25, Constitution of India, 1950.

120. Sumit Guha, "Wrongs and Rights in Maratha Country: Antiquity, Custom, and Power in Eighteenth-Century India," in *Changing Concepts of Rights and Justice in South Asia*, ed. M. R. Anderson and Sumit Guha (New Delhi: Oxford University Press, 2000), 14–29.

121. David Gilmartin and Jonathan K. Ocko, "State, Sovereignty, and the People: A Comparison of the 'Rule of Law' in China and India," *Journal of Asian Studies*, 68, no. 1 (February 2009): 55–133.

122. Pamela Price, *Kingship and Political Practice in Colonial India* (Cambridge, UK: Cambridge University Press, 1996).

123. Article 299, Government of India Act, 1935, guaranteed the right to property and contained safeguards against expropriation without compensation and against acquisition for a nonpublic purpose.

124. Jagat Narian, "Equal Protection Guarantee and the Right of Property under the Indian Constitution," *International and Comparative Law Quarterly* 15, no. 1 (1966): 199–230.; Jaivir Singh, *(Un) Constituting Property: Destruction of the Right to Property in India*, Centre for Studies in Law and Governance, CSLG/WP/04–05, http://www.jnu.ac.in/cslg/workingpaper /cslg%20wp%2004–05%20jaivir%20singh.pdf.

125. Ritu Birla, *Stages of Capital: Law, Culture, and Market Governance in Late Colonial India* (Durham, NC: Duke University Press, 2009).

126. Veena Das, *Critical Events: An Anthropological Perspective on Contemporary India* (New York: Oxford University Press, 1997), 6.

127. Hannah Arendt, *The Human Condition* (Chicago: University of Chicago Press, 1958), 34–35.

Chapter 1. The Case of the Constable's Nose: Policing Prohibition in Bombay

1. Judgment of the High Court, Criminal Appeal 1149, 1952, Supreme Court Record Room (SCRR).

2. The regional identity of the accident victims is significant. The Sindhis, like the Parsis (the community that Pesikaka belonged to), were a mercantile group and migrants to the city of Bombay from Sindh, particularly after partition. Both communities were famously litigious and were overrepresented in the legal profession.

3. Pesikaka had voluntarily and without prejudice to the trial compensated the victims with a sum of five thousand rupees.

4. Judgment of the High Court, Criminal Appeal 1149.

5. R. K. Karanjia, "There Is Money in the Racket," *Seminar*, August 1964.

6. Article 47, Constitution of India, 1950.

7. Mariana Valverde, *Diseases of the Will: Alcohol and the Dilemmas of Freedom* (New York: Cambridge University Press, 1998).

8. Ibid., 9. See also Robert Post, "Federalism, Positivism, and the Emergence of the American Administrative State: Prohibition in the Taft Court Era," *William and Mary Law Review* 48, no. 1 (2006): 1–184. Post's study of the US Supreme Court's decisions on Prohibition provide a model of such scholarship. It traces how an unusual coalition of conservative and progressive judges came together to uphold the constitutionalism of Prohibition, which sought to transform the nature of federal government in the United States.

9. Robert Eric Colvard. "A World without Drink: Temperance in Modern India, 1880–1940," PhD dissertation, University of Iowa, 2013; Nikhil Menon, "Battling the Bottle: Experiments in

Regulating Drink in Late Colonial Madras," *Indian Economic and Social History Review* 52, no. 1 (2015): 29–51; David Hardiman, *The Coming of the Devi: Adivasi Assertion in Western India* (New Delhi: Oxford University Press, 1987); David Hardiman, "From Custom to Crime: The Politics of Drinking in Colonial South Gujarat," in Ranajit Guha, ed., *Subaltern Studies IV* (New Delhi: Oxford University Press, 1985); Indra Munshi Saldanah, "On Drinking and Drunkenness: History of Liquor in Colonial India," *Economic and Political Weekly*, September 16, 1995.

10. Mausen Damodar Bhansali, *Prohibition Inquiry Report in Bombay State* (Bombay: Central Government Press, 1952), 5.

11. Bombay Prohibition Act, 1949.

12. The closest contemporary experience of Prohibition was in the United States. The National Prohibition Act of 1919 (also known as the Volstead Act) had been enacted to enforce the Eighteenth Amendment, which brought about the nationwide prohibition of alcohol in the United States. The act provided that "no person shall manufacture, sell, barter, transport, import, export, deliver, or furnish any intoxicating liquor except as authorized," but, significantly, it did not criminalize possession or consumption. See Ann-Mary Syzmanski, *Pathways to Prohibition: Radicals, Moderates, and Social Movement Outcomes* (Durham, NC: Duke University Press, 2003); Daniel Okrent, *Last Call: The Rise and Fall of Prohibition* (New York: Scribner, 2010).

13. For a detailed economic history of the Parsi community, see Amalendu Guha, "Parsi Seths as Entrepreneurs, 1750–1850," *Economic and Political Weekly*, August 29, 1970; Amalendu Guha, "More about the Parsi Seths: Their Roots, Entrepreneurship, and Comprador Role, 1650–1918," *Economic and Political Weekly*, January 21, 1984.

14. David Hardiman, *The Coming of the Devi: Adivasi Assertion in Western India* (Delhi: Oxford University Press, 1987) 110–12.

15. Indra Munshi Saldanah, "On Drinking and Drunkeness: History of Liquor in Colonial India,, *Economic and Political Weekly*, September 16, 1995.

16. *Queen Empress* v. *Pestanji Barjorji*, (1885) ILR 9 Bom 456.

17. *In re Limba Koya* (1885) ILR 9 Bom 556.

18. Hardiman, "From Custom to Crime."

19. Christopher Allan Bayly, *Recovering Liberties: Indian Thought in the Age of Liberalism and Empire* (Cambridge, UK: Cambridge University Press, 2012), 15–16.

20. David Shahey and Padma Manian, "Poverty and Purification: The Politics of Gandhi's Campaign for Prohibition," *Historian*, 67, no. 3 (2005) 489–506.

21. "Letter from Collector, Island of Bombay to Excise Commission, Bombay Presidency," June 21, 1930, File 750 (3) PL, Home Ministry Files, Maharashtra State Archives (MSA), Mumbai.

22. Mohandas K. Gandhi, "Total Prohibition," *Young India*, February 4, 1926, in *Collected Works of Mahatma Gandhi*, 33:49. It is difficult to estimate whether Indians drank less than other peoples, but some figures are suggestive. Hardiman, *Coming of the Devi*, 104, shows that the tribal populations of South Gujarat, who had few taboos on alcohol, drank 2.98 gallons of toddy and 0.5 gallons of daru per head, compared to Britons, whose per head consumption was 31.40 gallons of beer, 0.40 gallons of wine, and 1.03 gallons of hard liquor.

23. Mohandas K. Gandhi, "Letter to Herbert Anderson," April 3, 1926, in *Collected Works*, 35:5.

24. Mohandas K. Gandhi, "Speech of Prohibition—Madras, *Hindu*, March 24, 1925, in *Collected Works*, 31:32–38.

25. Mohandas K. Gandi, "To the Women of India," in *Collected Works*, 49:57.

26. Mohandas K. Gandhi, "To the Moderates," *Young India*, June 8, 1921, in *Collected Works*, 23:247.

27. Mohandas K. Gandhi, "Speech at Bardoli," August 12, 1928, in *Collected Works*, 42:362.

28. Mohandas K. Gandhi, "A Gentle Rebuke," *Young India*, June 25, 1931, in *Collected Works*, 47:53–54.

29. Karuna Mantena, "Gandhi and the Means-Ends Question in Politics," unpublished manuscript, June 2012, http://karunamantena.files.wordpress.com/2011/04/mantena -gandhimeansends.pdf.

30. Mohandas K. Gandhi, "Bombay the Beautiful," *Harijan*, January 4, 1939, in *Collected Works*, 75:210.

31. Gyan Prakash, *Another Reason: Science and the Imagination of Modern India* (Princeton, NJ: Princeton University Press, 2004), 201.

32. All India Women's Conference Annual Report, 1946, Hansa Mehta Papers, Nehru Memorial Museum and Library (NMML), New Delhi.

33. C. Rajagopalachari, *Indian Prohibition Manual* (Delhi: National Congress Committee, 1933); H. C. Mookherjee, *Why Prohibition? A Manual for Temperance, Social Service, and Congress Workers* (Calcutta: Book House, 1949), i.

34. N. G. Ranga, "The Madras Slum: A Study," *Mysore Economic Journal* 14, no. 3 (March 1928): 113.

35. Gandhi, "Bombay the Beautiful."

36. Mohandas K Gandhi, "Letter to Acharya Narendra Dev," August 2, 1934, in *Collected Works*, 64:250.

37. Marc Galanter, *Law and Society in Modern India* (Delhi: Oxford University Press, 1989), xxii.

38. Kengal Hanumanthaiya, *Constituent Assembly Debates*, November 17, 1949.

39. Kazi Syed Karimuddin, *Constituent Assembly Debates*, November 19, 1949.

40. Mohamed Ismail Sahib, *Constituent Assembly Debates*, November 19, 1949.

41. Mahavir Tyagi, *Constituent Assembly Debates*, November 19, 1949.

42. L. M. Patil, "The Need for Prohibition: Address to the Provincial Prohibition Board," in *New Lives for Old* (Bombay: Provincial Prohibition Board 1948), 31.

43. L. M. Patil, "A Historical Survey: Proceedings of the Bombay Legislative Assembly, February 28, 1947," in *New Lives for Old* (Bombay: Provincial Prohibition Board 1948), 51.

44. Morarji Desai, "A Word to the Prohibition Worker," in *New Lives for Old* (Bombay: Provincial Prohibition Board 1948), 127.

45. Austin, *Indian Constitution*, 101–4.

46. Article 19, Constitution of India, 1950.

47. Khandekar drew an interesting comparison of friends having a discussion over glasses of buttermilk versus an intellectual discussion over glasses of beer or wine in the evening. H. J Khandekar, *Constituent Assembly Debates*, November 24, 1948.

48. V. I Muniswamy Pillai, *Constituent Assembly Debates*, November 24, 1948. For reassurances to Christian and Jewish leaders, see Mohandas K. Gandhi, "Meaning of Prohibition," June 11, 1939, in *Collected Works*, 76:24–28.

49. B. G. Kher, *Constituent Assembly Debates*, November 24, 1948.

50. Pillai, *Constituent Assembly*.

51. Kher, *Constituent Assembly* .

52. Patil, "Need for Prohibition," 9.

53. Article 47, Constitution of India, 1950.

54. Planning Commission, *Prohibition Enquiry Committee Report* (New Delhi, 1955).

55. Ibid, 155–83.

56. "Decision on Total Prohibition in Bombay Reaffirmed," *Times of India*, February 20, 1949.

57. S.65, Bombay Prohibition Act, 1949.

58. S.84, Bombay Prohibition Act, 1949.

59. S.85, Bombay Prohibition Act, 1949.

60. S.23, Bombay Prohibition Act, 1949.

61. S.123, Bombay Prohibition Act, 1949.

62. S.139, Bombay Prohibition Act, 1949.

63. Bhansali, *Prohibition Inquiry Report*, 11.

64. State of Bombay, *Annual Police Administration Report, including the Railways, for the Year 1949* (Bombay: Central Government Press, 1950).

65. Bhansali, *Prohibition Inquiry Report*, 65–67.

66. "Prohibition Arrests" columns, *Times of India*, 1949–1960.

67. "Prohibition Arrests," *Times of India*, May 23, 1953.

68. Kher, *Constituent Assembly*.

69. Prof Shibban Lal Saxena, *Constituent Assembly Debates*, Vol VII, Wednesday, the 24th November 1948.

70. Roy, 20.

71. Morarji Desai, "A Word to the Prohibition Worker," in *New Lives for Old* (Bombay: Provincial Prohibition Board 1948), 127.

72. M. U. Mascarhenas, speech, *Proceedings of the Debate in the Bombay Legislative Assembly*, March 10, 1954, File 5/14/49, Judicial Branch, Ministry of Home Affairs Files, NAI.

73. H. S. Metgud, speech, *Proceedings of the Debate in the Bombay Legislative Assembly*, March 10, 1954, File 5/14/49, Judicial Branch, Ministry of Home Affairs Files, NAI.

74. C. J. Beamount, *Emperor v. Chinubhai Lalbhai*, (1940) 42 Bom LR 669. The Bombay High Court struck down attempts to impose Prohibition through notifications issued under the Abkari Act. Ruling that the Abkari Act was a piece of revenue legislation, the court found that the colonial legislature had not contemplated that it could be used for the 'prohibition of intoxicants as a measure of social reform.' The court did not make a distinction between the viceroy in council who had enacted the Abkari Act in 1878 and the elected Congress Party government that proposed the Prohibition amendment in 1939.

75. Civil Appeals 182 and 183, 1951, SCRR.

76. *Fram Nusserwanji Balsara v. State of Bombay*, AIR 1951 Bom 210.

77. *Fram Nusserwanji Balsara v. State of Bombay and M. D. Bhansali*, Miscellaneous Application 139, 1950, Bombay High Court, SCRR.

78. "Does Prohibition Act Violate Fundamental Rights," *Times of India*, August 1, 1950.

79. "Judgment Reserved in the Prohibition Test Case," *Times of India*, August 8, 1950.

80. S.136, Bombay Prohibition Act, 1949.

81. S.24, Bombay Prohibition Act, 1949.

82. "Bombay Prohibition Act, 1949," File 28/16/50, Judicial Branch, Ministry of Home Affairs Files, NAI; "Bombay Prohibition (Amendment) Bill," File 17/7/52, Judicial Branch, Ministry of Home Affairs Files, NAI; "Effect of the Judgment of the Bombay High Court on the Prohibition Act regarding Foreigners, Diplomats, and Counselor Officials in India," File 3(104) Police Branch II(50), Ministry of External Affairs Files, NAI.

83. Sardar Patel to B. G. Kher, "Judgment of the Bombay High Court in the Prohibition Case," File 5/156/50, Ministry of Home Affairs Files, NAI.

84. Sardar Patel to Rajendra Prasad, July 19, 1939, File 1-C/39, Patel Prasad Correspondence, Coll 2, Rajendra Prasad Papers, NAI.

85. Bhansali, *Prohibition Inquiry Report*, 4.

86. "Important Test Case in Sweepers Strike," *Times of India*, July 10, 1949, 9.

87. "Private Streets in Bombay: A Landlord's Appeal," *Times of India*, January 4, 1949. The advocate, Naushir Bharucha, was also a member of the legislative assembly and was one of the few who opposed the Bombay Prohibition Act.

88. "No License for Tea Vendors: Magistrate's Ruling in Test Case," *Times of India*, August 9, 1952.

89. "Administration of Justice: Danger of Hasty Changes," *Times of India*, September 30, 1946.

90. "Validity of House Requisition Order," *Times of India*, December 22, 1948. The case on appeal became one of the first rulings of the Supreme Court on the power of a high court to issue writs. See also *Province of Bombay v. Kushaldas S. Advani and Others*, AIR 1950 SC 222 For more on the Advani case, see Uttara Shahani, "Refugee Legal Challenges to Bombay Government's Land Requisitioning Scheme," *Economic and Political Weekly*, January 27, 2018,

91. "Use of Skimmed Milk Powder," *Times of India*, August 23, 1949.

92. "Moneylenders in Bombay: Prosecution Launched," *Times of India*, May 31, 1949.

93. "Petitioner's Right to Ask for Alternative Relief," *Times of India*, August 5, 1950.

94. *Sheoshankar* v. *State of Madhya Pradesh*, 1951 CriLJ 1140.

95. "Parts of 'Dry Law' Held Ultra Vires," *Times of India*, August 23, 1950.

96. "Violation of Rights," *Times of India*, December 31, 1953.

97. "Right of Privacy," *Times of India*, January 1, 1954.

98. "High Court Hears Petition of Jorurnalist," *Times of India*, August 1, 1950.

99. "Cabinet to Meet Soon," *Times of India*, August. 23, 1950.

100. Sharada Dwivedi and Rahul Mehrotra, *Bombay High Court: The Story of a Building, 1873-2003* (Mumbai: Emminence Designs, 2004), 200.

101. *Sheoshankar* v. *State of Madhya Pradesh*, 1951 CriLJ 1140.

102. "M.P. Dry Act Amendment, Sequel to Ruling in Bombay Case," *Times of India*, August 1, 1952.

103. "Liquor Stocks to Army Sealed," *Times of India*, August 25, 1950.

104. "Issue of Permits to Foreigners: Storm Brewing over Prohibition Laws," *Times of India*, September 16, 1950.

105. I am grateful to Barry Sen for sharing his reminisces of the early days of the Supreme Court. See also Barry Sen, *Six Decades of Law, Politics, and Diplomacy* (New Delhi: Jain, 2010).

106. Seervai succeeded Daphtary as the advocate general of Bombay and emerged as the leading authority on Indian constitutional law.

107. Noshirwan Engineer was perhaps colonial Bombay's leading lawyer and had served as the advocate general of India from 1945 to 1950. Joshi was a leading commercial and tax lawyer who also authored one of the early commentaries on the Constitution. Kolah was a leading practioner in the Bombay bar. This was one of the first cases in which Palkivalah appeared, but he was soon to emerge as India's leading constitutional lawyer and argue some of India's most prominent constitutional cases before the Supreme Court. Palkivalah was offered both a Supreme Court judgeship and the post of attorney general, which he declined.

108. *State of Bombay and Another v. F. N. Balsara,* AIR 1951 SC 318.

109. *State of Bombay v. Framji Nusserwanji Balsara,* AIR 1951 SC 318.

110. "Parts of 'Dry Law.' "

111. Bhansali, *Prohibition Inquiry Report,* 11.

112. Ibid., 12.

113. To give a sense of the relative alcohol content, the doctor, on cross-examination, stated that beer contains 2–9 percent alcohol, whereas sherry and port contained 15–20 percent. Evidence of witness Dr. Keval Kumar Beri, Criminal Appeal 42, 1953, SCRR.

114. "Toilet Goods and Medicines with Alcohol: Free Sale Now Allowed," *Times of India,* July 1, 1951.

115. "Tincture of Ginger Sales Up: Use as Alcohol Subsitute," *Times of India,* October 14, 1951.

116. "No Penal Action against Pharmacists Contemplated," *Times of India,* February 3, 1953.

117. Board of Experts to Secretary of Revenue Department, Government of Bombay, December 13, 1954, BPA 1654, Home Ministry File III, 1954, MSA.

118. Planning Commission, "Reply of Government of Bombay to General Questionnaire Issued by the Prohibition Enquiry Committee," in *Prohibition Enquiry Committee: State Government's Memoranda and Other Documents* (New Delhi, 1956), 85.

119. Written statement of the accused, B. K. Pesikaka, Criminal Appeal 1149, 1952, SCRR.

120. Judgment of presidency magistrate, 19 Court, Bombay, Criminal Appeal 1149, 1952, SCRR.

121. Oral judgment of Justice P. B. Gajendragatkar, Criminal Appeal 1149, 1952, Bombay High Court, SCRR.

122. "Burden of Proof," *Times of India,* February 23, 1954.

123. Case for the appellant, Criminal Appeal 1149, 1953, SCRR.

124. *Behram Khurshed Pesikaka v. State of Bombay,* AIR 1955 SC 123.

125. "New Ruling Will Make Dry Law Offenses Difficult to Prove," *Times of India,* September 26, 1954.

126. "Medical Evidence in Dry Case: Accused Freed," *Times of India,* March 19, 1954.

127. *State of Bombay v. Triambak Bhondu Dhoir,* (1955) 57 BOMLR 541.

128. BPA 1754, Home Ministry File III, 1954, MSA.

129. Planning Commission, *Report of the Study Team on Prohibition* (New Delhi, 1963), 192.

130. "People Cannot Be Forced into Medical Tests," *Times of India,* September 13, 1958.

131. "Doctors Oppose Prohibition," *Times of India,* December 21, 1950.

132. Planning Commission, *Report of the Study Team,* 109.

133. Ibid., 114, 127.

134. Ibid., 129.

135. Editorial, *Hindustan Times,* January 3, 1964; Editorial, *The Statesman,* January 5, 1964.

136. Editorial, *Times of India*, January 3, 1964.

137. Written statement of the accused, B. K. Pesiakaka.

138. Oral judgment of Justice Gajendragatkar.

139. "Policeman Turns Brewer," *Times of India*, March 31, 1950.

140. Tanya Luhrmann, *The Good Parsi: The Postcolonial Anxieties of an Indian Colonial Elite* (Cambridge, MA: Harvard University Press, 1996).

141. Mohandas Gandhi, "Speech at Meeting of Liquor Contractors, Bombay," July 12, 1921, in *Collected Works*, 23:408.

142. Mohandas Gandhi, "To the Parsis," March 23, 1921, in *Collected Works*, 22:456–57.

143. "Humble Petition from the Country Liquor, Foreign Liquor, and Toddy Merchants of Bombay," File No. 750 (30) P II Home Ministry Files, MSA.

144. Sapur F. Desai, *History of the Bombay Parsi Punchayet, 1860–1960* (Bombay: Parsi Panchayet, 1977), 104–8, 302–13.

145. "Parsis' Objection to Prohibition," *Times of India*, May 16, 1939.

146. "Petitions Agains Prohibition, Samast Parsi Anjuman, 29 March 1939" in Bomanjee B. Patel and Rustam B. Paymaster, eds., *Parsi Prakash: Important Events in the Growth of the Parsi Community, 1878-1942* (Bombay: Parsi Panchayat, 1945), 7:496–506.

147. "Parsi Women's Protest against Prohibition," *Times of India*, April 17, 1939.

148. S.299, Government of India Act, 1935.

149. "Prohibition Relief Committee," *Times of India*, April 23. 1950.

150. "Vote Congress Out of Power," *Times of India*, November 20, 1951.

151. "Mr. Munshi Warns Opponents of Prohibition," *Times of India*, June 13, 1939.

152. "Why Prohibiton Is Needed," *Times of India*, June 5, 1939.

153. "Parsis Desire Dry Law Probe," *Times of India*, February 14, 1954.

154. Mitra J. Sharafi, "Legal Consciousness and Strategies among Minorities: The Colonial Zoroastrian Experience," paper presented at the annual meeting of the the Law and Society Association, Chicago, February 17, 2011.

155. Sharafi shows that despite composing less than 6 percent of Bombay's population, the Parsis were 20 percent of all parties in reported cases. Mitra J.Sharafi, *Parsi Legal Culture in British India* (New York: Cambridge University Press, 2014), 3–4.

156. Ranabir Sammadar, *The Materiality of Politics: The Technologies of Rule* (London: Anthem Press, 2007), 1:9.

157. S.129-A, Bombay Prohibition Act, 1949 (as amended in 1959).

158. S.129-C, Bombay Prohibition Act, 1949 (as amended in 1959).

159. Jivraj Mehta, Proceedings of the Bombay Legislative Assembly, March 10, 1954, MSA.

160. Naushir Bharucha, Proceedings of the Bombay Legislative Assembly, March 10, 1954, MSA.

161. Planning Commission, "Reply of Government of Bombay," in Prohibition Enquiry Committee: State Government's Memoranda and Other Documents (Planning Commission, New Delhi, 1956) 85. (, please return to the original formulation),

162. Ibid., 89.

163. R. K. Karanjia, "There Is Money in the Racket," *Seminar*, August 1964.

164. "Curate's Egg," *Times of India*, January 29, 1959.

165. "All Around Welcome Gratifies Naik," *Times of India*, January 2 1964.

166. *New Lives for Old* (Bombay: Provincial Prohibition Board 1948), ii.

167. Uma Vasudev, "Prohibition: Case History of an Obsession," *Times of India*, April 5, 1964.

168. Planning Commission, "Reply of Government of Bombay," 93.

169. "Judgment Justifies Action," *Times of India*, August 23, 1950.

170. Planning Commission, *Report of the Study Team on Prohibition (they had over a dozen study teams)*, 293.

171. Dipesh Chakrabarty, "In the Name of Politics: Democracy and the Power of the Multitude in India," *From the Colonial to the Postcolonial: India and Pakistan in Transition*, ed. Dipesh Chakrabarti, Rochona Majumdar, and Andrew Sartori (New Delhi: Oxford University Press, 2007), 31–54.

172. K. N. Raj, "Evil of Prohibition," *Economic Weekly*, May 9, 1964.

173. Patil, "Need for Prohibition," 9.

174. Ibid.

175. "Doctors Oppose Prohibition," *Times of India*, December 21, 1951.

176. Khandekar, *Constituent Assembly*.

177. "Bombay Prohibition Act's Validity Challenged," *Times of India*, August 1, 1950.

178. Planning Commission, *Report of the Study Team*, 289.

179. U. N. Debhar, "Yesterday and Tomorrow," *Seminar*, August 1964.

180. R. K. Karanjia, "There Is Money in the Racket," *Seminar*, August 1964.

181. "Countering Ingenious Methods of Liquor Smugglers," *Times of India*, April 7, 1958.

Chapter 2. The Case of the Excess Baggage: Commodity Controls, Market Governance, and the Making of Administrative Law

1. Railway service wire, November 29, 1948, Criminal Appeal 7, 1953, SCRR.

2. First information report, Itarsi police station, Criminal Appeal 7, 1953, SCRR.

3. Secs. 14(1) and 15, Essential Supplies Act, 1946.

4. Sec. 17(1–2), Essential Supplies Act, 1946.

5. List of prosecution witnesses, Criminal Appeal 7, 1953, SCRR.

6. Article 19(1) of the Constitution guarantees basic civil liberties to all citizens of India: "(1) All citizens shall have the right to (a) freedom of speech and expression; (b) assemble peaceably and without arms; (c) form associations or unions; (d) move freely throughout the territory of India; (e) reside and settle in any part of the territory of India; (e) hold property; (g) practice any profession or carry on any occupation, trade, or business."

7. Lloyd Rudolph and Susan Rudolph, *In Pursuit of Lakshmi: The Political Economy of the Indian State* (New Delhi: Orient Blackswan, 1987); Terence J. Byres, ed., *The Indian Economy: Major Debates since Independence* (Delhi: Oxford University Press, 1998); Francine Frankel, *India's Political Economy, 1947–2004: A Gradual Revolution* (Oxford, UK: Oxford University Press, 1978); Vivek Chibber, *Locked in Place: State Building and Late Industrialization in India* (Princeton, NJ: Princeton University Press, 2006).

8. Paul Brass, *An Indian Political Life: Charan Singh and Congress Politics, 1937 to 1961* (New Delhi: Sage, 2011), 158.

9. Michel Foucault, *Security, Territory, Population: Lectures at the College De France, 1977–78*, trans. Graham Burchell (London: Palgrave Macmillan, 2009).

10. Recent scholarship on South Asia has begun to chart the processes through which the Indian economy was imagined and concretized. Such studies have focused on a range of sources, including the emergence of statistics, national accounting, the circulation of maps and globes, nationalist tracts on the economy, and the building of railways, but have all neglected to consider the role of law as an instrument of governance. For a pioneering study of market governance in late colonial India that is possibly the sole exception, see Ritu Birla, *Stages of Capital: Law, Culture, and Market Governance in Late Colonial India* (Durham, NC: Duke University Press, 2009), 23–24.

11. Stanley A. Kochanek, *Business and Politics in India* (Berkley: University of California Press, 1974); Chibber, *Locked in Place.*

12. For more details see Rohit De, " 'Commodities must be controlled': Economic Crimes and Market Discipline in India (1939–1955)," *International Journal of Law in Context* 10, no. 3 (2014): 277–94.

13. R. H. Tawney, "The Abolition of Economic Controls, 1918–1921," *Economic History Review* 13, nos. 1–2, (2008): 1–30.

14. Indivar Kamtekar, "A Different War Dance: State and Class in India, 1939–1945," " *Past & Present* 176 (2002): 187–221.

15. Entries 27 and 29, List 2, Schedule 7, Government of India Act, 1935.

16. S.102, Government of India Act, 1935.

17. Rule 81(2), Defense of India Act, 1939.

18. C. N. Vakil, J. J. Anjaria, and Dansukhlal Lakdawala, *Price Control and Food Supply with Special Reference to Bombay City* (Bombay: N. M. Tripathi, 1943), 15.

19. For a detailed account of the development of controls, see S. Muthilakshmi Reddi, *Report of the Commodity Controls Committee* (Delhi: Manager of Publications, 1953), 5–10.

20. M. A. Sreenivasan, *Controls and Freedom* (Bombay: Forum for Free Enterprise, 1960), 2.

21. This bureaucracy included the machine tool controller under the Machine Tool Control Order; the iron and steel controller under the Iron and Steel Order, 1943; the sugar controller under the Sugar Control Order, 1942; the wheat commissioner under the Wheat Control Order, 1942; the gur and molasses controller under the Gur Control Order, 1942; the vegetable oil products controller under the Vegetable Oil Products Order, 1946; the paper controller under the Paper Control Order, 1945; the textile commissioner under the Cotton Cloth and Yarn Order, 1943, and the Textile Industries (Miscellaneous Articles) Order, 1943; the director of paper under the Paper Control Order, 1943; the coal commissioner under the Colliery Control Order, 1945; and the controller general of civil supplies under the Prevention of Profiteering and Hoarding Ordinance, 1945, and the Consumer Goods Order, 1945.

22. M. P. Jain, *Administrative Process under the Essential Commodities Act, 1955* (Bombay: N. M. Tripathi, 1964), 15.

23. See, e.g., the requirements under the Cotton Textiles (Dyes and Chemicals) Control Order, 1945.

24. Jain, *Administrative Process*, mentions several examples, but perhaps most relevant to the Baglas' case was the Cotton Textiles (Sizing and Filing) Control Order, 1945, which provided conclusive proof that certain required tests (to determine the proportion of material to the weight of cotton) had been carried out A certificate was signed by an officer authorized to carry out the tests.

25. On the causes of the famine, see Amartya Sen, *Poverty and Famines: An Essay on Entitlement and Deprivation* (Oxford, UK: Oxford University Press, 1981); and Debarshi Das, "A Relook at the Bengal Famine," *Economic and Political Weekly*, August 2–8, 2008.

26. Jain, *Administrative Process*, 23.

27. Famine Inquiry Commission, *Report on Bengal* (Delhi: Manager of Publications, 1945), 107.

28. "India's Eventful Year: Testing Time Still to Come," *Times of India*, December 31, 1942.

29. "Cost of Living in Bombay: Rises in Prices in Foodstuffs," *Times of India*, May 26, 1942.

30. Letter to the editor, *Times of India*, November 5, 1942.

31. Vakil et al., *Price Control*, 40, 41.

32. Meg Jacobs, "How About Some Meat? The Office of Price Administration, Consumption Politics, and State Building from the Bottom Up, 1941–46," *Journal of American History* 84, no. 3 (December 1997): 910–41; Martin Hart-Landsberg, "Popular Mobilization and Progressive Policy Making: Lessons from World War II Price Control Struggles in the United States," *Science and Society* 67, no. 4 (Winter 2003–2004): 399–428.

33. Sreenivasan, *Controls and Freedom*.

34. William Gould, *Bureaucracy, Community, and Influence in India: Society and State, 1930s to 1960s* (London: Routledge, 2011), 22–46.

35. "National Campaign for Food Control Removal: Mahatma Gandhi's Plan," *Times of India*, November 7, 1947.

36. Mohandas K. Gandhi, "Discussion with a Friend," August 17, 1946, in *Collected Works*, 92:31.

37. Mohandas K. Gandhi, "Speech at Prayer Meeting," December 8, 1947, in *Collected Works*, 98:15.

38. "Cotton and Calico for Refugees: Merchants' Offer to Mahatma," *Times of India*, November 10, 1947.

39. Mohandas K. Gandhi, "Speech at Prayer Meeting," September 8, 1946, in *Collected Works*, 92:15.

40. Gandhi, "Speech at Prayer Meeting," December 8, 1947.

41. Gandhi, "Discussion with a Friend."

42. Sreenivasan, *Controls and Freedom*, 2.

43. "Food De-Control Not Overnight," *Times of India*, November 7, 1947.

44. "Food Controls May Go Soon," *Times of India*, November 25, 1947.

45. Murarji J. Vaidya, *Crisis of Controls* (Bombay: Forum for Free Enterprise, 1960), 3.

46. Central Government and Legislature Act, 1946.

47. S.3(1), Essential Supplies Act, 1946.

48. S.3(4), Essential Supplies Act, 1946.

49. S.6, Essential Supplies Act, 1946.

50. S.14(1), Essential Supplies Act, 1946

51. S.16(2), Essential Supplies Act, 1946.

52. Reddi, *Report of the Commodity Controls Committee*, 18.

53. Third Amendment Act, 1954, Constitution of India, 1950.

54. Giorgio Agamben, *State of Exception* (Chicago: University of Chicago Press, 2005).

55. For a recent survey of the literature, see Anil Kahlan, "Constitution and 'Extraconstitution': Colonial Emergency Regimes in Postcolonial India and Pakistan," in *Emergency Powers in*

Asia: Exploring the Limits of Legality, ed. Victor V. Ramraj and Arun K. Thiruvengadam (Cambridge, UK: Cambridge University Press, 2011), 89–120.

56. The Objectives Resolution adopted by the Constituent Assembly in 1946 stated, "Wherein shall be guaranteed and secured to all the people of India justice, social, economic, and political."

57. Lord Mountbatten, *Constituent Assembly Debates*, August 15, 1947.

58. Jawaharlal Nehru, *Constituent Assembly Debates*, January 22, 1947.

59. Moturi Satyanarayana, *Constituent Assembly Debates*, November 9, 1948.

60. Article 39(a–b), Constitution of India, 1950.

61. Advisory Sub-Committee of Fundamental Rights, *Fundamental Principles of Governance* (New Delhi, 1947).

62. The present-day Right to Food campaign in India provides an interesting contrast to the discussion on controls. A network of nongovernmental and civil society groups began a campaign in the late 1990s for recognition of the fundamental right of all Indian citizens to be free from hunger and to access nutrition. The realization of this right required not only equitable food distribution systems but also entitlements to job security, land reform, and social security. In 2001 the Supreme Court of India ruled the right to food a "justiciable" right, setting in motion legislation guaranteeing employment and enacting universal child-development services, several nutrition-related schemes, and social security arrangements. Although these entitlements were claimed from the state, they were articulated through civil society groups, and support for them was mobilized outside Parliament—through conventions, village-level mobilization, rallies, and public hearings. See Lauren Birchfield and Jessica Corsi, "Between Starvation and Globalizaiton: Realizing the Right to Food in India," *Michigan Journal of International Law*, 31 (2009): 691.

63. Ananthasayanam Ayyangar, *Constituent Assembly Debates*, November 9, 1948.

64. Partha Chatterjee, *The Nation and Its Fragments: Colonial and Postcolonial Histories* (New Delhi: Oxford University Press, 1993), 203–4.

65. Roy, *Beyond Belief*, 117.

66. A. D. Shroff, *Controls in a Planned Economy* (Bombay: Forum for Free Enterprise, 1960), 5.

67. The Commodity Controls Committee stated that it could do no better than to restate the findings of the Planning Commission on controls. Reddi, *Report of the Commodity Controls Committee*, 16.

68. Planning Commission, *Report on the First Five-Year Plan* (New Delhi, 1951).

69. Chatterjee, *Nation and Its Fragments*, 204.

70. Martin Hart-Landsberg, "Popular Mobilization and Progressive Policy Making: Lessons from World War II Price Control Struggles in the United States," *Science and Society* 67, no. .4 (Winter 2003–2004): 399–428.

71. Centre for South Asian Studies, *Controls: End or Mend? A Socialist Publication* (Cambridge, UK: Cambridge University, 1951).

72. "Cloth Removed from Corpses: Shortage in Calcutta," *Times of India*, March 2, 1945; "Danger of Cloth Riots in Delhi," *Times of India*, March 28, 1945.

73. Reddi,, *Report of the Commodity Controls Committee*, 81.

74. Ram Gopal Agrawal, *Price Controls in India since 1947* (Minneapolis: University of Minnesota, 1956), 98.

75. Ibid., 102.

76. Reddi, *Report of the Commodity Controls Committee*, 35, 82.

77. Law Commission of India, *29th Report* (New Delhi, 1966).

78. K. Santhanam, *Report on the Committee on the Prevention of Corruption* (New Delhi: Government of India, 1962), 54.

79. Law Commission of India, *47th Report: Trial and Punishment of Social and Economic Offenses* (New Delhi: 1972), 5.

80. Law Commission, *29th Report*, 5.

81. S.4, Essential Supplies Act, 1946.

82. S.9, Essential Supplies Act, 1946.

83. S.14(1), Essential Supplies Act, 1946.

84. S.12, Essential Supplies Act, 1946.

85. Essential Supplies Amendment Act, 1949.

86. Prabhu Dayal Himatsingka, "Extract from the Constituent Assembly of India (Legislative) Debates," March 25, 1949, Essential Supplies (Temporary Powers) Act, File 38-XXII/50-L, Ministry of Law, Justice, and Company Affairs Files, NAI.

87. Naziruddin Ahmad, "Extract from the Constituent Assembly of India (Legislative) Debates," March 25, 1949, Essential Supplies (Temporary Powers) Act, File 38-XXII/50-L, Ministry of Law, Justice, and Company Affairs Files, NAI.

88. R. K. Sidhwa, "Extract from the Constituent Assembly of India (Legislative) Debates," March 25, 1949, Essential Supplies (Temporary Powers) Act, File 38-XXII/50-L, Ministry of Law, Justice, and Company Affairs Files, NAI.

89. Naziruddin Ahmad, "Extract from the Constituent Assembly of India (Legislative) Debates," March 25, 1949, Essential Supplies (Temporary Powers Act, File 38-XXII/50-L, Ministry of Law, Justice, and Company Affairs Files, NAI.

90. B. P. Jhunjhunwala, "Extract from the Constituent Assembly of India (Legislative) Debates," March 25, 1949, Essential Supplies (Temporary Powers) Act, File 38-XXII/50-L, Ministry of Law, Justice, and Company Affairs Files, NAI.

91. Shibban Lal Saxena, "Extract from the Constituent Assembly of India (Legislative) Debates," March 25, 1949, Essential Supplies (Temporary Powers Act, Ministry of Law, File 38-XXII/50-L, Ministry of Law, Justice, and Company Affairs Files, NAI [NAI].

92. Advertising in South Asia has become the object of study only recently, with the emphasis on changing social milieus in contemporary South Asia. More historical engagements can be seen in Douglas Haynes, ed., "Creating the Consumer? Advertising, Capitalism, and the Middle Class in Urban Western India, 1914–40," in *Towards a History of Consumption in South Asia* (Oxford, UK: Oxford University Press, 2010) 188–89. For a review of the literature, see Rachel Berger, ""Between Digestion and Desire: Genealogies of food in nationalist North India." *Modern Asian Studies* 47, no. 5 (2013): 1622–43

93. *Citizens and Citizens* (1952), Films Division of India, Mumbai.

94. Preamble, Essential Commodities AmendmentAct, 1955.

95. Kochanek, *Business and Politics*, 198.

96. For more on the idea of native commerce as a class, see Ritu Birla, *Stages of Capital: Law, Culture, and Market Governance in Late Colonial India* (Durham, NC: Duke University Press, 2009).

97. The relationship of the Indian business class and the postcolonial Indian state has been the subject of much discussion. Recent scholarship has challenged the earlier consensus of a quiescent nationalist bourgeoisie. However, the focus in much of this literature has been on big industrialists and big business, and the role of petty traders and small-business owners has been ignored. This bias is apparent in the plethora of work done on industrial and investment controls, compared to the absence of any academic study on commodity controls. For a more detailed discussion see Chibber, *Locked in Place*.

98. Kochanek, *Business and Politics*, 198.

99. Birla, *Stages of Capital*, 18.

100. Charge sheet, May 27, 1949, Criminal Appeal 7, 1953, SCRR.

101. Thomas A. Timberg, *The Marwaris: From Traders to Industrialists* (Delhi: Vikas, 1977).

102. Anne Hardgrove, *Community and Public Culture: The Marwaris of Calcutta, c.1897–1997* (New York: Columbia University Press, 2004), 10–11.

103. The literature on these riots is extensive, but see especially David Hardiman, *Feeding the Baniya: Peasants and Usurers in Western India* (Delhi: Oxford University Press, 1996).

104. Tanya Luhrmann, *The Good Parsi: The Fate of a Colonial Elite in a Postcolonial Society* (Cambridge, MA: Harvard University Press, 1996).

105. Omkar Goswami, "Then Came the Marwaris: Some Aspects of the Changes in the Pattern of Industrial Control in Eastern India," *Indian Economic and Social History Review* 22, no. 3 (1985): 225.

106. Helen B. Lamb, "The Role of Business Communities in the Evolution of Indian Industrialist Class," *Pacific Affairs*, June 1955.

107. Selig G. Harrison, *India: The Most Dangerous Decades* (Princeton, NJ: Princeton University Press, 1960), 116–17.

108. Hardgrove, *Community and Public Culture*, 162–63.

109. "Govt Assured of Suppoert: Marwardi Conference" *Times of India*, February 11, 1956.

110. Harrison, *India*, 121.

111. Birla, *Stages of Capital*, 139.

112. "War Time Controls Being Perpetuated," *Times of India*, April 25, 1945.

113. Prabhu Dayal Himatsingka was a lawyer and businessman from Bengal who had a long career as a member of the legislative assemblies of Bengal and Assam before becoming a member of the Constituent Assembly and subsequently being elected to both houses of parliament from Bengal. Banasri Prasad Jhunjhunwala was a member of parliament from Bihar.

114. "Do Not Set Your Minds on Profits: Dr. Prasad's Plea to Marwaris," *Times of India*, April 15, 1947.

115. Claude Markovits, *Indian Business and Nationalist Politics, 1931–39: The Indigenous Capitalist Class and the Rise of the Congress Party* (Cambridge, UK: Cambridge University Press, 1985).

116. "Relaxation of Cloth Control Essential: Piecegoods Market," *Times of India*, January 12, 1946.

117. "Millionaire Cloth Dealers Arrested: Public Humiliation," *Times of India*, October 7, 1950.

118. "Rs 2 Lakh Fine and Jail," *Times of India*, November 26, 1947.

119. "Bombay's War on the Black Market," *Times of India*, May 22, 1946.

120. "Cawnpore Raids on the Black Market," *Times of India*, June 3, 1943.

121. "Two Millionaire Mill Owners Arrested: Charge of Selling at High Price," *Times of India*, February 6, 1951.

122. "Cloth Smuggling Gang Cornered," *Times of India*, January 24, 1947.

123. "UP Nominations," *Times of India*, October 29, 1945; "UP Elections: Results and Analysis," *Times of India*, April 13, 1946.

124. *Harish Chandra Bagla v. King Emperor*, AIR 1945 All 90.

125. "Mill Directors: Kanpur Judge Accepts Bail Applications," *Times of India*, July 14, 1950.

126. "Order of the High Court in Criminal Revision No. 659 of 1949," Criminal Appeal 7, 1953, SCRR.

127. Gopal Swarup Pathak was a leading lawyer in Allahabad and had even briefly served as an additional judge in the Allahabad High Court in 1945–1946. A decade after the Bagla case, he was elected to the Rajya Sabha (the upper house of the Indian Parliament) and became the minister of law in Indira Gandhi's cabinet. In 1974 he was elected vice president of India.

128. For instance, the Supreme Court and the Bombay High Court both ruled that the life of the ESA could be validly extended through parliamentary resolutions. *Joylal Agarwala v. Union of India*, SCR 127; *State of Bombay v. Hiralal*, AIR 1951 Bom 369.

129. Laura Bear, *Lines of the Nation: Indian Railway Workers, Bureaucracy, and the Intimate Historical Self* (New York: Columbia University Press, 2007).

130. *Niharendu Dutt Mazumdar v. King Emperor*, AIR (29) 1942 PC 22; *Bimal Protiva Debi v. Emperor*, 43 CrLJ 793; *Baldev Mitter v. King Emperor*, AIR (31) 1944 Lah 142.

131. *King Emperor v. Meer Singh*, ILR 1941 All 617.

132. *Gopal Narain v. Emperor*, AIR (30) 1943 Oudh 227; *King Emperor v. Sibnath Banerjee*, AIR (30) 1943 PC 75; *Haveliram v. Maharaja of Morvi*, AIR (32) 1945 Bom 88; *Harkishan Das v. Emperor*, AIR (31) 1944 Lah 33; *H. N. Nolan v. Emperor*, AIR (31) 1944 All 118.

133. *Benoari Lal Sharma v. King Emperor*, AIR (30) 1943 FC 36.

134. *King Emperor v. Meer Singh*, ILR 1941 All 617.

135. *Ramananda Agarwala v. State of West Bengal*, AIR 1951 Cal 120.

136. *Monomohan v. Gobinda Das*, 55 CWN 6; *Haveliram Shetty v. His Highness, Shri Lukhdhirji, the Maharajsaheb of Morvi*, ILR 1944 Bom 487.

137. *State of Uttar Pradesh v. Basdeo Bajoria*, AIR 1951 All 44.

138. Bernard L. Schwartz, *American Administrative Law* (London: Pitman, 1950), 23. In the 1950s, just after writing the book, Schwartz served for two years as the chief counsel for a congressional subcommission on legislative oversight looking for misconduct in federal regulatory agencies. Woflgang Saxon, "Bernard Schwartz Dies at 74: Legal Scholar and Historian," *New York Times*, December 26, 1997.

139. Schwartz, *American Administrative Law*, 22.

140. *A.L.A. Schechter Poultry Corp v. United States*, 295 U.S. 495.

141. Schwartz, *American Administrative Law*, 31.

142. *Hodge v. Regina*, (1883) 9 AC 117.

143. A few exceptions remained to this general trend, such as the behavior of the Federal Court of India, established in 1939. For a more detailed account, see Rohit De, "The Federal Court and Civil Liberties in Late Colonial India," in *The Legal Complex in Postcolonial Struggles for*

Political Freedom, ed. Terrence Halliday, Lucien Karpik, and Malcolm Feeley (Cambridge, UK: Cambridge University Press, 2012), 59–90.

144. Dhavan, *Nehru and the Constitution*, xxxi.

145. Justice M. R. Jayakar to B. L. Mitter, April 6, 1937, Justice M. R. Jayakar Papers, NAI.

146. *In re Delhi Laws Act*, AIR 1951 SC 332.

147. *Queen v. Boorah*, 3 App. Cas. 889 (PC 1878).

148. Treatise writers focused on the decisions of Justices Kania and Fazl Ali and not the other judges; see A. T. Markose, *Cases and Materials in Administrative Law* (New Delhi: Indian Law Institute, 1966), 219.

149. *In re Delhi Laws Act*, AIR 1951 SC 332.

150. *Yick Wo v. Hopkins*, (1886) 118 U.S. 356.

151. *Harishankar Bagla and Another v. State of Madhya Pradesh*, AIR 1954 SC 465.

152. "Essential Supplies Act Held Valid; Supreme Court Dismisses Appeal," *Times of India*, May 17, 1954.

153. Uttar Pradesh Coal Control Order, 1943.

154. *Messrs. Dwarka Prasad Laxmi Narain v. State of Uttar Pradesh*, AIR 1954 SC 224.

155. Ibid.

156. *State of Rajasthan v. Nathmal*, AIR 1954 SC 307.

157. Jain, *Administrative Process*, 47.

158. *State of Rajasthan v. Nathmal*, AIR 1954 SC 307; *Union of India v. Bhanamal Gulzarimal*, AIR 1961 SC 475; *Bhagwati Saran v. State of Uttar Pradesh*, AIR 1961 SC 928.

159. This trend is evident from the very early case of *Santosh Kumar Jain v. State of Bihar*, AIR 1951 SC 201; see also *State of Rajasthan v. Nathmal*, AIR 1954 SC 307.

160. D. R. Gadgil, "Wartime Controls and Peacetime Ends in Government of India, Ministry of Labor," *Problems of Indian Labor: A Symposium* (Simla: Government of India, 1950), 5.

161. Nicole Sackley, "Passage to Modernity: American Social Scientists, India, and the Pursuit of Development, 1945–1961," PhD dissertation, Princeton University, 2004; Michael Latham, *Modernization as Ideology: American Social Science and "Nation Building" in the Kennedy Era* (Chapel Hill: University of North Carolina Press, 2000).

162. Don Price, *Special Report to the Officers: International Legal Studies*, October 26, 1955, Ford Foundation Collection, Rockefeller Archives; see also Jayanth Krishnan, "Prof. Kingsfield Goes to Delhi: American Academics, the Ford Foundation, and the Development of Legal Education in India," *American Journal of Legal History* 46 (2004): 447.

163. Jayanth Krishnan, "From the ALI to the ILI: The Efforts to Export an American Legal Institution," *Vanderbilt Journal of Transnational Law* 38 (2005): 1255.

164. *Final Report*, 17, Spaeth Merrilat Papers, Rockefeller Archives.

165. Markose, *Judicial Control*; Markose, *Cases and Materials*.

166. Jain, *Administrative Process*. The other studies addressed delegated legislation in India, administrative procedure under labor conciliation, disciplinary proceedings against government servants, and judicial review through writ petitions. For a detailed research report, see A. T. Markose, "Report of the Research Director on the Working of the Indian Law Institute from May 1960 to July 1962," *Journal of the Indian Law Institute* 3: 602–10.

167. M. Ramaswami, "Rule of Law and a Planned Society," *Journal of the Indian Law Institute* 1 (1958–1959): 31–32.

168. On the early generation of Indian legal scholarship, see Rajeev Dhavan, "Borrowed Ideas: On the Impact of American Scholarship on Indian Law," *American Journal of Comparative Law* 33, no. 3 (Summer 1985): 505–26.

169. Upendra Baxi, "Introduction," in M. Rama Jois, *Services under the State* (Bombay: N. M. Tripathi, 1987), xliii–lxii. In contrast, in the United States this common-law system of case-by-case decision making had been attacked as slow and expensive; see John Landis, *The Administrative Process* (New Haven, CT: Yale University Press, 1938), 34.

170. For the impact of partition and refugee resettlement on the creation of the modern Indian and Pakistani states, see Rohit De, "Evacuee Property and the Management of Economic Life in Postcolonial India," in Gyan Prakash, Michael Laffan, and Nikhil Menon, eds., The Postcolonial Moment in South and Southeast Asia (London: Bloomsbury, 2017), 87–106.

171. *Durga Prasad v. State of Uttar Pradesh*, AIR 1955 All 9.

172. *Jyoti Pershad v. Administrator for the Union Territory of Delhi*, AIR 1961 SC 1602.

173. *Amir Chand v. State of Uttar Pradesh*, AIR 1956 All 562.

174. The *Bagla* decision was cited as an authority in at least 194 cases (33 of them Supreme Court), and the *Dwarka Prasad* decision was cited as a precedent in 50 cases.

175. Upendra Baxi, "Developments in Administrative Law," in A. G. Noorani, ed., *Public Law in India* (Hamburg: Institut fur Aseinkunde, 1982), 149.

176. Morton Horwitz, *The Transformation of American Law, 1870–1960: The Crisis of Legal Orthodoxy* (Oxford, UK: Oxford University Press, 1992), 222.

177. Elizabeth Kolsky, "Codification and the Rule of Colonial Difference: Criminal Procedure in British India," *Law and History Review* 23, no. 3 (2005): 631–83.

178. Upendra Baxi, "Taking Suffering Seriously," in *Judges and Judicial Power: Essays in Honour of Justice V.R. Krishna Iyer*, ed. Rajeev Dhavan and R. Sudarshan (Bombay: N. M. Tripathi, 1985), 293.

179. George Gadbois, "The Supreme Court of India: A Preliminary Report of an Empirical Study," *Journal of Constitutional and Parliamentary Studies* 4, no. 1 (January–March 1970): 33–54.

180. Pranab Bardhan, *The Political Economy of Development in India* (New York: Basil Blackwell, 1984); Achin Vanaik, *The Painful Transition: Bourgeois Democracy in India* (New York: Verso Books, 1990).

181. Barbara Harris-White, *India Working: Essays on Society and Economy* (Cambridge, UK: Cambridge University Press, 2003).

182. Nasir Tyabji, *Forging Capitalism in Nehru's India: Neocolonialism and the State, c. 1940–1970* (New Delhi: Oxford University Press, 2015).

Chapter 3. The Case of the Invisible Butchers: Religious Rites and Economic Rights

1. *Bidi Supply Company v. Union of India*, AIR 1956 SC 479.

2. S. P. Sathe, "Cow Slaughter: The Legal Aspect," in *Cow-Slaughter: Horns of a Dilemma*, ed. Amritlal Shah (Bombay: Lalvani, 1967), 69–82.

3. *Mohd. Hanif Qureshi v. State of Bihar*, AIR 1958 SC 731.

4. Rajeev Dhavan, "Religious Freedom in India," *American Journal of Comparative Law* 35, no. 1 (1987): 209–54; H. Seervai, *Constitutional Law of India: A Critical Commentary*, 3rd ed.

(Bombay: N. M. Tripathi, 1983), 834–38; Durga Basu, *Commentary on the Constitution of India*, 3rd ed. (Calcutta: Sarkar, 1955), 238.

5. Baxi, "The Little Done," 348; Shradha Chigateri, "Negotiating the Sacred Cow: Cow Slaughter and the Regulation of Difference in India," in *Democracy, Religious Pluralism, and the Liberal Dilemma of Accommodation*, ed. Monica Mookherjee (New York: Springer, 2011), 143–50. Justice Barak-Erez compares the strictness shown by the Indian Supreme Court over the cow protection laws and the leniency of the Israeli Courts on pig prohibition as evidence of their majoritarian leanings towards Hindus and secular Jews , see Daphne Barak-Erez, "Symbolic Constitutionalism: On Sacred Cows and Abominable Pigs," *Law Culture and the Humanities* 6 (2010): 420–35.

6. The other petitions were *Mohd Ilias v. State of Bihar*, CMP 1161 of 1956, Writ Petition 58 of 1956; *Ghani Mahajan and Others v. State of Bihar*, CMP 1162 of 1956 and CMP 424 of 1957, Writ Petition of 1956; *Nasir ud Din v. State of Uttar Pradesh*, CMP 879 and 880 of 1956, Writ Petition 103 of 1956; *Mohd. Jan v. State of Uttar Pradesh*, CMP 129 of 1957, Writ Petition 129 of 1956, *Sheikh Hussain Qurashi v. State of Bombay*, CMP 882, 1174, and 1175, Writ Petition 117 of 1956; and *Sheikh Sobhan v State of Bombay*, CMP 881 of 1956, Writ Petition 126 of 1956.

7. The debates over the *Hanif Qureshi* case highlight the way in which constitutional cases are labeled or categorized. *Hanif Qureshi* is frequently cited in discussions about freedom of religion, thus effacing the caste and professional identity of the butchers and highlighting only their religious identity. The fixity of the final text of the judgment makes it easy to ignore the number of petitioners and the geographical range they covered, both of which are hard to miss when one looks at the actual petitions.

8. C. A. Bayly, "The Pre-History of 'Communalism'? Religious Conflict in India, 1700–1860," *Modern Asian Studies* 19, no. 2 (1985): 177–203.

9. Sandria Freitag critiques Bayly's (ibid.) suggestion that the riots of the eighteenth century form a prehistory of communalism. Through a reexamination of his sources in addition to her own research, she suggests that the key difference lies in the changing meanings of the same symbols. Sandria Freitag, *Collective Action and Community: Public Arenas and the Emergence of Communalism in North India* (Berkeley: University of California Press, 1989), 95.

10. Arjun Appadurai, "Gastro-Politics in Hindu South Asia," *American Ethnologist* 8, no. 3 (1981): 494–511.

11. A. A. Yang, "Sacred Symbol and Sacred Space in Rural India: Community Mobilization in the 'Anti-Cow Killing' Riot of 1893," *Comparative Studies in Society and History* 22, no. 4 (1980): 583.

12. Charles Metcalfe, resident of Delhi, to J. Adam, secretary to the governor-general, January 18, 1818, quoted in T. Dharampal and T. M. Mukundan, *The British Origin of Cow-Slaughter in India : With Some British Documents on the Anti-Kine-Killing Movement, 1880–1894* (Mussoorie: Society for Integrated Development of Himalayas, 2002), 85.

13. Mitra Dayananda Sarasvati, *Gōkaruṇānidhi* (Tenali: Satya Mitra Arya, 1938); see also Mitra Dayananda Sarasvati, *The Ocean of Mercy: An English Translation of Maharshi Swami Dayananda Saraswati's "Gocaruna Nidhi" by Durga Prasad* (Lahore: Virajanand Press, 1889). For a deeper engagement with both English and vernacular pamphlet literature on cow protection in the nineteenth and early twentieth centuries, see Cassie Adcock, "Sacred Cows and Secular History: Cow Protection Debates in Colonial North India," *CSSAAME* 30, no. 2 (2010): 297–311.

14. D. J. Lyall, Home Department secretary, to advocate general, IOR/L/PJ/6/376, 1894, file 298, India Office Records, British Library Asian and African Studies Collection, London.

15. Records of these trials are published as *Gau Maharani v. Sita Ram Ahir* and *Gau Maharani v. Sheo Lochan*, India Office Records, British Library Asian and African Studies Collection.

16. John R. McLane, *Indian Nationalism and the Early Congress* (Princeton, NJ: Princeton University Press, 1977); Francis Robinson, *Separatism among Indian Muslims: The Politics of the United Provinces' Muslims, 1860–1923* (Cambridge, UK: Cambridge University Press, 2007).

17. D. F. McCracken, officiating general superintendent, Thagi and Dacoity Department, IOR:L/PJ/254/1894, , India Office Records, British Library Asian and African Studies Collection.

18. D. F. McCracken, "Note on the Anti–Kine Killing Agitation," L/P&J/254/1894, India Office Records, British Library Asian and African Studies Collection.

19. "Note on Agitation regarding the Cow Question," Office of the Assistant to the Inspector General Police, Punjab, Special Branch, L/P&J/298/1984, India Office Records, British Library Asian and African Studies Collection.

20. Lord Lansdowne's minutes on the anti–kine killing movement, December 28, 1893, L/P&J/257, 1894, India Office Records, British Library Asian and African Studies Collection. .

21. Freitag, *Collective Action and Community*, 150.

22. Christopher Pinney, *"Photos of the Gods": The Printed Image and Political Struggle in India* (London: Reaktion Books, 2004), 108.

23. "Note on Agitation regarding the Cow Question."

24. *Naubahar Singh and Others v. Qadir Bux and Others*, AIR 1930 All 753.

25. "Note on Agitation regarding the Cow Question."

26. *Naubahar Singh and Others v. Qadir Bux and Others*, AIR 1930 All 753.

27. *Shahbaz Khan and Others v. Umrao Puri and Others*, (1908) ILR 30 All 81.

28. *Sheikh Muhammad Yakub v. Mangru Rai and Others*, 7 Ind Cas 318.

29. *Sheikh Muhammad Yakub v. King Emperor*, 6 Ind Cas 454.

30. *Subhan Mochi v. Babu Ram Singh and Others*, AIR 1930 All 121.

31. Common law also provided a category of public nuisance, but its recognition depended on legislation and custom. Hendrik Hartog, "Pigs and Positivism," *Wisconsin Law Review* (1985): 899–935.

32. *Queen Empress v. Zakiuddin and Another*, (1888) ILR 10 All 44.

33. *Abdullah v. King Emperor*, 49 Ind Cas 776 (1919).

34. *Khan Baputi Dewan v. Bispait Pundit*, (1900) ILR 27 Cal 655.

35. Mohandas K. Gandhi, "Befriend Musulmans," *Young India*, October 6, 1921, in Mohandas Gandhi, *How to Serve the Cow* (Ahmedbad: Navjivan, 1954), 18.

36. Mohandas Gandhi, *Freedom's Battle: Being A Comprehensive Collection of Writings and Speeches on the Present Situation*, 2nd ed. (Madras: Ganesh, 1922).

37. Mohanda K. Gandhi, "Save the Cow," *Young India*, June 8, 1921, in *Collected Works*, 23:251.

38. Mohandas K. Gandhi, "Cow Protection," *Young India*, January 29, 1925, in Mohandas Gandhi, *How to Serve the Cow* (Ahmedbad, Navjivan Publishing, 1954), 18.

39. Rao, *Framing of Indian Constitution*, 4:56.

40. Mohandas K. Gandhi, "Speech at Prayer Meeting," July 25, 1947, in *Collected Works* 96:86.

41. R. V. Dhulekar, *Constituent Assembly Debates*, November 24, 1948.

42. Thakur Das Bhargava, *Constituent Assembly Debates*, November 24, 1948. In 1940, there were 115,600,960 oxen in India and in 1945 only 111, 900,000 were left. During five years there was a decrease of thirty-seven oxen. Similiarly the number of buffaloes in 1940 were 32,891,3000 and in 1945 this was reduced to 32,533,400.

43. Benjamin Zachariah, "Uses of Scientific Argument: The Case of 'Development' in India, c. 1930–1950," *Economic and Political Weekly*, September 29, 2001.

44. Bhargava, *Constituent Assembly*.

45. The concern with India's hunger became both a focus of intervention and the basis of legitimacy for the Nehruvian state. Siegel, *Hungry Nation*); Sunil Amrith "Food and Welfare in India, c. 1900–1950." *Comparative Studies in Society and History* 50, no. 4 (2008): 1010–35.

46. Ministry of Agriculture, *Report of the Cattle Preservation and Development Committee* (New Delhi, 1949), 3.

47. Shibban Lal Saxena, *Constituent Assembly Debates*, November 24, 1948.

48. Seth Govind Das, *Constituent Assembly Debates*, November 24, 1948. Das was an influential Marwari businessman and had served as a legislator for thirty-two years. His two main agendas were the adoption of Hindi as the national language and cow protection. He raised the issue in the Council of States as early as 1927, held several terms as president of the All India Cow Protection Society, and was appointed a member of the Cattle Preservation and Development Committee by the Ministry of Agriculture in 1947. In the 1950s he introduced a number of private member bills for a national ban on cow slaughter. Bhupendra Hooda, *A Life Dedicated: Biography of Govind Das* (Delhi: Seth Govind Das Diamond Jubilee Celebrations Committee, 1956).

49. Bhargava, *Constituent Assembly*; Dhulekar, *Constituent Assembly*.

50. Bhargava, *Constituent Assembly*; Das, *Constituent Assembly*.

51. Rochana Bajpai, "Constituent Assembly Debates and Minority Rights," *Economic and Political Weekly*, May 27, 2000; Aditya Nigam, "A Text without Author: Locating Constituent Assembly as Event," *Economic and Political Weekly*, May 22, 2004.

52. It is surprising that none of the Congress Party members like Nehru, who were otherwise opposed to or contemptuous of cow protection, spoke during the debate. They were possibly involved in backroom negotiations to get cow protection moved from fundamental rights to directive principles.

53. Cassie Adcock, "Sacred Cows and Secular History: Cow Protection Debates in Colonial North India," *CSSAAME* 30, no. 2 (2010): 297–311.

54. Zairul Hasan Lari, *Constituent Assembly Debates*, November 24, 1948.

55. "Nehru Stakes His Position to Oppose Cattle Slaughter Ban," *Times of India*, April 3, 1955. See also Subrata Kumar Mitra, "Desecularizing the State: Religion and Politics in India after Independence," *Comparative Studies in Society and History* 33, no. 4 (1991): 755, 770–772

56. Jawaharlal Nehru, April 2, 1955, in Lok Sabha Secretariat, *A Selection from Questions and Answers in Lok Sabha, First to Fifteenth Sessions (1952–1957)* (New Delhi, 1957).

57. William Gould, "Contesting Secularism in Colonial and Postcolonial North India between the 1930 and 1950s," *Contemporary South Asia* 14 (December 2005): 483.

58. *Babulal Sharma v.. Brijnarain Brajesh and Others*, AIR 1958 MP 175.

59. "Hindu Right Wing Condemns Nehru: Election Manifesto of Most Extreme Party Strives for Wide Appeal," *New York Times*, February 20, 1957.

60. A. M. Rosenthal, "Cow Again Focus of Indian Debate: Slaughter Ban Urged Anew by Friend of Nehru," *New York Times*, July 23, 1956.

61. "Reds Join Hindu Protest: Parade Assails Slaughtering of Cows and Serving of Beef," *New York Times*, January 23, 1955.

62. Rosenthal, "Cow Again Focus."

63. "Fast for Ban on Cow Slaughter: More Workers Go on Sympathetic Strike," *Indian Express*, March 15, 1951.

64. Uttar Pradesh, *Gosamvardhan Enquiry Committee Report* (Allahabad: Government of India Press, 1955), 37.

65. *Mangru Meya and Others v. Commissioners of the Budge Budge Municipality*, AIR 1953 Cal 333.

66. *Madran Kassab v. King Emperor*, 86 Ind Cas 964.

67. S.370(2), Bengal Municipal Act, 1932.

68. *Madran Kassab v. King Emperor*, 86 Ind Cas 964.

69. *Chairman, Budge Budge Municipality v. Mangru Meya and Others*, AIR 1953 Cal 433

70. *Haji Ahmad Raza and Others v. Municipal Board, Allahabad*, AIR 1952 All 1.

71. *Buddhu v. Municipal Board*, AIR 1952 All 753.

72. S.326, United Provinces Municipalities Act, 1916.

73. *Haji Ahmad Raza and Others v. Municipal Board, Allahabad*, AIR 1952 All 1.

74. *Kruse v. Johnson*, (1898) 2 QB 91.

75. The court cited J. B. Sampat Kumaran, *Artificial Insemination and Animal Production* (Jubblepore: Mission Press, 1951).

76. Kumaran, *Artificial Insemination*, 248.

77. *Buddhu v. Municipal Board*, AIR 1952 All 753.

78. Justice Dayal would later be elevated to the Supreme Court of India.

79. S.238, Uttar Pradesh Municipalities Act, 1916.

80. *Hamid and Another v. State of Uttar Pradesh*, 1958 CriLJ 115.

81. The court considered the precedent of *Buddhu v. Municipal Board* as binding in part, but it distinguished the case before it on the grounds that the case involved a town committee set up under the Town Area Committee Act rather than a municipality set up under the Uttar Pradesh Municipalities Act.

82. S.29(1), Town Area Committee Act, 1914.

83. Uttar Pradesh, *Gosamvardhan*, 49.

84. Mariana Valverde, "Jurisdiction and Scale: Using Law's Technicalities as Theoretical Resources." *Social and Legal Studies* 18, no. 2 (2009): 139–57.

85. Ministry of Agriculture, *Report of the Cattle Preservation*, 12.

86. Reply by Rafi Ahmad Kidwai, food minister, December 15, 1952, in Lok Sabha Secretariat, *Selection from Questions and Answers*, 115.

87. Saurasthra Ordinance, L and A FN 1(6) L/50, Ministry of State Files, NAI.

88. N. Bonarji, chief commissioner, Bhopal, to undersecretary, Ministry of State, November 21, 1949, Prohibition of cattle slaughter- recommendations made by the cattle preservation and Development committee, L and A FN 1(6) L/50, Ministry of State Files, NAI.

89. Uttar Pradesh, *Gosamvardhan*, 17.

90. William Gould, "Contesting Secularism in Colonial and Postcolonial North India between the 1930 and 1950s," *Contemporary South Asia* 14, no. 4 (2005): 481–94; William Gould, *Bureaucracy, Community, and Influence in India Society and the State, 1930s–1960s* (London: Routledge, 2010).

91. "Prevention of Cow Slaughter Urged," *Times of India,* February 27, 1954.

92. Uttar Pradesh, *Gosamvardhan*, 2.

93. These included the Central Dairy Farm in Aligarh, the College of Veterinary Science and Animal Husbandry in Mathura, the Mechanized State Fair at Madhurikund, and the Dairy at the Dayal Bagh Insttute in Agra to learn about new technology. The chairman and the Nawab of Chhatari visited the hide-flaying and -curing centers at the Bakshi-ka-Talab at Lucknow. The committee toured several districts of Uttar Pradesh, visited homes for abandoned cattle, and issued questions to heads of political parties, various religious leaders, members of central and state legislatures, officers of the Indian Administrative Service serving within the states, heads of departments, the vice chancellor of universities, and several individuals. Furthermore, 250 witnesses were examined by the committee, including S. C. Das Gupta, the author of the earliest scientific work on the cow in India; Seth Govind Das and Thakurdas Bhargava, the advocates of cow protection in parliament; the president of the Jamiat-e-Ulema Hind (Association of Indian Muslim Clerics) and the head of the influential Sunni Muslim seminary in Deoband; and Mira Behn, one of Gandhi's closest associates.

94. Uttar Pradesh, *Gosamvardhan*, 71, 74.

95. S.4, Uttar Pradesh Cow Protection Act, 1950.

96. Bihar Preservation and Improvement of Animals Act, 1955

97. File 17/132/55, Judicial Branch, Ministry of Home Affairs Files, NAI.

98. "Memorandum from Law Ministry," October 20, 1955, File 17/132/55, Judicial Branch, Files, NAI.

99. The Ministry of Agriculture concurred with the Ministry of Law. "Memorandum from A. B Lal, undersecretary, Ministry of Food and Agriculture, October 19, 1955, File 17/132/55, Judicial Branch, Ministry of Home Affairs Files, NAI. Pataskar was a long-term member of the Congress Party, had a successful legal practice before the Bombay High Court and the Supreme Court, and had been a member of the Constituent Assembly.

100. Writ Petition 144, 1956, SCRR.

101. K. Singh, ed., *People of India: Uttar Pradesh* (New Delhi: Anthropological Survey of India, 2005), 2.

102. Ahmed Said Khan was one of the largest landlords in the province, had been a member of the Muslim League before independence, and had served as the premier of Uttar Pradesh and the state of Hyderabad. Akhtar Hussein was a Congress Party member nominated to the upper house of parliament. Mohammed Habib was a politically active professor of history at Aligarh Muslim University, the intellectual home for north Indian Muslims.

103. Writ Petitions No. 136 of 1956, 128 of 1956, 144 of 1956, and 129 of 1957, SCRR.

104. "Cow Slaughter Banned," *Boston Globe*, January 9, 1953.

105. Article 25(1), Constitution of India, 1950.

106. *Mohd. Hanif Qureshi v. State of Bihar*, AIR 1958 SC 731.

107. "Counter Affidavit on Behalf of the State of UP," Writ Petition 144, 1956, SCRR.

108. *Sastri Yagnapurusha Dasji v. Mooldas*, AIR 1966 SC 1119.

109. *State of Madras v. V. G Row*, [1952] SCR 607.

110. The court resorted to amateur linguistics to argue the value of cattle. Cattle in Sankrit were called *pasus*, which was similar to the Latin word *pecus*, the root of the English words *pecuniary* and *impecunious*. According to the court's reasoning, the Latin word was also derived from "cattle" and emphasized their value. The court referred to the Hindu epic Ramayana, the Arthashastra, the classic Mauryan treatise on political economy, and works on Hindu law, all of which all emphasized the importance of cattle.

111. Mitra Sharafi, "A New History of Colonial Lawyering: Likhovski and Legal Identities in the British Empire," *Law and Social Inquiry* 32, no. 4 (2007): 1059–94.

112. Rajeev Dhavan, *The Supreme Court of India: A Socio-Legal Critique of Its Juristic Techniques* (Bombay: N. M. Tripathi, 1977); George Gadbois, *Judges of the Supreme Court of India (1950–1989)* (New Delhi: Oxford University Press, 2011).

113. Ronojoy Sen, *Articles of Faith: Religion, Secularism, and the Indian Supreme Court* (New Delhi: Oxford University Press, 2010).

114. Rohit De, "The Two Husbands of Vera Tiscenko: Apostasy, Conversion, and Divorce in Late Colonial India," *Law and History Review* 28, no. 4 (2010): 1011.

115. Abinas Das, *Rig-Vedic India* (Calcutta: University of Calcutta, 1921); Pāṇḍuraṅga Kāṇe, *History of the Dharmasastra: Ancient and Medieval Religious and Civil Law in India* (Poona: Bhandarkar Oriental Research Institute, 1953).

116. Rafiq Zakaria, "Legal Notes: Reasonable Classes in Good Faith," *Times of India*, October 4, 1958.

117. Baxi, "The Little Done," 348.

118. Surendra Gopal and Hetukhar Jha, eds., *People of India: Bihar including Jharkhand* (Calcutta: Seagull Books, 2008), 476.

119. Under Article 340 of the Constitution, the government is required to set up a commission to investigate the conditions of socially and educationally "backward" classes and to take steps for their welfare. Since 1950 the central government has maintained a list of groups that it identifies as socially and educationally "backward." The list is dynamic, and groups and communities can be added or removed depending on their development. Among the benefits they receive are quotas reserved for them in public-sector employment and higher education.

120. "Conference of Butchers: Seeking Redress by Persuasion," *Times of India*, April 15, 1955.

121. *Haji Ahmad Raza and Others v. Municipal Board, Allahabad*, AIR 1952 All 1.

122. Directorate of Marketing and Inspection, *Report on the Marketing of Cattle in India* (Delhi: Manager of Publications, 1946).

123. *Mohd. Hanif Qureshi v. State of Bihar*, AIR 1958 SC 731.

124. Emma Tarlo, *Clothing Matters: Dress and Identity in India* (Chicago: University of Chicago Press, 1996).

125. Union minister for food and agriculture, Lok Sabha, December 5, 1953, SCRR.

126. Writ Petition 144, 1956, [SCRR.].

127. Uttar Pradesh, *Gosamvardhan*, 71; *Mohd. Hanif Qureshi v. State of Bihar*, AIR 1958 SC 731.

128. *Mohd. Hanif Qureshi v. State of Bihar*, AIR 1958 SC 731.

129. Shiv Visvanathan, "The Great Indian Novel: Reflections on the Lentin Report," *Economic and Political Weekly* January 30, 1999.

130. In contrast, a cow yielded eight thousand pounds of milk in the Netherlands, seven thousand pounds in Australia, and five thousand pounds in the United States.

131. Uttar Pradesh, *Gosamvardhan*, 12.

132. Mohandas K. Gandhi, "Address to Gosewa Sangh," 1930.{Newspaper source? *Collected Works*?}

133. Ibid.

134. *Saghir Ahmad v. State of Uttar Pradesh*, [1955] 1 SCR 707.

135. Directorate of Marketing and Inspection, *Report on the Marketing of Cattle*, 24.

136. The Gosamvardhan Committee noted that in the state of Uttar Pradesh there was a deficiency of 60 million tons of straw, 104 million tons of green fodder, and 26.5 million tons in concentrates such as oil cakes, bran, and oil seeds. The court devoted considerable time to estimating what the actual gap in available feed was.

137. *Mohd. Hanif Qureshi v. State of Bihar*, AIR 1958 SC 731.

138. Uttar Pradesh, *Gosamvardhan*, 44.

139. Ministry of Agriculture, *Report of the Cattle Preservation*, 47.

140. *Mohd. Hanif Qureshi v. State of Bihar*, AIR 1958 SC 731. The court quoted approvingly from the Assam Cattle Protection Act of 1950, the Bombay Animal Preservation Act of 1948, the West Bengal Animal Slaughter Control Act of 1950, the Hyderabad Slaughter of Animals Act of 1950, and the Tranvancore and Cochin Notification of 1951.

141. "Indian Court Upholds Ban," *Calgary Herald*, April 26, 1958.

142. "Cows Win Fight in India Court," *St. Petersburg Independent*, May 4, 1958.

143. Baxi, "The Little Done"; Chigateri, "Negotiating the Sacred Cow"; Salman Khurshid, *At Home in India: A Restatement of Indian Muslims* (New Delhi: Vikas Pub. House, 1986).

144. S.4(1)(b), Madhya Pradesh Agricultural Cattle Preservation Act, 1958.

145. Writ Petitions No. 15 of 1959, 14 of 1960, and 21 of 1959, SCRR.

146. For instance, in *Mohd. Jan v. State of Uttar Pradesh*, Writ Petitions Nos. 15 and 129 of 1956, the petitioners were identified as gut merchants, cattle dealers, *kasais*, beef vendors, and hide merchants.

147. *Dulla and Others v. State of Uttar Pradesh*, AIR 1958 All 198.

148. *Adamji Umar Dalai v. State of Bombay*, 1952 SCR 172; *Emperor v. Yar Mohammad*, AIR 1931 Cal 448; *Emperor v. Sakinabai Baddurddin*, AIR 1931 Bom 70; *Emperor v. Maiku*, AIR 1930 All 279.

149. *Ayub v. State of Uttar Pradesh*, AIR 1962 All 141.

150. For a detailed ethnography of a Qureshi community in Delhi, see Zarin Ahmad, *Delhi Meatscapes: Muslim Butchers in a Transforming Megacity* (New Delhi: Oxford University Press, 2018).

151. Lala Hardev Sahai, "Savrocha Nyalaya ka Nridnay Godhan ko Ko Katal Se Naheen Bacha Sakta: Pashu Visheshagyon ka Safal Shadyantra" [Supreme Court Decision Could Not Save Cows from Slaughter: Animal Expert's Conspiracy Successful], File 277, Purushottam Das Tandon Papers, NAI.

152. FAO Statistics Division, 2007, http://faostat.fao.org/site/336/default.aspx.

153. For an examination of how cow protection politics interacted with the courts from 1958 till 2017, see De, "Cows and Constitutionalism," *Modern Asian Studies* 53, no. 1 (forthcoming, 2019).

Chapter 4. The Case of the Honest Prostitute:
Sex, Work, and Freedom

1. "Prostitute Files Writ Petition: Fundamental Right 'Offended,' " *Statesman*, May 2, 1958.

2. "Premature Petition by Prostitute," *Statesman*, May 27, 1958.

3. "Writ Petition by a Prostitute," File 3/7/58 (1958), Police Branch IV, Ministry of Home Affairs Files, NAI.

4. Durgabai Deshmukh to Jawaharlal Nehru, September 7, 1954, Durgabai Deshmukh Papers, Nehru Memorial Museum and Library (NMML), New Delhi.

5. Durgabai Deshmukh had been active in social work and nationalist politics since her teenage years and rose to prominence during the civil disobedience movement of 1932. She was one of India's first female lawyers and had built up a considerable criminal-law practice in Madras by the mid-1940s. Deshmukh was the first female advocate before the Federal Court at Delhi, was elected a member of the Constituent Assembly in 1946, and played a prominent role in the processes of drafting and debating bills. After independence she was appointed a member of the Planning Commission and later became the chairwoman of the Central Social Welfare Board. See Durgabai Deshmukh, *Chintaman and I* (New Delhi: Allied, 1980).

6. The Constituent Assembly had already foreseen that the fundamental rights could come into conflict with some parts of the government's plan to bring about economic and social change. Assembly debates indicate that they imagined these challenges would come from vested interests representing the old order. Discussion mostly revolved around the possibility of the landed aristocracy challenging the proposed land reforms through the right to property. In addition, the religious orthodoxy could challenge social reforms through the right to religion. In an attempt to stave off these challenges, both the right to property and the right to practice one's religion were accordingly circumscribed in the very text of the Constitution.

7. Swati Ghosh, "The Shadow Lines of Citizenship: Prostitutes' Struggle over Workers' Rights," *Identity, Culture, and Politics* 5, nos.1–2 (2004): 105–23.

8. Philippa Levine, *Prostitution, Race, and Politics: Policing Venereal Disease in the British Empire* (New York: Routledge, 2003); Janaki Nair, *Women and Law in Colonial India: A Social History* (New Delhi: Kali for Women, 1996); Kunal Parker, " 'A Corporation of Superior Prostitutes': Anglo-Indian Legal Conceptions of Temple Dancing Girls, 1800–1914," *Modern Asian Studies* 32, no. 3 (1998): 559–633; Erica Wald, "From *Begums* and *Bibis* to Abandoned Females and Idle Women: Sexual Relationships, Venereal Disease, and the Redefinition of Prostitution in Early Nineteenth-Century India," *Indian Economic Social History Review* 46, no. 1 (2009): 5–25; Kalpana Muvalar Ramamirthammal, *Muvalur Ramamirthammal's Web of Deceit: Devadasi Reform in Colonial India* (New Delhi: Kali for Women, 2003); Ashwini Tambe, "The Elusive Ingénue: A Transnational Feminist Analysis of European Prostitution in Colonial Bombay," *Gender and Society* 19, no. 2 (2005).

9. There is a considerable body of work on both these topics. On family law, see Eleanor Newbigin, *The Hindu Family and the Emergence of Modern India: Law, Citizenship, and Community* (Cambridge, UK: Cambridge University Press, 2013); and Rochana Majumdar, *Marriage and Modernity: Family Values in Colonial Bengal* (Durham, NC: Duke University Press, 2009). On partition, see Ritu Menon, *Abducted Women, the State, and Questions of Honour: Three*

Perspectives on the Recovery Operation in Post-Partition India (Canberra, Australia: Research School of Pacific Studies, 1993); and Urvashi Butalia, *The Other Side of Silence: Voices from the Partition of India* (Durham, NC: Duke University Press, 2001).

10. Roy, *Beyond Belief*, 33.

11. A notable exception is the Emancipation Edict for Female Performers and Prostitutes, proclaimed during the Meiji period (1868–1912) in Japan. Daniel V. Botsman, "Freedom without Slavery? 'Coolies,' Prostitutes, and Outcasts in Meiji Japan's 'Emancipation Moment,' " *American Historical Review* 116, no. 5 (December 2011): 1323–47.

12. For an overview, see Wald, From *Begums* and *Bibis*; and Ashwini Tambe, *Codes of Misconduct: Regulating Prostitution in Late Colonial Bombay* (Minneapolis: University of Minnesota Press, 2009).

13. Ibid., xxvi.

14. The Constituent Assembly had fifteen female members, at least two-thirds of whom had been members of the All India Women's Conference. The Constituent Assembly of Pakistan, established in 1947, had two female members, Begum Jahanara Shahnawaz and Shaista Suhrawardy Ikramullah, representing the two largest provinces of the country, Punjab and Bengal. However, both had resigned by the early 1950s, and the assembly itself was dismissed by the governor-general in 1952. The second and third constituent assemblies in Pakistan did not have female members. The Knesset, the parliament of Israel, was set up in early 1949 and had twelve female members, but it failed to enact a constitution.

15. "Bulletin of the Indian Women's Movement," January 1946, File No. 7, Hansa Mehta Papers NMML.

16. Lakshmi N. Menon to Hansa Mehta, October 11, 1946, File No. 6, Hansa Mehta Papers, NMML.

17. "Draft Charter of Rights and Duties for Indian Women," File No. 9-A, Hansa Mehta Papers, NMML.

18. "AIWC Memorandum to Central and Provincial Governments," File No. 7, Hansa Mehta Papers, NMML.

19. Purnima Banerjee, *Constituent Assembly Debates*, October 11, 1949.

20. Shakuntala Lall, "ASMH: What it Stands For," *Social Health* 1 (July 1962): 7.

21. "Draft Charter of Rights and Duties for Indian Women."

22. Rohit De, "The Birth of SITA: Sex Work, Social Work, and Social Science in the Indian Republic (1947–1960)," in *Political Imaginaries of Modern India*, ed. Manu Goswami and Mrinalini Sinha (forthcoming).

23. T. T. K. Krishnamachari, *Constitutent Assembly Debates*, March 1, 1947

24. Biswanath Das, *Constitutent Assembyl Debates*, May 1, 1947

25. Gyan Prakash, *Bonded Histories: Genealogies of Labor Servitude in Colonial India* (Cambridge, UK: Cambridge University Press, 1990), xxii.

26. Botsman, "Freedom without Slavery?", 1344.

27. David Scott, *Refashioning Futures: Criticism after Postcoloniality* (Princeton, NJ: Princeton University Press, 1999), 82–83.

28. Article 35, Constitution of India, 1950.

29. "Statements of Objects and Reasons," SITA, 1956.

30. De, "Birth of SITA."

31. Deshmukh, *Chintaman*; Durgabai Deshmukh to G. B Pant, File 46/53, Vol. 3, 1953, Police Branch II, Ministry of Home Affairs Files, NAI.

32. Julia Laite, "The Association for Moral and Social Hygiene: Abolitionism and Prostitution Law in Britain (1915–1959)," *Women's History Review* 17, no. 2 (April 2008): 207–23.

33. Stephen Legg, "An Intimate and Imperial Feminism: Meliscent Shephard and the Regulation of Prostitution in Colonial India," *Environment and Planning: Society and Space*, 28 (2010): 68–94.

34. "Indian Women Leaders: Mrs. Rameshwari Nehru," *Times of India*, May 29, 1953.

35. Durgabai Deshmukh, "Presidential Address," Fifth All India Conference, 1956, Durgabai Deshmukh Papers, NMML.

36. It is notable that the Home Ministry's files on SITA seem to have been acted upon by bureaucratcs only before an impending visit by Rameshwari Nehru or Durgabai Deshmukh. See, e.g., File 46/53, Volume 3, 1953, Police Branch II, Ministry of Home Affairs Files, NAI.

37. Durgabai Deshmukh to Jawaharlal Nehru, September 7, 1954, Durgabai Deshmukh Papers, NMML.

38. These include the Bombay Prevention of Prostitution Act, 1923; the Madras Suppression of Immoral Traffic Act, 1930; the Bengal Suppression of Immoral Traffic Act, 1933; the Uttar Pradesh Suppression of Immoral Traffic Act, 1933; the Punjab Suppression of Immoral Traffic Act, 1935; the Madhya Pradesh Suppression of Immoral Traffic Act, 1953; the Bihar Suppression of Immoral Traffic Act, 1948; the Mysore Suppression of Immoral Traffic Act, 1936; the Travancore-Cochin Suppression of Immoral Traffic Act, 1952; the Hyderabad Suppression of Immoral Traffic Act, 1952; the Ajmer Prevention of Prostitution Act, 1953; the Patiala Suppression of Immoral Traffic Act, 1940; and the Suppression of Immoral Traffic Act (Jammu and Kashmir), 1934. The Bombay Devadasi Protection Act of 1934 and the Madras Devadasi Prevention of Dedication Act of 1938 were special statutes enacted to invalidate the dedication of women to temples. Finally, to check the practice of training minor girls in prostitution, the Uttar Pradesh Naik Girls Protection Act of 1929 authorized the magistrate to receive details about all girls under eighteen years of age and to restrict and regulate their movements.

39. Central Social Welfare Board, *Report of the Advisory Committee*.

40. Regina Kuenzel, *Fallen Women, Problem Girls: Unmarried Mothers and the Professionalization of Social Work, 1890–1945* (New Haven, CT: Yale University Press, 1993).

41. S.5, SITA, 1956.

42. S.8, SITA, 1956.

43. S.10(1)(a), SITA, 1956.

44. *In re Shantibai Rani Benoor*, AIR 1951 Bom 337; *Smt Sona Bai and Others v. Municipality of Agra*, AIR 1956 All 736.

45. A. S. Mathur and B. L. Gupta, *Prostitutes and Prostitution* (Agra, India: Ram Prasad, 1965), 189.

46. Vidyadhar Agnihotri, *Fallen Women: A Study with Special Reference to Kanpur* (Kanpur: Maharajas, 1954), 17.

47. "Brothel Owners Get Ready for Legal Battle: Implementation of Immoral Traffic Act Difficult," *Statesman*, April 25, 1958.

48. "Immoral Traffic Suppression Protest in Delhi," *Times of India*, April 30, 1958.

49. "Allahabad Dancing Girls Form Union," *Hindustan Times*, May 3, 1958.

50. "Prostitute Files Writ Petition: Fundamental Right Offended," *Statesman*, May 2, 1958.

51. "Prostitutes' Plea Rejected: Circuit Court Decision," *Times of India*, May 8, 1958.

52. Note to Joint Secretary, Serial No. 4, File 37/3/58, 1958, Police Branch IV, Ministry of Home Affairs Files, NAI.

53. "Immoral Traffic," *Times of India*, May 7, 1958.

54. Julia Laite, *Common Prostitutes and Ordinary Citizens: Commercial Sex in London, 1885–1960* (London: Palgrave Macmillan, 2010).

55. Tambe, *Codes of Misconduct*, 39.

56. The interviewers noted that questions about relations with the police aroused suspicion and fear among the respondents, and only a minority chose to respond. S. D. Punekar and Kamala Rao, *A Study of Prostitutes in Bombay (With Reference to Family Background)* (Bombay: Allied, 1962), 154.

57. Tambe, *Codes of Misconduct*, 117.

58. "Prostitutes in Indian Censuses," File 46/53, Vol. 3, 1953, Police Branch II, Ministry of Home Affairs Files, NAI.

59. Rameshwari Nehru to G. B. Pant, January 10, 1959 Subject File 31, Rameshwari Nehru Papers, NMML.

60. "Steps to Suppress Immoral Traffic: Dissatisfaction Voiced in Lok Sabha," *Times of India*, September 24, 1958.

61. Petition from Bismillah, a prostitute formerly residing in Agra Cantonment, against her expulsion from that cantonment, 1918, Legislative Branch, Ministry of Home Affairs Files, NAI.

62. Nationalist politics were closed to prostitutes. Gandhi famously refused to allow 350 prostitutes from East Bengal, who were Congress Party members and contributed funds, from seeking organizational positions on the grounds that only those "who had pure hands" could lead the battle for *swaraj*. Ashwini Tambe, "Gandhi's 'Fallen' Sisters: Difference and the National Body Politic," *Social Scientist* 37, nos. 1/2 (2009): 21–38.

63. Tambe, *Codes of Misconduct*, 39.

64. Stephen Legg, *Scales of Prostitution: International Governmentalities and Interwar India* (Durham, NC: Duke University Press, 2014).

65. *Municipal Committee of Delhi v. Moti Jan*, (1930) 123 IC 536; *Moti Jan v. Municipal Committee, Delhi* (1926) 93 IC 827.

66. Wald, "From *Begums* and *Bibis*"; Veena Talwar-Oldenburg, "Lifestyle as Resistance: The Case of the Courtesans of Lucknow, India," *Feminist Studies* 16 (1990): 259–87; Kunal M. Parker, " 'A Corporation of Superior Prostitutes': Anglo-Indian Legal Conceptions of Temple Dancing Girls, 1800–1914," *Modern Asian Studies* 32, no. 3 (1998): 559–633.

67. Amanda Weidman, *Singing the Classical, Voicing the Modern: The Postcolonial Politics of Music in South India* (Durham, NC: Duke University Press, 2006).

68. Amanda Weidman, "Stage Goddesses and Studio Divas: Agency and the Politics of Voice," in *Words, Worlds, and Material Girls: Essays on Language, Gender, Globalization*, ed. Bonnie McElhinny (Berlin: Mouton de Gruyter Press, 2007), 131–56; Vikram Sampath, *My Name Is Gauhar Jaan: Life and Times of a Musician* (Delhi: Rupa, 2010).

69. *Parbatti Dassi v. King Emperor*, AIR 1934 Cal 198.

70. Mazhar Husain, *The Suppression of Immoral Traffic in Women and Girls Act, 1956: With Commentary and Case Law* (Lucknow: Eastern Book, 1958), 5; B. R. Beotra, *The Suppression*

of Immoral Traffic in Women and Girls Act, 1956 (with State Rules) (Allahabad: Law Book, 1962), 12.

71. The case was cited in *Razia v. State of Uttar Pradesh*, AIR 1957 All 340; and *Balwant and Others v. Deputy Director*, AIR 1975 All 295.

72. S.247, United Provinces Municipalities Act, 1917.

73. *Municipal Board, Etah v. Asghari Jaan and Mt. Bismillah*, AIR 1932 All 264.

74. Ibid.

75. Ibid.

76. Feminist scholars caution against strategies that are predicated on the state distinguishing between good female behavior and bad female behavior, in this case between a courtesan and a prostitute. Prabha Kotiswaran, "Labours in Vice or Virtue? Neo-Liberalism, Sexual Commerce, and the Case of Indian Bar Dancing," *Journal of Law and Society* 37, no. 1 (March 2010): 105–24.

77. *Sona Bai and others v. Municipal Board, Agra*, 1956 AIR (All) 76.

78. Since the 1920s, prostitutes had been categorized with other forms of unproductive labor in the Indian census. "Prostitutes in Indian Censuses," File 46/53, Vol. 3, 1953, Police Branch II, Ministry of Home Affairs Files, NAI.

79. Rajeshwari Sundar Rajan, "The Prostitution Question(s): Female Agency, Sexuality and Work," in *Sex Work: Issues in Contemporary Indian Feminism*, ed. Prabha Kotiswaran (Delhi: Women Unlimited, 2011), 130.

80. See, e.g., *Kamalabai Jethamal v. State of Maharasthra*, AIR 1962 SC 1189; and *State of Uttar Pradesh v. Kaushalya Devi*, AIR 1964 SC 416. Both took two years from the initiation of the petition before the high court to the final disposal of the appeal by the Supreme Court.

81. Central Social Welfare Board. *Report of the Advisory Committee*, 11.

82. See Mathur and Gupta, *Prostitutes*, 3; Agnihotri, *Fallen Women*, 3.

83. Kamaladevi Chattopadhyay, "Presidential Address," All India Conference of the ASMH, Kamaladevi Chattopadhyay Papers, NMML.

84. Central Social Welfare Board. *Report of the Advisory Committee*, 4.

85. Agnihotri, *Fallen Women*, 8.

86. Central Social Welfare Board. *Report of the Advisory Committee*, 6.

87. S. D. Punekar and Kamala Rao, *A Study of Prostitutes in Bombay: With Reference to Family Background*. (Bombay: Lalvani Pub. House, 1967) 142.

88. S.7(2)(a), SITA, 1956.

89. S.372, Indian Penal Code, 1875.

90. *Chiranjit Lal Chowdhury v. Union of India*, AIR 1951 SC 41.

91. Justice Sahai cited *Rashid Ahmad* v. *Municipal Board, Kairana*, AIR 1963 SC 163, one of the early vegetable-seller petitions (discussed in the introduction) as a precedent on this point.

92. S.18, S.20, SITA, 1956.

93. Agnihotri, *Fallen Women*, 97.

94. Serials 8 and 9, 37/3/58, 1958, Police Branch IV, Ministry of Home Affairs Files, NAI.

95. AIWC Opinion of Mrs. Mithan J. Lam (Bill No. 58 of 1954), File No. 138, Installment IV, All India Women's Conference Papers, NMML.

96. Central Social Welfare Board, *Report of the Advisory Committee*, 4.

97. Ashwini Tambe, "Brothels as Families: Reflections on the History of Bombay's *Kothas*," *International Feminist Journal of Politics* 8, no. 2 (2006): 223.

98. Punekar and Rao, *Study of Prostitutes,*144.

99. B. N. Data, Minister for Law and Justice, note, File 37/3/58, 1958, Police Branch IV, Ministry of Home Affairs, NAI.

100. Mazhar Hussein (1958), *The Suppression of Immoral Traffic in Women and Girls Act, 1956: With Commentary and Case Law* (Lucknow: Eastern Book, 1958), 62.

101. Alishon Bashford, *Imperial Hygiene: A Critical History of Colonialism, Nationalism, and Public Health* (Basingstoke, UK: Palgrave Macmillan, 2004).

102. Stephen Legg, "Stimulation, Segregation and Scandal: Geographies of Prostitution Regulation in British India, Between Registration (1888) and Suppression (1923)," *Modern Asian Studies* 46, no. 6 (2012): 1459–1505.

103. *Municipal Board, Etah v. Asghari Jaan and Mt. Bismillah*, AIR 1932 All 264.

104. *Kachanmala Dassi v. Lilabati Debi*, AIR 1951 Cal 164.

105. *Municipal Committee, Malerkotla v. Mohd. Mustaq and Others*, AIR 1960 Punjab and Hisraela 18.

106. *In re Shantabai Rani Benoor*, AIR 1951 Bom 337.

107. "Order on Poona Women Void: Case under Prevention of Prostitution Act," *Times of India*, November 29, 1950.

108. *Jesinghbhai Ishwarlal v. King Emperor*, AIR 1950 Bom 363.

109. Durgabai Deshmukh to Jawaharlal Nehru, September 7, 1954, Durgabai Deshmukh Papers, NMML.

110. *Shama Bai and Another v. State of Uttar Pradesh*, AIR 1959 All 57.

111. *Mt. Chanchal v. King Emperor*, AIR 1932 All 70.

112. *Mt. Muhammadi v. King Emperor*, AIR 1932 All 110; *Mt Naziran v. King Emperor*, AIR 1932 All 537.

113. *State of West Bengal v. Anwar Ali Sarkar*, AIR 1952 SC 75; Rohit De, "Rebellion, Dacoity, and Equality: The Emergence of the Constitutional Field in Postcolonial India," *CSSAAME* 34, no. 2 (2014): 260–78.

114. *Yick Wo v. Hopkins* (1886) 118 U.S. 356.

115. "Proposed Law Minister Conference: Separation of Judiciary from the Executive," File 9/1/60, Judicial Branch, Ministry of Home Affairs Files, NAI.

116. Bombay Prevention of Prostitution Act, File 13/13/55, 1955, Police Branch II, Ministry of Home Affairs Files, NAI.

117. S.20(2), SITA, 1956.

118. Minister of law to minister of home affairs, note, September 17, 1958, File 37/3/58, 1958, Police Branch IV, Ministry of Home Affairs, NAI.

119. Ibid.

120. *State of West Bengal v. Anwar Ali Sarkar*, AIR 1952 SC 75.

121. *Mt. Chanchal v. King Emperor*, AIR 1932 All 70

122. *Chiranjit Lal Chowdhury v. Union of India*, AIR 1951 SC 41.

123. For example, "Suppression of Immoral Traffic Act Held Valid: Woman's Plea Fails," *Times of India*, May 27, 1958.

124. S. Balakrishna, Assistant Legal Advisor, note, File 37/3/58, 1958, Police Branch IV, Ministry of Home Affairs Files, NAI.

125. "State's Appeal Dismissed: Case against Prostitute," *Times of India*, July 13, 1960.

126. *Municipal Committee, Malterkotla v. Mod Mushtaq and Others*, AIR 1960 Punjab and Haryana 18.

127. *Kamla China v. State of Delhi*, AIR 1963 Punjab and Haryana 36.

128. *Begum Do Hussain Saheb Kalawat and Another v. State of Bombay*, 1963 (1) CrLJ 148.

129. *Cooverjee v. Excise Commissioner, Ajmer*, AIR 1954 SC 220.

130. Central Social Welfare Board, *Report of the Advisory Committee*, 32.

131. *Kaushalya v. State of Uttar Pradesh*, AIR 1963 All 71.

132. The precedent was *Phool Din. v. State of Uttar Pradesh*, AIR 1952 All 491.

133. *Narenda Kumar v. Union of India*, AIR 1960 SC 430.

134. Justice William Broome was the last British judge in India and the only one to be appointed to a high court after independence. He fully assimilated into the Indian polity, marrying an Indian woman and raising his children as Hindus. Douglas McDonald, "Becoming Indian: William Broome and Colonial Continuity in Postindependence India" *Indian Historical Review* 42, no. 2 (2015) 303–31.

135. *Hari Khemu Gawali v. Deputy Commissioner of Police, Bombay*, AIR 1956 SC 559.

136. "Curbs Held Void; Women's Petitions Allowed," *Times of India*, November 20, 1961.

137. *Kaushalya v. State of Uttar Pradesh*, AIR 1963 All 71.

138. *Vanga Seetharamamma v. Chitta Sambasiva Rao and Another*, AIR 1964 AP 400.

139. Ibid.

140. *State of Uttar Pradesh v. Kaushaliya and Others*, AIR 1964 SC 416.

141. Ibid.

142. *Sahyog Mahila Mandal v. State of Gujarat*, (2004) 2 GLR 1764.

143. *State of Uttar Pradesh v. Kaushaliya and Others*, AIR 1964 SC 416.

144. Nivedita Menon, *Subversive Sites: Feminist Politics beyond the Law* (Chicago: University of Illinois Press, 2004).

145. The classic statements of this position can be found in Stuart A. Scheingold, *The Politics of Rights: Lawyers, Public Policy, and Social Change* (New Haven, CT: Yale University Press, 1974); and Gerald Rosenberg, *The Hollow Hope: Can Courts Bring about Social Change?* (Chicago: University of Chicago Press, 1990).

146. Prabha Kottiswaran, "Sword or Shield? The Role of Law in the Indian Sex Worker's Movement," *Interventions* 15, no. 4 (2013): 530-548.; For a similar argument on bar dancers see Anna Morcom, "'The Cure is Worse than the Disease': Mumbai Dance Bars, and New Forms of Justice in the History of Female Public Performers in India." *Cultural and Social History* 14, no. 4 (2017): 499-512.

147. Martha Minow, "Interpreting Rights: An Essay for Robert Cover," *Yale Law Journal*, 96 (1987): 1860–1915.

148. Rameshwari Nehru, "Presidential Address," All India Conference on Social and Moral Hygiene, 1960, 110. File 29, Rameshwari Nehru Papers, NMML.

149. Nita Verma Prasad, *Defensive Widows, Litigous Widows, Imagined Widows: Inheritance Disputes in the Courts of the Raj, 1875–1911* (Berkeley: University of California, ,2006).

150. Mathur and Gupta, *Prostitutes,*189.

151. Michal McCann, *Rights at Work: Pay Equity Reform and the Politics of Legal Mobilization* (Chicago: University of Chicago Press, 1994).

152. Punekar and Rao, *Study of Prostitutes*, 179.

153. *National Legal Services Authority v. Union of India*, (2014) 5 SCC 438.

154. McCann, *Rights at Work*, 305.

155. Ibid., 308.

156. "Voluntary Vice," *Times of India*, December 11, 1959.

157. Central Social Welfare Board, *Report of the Advisory Committee*, 33.

158. Deshmukh, "President Address.".

159. Durgabai Deshmukh to G. B. Pant, File 46/53, Vol. 3, 1953, Police Branch II, Ministry of Home Affairs Files, NAI.

160. Rameshwari Nehru to G. B. Pant, January 10, 1959, Subject File 31, Rameshwari Nehru Papers, NMML.

161. Chaitanya Lakkimsetti, "HIV Is Our Friend": Prostitution, Biopower, and the State in Postcolonial India," *Signs* 40, no. 1 (2014): 201–26; Moni Nag, "Sex Workers in Sonagachi: Pioneers of a Revolution," *Economic and Political Weekly*, January 2005.

Epilogue

1. *Mohd. Hasan v. Notified Area Committee, Kandla*, and *Rashid Ahmad Khan v. Municipal Board, Kariana*, AIR 1963 SC 163.

2. There is a small but growing body of work that builds on this approach, tracing, for instance, how enlightenment principles were articulated outside the republic of letters in the Iberian empire or how action by hundreds of disparate actors clashing with the police led to changes in American vagrancy law in the 1960s. Biana Premo, *The Enlightenment on Trial: Ordinary Litigants and the Spanish Empire* (New York: Oxford University Press, 2017); Risa Goluboff, *Vagrant Nation: Police Power, Constitutional Change, and the Making of the 1960s* (Cambridge, MA: Harvard University Press, 2016).

3. There are several versions of the heroic judge narrative, but perhaps the most prominent is Jennifer Widner, *Building the Rule of Law: Francis Nyali and the Road to Judicial Independence in Africa.* (New York: W. W. Norton, 2001).

4. Hendrik Hartog, *Man and Wife in America: A History* (Cambridge, MA: Harvard University Press, 2002), 2.

5. *Mohammad Yasin v. Town Area Committee, Jalalabad*, Writ Petition 132, 1951, SCRR.

6. File 30/43/58 Judicial Branch, Ministry of Home Affairs Files, NAI.

7. Krishan Wadhwa, director of Wadhwa Publishers in Nagpur, interview with author, 2009.

8. B. R Ambedkar, *Constituent Assembly Debates*, November 4, 1948.

9. Roy, *Beyond Belief; Our Constitution* (1950), *The Case of Mr. X* (1952), and *The Case of Mr. Critic* (1952), Films Division of India, Mumbai.

10. Zairul Hassan Lari, *Constituent Assembly Debates*, November 8, 1948.

11. Upendra Baxi, "Accumulation and Legitimacy: The Indian Constitution and State Formation," *Delhi Law Review* 12 (1991): 72–84.

12. Planning Commission, "Reply of Government of Bombay," 89.

13. Sahai, "Savrocha Nyalaya ka Nridnay Godhan ko Ko Katal Se Naheen Bacha Sakta."

14. Durgabai Deshmukh to G. B. Pant, File 46/53, Vol. 3, 1953, Police Branch II, Ministry of Home Affairs Files, NAI.

15. I draw on these categories from Leslie Pierce, *Morality Tales: Law and Gender in the Ottoman Court of Aintab* (Berkeley: University of California Press, 2003), 5–7.

16. Hendrik Hartog, "The Constitution of Aspiration and the Rights That Belong to Us All, *Journal of American History* 74, no. 3 (1987): 1016.

17. BPA 1654, File III, 1954, Home Ministry Files, MSA.

18. Bhansali, *Prohibition Inquiry Report*; Planning Commission, *Prohibition Enquiry Committee Report*; Planning Commission, *Report of the Study Team*.

19. "The Orissa Prevention of Cow Slaughter Act," File 17/284/60, "Prevention of Cow Slaughter Bill," File 43/3/54, and "Mysore Prevention of Cow Slaughter Act," File 17/18/64, Judicial Branch, Ministry of Home Affairs Files, NAI:, "Gujarat Prevention of Cow Slaughter Bill," File Parl6 (13) 67, Ministry of Commerce Files, NAI.

20. File 46/53, Vol. 2, Police Branch II, Ministry of Home Affairs Files, NAI.

21. Nivedita Menon, "Citizenship and the Passive Revolution," in *Politics and Ethics of the Indian Constitution*, ed. Rajeev Bhargava (New Delhi: Oxford University Press, 2008), 189–211.

22. Article 21, Constitution of India, 1950. For an account of how due process played out in the Constituent Assembly, see Austin, *Indian Constitution*, 101–11.

23. "Proposed Law Minister Conference: Separation of Judiciary from the Executive," File 9/1/60, Judicial Branch, Ministry of Home Affairs Files, NAI.

24. Karen Orren, "Officers' Rights: Towards a Unified Field Theory of Constitutional Development," *Law and Society Review* 34, no. 4 (2000): 877.

25. Baxi, "Accumulation and Legitimacy," 80.

26. Julia Eckert, "From Subjects to Citizens: Legalism from Below and the Homogenization of the Legal Sphere," *Journal of Legal Pluralism* 53 (2006): 45–70.

27. Welfare recipients demonstrated a significant degree of legal consciousness. Austin Sarat, "Law Is All Over: Power, Resistance, and the Legal Consciousness of the Welfare Poor," *Yale Journal of Law and the Humanities* 2 (1990): 343.

28. B. R. Ambedkar, *Draft Articles on the Rights of States and Minorities*, March 24, 1947. I am grateful to Gautam Bhatia for drawing my attention to this statement.

29. Ashis S. Koul, "Making New Muslim Arian: Reform and Social Mobility in Colonial Punjab, 1890s–1910s," *South Asian History and Culture* 8, no. 1 (2017): 1–18.

30. Javeed Alam, *Who Wants Democracy?* (Delhi: Orient Blackswan, 2012).

31. The literature on dalit constitutionalism remains sparse but for some early engagements, see Rohit De, "Lawyering as Politics: The Legal Career of Dr. Ambedkar, Bar-at-Law," in Anand Teltumbe and Suraj Yengde, eds., *Ambedkar at 123* (New Delhi: Penguin, 2019); Amita Sinha and Rajat Kant, "Mayawati and Memorial Parks in Lucknow, India: Landscapes of Empowerment," *Studies in the History of Gardens & Designed Landscapes* 35, no. 1 (2015): 43–58. On tribal engagements with the constitution, see Anand Vaidya, "Word Traps and the Drafting of the Indian Forest Rights Act" in Uday Chandra and Daniel Taghioff, eds., *Staking Claims: The Politics of Social Movements in Contemporary Rural India* (Delhi: Oxford University Press, 2018) 292–316; Sundar, "Pathalgadi Is Nothing but Constitutional Messianism"; Sahu, " The Constitution Set in Stone."

32. *Moti Ram v. State of Madhya Pradesh*, AIR 1978 SC 1594.

33. *Bidi Supply Company v. Union of India*, AIR 1956 SC 479.

34. Baxi, "Taking Suffering Seriously," 293.

35. Robert Cover, "The Supreme Court, 1982 Term—Foreword: Nomos and Narrative," *Harvard Law Review* 97, no. 4 (1983): 4–68.

36. Nandini Sundar, "The Constitution as a Living Document," *Wire,* January 28, 2018, https://thewire.in/featured/constitution-living-document.

SELECTED BIBLIOGRAPHY

Archives

Alkazi Foundation for the Arts, New Delhi

Homai Vyarawalla Collection

British Library, Asian and African Studies Collection, London

India Office Records

Centre for South Asian Studies, Cambridge University

N. G. Barrier Political Pamphlets Collection

Films Division of India, Mumbai

The Case of Mr. Critic (1948)
The Case of Mr. X (1952)
Citizens and Citizens (1952)
Our Constitution (1950)
Rights and Responsibilities (1952)

Maharashtra State Archives, Mumbai

Home Ministry Files
Proceedings of the Bombay Legislative Assembly

National Archives of India, New Delhi

Justice M. R. Jayakar Papers
Ministry of Commerce Files
Ministry of External Affairs Files
Ministry of Finance Files
Ministry of Home Affairs Files

Ministry of Law, Justice, and Company Affairs Files
Ministry of Refugee and Rehabilitation Files
Ministry of State Files
Purushottam Das Tandon Papers
Rajendra Prasad Papers
Sir Sita Ram Papers

Nehru Memorial Museum and Library, New Delhi

All India Congress Committee Papers
All India Women's Conference Papers
B. G. Kher Papers
Bombay Pradesh Congress Committee Papers
Durgabai Deshmukh Oral History Transcript
Durgabai Deshmukh Papers
Frank Anthony Oral History Transcript
Hansa Mehta Papers
Indian Merchant Chambers Papers
Kamaladevi Chattopadhyay Papers
Rameshwari Nehru Papers
Renuka Ray Papers
Sir Sita Ram Oral History Transcript

Punjab State Archives, Chandigarh

District Commissioner Records of Jullunder

Rockefeller Foundation Archives, New York

Ford Foundation Collection
Spaeth-Merrilat Papers

Supreme Court of India Record Room, Delhi

Writ Petitions
Civil Appeals
Criminal Appeals
Supreme Court Museum Collection

Women's Library, London Metropolitan University

Records of the Association for Social and Moral Hygiene

Statutes

Abducted Persons (Recovery and Restoration) Act, 1949
Administration of Evacuee Property Act, 1950
Bihar Preservation and Improvement of Animals Act, 1955
Bombay Abkari Act, 1878
Bombay Prevention of Prostitution Act, 1923
Bombay Prohibition Act, 1949
Central Provinces and Berar Animal Preservation Act, 1949
Constitution of India, 1950
Defense of India Act, 1939 (and associated rules)
Essential Supplies (Temporary Powers) Act, 1946 (and associated state rules)
Essential Supplies (Temporary Powers) Amendment Act, 1949
Government of India Act, 1935
Indian Penal Code, 1860
Karnataka Prevention of Slaughter and Preservation of Cattle Act, 2010
Mhwora Act, 1892
Specific Relief Act, 1861
Suppression of Immoral Traffic in Women and Girls Act, 1956
Uttar Pradesh Cow Protection Act 1955
Uttar Pradesh Municipalities Act, 1916
Women and Children's Institutions (Licensing Act), 1956

Court Cases

Abdullah v. King Emperor, 49 Ind Cas 776 (1919).
Adamji Umar Dalai v. State of Bombay, 1952 SCR 172.
A. L. A. Schechter Poultry Corp v. United States, 295 U.S. 495.
Amir Chand v. State of Uttar Pradesh, AIR 1956 All 562.
Ayub v. State of Uttar Pradesh, AIR 1962 All 141.
Babulal Sharma v. Brijnarain Brajesh and Others, AIR 1958 MP 175.
Baldev Mitter v. King Emperor, AIR (31) 1944 Lah 142.
Balla and Others v. State of Uttar Pradesh, AIR 1956 All 335.
Balwant and Others v. Deputy Director, AIR 1975 All 295.
Begum Do Hussain Saheb Kalawat and Another v. State of Bombay, 1963 (1) CrLJ 148.
Behram Khurshed Pesikaka v. State of Bombay, AIR 1955 SC 123.
Benoari Lal Sharma v. King Emperor, AIR (30) 1943 FC 36.
Bhagwati Saran v. State of Uttar Pradesh, AIR 1961 SC 928.
Bidi Supply Company v. Union of India, AIR 1956 SC 479.
Bimal Protiva Debi v. Emperor, 43 CrLJ 793.
Buddhu v. Municipal Board, AIR 1952 All 753.
Centre for Public Interest Litigation v. Union of India, Writ Petition (Civil) No. 423 of 2010.
Chairman, Budge Budge Municipality v. Mangru Meya and Others, AIR 1953 Cal 433.
Chinubhai Lalbhai v. Emperor, (1940) 42 BOMLR 669.

Chiranjit Lal Chowdhury v. Union of India, AIR 1951 SC 41.

Cooverjee v. Excise Commissioner, Ajmer, AIR 1954 SC 220.

Deputy Legal Remembrancer v. Kailash Chandra Ghosh, (1915) ILR 42 Cal 760.

Dulla and Others v. State of Uttar Pradesh, AIR 1958 All 198.

Durga Prasad v. State of Uttar Pradesh, AIR 1955 All 9.

Emperor v. Chinubhai Lalbhai, (1940) 42 Bom LR 669.

Emperor v. Maiku, AIR 1930 All 279.

Emperor v. Sakinabai Baddurddin, AIR 1931 Bom 70.

Emperor v. Yar Mohammad, AIR 1931 Cal 448.

Fram Nusserwanji Balsara v. State of Bombay, AIR 1951 Bom 210.

Ghani Mahajan and Others v. State of Bihar, CMP 1162 of 1956 and CMP 424 of 1957, Writ Petition No. 72 of 1956.

Ghazi v. State of Uttar Pradesh, Crim. Revision No. 1742 of 1959, August 30, 1960.

Gopal Narain v. Emperor, AIR (30) 1943 Oudh 227.

Hadjee Mazdur Ali v. Gundowree Sahoo, (1876) 25 WR CrR 72.

Haji Ahmad Raza and Others v. Municipal Board, Allahabad, AIR 1952 All 1.

Hamid and Another v. State of Uttar Pradesh, 1958 CriLJ 115.

Hari Khemu Gawali v. Deputy Commissioner of Police, Bombay, AIR 1956 SC 559.

Harishankar Bagla and Another v. State of Madhya Pradesh, AIR 1954 SC 465.

Harish Chandra Bagla v. King Emperor, AIR 1945 All 90.

Harkishan Das v. Emperor, AIR (31) 1944 Lah 33.

Haveliram v. Maharaja of Morvi, AIR (32) 1945 Bom 88.

Haveliram Shetty v. His Highness, Shri Lukhdhirji, the Maharajsaheb of Morvi, ILR 1944 Bom 487.

H. N. Nolan v. Emperor, AIR (31) 1944 All 118.

Hodge v. Regina, (1883) 9 AC 117.

In re Benoarilal Roy, (1944) 48 CWN 766.

In re Delhi Laws Act, AIR 1951 SC 332.

In re Limba Koya, (1885) ILR 9 Bom 556.

In re Shantabai Rani Benoor, AIR 1951 Bom 337.

Jesinghbhai Ishwarlal v. King Emperor, AIR 1950 Bom 363.

Joylal Agarwala v. Union of India, SCR 127.

Jyoti Pershad v. Administrator for the Union Territory of Delhi, AIR 1961 SC 1602.

Kachanmala Dassi v. Lilabati Debi, AIR 1951 Cal 164.

Kamalabai Jethamal v. State of Maharasthra, AIR 1962 SC 1189.

Kamla China v. State of Delhi, AIR 1963 Punjab and Haryana 36.

Kande and Others v. Jhanjhan Lal and Others, AIR 1936 All 1.

Kaushalya Devi v. State of Uttar Pradesh, AIR 1963 All 71.

Kesavananda Bharti v. State of Kerala, AIR 1973 SC 1461.

Khan Baputi Dewan v. Bispait Pundit, (1900) ILR 27 Cal 655.

King Emperor v. Meer Singh, ILR 1941 All 617.

King Emperor v. Sibnath Banerjee, AIR (30) 1943 PC 75.

Kruse v. Johnson, (1898) 2 QB 91.

L. A. Schechter Poultry Corp v. United States, 295 U.S. 495.

Madran Kassab v. King Emperor, 86 Ind Cas 964.

Mangru Meya and Others v. Commissioners of the Budge Budge Municipality, AIR 1953 Cal 333.

Messrs. Dwarka Prasad Laxmi Narain v. State of Uttar Pradesh, AIR 1954 SC 224.

Mir Chittan v. King Emperor, 166 Ind Cas 373.

Mohammed Yasin v. Town Area Committee, Jalalabad, AIR 1952 SC 115.

Mohd. Hanif Qureshi v. State of Bihar, AIR 1958 SC 731.

Mohd. Hasan v. Notified Area Committee, Kandla, and *Rashid Ahmad Khan v. Municipal Board, Kairana*, AIR 1963 SC 163.

Mohd. Ilias v. State of Bihar, CMP 1161 of 1956, Writ Petition No. 58 of 1956.

Mohd. Jan v. State of Uttar Pradesh, Writ Petition No. 129 of 1956.

Monomohan v. Gobinda Das, 55 CWN 6.

Moti Jan v. Municipal Committee, Delhi (1926) 93 IC 827.

Moti Ram v. State of Madhya Pradesh, AIR 1978 SC 1594.

Mt. Chanchal v. King Emperor, AIR 1932 All 70.

Mt. Muhammadi v. King Emperor, AIR 1932 All 110.

Mt. Naziran v. King Emperor, AIR 1932 All 537.

Muhammad Salim v. Ramkumar Singh and Others, AIR 1928 All 710.

Municipal Board, Etah v. Asghari Jaan and Mt. Bismillah, AIR 1932 All 264.

Municipal Committee, Malerkotla v. Mohd. Mustaq and Others, AIR 1960 Punjab and Haryana 18.

Municipal Committee of Delhi v. Moti Jan, (1930) 123 IC 536.

Nanbahar Singh v. Kabir Bux, AIR 1930 All 753.

Narasu Appa Mali v. State of Bombay, AIR 1952 Bom 84.

Narenda Kumar v. Union of India, AIR 1960 SC 430.

Nasir ud Din v. State of Uttar Pradesh, CMP 879 and 880 of 1956, Writ Petition No. 103 of 1956.

National Legal Services Authority v. Union of India, (2014) 5 SCC 438.

Naubahar Singh and Others v. Qadir Bux and Others, AIR 1930 All 753.

Niharendu Dutt Mazumdar v. King Emperor, AIR (29) 1942 PC 22.

Ori Lal v. Muhammad Yakub, [1914] 17 OC 354.

Parbatti Dassi v. King Emperor, AIR 1934 Cal 198.

Phool Din. v. State of Uttar Pradesh, AIR 1952 All 491.

Pir Ali Kasab and Others v. King Emperor, 56 Ind Cas 437.

Province of Bombay v. Kushaldas S. Advani and Others, AIR 1950 SC 222.

Queen v. Boorah, 3 App. Cas. 889 (PC 1878).

Queen Empress v. Iman Ali, (1888) ILR 10 All 150.

Queen Empress v. Pestanji Barjorji, (1885) ILR 9 Bom 456.

Queen Empress v. Zakiuddin and Another, (1888) ILR 10 All 44.

Queen Romesh Chunder Sanyal v. Hiru Mondal and Another, (1890) ILR 17 Cal 852.

Raghubar Dayal v. Ameeran Jahan, Second Appeal No. 1023 of 1881, Allahabad High Court, May 4, 1882.

Ramananda Agarwala v. State of West Bengal, AIR 1951 Cal 120.

Ram Jawaya Kapur v. State of Punjab, AIR 1955 SC 549.

Razia v. State of Uttar Pradesh, AIR 1957 All 340.

Romesh Thapar v. State of Madras, [1950] SCR 549.

Saghir Ahmad v. State of Uttar Pradesh, [1955] 1 SCR 707.

Sahyog Mahila Mandal v. State of Gujarat, (2004) 2 GLR 1764.

Santosh Kumar Jain v. State of Bihar, AIR 1951 SC 201.

Sastri Yagnapurusha Dasji v. Mooldas, AIR 1966 SC 1119.

Shahbaz Khan and Others v. Umrao Puri and Others, (1908) ILR 30 All 81.

Sheikh Hussain Qureshi v. State of Bombay, CMP 882, 1174, and 1175 of Writ Petition No. 117 of 1956.

Sheikh Muhammad Yakub v. King Emperor, 6 Ind Cas 454.

Sheikh Muhammad Yakub v. Mangru Rai and Others, 7 Ind Cas 318.

Sheikh Sobhan v. State of Bombay, CMP 881 of 1956.

Sheoshankar v. State of Madhya Pradesh, 1951 CriLJ 1140.

Smt Sona Bai and Others v. Municipality of Agra, AIR 1956 All 736.

Sona Bai and Others v. Municipal Board, Agra, AIR 1956 All 76.

State of Bombay v. Bombay Education Society and Others, AIR 1954 SC 561.

State of Bombay v. Framji Nusserwanji Balsara, AIR 1951 SC 518.

State of Bombay v. Hiralal, AIR 1951 Bom 369.

State of Bombay v. Triambak Bhondu Dhoir, (1955) 57 BOMLR 541.

State of Bombay and Another v. F. N. Balsara, AIR 1951 SC 318.

State of Madras v. Champakam Dorairajam, AIR 1951 SC 226.

State of Madras v. V. G. Row, [1952] SCR 607.

State of Rajasthan v. Nathmal, AIR 1954 SC 307.

State of Uttar Pradesh v. Basdeo Bajoria, AIR 1951 All 44.

State of Uttar Pradesh v. Kaushaliya and Others, AIR 1964 SC 416.

State of Uttar Pradesh v. Kaushalya Devi, AIR 1964 SC 416.

State of West Bengal v. Anwar Ali Sarkar, AIR 1952 SC 75.

Subhan Mochi v. Babu Ram Singh and Others, AIR 1930 All 121.

Subramaniam Swamy v. A. Raja, Civil Appeal No. 10660 of 2010.

Sudhir Chandra Neogy v. Calcutta Tramways, AIR 1960 Cal 396.

Union of India v. Bhanamal Gulzarimal, AIR 1961 SC 475.

Union of India v. Shirinbai Aspandier Irani, Civil Appeal No. 154 of 1953.

Vanga Seetharamamma v. Chitta Sambasiva Rao and Another, AIR 1964 AP 400.

Virendra Singh v. State of Uttar Pradesh [1955] 1 SCR 415.

Yick Wo v. Hopkins (1886) 118 U.S. 356.

Newspapers and Periodicals

All India Reporter

Blitz

Bombay Chronicle

Hindustan Times

National Herald

New York Times

Shankar's Weekly

Social Health

Statesman

Times of India

Young India

Primary Sources

Agnihotri, Vidyadhar. *Fallen Women: A Study with Special Reference to Kanpur*. Kanpur: Maharaja, 1954.

Agrawal, Ram Gopal. *Price Controls in India since 1947*. Minneapolis: University of Minnesota, 1956.

Bayley, David H. *Preventive Detention in India: A Case Study in Democratic Social Control*. Calcutta: F. L. Mukhopadhay, 1962.

Beotra, B. R. *The Suppression of Immoral Traffic in Women and Girls Act, 1956 (with State Rules)*. Allahabad: Law Book, 1962.

Bhansali, Mausen Damodar. *Prohibition Inquiry Report in Bombay State*. Bombay: Central Government Press, 1952.

Central Social Welfare Board. *Report of the Advisory Committee on Social and Moral Hygiene*. New Delhi, 1956.

Collected Works of Mahatma Gandhi. 98 vols. New Delhi: Government of India, 1999.

Constituent Assembly Debates. New Delhi: Lok Sabha Secretariat, 1989.

Desai, Morarji, ed. "A Word to the Prohibition Worker." In *New Lives for Old*, 127. Bombay: Provincial Prohibition Board, 1948.

Deshmukh, Durgabai. *Chintaman and I*. New Delhi: Allied, 1980.

Directorate of Marketing and Inspection. *Report on the Marketing of Cattle in India*. Delhi: Manager of Publications, 1946.

Famine Inquiry Commission. *Report on Bengal*. Delhi: Manager of Publications, 1945.

Gadbois, George. "The Supreme Court of India: A Preliminary Report of an Empirical Study." *Journal of Constitutional and Parliamentary Studies* 4, no. 1 (January–March 1970): 34–50.

Gandhi, Mohandas K. *Freedom's Battle: Being a Comprehensive Collection of Writings and Speeches on the Present Situation*. 2nd ed. Madras: Ganesh, 1922.

———. "A Gentle Rebuke." *Young India*, June 25, 1931; in *Collected Works*, 47: 53–54.

———. *How to Serve the Cow*. Ahmedabad: Navajivan, 1954.

———. "Letter to Herbert Anderson." April 3, 1926. In Collected Works, 35: 5.

———. "Speech at Bardoli." August 12, 1928. In *Collected Works*, 42: 362.

———. "Speech of Prohibition—Madras." *Hindu*, March 24, 1925; in *Collected Works*, 31: 32–38.

———. "Total Prohibition." *Young India*, February 4, 1926; in *Collected Works*, 33: 49.

———. "To the Women of India." In *Collected Works*, 49: 57.

———. *Women and Social Injustice*. Ahmedabad: Navjivan, 1942.

Gorwalla, A. D. *The Role of the Administrator: Past, Present and Future*. Pune: Gokhale Institute of Politics and Economics, 1952.

Husain, Mazhar. *The Suppression of Immoral Traffic in Women and Girls Act, 1956: With Commentary and Case Law*. Lucknow: Eastern Book, 1958.

Ikramullah, Begum Shaista. *From Purdah to Parliament*. London: Cresset Press, 1963.

Indian Institute of Public Opinion. "The Structure of Urban Opinion on the Socialist Pattern of Society." *Monthly Public Opinion Surveys* I (1956): 36–39.

Jain, M. P. *Administrative Process under the Essential Commodities Act, 1955*. New Delhi: Indian Law Institute, 1964.

Kāṇe, Pāṇḍuraṅga. *History of the Dharmasastra (Ancient and Medieval Religions and Civil Law in India.* Poona: Bhandarkar Oriental Research Institute, 1953.

Kumaran, J. B. Sampat. *Artificial Insemination and Animal Production.* Jubbulpore: Mission Press, 1951.

Law Commission of India. *14th Report: Reform of Judicial Administration.* New Delhi, 1958.

———. *29th Report.* Proposal to include certain Social and Economic Offences in the Indian Penal Code. New Delhi, 1966.

———. *47th Report: Trial and Punishment of Social and Economic Offenses.* New Delhi, 1972.

Lok Sabha Secretariat. *A Selection from Questions and Answers in Lok Sabha, First to Fifteenth Sessions (1952–1957).* New Delhi, 1957.

Markose, A. T. *Cases and Materials in Administrative Law.* New Delhi: Indian Law Institute, 1966.

———. *Judicial Control of Administrative Action in India.* Bombay: N. M. Tripathi, 1956.

———. "Report of the Research Director on the Working of the Indian Law Institute from May 1960 to July 1962." *Journal of the Indian Law Institute* 3 (1963): 602–10.

Ministry of Agriculture. *Report of the Cattle Preservation and Development Committee.* New Delhi, 1949.

Ministry of Food and Agriculture. *Supplement to the Report of the G.M.F. Enquiry Committee: Notes.* New Delhi, 1952.

Mookherjee, H. C. *Why Prohibition? A Manual for Temperance, Social Service and Congress Workers.* Calcutta: Book House, 1949.

Pandit, Vijaya Lakshmi. *The Scope of Happiness: A Personal Memoir.* New York: Crown, 1969.

Planning Commission. *Prohibition Enquiry Committee Report.* New Delhi, 1955.

———. *Prohibition Enquiry Committee: State Government's Memoranda and Other Documents.* New Delhi, 1956.

———. *Report of the Study Team on Prohibition.* New Delhi, 1963.

———. *Report on the First Five-Year Plan.* New Delhi, 1951.

Rajagopalachari, C. *Indian Prohibition Manual.* Delhi: National Congress Committee, 1933.

Ramaswami, M. "Rule of Law and a Planned Society." *Journal of the Indian Law Institute* 1 (1958–1959): 31–32.

Rao, B. Shiva. *The Framing of India's Constitution: A Study.* 4 vols. Nashik: Government of India Press, 1968.

Reddi, S. Muthilakshmi. *Report of the Commodity Controls Committee.* Delhi: Manager of Publications, 1953.

———. *Why Should the Devadasi Institution in the Hindu Temples Be Abolished?* Chintradipet: Co-Operative Printing Works, 1920.

Sarasvati, Mitra Dayananda. *Gōkaruṇānidhi.* Tenali: Satya Mitra Arya, 1938.

———. *The Ocean of Mercy: An English Translation of Maharshi Swami Dayananda Saraswati's "Gocaruna Nidhi" by Durga Prasad.* Lahore: Virajanand Press, 1889.

Shroff, A. D. *Controls in a Planned Economy.* Bombay: Forum for Free Enterprise, 1960.

State of Bombay. *Annual Police Administration Report, including the Railways, for the Year 1949.* Bombay: Central Government Press, 1950.

Tribhuwan, Jyotsna. *The Law Relating to Women in India.* Poona: P. R. Ambike, 1965.

Tripathi, P. K. "Preventive Detention: The Indian Experience." *American Journal of Comparative Law* 9 (1960): 219–48.

Uttar Pradesh. *Gosamvardhan Enquiry Committee Report.* Allahabad: Government of India Press, 1955.

Vaidya, Murarji J. *Crisis of Controls.* Bombay: Forum for Free Enterprise, 1960.

Vakil, C. N., J. J. Anjaria, and Dansukhlal Lakdawala. *Price Control and Food Supply with Special Reference to Bombay City.* Bombay: N. M. Tripathi, 1943.

INDEX

Aanandi, Ghulam Abbas, 184, 211
Abkari Act, 246n74
administrative law, 79, 110, 117–22
Administrative Procedure Act, 118
Advisory Committee on Social and Moral
    Hygiene, 191, 210
Advocates-on-Record, 16
ajlaf (common birth), 154
Ali, Ameer, 13
Ali, Fazl, 57
Allahabad Dancing Girls Union, 170, 181,
    212, 223. *See also* prostitution
Allahabad High Court, 205; commodity-
    controls and, 109–10, 119; cow protection
    and, 129, 140–41, 155, 165; prostitution
    and, 169, 189, 201, 203; Suppression of
    Immoral Traffic of Women and Girls Act
    and, 206–7, 221
All India Anti-Cow Slaughter Movement
    Committee, 149, 159
All India Cow Protection Society, 15, 135
All India Guts Manufacturers Association,
    154
All India Hindu Raj Party, 154
All India Jamitaul Quresh Action Commit-
    tee, 154, 223
All India Women's Conference (AIWC), 39,
    173–75, 194
Ambedkar, Bhimrao Ramji, 6, 40, 217, 223
American Administrative Law (Schwartz),
    110, 256n138
American Civil Liberties Union (ACLU), 27
American Law Institute, 117

Andhra Pradesh High Court, 207, 221
anjuman (village council), 154
anti–kine killing movement, 260n20
anti-trafficking. *See* forced labor; human
    trafficking
Arendt, Hannah, 31
Article 14 (of the Indian Constitution), 140,
    199, 208
Article 15 (of the Indian Constitution),
    174, 204
Article 19 (of the Indian Constitution), 49,
    141–43, 151, 169, 193, 199, 204–6, 214,
    250n6
Article 20 (of the Indian Constitution), 62
Article 21 (of the Indian Constitution), 214
Article 23 (of the Indian Constitution), 20,
    170–72, 176–77, 205–7
Article 25 (of the Indian Constitution), 124
Article 32 (of the Indian Constitution), 155
Article 38 (of the Indian Constitution), 132
Article 42 (of the Indian Constitution), 31
Article 47 (of the Indian Constitution),
    19, 43
Article 48 (of the Indian Constitution), 19,
    123, 135, 139–41, 157
Article 50 (of the Indian Constitution),
    201
Article 225 (of the Indian Constitution), 14
Article 226 (of the Indian Constitution),
    48, 139
Article 340 (of the Indian Constitution),
    264n119
Arya Samaj, 126

Cattle Preservation and Development
Committee, 133
Central List, the, 80
Central Provinces, the, 33, 38, 56
Central Social Welfare Board, 170
Chand, Amir, 119–20
Chand, Mehr, 217
Chand, Tek, 74
Charter of Rights of and Duties for Indian
Women, 173
Chattopadhyaya, Kamaladevi, 191
chikwas (chickens), 148, 156
China, Kamla, 204
Citizens and Citizens (film), 96–97
civil disobedience, 36–37, 265n5
Civil Procedure Code, 128, 140, 155, 187
civil-service employment, 118
class: backwardness and, 84, 164, 166,
264n119; intellectual, 37; lower, 3, 27,
34, 36, 47, 72, 77, 121; middle, 24, 46, 53,
68, 71; prostitutes, 148, 172–73, 188–89,
192; working, 38, 95–96, 121. *See also*
caste
class-action lawsuits, 20, 125
Coal Control Order, 114–15
colonialism, 68, 216; economics and, 97;
inequality and, 30; law and, 120; liquor
and, 36; litigation and, 13; oppression
and, 23; rights and, 67; war and, 80
Commodities Act (1955), 88, 93, 96, 109
commodity-control operations: administration of, 83–84, 87–88, 91, 116; advertisements and, 95–97, 254n92; black markets
and, 86, 94, 105; cloth and, 85, 89;
corruption and, 85, 92–99; farmers and,
85–86; Gandhi, Mohandas, and, 78–79,
84–86; licensing and, 81–82, 91, 104–5;
price controls and, 83–84, 86; trade and,
90–92, 97; violations of, 94–95, 105–6.
See also black markets
Commodity Controls Committee, 90
common law, 221, 258n169
communalism, 259n9
Communist Party, 8, 177, 236n18

Congress Party: commodity controls and,
86, 95, 104, 130; Constituent Assembly
and, 2, 15, 22, 73, 108; cow protection and,
130, 134–38, 145, 167, 261n52; prohibition
and, 35–39, 41, 46, 66–67, 73–74, 246n74;
prostitution and, 172, 177, 181, 269n62
Congress Socialist Party, 39
Constituent Assembly: cow protection and,
131–34, 145; Indian Constitution and, 2, 5,
8, 39–40, 88, 94, 110–11, 266n6; prohibition and, 41–42, 73; prostitution and,
170–76; women and, 173–74, 266n5,
267n14. *See also* Indian Parliament
Constitutional Faith (Levinson), 240n79
Contagious Diseases Act, 177, 183, 185, 196
Controlled Cotton Cloth and Yarn Dealers
Licensing Order (1948), 119
Cotton Cloth and Yarn Order of 1942,
251n21
Cotton Textile Order (1948), 77, 80, 91–92,
104–5, 107, 112, 119–20
Cotton Textiles (Sizing and Filing) Control
Order (1945), 251n24
Council of States, 11, 261n48
Council of the Parsi Central Association,
67–68
Country Liquor, Foreign Liquor, and
Toddy Merchants of Bombay, 64
Cover, Robert, 4
cows: butchers and, 148–49, 156–57, 222;
cattle effluence and, 161; cow protection
and, 130–35, 151–52, 155–56, 168, 219;
economic rights and, 140–41, 145–46,
148, 150–56, 158–59, 161–63; Hinduism
and, 124–25, 129–31, 134, 136, 149, 152, 157,
165–66; Indian Constitution and, 130–35,
151–53, 155–56, 168, 219; Islam and, 125–28,
130–36, 142, 145, 148–53, 167, 219, 222;
litigation and, 130–31, 144, 220; milk cows
and, 160, 265n150; municipal management and, 135–45; nutrition and, 160–62,
166; protection of, 124–27, 131–36, 139,
145, 160, 167–68, 262n88, 263n93;
Provincial Assembly and, 144–48;

Sahib, Mohamed Ismail, 40
Samaj, Bharat Go Sevak, 159
Sarawati, Swami Dayanand, 126
Saxena, Shibban Lal, 133, 145
Schwartz, Bernard, 110, 256n138
Seervai, Hormasji M., 57
Sen, Ashoke, 184
Sen, Barry, 247n105
Setalvad, Motilal, 57
Seth, Damodar Swarup, 238n47
Shankar's Weekly, 74–75, 136–38, 218
Sharafi, Mitra, 68, 211, 249n155
sharia, 150
shastras (scriptures), 41
Shepherd, Meliscent, 177
Siddiq, Mohammed, 158
Simon Commission (1930), 239n68
Sindhis, 32, 243n2
slavish imitation, 238n47
social change, 36–38, 41, 72, 74, 216, 218–19, 226–27
Socialist Party, 91
social workers, 20, 24, 174, 179–81, 211, 214, 266n5
Sorabji, Soli, 55
Sreenivasan, M. A., 85–86
State of Rajasthan v. Nathmal, 116
State of Uttar Pradesh v. Kaushalya Devi, 209
Subbarao, Koka, 208–9
Sugar Control Order (1942), 251n21
Sulaiman, Shah, 200
Suppression of Immoral Traffic of Women and Girls Act (SITA): Association for Social and Moral Hygiene and, 177–81, 184, 191–94, 205, 210, 213; Bai, Husna, and, 169–71, 176–82, 190–202, 211–12; enactment of, 176–80, 210; Indian Constitution and, 176, 190–91, 193, 203–10; morality and, 176–77; protests against, 182, 184, 186; rehabilitation and, 179–80; Section 4, 194, 196, 203; Section 20, 198–99, 201–2, 204–5, 207–8, 221. *See also* Association for Social and Moral Hygiene (ASMH); prostitution

Sutwala, Hiralal, 93, 99
Swadeshi Cotton Mills, 106
swaraj (self-governance), 37–38, 131

Tambe, Ashwini, 195
Tandon, Purushottam Das, 135
Tendolkar, S. R., 54
Textile Industries (Miscellaneous Articles) Order (1942), 251n21
Tinctura Zingiberis Mitis, 58
toddy, 35–38, 70, 244n22
Town Area Committee Act, 143
tribals, 3, 224
Tyagi, Mahavir, 40–41

ultra vires, 1, 49, 106, 111–13, 141–42, 169, 200
UN Declaration of Human Rights, 55
UP Coal Control Order, 115
US Constitution, 111, 217, 238n45
US Office of Price Administration, 84
US Supreme Court, 11, 20, 201, 243n8
Uttar Pradesh Coal Control Order (1953), 114–15
Uttar Pradesh Controlled Cotton Cloth and Yarn Dealers Licensing Order (1948), 119
Uttar Pradesh Cow Protection Act, 154
Uttar Pradesh Legislative Assembly, 145
Uttar Pradesh Municipalities Act (1916), 140, 142
Uttar Pradesh Prevention of Cow Slaughter Act (1955), 148
Uttar Pradesh Prevention of Cow Slaughter Act (1958), 156
Uttar Pradesh Prevention of Cow Slaughter (Amendment) Act (1958), 163

Vaidya, Murarji J., 86
Victoria (Queen), 66, 128, 134

women: Constituent Assembly and, 173–75, 266n5, 267n14; Indian Constitution and, 9, 17, 29–30, 171–75; prostitution and, 175; rights and, 9, 201–3; violence against, 175. *See also* feminism